MATLAB
Easy Way of Learning

S. SWAPNA KUMAR

Professor and Head
Department of Electronics and Communication Engineering
Vidya Academy of Science and Technology
Thrissur, Kerala

LENINA S V B

Assistant Professor
Department of Electronics and Telecommunication Engineering
Shri Guru Gobind Singhji Institute of Engineering and Technology
Nanded, Maharashtra

PHI Learning Private Limited

Delhi-110092
2016

₹ 395.00

MATLAB—Easy Way of Learning
S. Swapna Kumar and Lenina S V B

© 2016 by PHI Learning Private Limited, Delhi. All rights reserved. No part of this book may be reproduced in any form, by mimeograph or any other means, without permission in writing from the publisher.

ISBN-978-81-203-5165-3

The export rights of this book are vested solely with the publisher.

Published by Asoke K. Ghosh, PHI Learning Private Limited, Rimjhim House, 111, Patparganj Industrial Estate, Delhi-110092 and Printed by Mohan Makhijani at Rekha Printers Private Limited, New Delhi-110020.

To
My great teachers and dear students
and
My constant companions
Dr. Sona Ram T.R., Adarsh Roshan S., Ardra S. Kumar, K.S. Omana Kutty, and Beebi
(In the memory of K. Surendran, S. Sudarsh Kumar, and Rishi Ram T.K.)

—Dr. S. Swapna Kumar

To
My wonderful family, for all their motivation and continuous support.

—Dr. Lenina S V B

Contents

2. Building MATLAB Expression

27–70

3. MATLAB Vector and Matrix

71–141

6. Graphics in MATLAB   **187–235**

7. Flow Logic   **236–257**

8.   MATLAB Programming: Introduction to M-files   258–281

9.   MATLAB in Filter Application   282–311

10.   Digital Signal and Image Processing with MATLAB   312–331

11.   MATLAB and Simulink   332–364

13.　MATLAB in Neural Network

14.　MATLAB Graphical User Interfaces

Preface

MATLAB stands for MATrix LABoratory. It is a very powerful technical programming language used by scientific, engineering and non-engineering community all over the world. This is one of the most versatile user-friendly software for solving any complex problem in an easy way. MATLAB emerged over the year as a tool that has aids for scientists, engineers and professionals in their field of study and research. MATLAB has also become popular technical language for teachers and students to use. Nearly, all disciplines extent MATLAB in curriculum of their undergraduate, postgraduate and research academic pursuit.

Objective

Presently, MATLAB can be used for image processing, signal processing, data analysis, data acquisition, graphical visualisation, numerical analysis, algorithm development and many other applications. Writing programs in MATLAB is easier as compared to other programming languages like FORTRAN, C, C++, Java, etc. This is because MATLAB keeps aside declaration statement requirements which are the main source for any other programming languages. The use of MATLAB is convenient as it provides vast source of tools whose information is available from library and supporting documentation.

There are several books available in the market on MATLAB in different areas of application. This book (**MATLAB—Easy Way of Learning**) is specifically written for the beginners in easy to read and simple language. This book is designed to develop background knowledge and expertise in MATLAB domain which is one of the fastest growing tools in the world. This book presents a comprehensive account of MATLAB basic, design and analysis. It is written as a textbook as well as a reference book that can be used for theoretical learning and for laboratory course. It is easy to read, logical and has step-by-step approach that enables readers to follow the concepts clearly.

While writing this book, we have tried to address most of the difficulties faced by us during our studentship as well as when we were research scholars. Also, we have tried to address the issues which we have come across when teaching MATLAB to students in our academic career.

About the book

In this book, we presented each topic in simple language. This book provides good introduction to MATLAB programming concepts with several workout examples. Each topic is explained in such a way that make reader involved in reading this text with more interest. At the same time, we covered all the essentials required in initial learning of MATLAB concepts. This book is aimed to provide programming skills from basic level onwards. The examples in all the chapters have been explained in a logical manner. We believe after reading all the chapters of this book, reader will be able to write their own programs in MATLAB easily.

This book consists of fourteen chapters, divided into two parts. First eight chapters of the book are devoted to the MATLAB basic, which are very essential for beginners. The remaining six chapters cover applications of MATLAB. All chapters cover with several examples that illustrate the topics in-depth. These examples and programming illustrations are provided to introduce fundamental concepts of MATLAB. Moreover, all the chapters contain review questions and practice exercises at the end. Also at the end of each chapter, students will have a chance to review a summary of the presented features. In addition to these, this book contains graphic user interface figures. The book also discussed advanced topics such as Simulink, Fuzzy Logic, Neural Network and Signal and Image Processing in self-contained and reader friendly manner.

The chapter-wise organisation of the book is as follows:

Chapter 1 provides an introduction of different aspects of MATLAB and its various windows. It describes different components of MATLAB and its desktop in an easy way. The chapter covers different windows, editor and certain basic operations of MATLAB. Screenshots are provided for easy understanding of MATLAB software windows and tools.

Chapter 2 deals with the information of variables and basic system commands, which would require for smooth handling of the MATLAB. In the later part of this chapter, we discussed various mathematical functions and the mode of operations. The chapter is covered with several workout examples that help the reader to understand the topic easily.

Chapter 3 is related to scalar, vector and matrix. It also describes different operations namely mathematical types, handling of scalar, vector and arrays, matrix, etc. Further, we discussed different set of operations using array. The coverage of this chapter with examples, make the concepts self-explanatory.

Chapter 4 deals with polynomials and algebraic expressions. This chapter introduces the MATLAB commands that enable us to perform polynomial operations. Also, we explained about polynomial equation, characteristic polynomial, polynomial differentiation, polynomial integration, polynomial curve and polynomial matrix.

Chapter 5 explores input and output functions provided by MATLAB including operations with files.

Chapter 6 introduces MATLAB technique to draw the graph of functions in a variety of formats. In this chapter, we begin our discussion by plotting the graphs of function, defined by parametric and polar equations in xy-plane. Later, we discussed and investigate the nature of curves and surfaces in 3D space.

Chapter 7 deals with the Flow Logic. MATLAB flow control is almost identical to flow control in C. The idea of program flow becomes simple by using flow techniques effectively. So, we explained flow control techniques with programming codes examples for easy understanding with emphasis on practice of these examples.

Chapter 8 is related to the introduction of m-file. This chapter shows how to create m-files that contain MATLAB commands. These m-files are run at the MATLAB prompt to produce fast and efficient outputs. This is helpful to understand the programming technique in many cases.

Chapter 9 is written for introductory understanding of MATLAB in Filters Applications. Also, we discussed their workings with the help of workout examples.

Chapter 10 introduces the concept of Digital Signal and Image Processing with MATLAB. This chapter presents the theoretical aspects of Image and Signal Processing (ISP) with supported exercises based on practical applications. Thus, allowing readers to develop a deeper understanding of both the theoretical and practical aspects of this subject.

Chapter 11 deals with the MATLAB and Simulink. Simulink is a programming language specifically designed for simulating dynamical systems using standard block diagram notation. This chapter describes the SIMULINK toolboxes. Further in the chapter, we simulate block diagrams using these Simulink toolboxes.

Chapter 12 is meant for MATLAB in Fuzzy Logic. The readers learn basic techniques of Fuzzy systems. It also deals with the in-depth information for solving Fuzzy problems using MATLAB.

Chapter 13 discusses MATLAB in Neural Network. This chapter provides a comprehensive overview of the field of neural networks with their applications. Topics that are covered include fundamental models of artificial neural networks and perception networks theory.

Chapter 14 is the last chapter focused on MATLAB graphical user interfaces. This chapter gives readers the ideas of GUI (graphical user interface) tools to construct and design their own GUI.

All the suggestions and comments about the book from readers, faculty members, research scholars, engineers and students would definitely be used for further improvements in the book. We would appreciate and love to hear from you. This would definitely fulfill our aim of making MATLAB learning really easy.

S. SWAPNA KUMAR
LENINA S V B

Acknowledgements

At the outset, we thank everyone who directly or indirectly has shown the rays of hopes for writing this book till its smooth completion. Since we began writing, we have received many indispensable inputs directly or indirectly in materialising this book from learned societies of different corners all over the world. **A Very Huge Thanks** to each of them.

This is really an inspiration and memorable moments that add to our profession life.

We express our sincere gratitude to all the members of Vidya Academy of Science and Technology, Thrissur; Vidya International Charitable Trust; VAST, Kilimanoor and Shri Guru Gobind Singhji Institute of Engineering and Technology, Vishnupuri; for motivating us to contribute towards academic excellence. Our acknowledgements would be incomplete, if we specially do not remember the trust members, management, director, principal, teachers, technical staff and office staff members for rendering their cooperation in completion of this book.

We are immensely grateful and thankful to MathWorks, Inc., CoreEL Technologies (I) Pvt. Ltd., Bangalore for supporting us to use the resources in writing this book. We express our gratitude to Naomi Fernandes, MathWorks Book Program, US, and Bobban Ignatius, CoreEL Technologies (I) Pvt. Ltd., Bangalore for extending their support.

We are also greatly thankful to our family members and friends for their love and moral support in successful completion of the book. We are really indebted to our parents for their constant encouragement.

Finally, we express our sincere gratitude to the publisher, PHI Learning Private Limited, Delhi for improving the presentation of this book. Their continuous support, led by Malaya Ranjan Parida, Shivani Garg, and Lakshmi Kumar made us possible to organise the book chapters so well.

This book is written as a means for understanding the MATLAB basics easily. So we welcome all, to write us comments and suggestions for future enhancement of the book.

S. SWAPNA KUMAR
LENINA S V B

CHAPTER 1

MATLAB
An Overview

LEARNING OBJECTIVES

The aim of this chapter is to provide the basic ideas on MATLAB. At the end of this chapter, we should able to understand:

- The MATLAB and some of its toolboxes.
- How to start a new MATLAB session, use the desktop environment and terminate the session.
- The environment of MATLAB and its components.
- The ideas behind the various MATLAB toolboxes.

INTRODUCTION

When one is in search of programming software for quantitative analysis in the field of engineering, statistics, finance, research applications and study of design in industrial intelligent device, then MATLAB software is the better option. MATLAB has evolved over a period of years with input from many contributes. It has tools for almost all applications. The name MATLAB stands for MATrix LABoratory. MATLAB was originally written to provide easy access to matrix software developed by the LINPACK and EISPACK projects, which together represent the state-of-the-art in software for matrix computation.

This book is designed to provide basic tools for beginners whether they are students or researchers. It is also designed to meet the difficulties of understanding the basics of MATLAB and does not assume one shall have any prior knowledge of any programming software. The basic concepts are explained step-by-step from the first chapter till the last as the chapters progress. However, it is assumed that MATLAB is installed in the computer system. It is also expected that one has average level of general computer experience. In this book, we will learn how to solve simple quantitative problems using MATLAB. This includes how to load data into the program, how to do the programming and how to create the graphs. Even we can troubleshoot the errors. Through this book the learning of MATLAB is a fun and develops an interest in solving the complex problems. Further, this book will not let us to any annoyance rather make us feel that learning of MATLAB is possible by mimicking. We can mimic many examples given in this book which will lead us to learn like a child learning by mimicking its parents. This way we can learn any language.

1.1   MAPPING OF THE BOOK

This book is focussed on certain desktop tools, mathematical functions, graphics and methods to write programs. There are several toolbox packages of program that provide functionality to MATLAB, such as Optimisation toolbox for minimisation function and statistical function toolbox. Many toolbox tasks can be performed using drop-down menus, using keyboard shortcuts or using commands.

At the beginning of the book, several descriptions are explained in less detail but later more detail explanation are provided as the progress of chapters takes place. Some of the basic information discussed as move through the chapters are follows:

- Initially the understanding of DESKTOP blocks in different parts is explained.
- The algebraic problem expression and its solution using MATLAB are explained in Chapter 2.
- More on variables that are used to store information are explained in Chapter 3.
- The matrix manipulation technique using MATLAB is also explained in Chapter 3. This is followed by matrix algebra and use of linear equation and linear regression coefficients.
- Chapter 5 focusses on data import into the program and exported out of it for analysis.
- Further Chapter 6 shows the ways to produce two dimensional graphs.
- Flow logic is explained in Chapter 7.
- In Chapter 8 scripts and functions are explained with different programming techniques.
- Several numerical analyses are performed to solve equation based filter, digital signal and image processing using MATLAB in Chapters 9 and 10.
- Few of the toolboxes uses are explained and also dealt with Simulink in Chapters 11, 12 and 13.
- Finally, error checking, debugging and searching for help are explained in Chapter 14.

Further, MATLAB also provides an extensible programming visualisation environment for easy mode of learning. At the end of chapter, it simplifies the analysis of mathematical models to let you free from coding in high-level languages, to save time and improve computational speed.

1.2   BRIEF HISTORY OF MATLAB

Cleve Moler, the chairman of the computer science department at the University of New Mexica developed a program known as MATLAB in late 1970s. The purpose of this program initiation was to make students to learn LINPACK (a software library for performing numerical linear algebra on digital computers) and EISPACK (a software library for numerical computation of eigenvalues and eigenvectors of matrices, written in FORTRAN) without learning FORTRAN (Formula Translating System—a programming language). When the popularity of this program language spread then later Jack Little, an engineer joined with Cleve and Steve Banger rewrote MATLAB in C (a middle-level language used to interact with computers) and founded MathWorks in 1984.

1.2.1 MATLAB Foundations: The MathWorks

MathWorks, employs more than 3000 people in 15 countries, with headquarters in Natick, Massachusetts, USA. MATLAB developed by 'The MathWorksInc' is a software package. It is a high-performance language for technical computing (MathWorks, 1998). It is platform independent software. It is the software used in interactive mode or in compiled version. MATLAB is a case sensitive language and it acts as a tool for performing matrix algebra.

MATLAB was first adopted by researchers and practitioners in control engineering. It is now used in education, for learning and teaching linear algebra, numerical analysis and image processing. Engineers, structural geologists and scientists worldwide use these product families to do research, innovation and development in various sectors of automotive, aerospace, electronics, engineering field, financial services, biotech-pharmaceutical, structural geology and other industries.

Today, MathWorks is the leading developer of mathematical computing software and other supporting tools. MATLAB and Simulink are also fundamental teaching and research tools in various universities and learning institutions around the world. The MATLAB and Simulink product families R2014a, with supporting tools are as summarised in Figure 1.1.

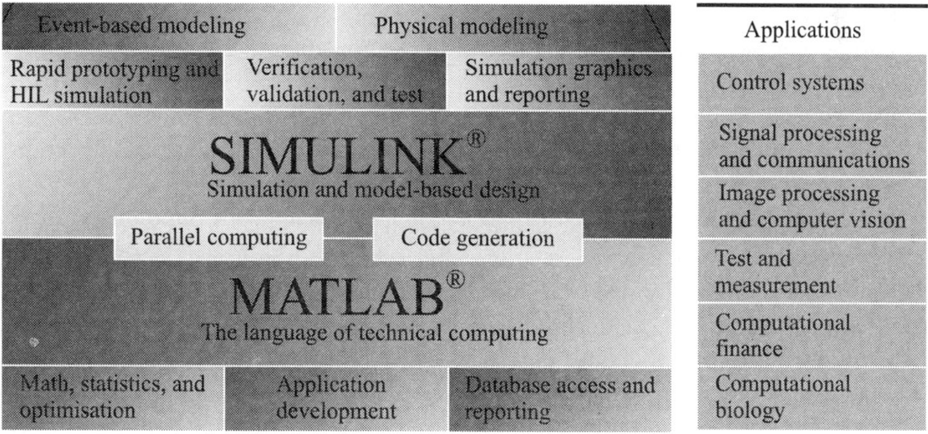

FIGURE 1.1 MATLAB and Simulink product families.

MathWorks product family is subdivided into three sections which are as follows:

- *MATLAB:* It is a computational language, for math and visualisation.
- *Simulink:* It is used for graphical modelling, simulation of continuous and discrete systems.
- *State flow:* It is the simulation of event driven systems to complement Simulink.

Simulink is a graphical environment for simulation and Model-based Design for multi-domain dynamic and embedded systems.

State flow software is an interactive, graphical design tool for developing and simulating event-driven systems based on finite-state machine theory.

MATLAB supports various features such as a family of application-specific solutions using toolboxes that allow us to learn and apply specialised technology. Toolboxes are comprehensive collections of MATLAB functions to solve particular class of problems that include signal processing, control systems, neural networks, fuzzy logic, wavelets, simulation, and many others. Few of them shall be discussed later in the chapters.

1.3   ABOUT THE MATLAB

MATLAB is a high-performance language for technical computing. It integrates programming, computation and visualisation in an easy-to-use environment where problems and solutions are expressed in familiar mathematical notation. The key feature of MATLAB that differentiates it from other software is the easy way of interactive environment. This optimise problems of statistics, Fourier analysis, filtering, numerical integration, ordinary differential equations, etc. It has built-in graphics for visualising data and tools for creating custom plots, development tools for improving code quality and maintainability, and maximising performance. MATLAB also supports tools for building applications with custom graphical interfaces. MATLAB based algorithms with external applications and languages such as C, Java, .NET, and Microsoft's Excel.

Typical uses of MATLAB in brief are as follows:

- Solving mathematical computations
- Development of algorithmic program
- Prototype model creation for solving complex problem
- Data analysis and synthesis for analysis
- Generation of scientific and engineering graphics for analysis
- Complex data analysis using MATLAB toolboxes (i.e., statistics, neural networks, fuzzy logic, H-infinity control, economics, etc.)

MATLAB in university environment is the standard instructional tool for introductory and advanced courses in mathematics, engineering, and science. In industry, MATLAB is the tool of choice for high-productivity research, development and analysis.

In nut shell, MATLAB is a high-level language for application development, data analysis, numerical computations and visualisations. The reader practicing this book will be enabled to solve quantitative problems using MATLAB. This includes programming, data loading and graph creation. This chapter introduces tools that we need to begin using MATLAB effectively. It also includes brief description on launch of MATLAB program, use of help menu, command window usage and finally, to quit the software. After completion of this chapter, we will understand the front end of the MATLAB and its functionality.

1.3.1   Platform and Version

MATLAB can be installed on any of the operating system (OS), like Windows, UNIX, (UNICS later became Unix, UNICS—UNiplexed Information Computing System), Mac OS X (Macintosh operating system). Initially, MATLAB versions were supporting only for Macintosh.

MATLAB version 6 supports Windows and UNIX platforms. For effectiveness of MATLAB, it is better to prefer Windows environment. Windows operating system flavor is Windows 95, Windows 2000, Windows Millennium Edition, and Windows NT. This book compatible with the current version of MATLAB 2015b or MATLAB 2010.

Today, MATLAB engines incorporate the LAPACK and BLAS libraries, embedding the state-of-the-art in software for matrix computation. MATLAB was created to be a numerical computation package based on the LINPACK routines. This is usually faster than Mathematica (mathematical engine) and Maple (mathematical engine) in numeric intensive tasks. There are different versions of MATLAB. Every newer version adds new features to the older one. The **release number** is the version reported by Concurrent License Manager Program, *FLEXlm*. FlexNet Publisher (formerly known as *FLEXlm*) is a software license manager from Flexera Software which implements license and is intended to be used in corporate environments to provide floating licenses to multiple end users of computer software.

Version command

Typing version on the command prompt shows on which version of MATLAB we are working with. Various versions of MATLAB are listed in Table 1.1 (can be obtained by typing version command on the command prompt. The reader shall come to know about the command prompt shortly in this chapter itself).

TABLE 1.1 The MATLAB version

Version—Year	Version—Year
MATLAB 1.0—1984	MATLAB 7.2 (R2006a)—Mar. 1, 2006
MATLAB 2.0—1986	MATLAB 7.3 (R2006b)—Sep. 1, 2006
MATLAB 3.0—1987	MATLAB 7.4 (R2007a)—Mar. 1, 2007
MATLAB 3.5—1990	MATLAB 7.5 (R2007b)—Sep. 1, 2007
MATLAB 4.0—1992	MATLAB 7.6 (R2008a)—Mar. 1, 2008
MATLAB 4.2c—1994	MATLAB 7.7 (R2008b)—Oct. 9, 2008
MATLAB 5.0 (Volume 8)—Dec., 1996	MATLAB 7.8 (R2009a)—Mar. 6, 2009
MATLAB 5.1—May, 1997	MATLAB 7.9 (R2009b)—Sep. 4, 2009
MATLAB 5.1.1—1997	MATLAB 7.9.1 (R2009bSP1)—Apr. 1, 2010
MATLAB 5.2—1998	MATLAB 7.10 (R2010a)—Mar. 5, 2010
MATLAB 5.2.1—1999	MATLAB 7.11(R2010b)—Sep. 3, 2010
MATLAB 5.3—1999	MATLAB 7.11.1 (R2010bSP1)—Mar. 17, 2011
MATLAB 5.3.1—1999	MATLAB 7.11.2 (R2010bSP2)—Apr. 5, 2012
MATLAB 6.0 (R12)—Nov., 2000	MATLAB 7.12 (R2011a)—Apr. 8, 2011
MATLAB 6.1 (R12.1)—June, 2001	MATLAB 7.13 (R2011b)—Sep. 1, 2011
MATLAB 6.5 (R13)—July, 2002	MATLAB 7.14 (R2012a)—Mar. 1, 2012
MATLAB 6.5.1 (R13SP1)—2003	MATLAB 8.0 (R2012b)—Sep. 11, 2012
MATLAB 6.5.2 (R13SP2)—2003	MATLAB 8.1 (R2013a)—Mar. 7, 2013
MATLAB 7.0 (R14)—June, 2004	MATLAB 8.2 (R2013b)—Sep. 6, 2013
MATLAB 7.0.1 (R14SP1)—Oct., 2004	MATLAB 8.3 (R2014a)—Mar. 7, 2014
MATLAB 7.0.4 (R14SP2)—Mar. 7, 2005	MATLAB 8.4 (R2014b)—Oct. 2, 2014
MATLAB 7.1 (R14SP3)—Sep. 1, 2005	MATLAB 8.5 (R2015a)—Mar. 5, 2015

1.3.2   MATLAB Scope in Computational Mathematics

MATLAB is a platform independent system that provides interactive environment for computation, visualisation, and animation. MATLAB has a 'natural language' interface that is easy to use with built-in functions and toolboxes. It solves the problems in matrix format. MATLAB is used in every facet of computational mathematics. The mathematics that we typically learn in math class environment is based on manipulation of symbols to find solutions. MATLAB, however, uses numerical methods to solve such types of problems. The solutions are generally end up being the same, but the method of arriving at them differs.

Following are some commonly used mathematical calculations where MATLAB is used:

- Handling with matrices and arrays
- Linear algebra and equations
- Nonlinear functions
- Statistics and data analysis
- Calculus and differential equations
- Numerical calculations
- Integration
- Transformation
- Curve fitting
- 2D and 3D plotting and graphics
- Various other special functions

1.3.3   The MATLAB System

The MATLAB system is broadly classified into the following five main sections:

1. The MATLAB development environment
2. The MATLAB mathematical function library
3. The MATLAB language
4. The MATLAB graphics
5. The MATLAB external interfaces/API (Application Programming Interface)

Following explanation gives the brief ideas of the above sections:

The MATLAB development environment: This is the set of tools and facilities that help to use MATLAB functions and files. Many of these tools are graphical user interfaces. It includes the MATLAB desktop and command window, a command history, an editor and debugger, and browsers for viewing help, the workspace, files, and the search path.

The MATLAB mathematical function library: MATLAB supports mathematical function using toolbox. Toolbox is a vast collection of computational algorithms ranging from elementary functions like sum, sine, cosine and complex arithmetic to more sophisticated functions like matrix inverse, matrix eigenvalues, Bessel functions and Fast Fourier transforms.

The MATLAB language: This is a high-level matrix/array language with control flow statements, functions, data structures, input/output, and object-oriented programming features. It allows creation of large and complex application programs.

The MATLAB graphics: MATLAB has extensive facilities for displaying vectors and matrices as graphs. It includes high-level functions for two-dimensional and three-dimensional data visualisation, image processing, animation, and graphics presentation. It also includes low-level functions that allow us to fully customise the appearance of graphics as well as graphical user interfaces on MATLAB applications.

The MATLAB external interfaces/API: MATLAB has an inbuilt library function that allows us to write C and FORTRAN programs that interact with MATLAB. It includes facilities for calling routines from MATLAB as a computational engine for reading and writing MAT-files.

1.3.4   Features of MATLAB

Following are some of the basic features of MATLAB discussed in earlier sections:

- It is a high-level language for numerical computation, visualisation and application development.
- It provides an interactive environment for iterative exploration, design and problem solving.
- It provides vast library of mathematical functions for solving problems on linear algebra, statistics, Fourier analysis, filtering, optimisation, numerical integration and ordinary differential equations.
- MATLAB programming interface gives development tools for optimisation of performance.
- It provides tools for building applications with custom graphical interfaces along with visualising data.
- It provides functions for integrating MATLAB based algorithms with external applications and supports languages, such as C, Java, .NET and Microsoft Excel.
- The language tools, inbuilt functions provide faster solution than spreadsheets or traditional programming languages such as C/C++ or Java.
- MATLAB is used for range of applications such as in signal processing and communications, image and video processing, control system, test and measurement, computational biology and computational finance.

1.3.5   Uses of MATLAB

MATLAB is widely used as a computational tool in science and engineering. It is also encompassing the fields of non-engineering streams. It is used in a range of fields some of them are listed as follows:

- All engineering branches
- Medical electronics

- Math and computation
- Signal processing and communications
- Image and video processing
- Robotics
- Modelling, simulation and prototyping
- Control systems
- Algorithm development
- Test and measurement
- Data acquisition, data analysis, exploration and visualisation
- Power systems
- Computational finance
- Scientific and engineering graphics
- Chemical engineering
- Computational biology
- Application development, including graphical user interface building

1.4   INSTALLATION OF MATLAB

MATLAB can be installed on Windows or Linux or Macintosh platform. The simplest way to setup MATLAB is to run '*SetupSimple.exe*'. At the end of setup process, when the activation question will appear then activate MATLAB manually according to the steps 6–7 in the list below. If simplified setup does not work then execute steps 2–6 manually. To install, subsequent steps are needed to follow:

Step 1   Open the folder with MATLAB setup.

Step 2   Run 'setup.exe' (or 'bin\win32\setup.exe' to install 32-bit MATLAB under 64-bit Windows).

Step 3   Choose 'install manually without using the internet'.

Step 4   Set the 'file installation key' that is provided during purchase of MATLAB software. For example, set up 25716-63335-16746-06072.

Step 5   Install MATLAB with required components.

Step 6   When asked to activate the product select 'Activate manually without internet'

Step 7   Select 'X:\serial\license.lic' when asked for license file.

1.4.1   MATLAB Startup

MATLAB is a programming language that built with a working environment. This includes facilities to manage the variables for importing and exporting data of work source. MATLAB also includes many supporting features like tools for developing and managing M-files based on the MATLAB applications depend on specific platform. The MATLAB can run on Microsoft Windows information or UNIX information.

To start, double-click on shortcut icon of the MATLAB shown in Figure 1.2.

FIGURE 1.2   The default view of MATLAB icon.

On start, the MATLAB logo will display product information and desktop window will appear before as an intermediate screen. On a UNIX machine, generally we need to type MATLAB in a terminal window by setting up the directory path initially.

1.4.2   Starting and Quitting MATLAB

Starting MATLAB

If we are working on Windows or Mac OS X platform, we can start MATLAB by choosing it from the menu. If we like to install the MATLAB software on Windows platforms, the installer will create a shortcut of the program file in the installation directory. This shortcut icon can be moved to desktop, if we desire so. Any version of MATLAB after installation can be started by simple double-click on the shortcut generated on our desktop.

We can also customise MATLAB startup by changing the directory in which MATLAB starts or automatically execute MATLAB statements in a script file named *startup.m*. We can write text that follows, with two greater than signs (>>) used to denote the MATLAB command prompt where we can enter our commands as shown in Figure 1.3.

On UNIX platforms, start MATLAB by typing `matlab` at the operating system prompt. Clearly, to start MATLAB on a UNIX system, open up a UNIX shell and type the command `matlab`. This will start up the software, and wait for us to write our commands.

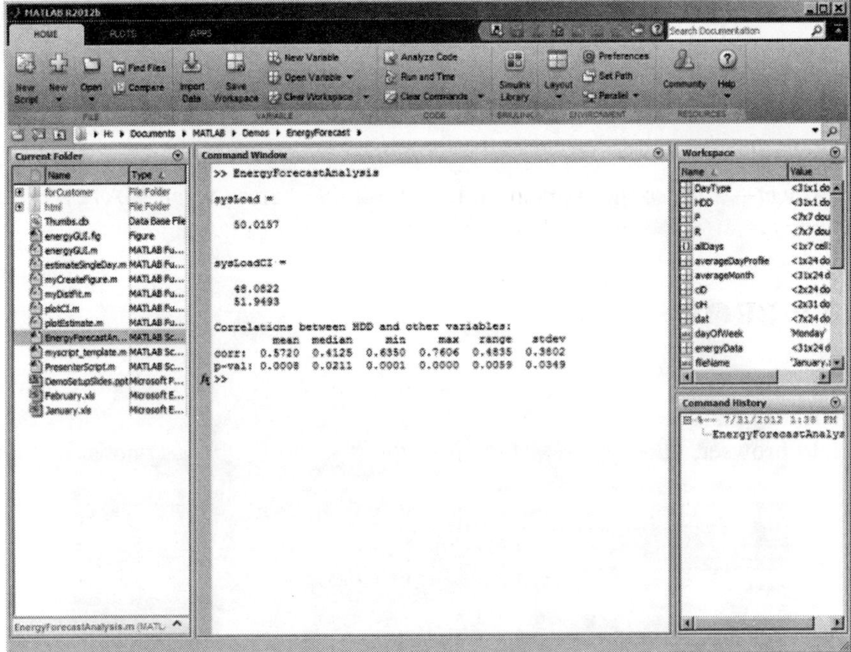

FIGURE 1.3 The default view of MATLAB shortcut on desktop.

Terminating MATLAB

Once we have finished the work and like to terminate the MATLAB application type quit in the command window. Alternatively, select Exit MATLAB from the File menu. So, there are two ways end our MATLAB session, the one ways is select File toolbar and click on Exit tab from the MATLAB desktop as shown in Figure 1.4, or other way is type quit in the Command Window (i.e., >> quit).

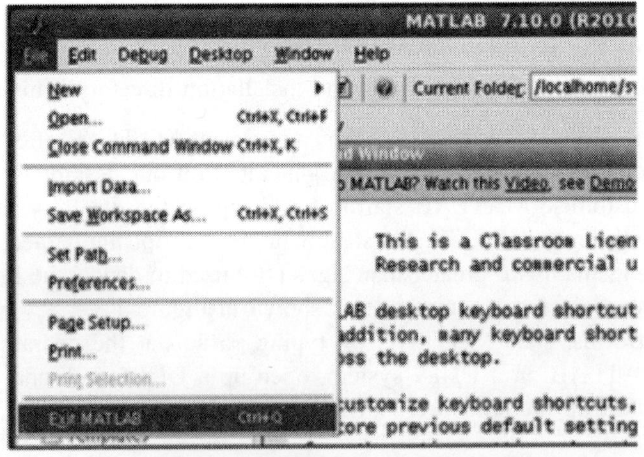

FIGURE 1.4 Toolbar to display Exit tab.

We can also terminate the MATLAB application, even by running a script file named *finish.m* each time MATLAB quits. *finish.m* is a file user create, that contains commands user want to run when MATLAB terminates. For example, users can include a save command in their *finish.m* file to save the workspace when MATLAB quits.

Two sample *finish.m* files that are in/toolbox/local are as follows:

- *finishsav.m*—It saves the workspace to a MAT-file before when MATLAB quits.
- *finishdlg.m*—It displays a dialog that allow us to cancel quitting.

1.5 HELP BROWSER

Use the Help browser to search and view documentation and demos for all our MathWorks products. The Help browser is an HTML viewer integrated into the MATLAB desktop. To open the Help browser, click the help button in the desktop toolbar as shown in Figure 1.5.

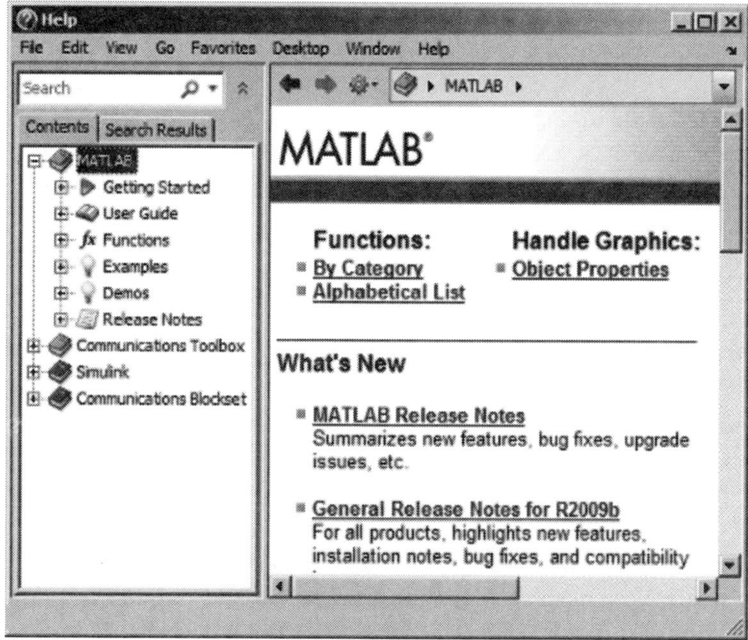

FIGURE 1.5   Help browser.

The Help browser consists of two panes, the Help Navigator which we use to find information and the display pane where we view the information. These are having the following key features:

- *Contents tab* — To view the titles and tables of contents of the documentation.
- *Index tab* — To find specific index entries (selected keywords) in the documentation.
- *Search tab* — To look for specific words in the documentation.
- *Demos tab* — To view and run demonstrations for our MathWorks products.

1.5.1   MATLAB Environment

The most important features of the MATLAB development environment are highly configurable, which means that it may appear in different forms on machine. We can try that by selecting Desktop → Desktop Layout → Default from the menu bar, but that may still not give us the exact configuration, depending on our particular version.

MATLAB desktop default window environment pop up as shown in Figure 1.6, when the program starts. The following screen shows the default desktop. We can customise the arrangement of tools and documents to suit our needs.

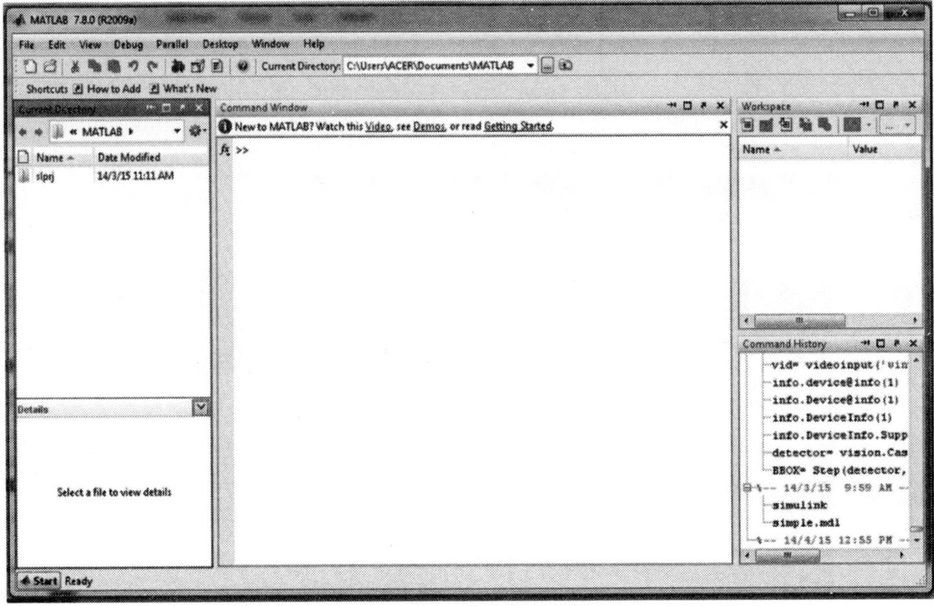

FIGURE 1.6   The MATLAB work environment.

Once the MATLAB initialising process is completed, a MATLAB desktop environment will appear providing a set of sub-windows and a browser. In this desktop environment, we you may define variables, manage files and objects, execute programs, and view command history. The desktop also contain tools (graphical user interfaces) that appear for managing files, variables, and applications associated with MATLAB.

1.5.2   Composite MATLAB Window Environment

MATLAB based GUI environment allows user to easily navigate between various windows. Composite MATLAB Window Environment is as shown in Figure 1.7. This view shows all the windows of MATLAB in single window, which is very easy for navigation from one window to another.

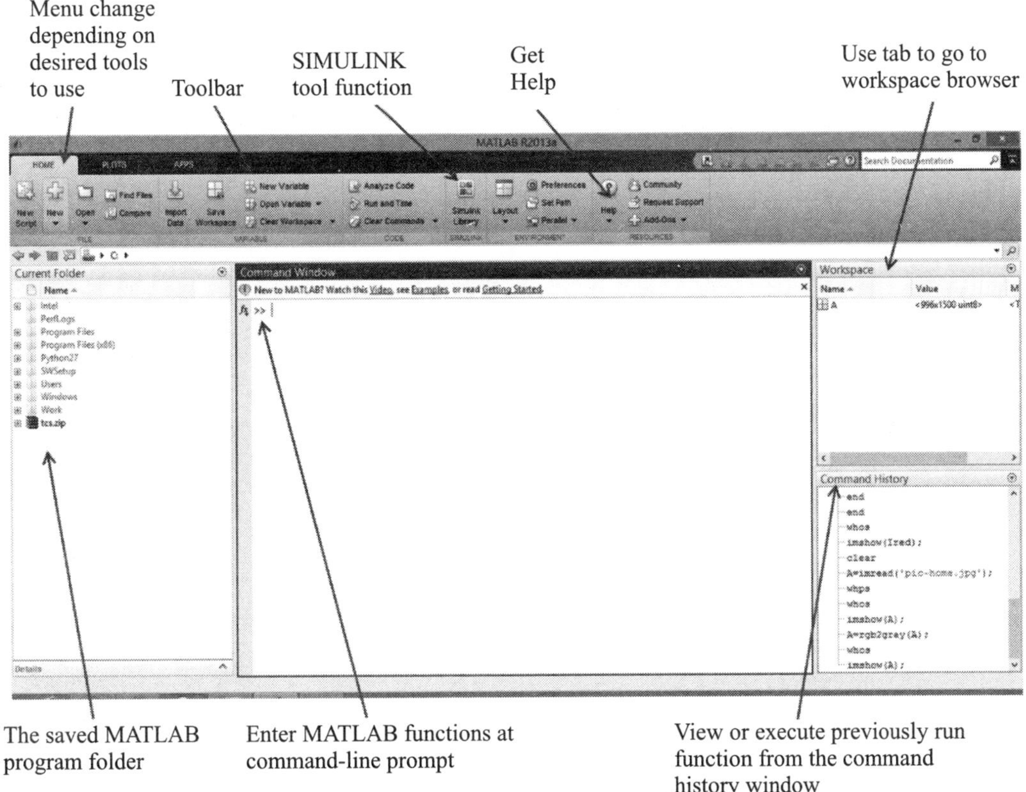

FIGURE 1.7   Composite MATLAB window environment.

A typical MATLAB desktop includes a Command Window where we can type MATLAB commands. Even we take the MATLAB help by clicking on the 'Help toolbar'.

1.5.3   Basic Components of the MATLAB Environment

The MATLAB window will contain a title bar, a menu bar, a toolbar and five embedded windows, out of which one window is hidden. The largest window is the Command Window and it is the important window. The other four windows are the 'Launch Pad' (hidden), the 'Workspace', the 'Command History' window, and the 'Current Folder' window. If the Command Window is active, its title bar will be dark, and the prompt will follow a cursor. If the Command Window is not active, just click anywhere in it, it gets activated.

The following screen shows the default configuration of the MATLAB (2009a version) Desktop front screen in Figure 1.8.

MATLAB displays the following basic window components once it is pop-up.

- Launch pad window
- Command window

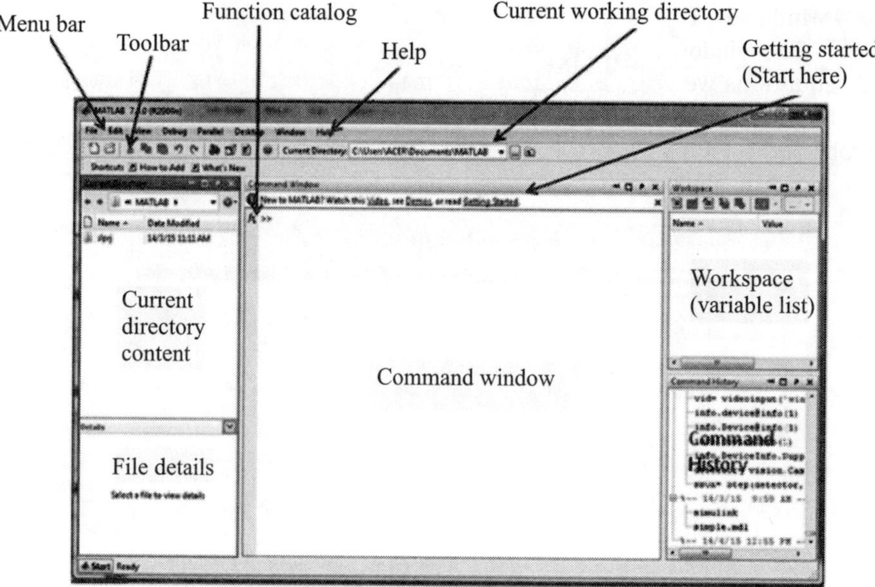

FIGURE 1.8   The MATLAB (2009a version) desktop front screen.

- Command history window
- Workspace window
- Current directory window

Launch pad window: This is used to access all MATLAB services and toolboxes quickly as shown in Figure 1.9. It is easy to access MATLAB and three installed toolboxes in the launch window environment. It is also easy to run tools and access documentation for all our MathWorks products. Launch pad window expands a listing to show the documentation, demos, and tools for that product.

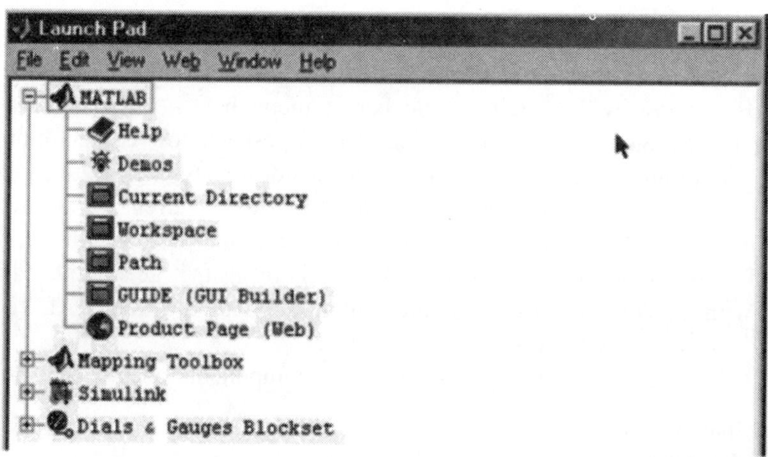

FIGURE 1.9   The Launch pad window.

Command window: This runs MATLAB functions. It is to execute commands in the MATLAB environment. The window is used to write the command and run to observe the result. These can be simple equations we want to evaluate, or more complex expressions involving MATLAB scripts or functions. For repeating the task, we can use 'up-down' arrow keys to execute the previous operation. We can also cut and paste the operations to be executed on the command prompt as shown in Figure 1.10.

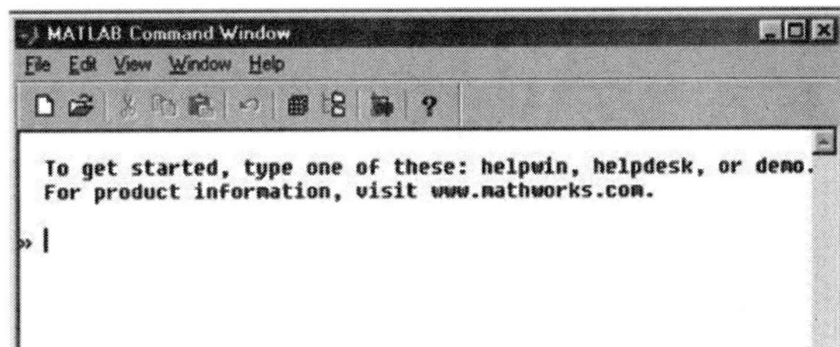

FIGURE 1.10   The command window.

Command history window: The Command history window shows the commands which we have entered in MATLAB since the last session. This window will retain all the information even though the system is put off and restore back. We can repeat any of these commands by double-clicking on them, or by dragging them from the Command history window into the Command window. We can also scroll back to previous commands by using the up arrow in the Command window. Even using MATLAB script files or functions, we can also drag commands from the Command history window into a file.

Workspace window: The Workspace shows the list of variables built-up during a session while using the MATLAB software to store in memory. This is used to view variable definitions and variable memory allocations in matrix form. Further, we can add variables (a simple scalar, a vector, or a matrix, and the size of all arrays) to the workspace by using functions, running M-files, and loading saved workspaces. Work space performs related operations using the Workspace browser. To open the Workspace browser, select Workspace from the Desktop menu in the MATLAB desktop, or type Workspace at the commend Window prompt or type workspace at the Command Window prompt. If any of the variables in the Workspace are plot able, they may be plotted quickly and easily by right-clicking on the variable name and selecting a plot type.

Current directory window: The Current directory window shows the contents of the current working directory. This window also shows all the files related to current set of operation of script/function files. If we double-click on any of these file, it will open in a (text) editor. This way we can quickly access files on the MATLAB path by right-click on MATLAB scripts and function files to execute the commands contained therein. We can also change directories by clicking on folders or use the Current working directory text box at the top of the MATLAB working environment.

Some of the other important features of the MATLAB icon is pop-ups are highlighted as follows.

Figure window: It displays graphical output from the MATLAB code. When the command is executed the Figure window appears in separate screen.

Getting started: It is the link that leads users towards the MATLAB tutorial system. It helps the new users to go through the tutorials in the order in which they are presented.

M-File editor/debugger window: It is used to write M-files (includes colour-coded syntax features). The M-files can be used to debug interactively by using the break points.

Help: The *Help* menu provides a wide variety of useful sources of help. We can also use this menu to get guidelines to solve issues.

MATLAB path window: It is to add and delete folders to the MATLAB path. When the path is proper, the script or function file that is saved will be appeared in the current folder.

File details window: The File details window shows complete detail of the files in the current working directory.

Function catalog: The Function catalog provides a complete list of every MATLAB function description along with installed toolboxes.

By considering the menu bar and toolbar the five basic window components can be selected according to our personal preferences.

1.5.4   Desktop Environment of MATLAB R2013a/R2013b

When we start R2013a/R 2013b MATLAB, it shows a new environment called the MATLAB desktop, containing tools (graphical user interfaces) for managing files, variables, and applications associated with MATLAB. In the MATLAB, the desktop appears in its default layout as shown in Figure 1.11.

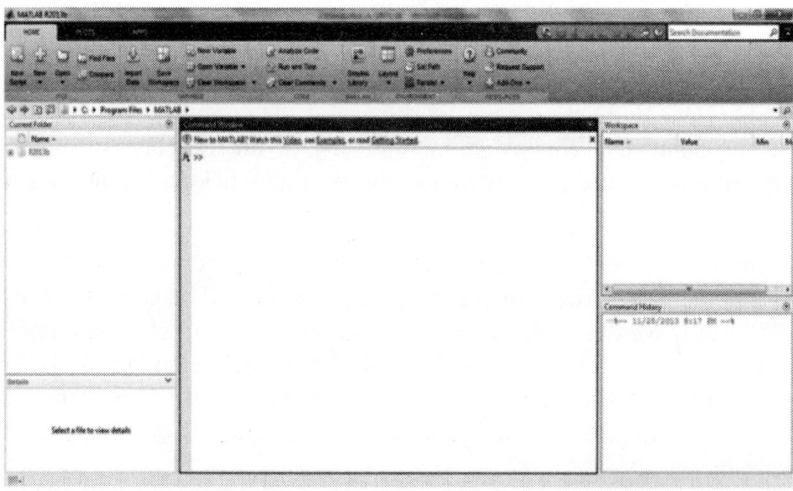

FIGURE 1.11   MATLAB R2013b desktop layout.

The Toolstrip organises MATLAB functionality in a series of tabs. One of the objectives of the Toolstrip is to make important MATLAB functionality easier to find and use. Tabs are divided into sections that contain a series of related controls. The controls are buttons, drop-down menus and other user interface elements in MATLAB.

Following are the tabs that support the MATLAB R2013a/R2013b version.

Global tabs

When we open R2013a/R2013b for the first time, we will notice three tabs—the Home tab, the Plots tab, and the Apps tab. We may notice the light blue bar in the upper right corner. That is called the *Quick Access Toolbar*. These three tabs are always there no matter what we are doing in MATLAB. For that reason, they are called *global tabs*.

The **Home tab**, shown in Figure 1.12 is a tab where general purpose operations like creating new files, importing data, managing workspace, and setting of Desktop layout are present which every user use.

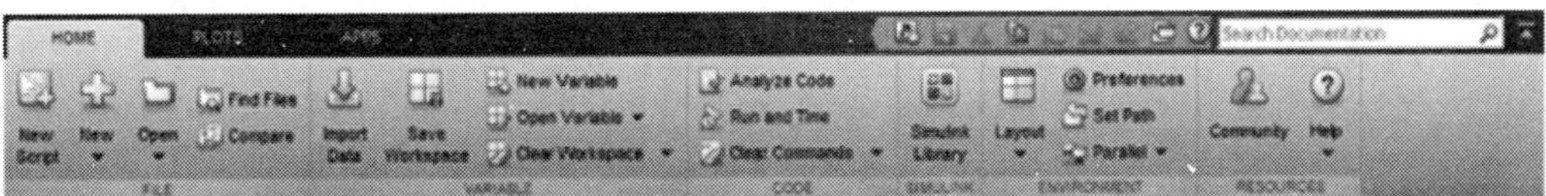

FIGURE 1.12   Home tab.

The Home tab has sections for operations on files, variables, code and so forth. The `File` section has controls to do file related operations including creating scripts (`New Script`), opening files (`Open`), and comparing two files (`Compare`).

The **Plots tab**, shown in Figure 1.13 is a tab which we use to create MATLAB Plots.

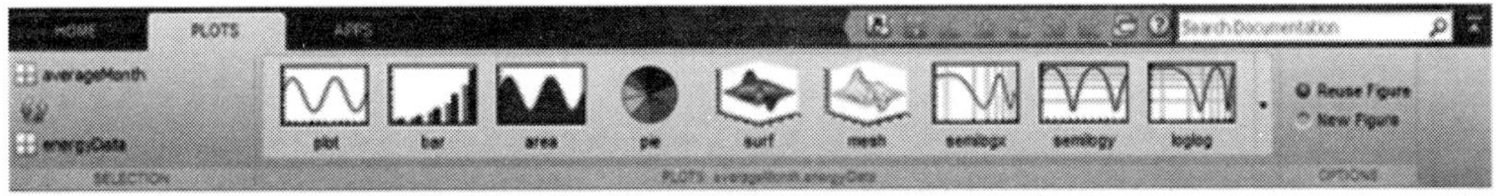

FIGURE 1.13   Plots tab.

The Plots tab displays a gallery of plots available in MATLAB and any toolboxes that have installed. To create a plot from the gallery, select the variables in the workspace that we need to plot and then select the type of visualisation that we want to use for that data. The gallery showing plots that are appropriate for the data, we select as per requirements. The downward facing arrow on the far right brings down the full extent of the plot gallery with many more choices.

The last tab of the global tabs is the **Apps tab**, shown in Figure 1.14.

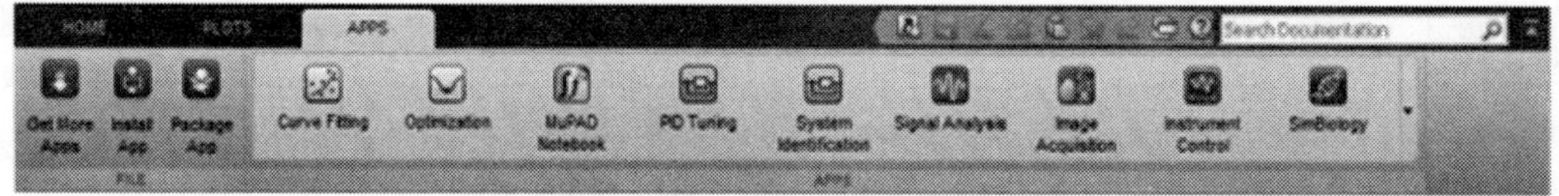

FIGURE 1.14   Apps tab.

It is the place to run interactive MATLAB applications. Some of those applications come from MathWorks automatically with toolboxes that we purchase and have installed. The Apps tab presents a gallery of apps that we have installed. The downward facing arrow on the far right brings down the full extent of the apps gallery with many more choices. We simply click on the icon of our favorite app (e.g., Optimisation) and the app will start.

Contextual tabs

The MATLAB has another important tab known as **Contextual tabs**. When we click the Home tab followed by clicking on → New Script; three new tabs appear—the Editor tab, Publish tab, and View tab as shown in Figure 1.15. The Editor tab contains all the functions that are needed when we are editing our file. All great capabilities of the Editor tab are organised in a way that is easier to use.

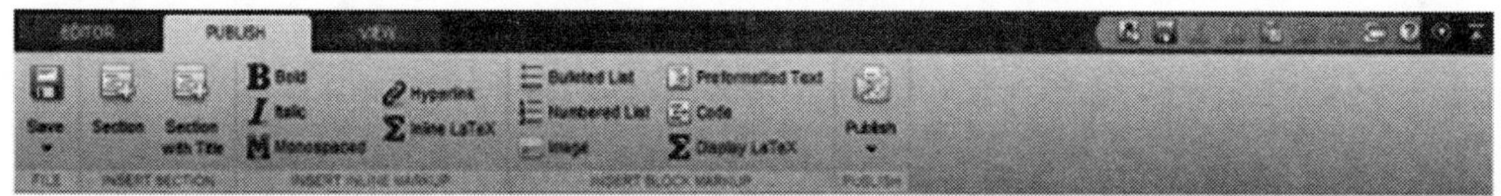

FIGURE 1.15   Contextual tabs.

The **Publish tab**, as shown in Figure 1.16, is another tab associated with the Editor. The publish tab has the formatting controls that can create MATLAB documents using Publish tools all documents can put in a single place.

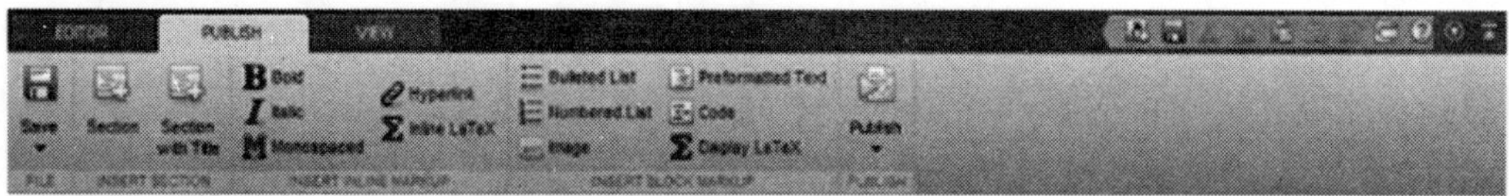

FIGURE 1.16   Publishing tab.

Publishing is a very useful feature in MATLAB that has been in the product for several years.

The **View tab** is the last of the Editor contextual tabs. It is used to control the layout and appearance of files in the Editor as shown in Figure 1.17.

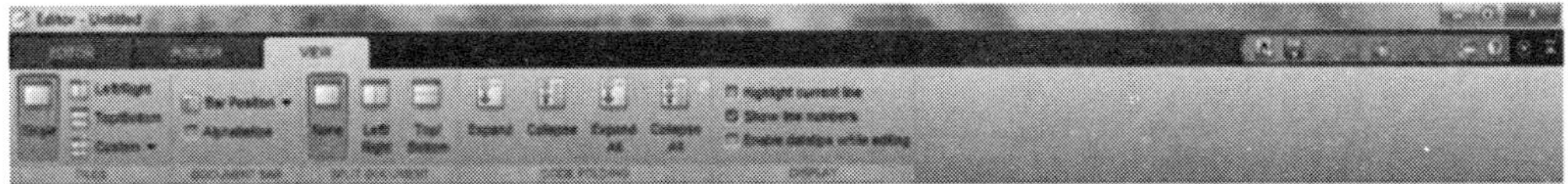

FIGURE 1.17   View tab.

Minimising the Toolstrip

The toolstrip is used when there is limited screen real space in laptop or desktop computers. We can do that by right-clicking anywhere in the toolstrip and selecting 'Minimize Toolstrip' or by double-clicking on any of the tabs. When the toolstrip is minimised it appears as shown in Figure 1.18.

FIGURE 1.18   Toolstrip.

Clicking on the above tab will temporarily restore to important functions. We can permanently restore the toolstrip by right-clicking anywhere on the toolstrip and selecting 'Restore Toolstrip' or by double-clicking on any of the tabs.

1.6   ARRANGING THE DESKTOP

It is always better to follow the default mode of operation of the MATLAB windows on the desktop. When we open the MATLAB desktop all the five window pop-up some time certain window may not seen, so to restore those window it is better to click the default mode from the desktop. A visual representation of this layout is appeared in Figure 1.19.

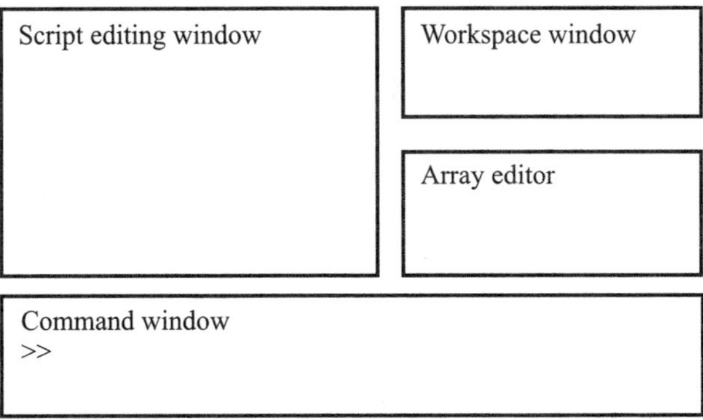

FIGURE 1.19   A convenient arrangement of the desktop.

Following ways can be used to arrange the desktop conveniently:

1. Keep the command window wide and not very tall, by stretching across the bottom of the desktop.

2. Keep the script editing window on the left side, just above the command window by click on the open-a-file icon on the toolbar.
3. Click on View on the toolbar, to place workspace window at the upper right corner, and array editor below it.

Using these windows we can simultaneously edit our script, watch the command window, programs and view the variables values in the array editor. Such arrangements is very helpful in the complicated script for easy debug.

1.6.1   Desktop Basic

The desktop includes the following panels:

- *Current folder:* To access the user files.
- *Command window:* To enter commands at the command line, using the command prompt (>>).
- *Workspace:* To explore the data that is created or import from files.

1.7   BASIC FUNCTIONS OF MATLAB

In the MATLAB, there are many types of functions such as display function, date function etc. Here we have listed some definitions for beginners of any programming language which help in understanding the MATLAB functions in better way:

- *Functions:* A block of statements grouped to perform a particular task.
- *Input:* Any parameters that is fed to the computer through the input devices for getting processed by the computer.
- *Output:* Any parameters that is processed by the computer and displayed or performed for the user.
- *Variables:* They are not constants. Variables in MATLAB can be of maximum 63 characters. Variable name cannot start with a number or character. It always starts with an alphabet. It can be followed by numeric or under score. MATLAB has few special variables like ans, pi, eps, NaN, realmin, realmax, etc.
- *Characters:* These can be alphabets, special characters like !, @, #, etc.
- *Constants:* These are not variable once defined will remain same throughout the program.
- *Computer program:* Sequence of steps that is written for a computer. They help in interacting with computers.

Following are some of the basic functions of MATLAB:

Display function: MATLAB prompt can display any statement by calling this function. We can start MATLAB environment by displaying the welcome statement as shown in Example 1.1.

EXAMPLE 1.1

```
>> display('@@@@@*****Hearty Welcome to MATLAB Learning*****@@@@@@')
@@@@@*****Hearty Welcome to MATLAB Learning*****@@@@@@
```

In MATLAB, display(X) prints the value of a variable or expression, X. The MATLAB software calls display(X) when it interprets a variable or expression X, that is, not terminated by a semicolon.

Date function: It gives current date of the system. Date function returns a string containing the date in dd-mm-yyyy format.

For example, typing date on command prompt is as shown below.

EXAMPLE 1.2

```
>> date
ans =
17-Dec-2014
```

Note: The MATLAB software creates the variable automatically when there is no specified output argument.

Doc function: Type doc MATLAB at command prompt, that will popup the helps windows shown in Figure 1.20. The word MATLAB in the contents is highlighted, and it displays the contents in it. A learner can select any content and read its details in the right side of the help window. This would be of great help to the beginners while beginning.

For example if we type doc MATLAB at the command and press enter key on the keyboard then we will get the screen as shown in Figure 1.20.

So right part of help window will get displayed, using the command:

```
>> doc MATLAB
```

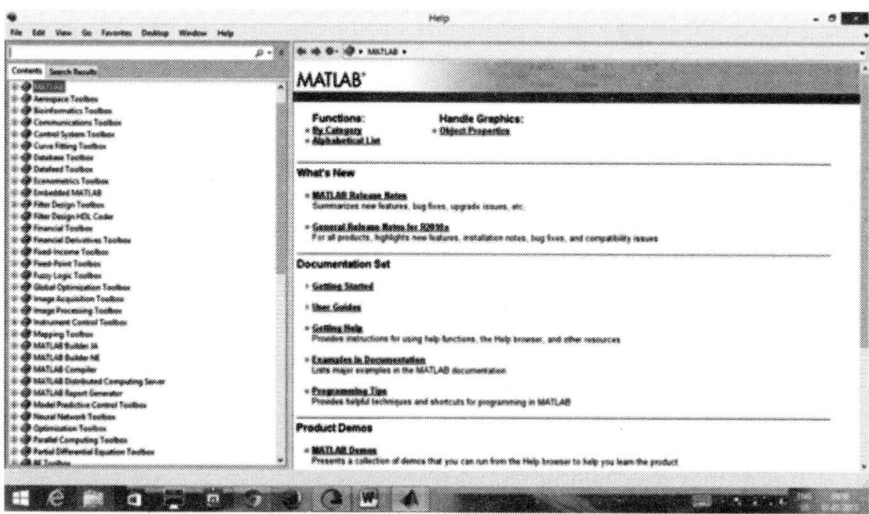

FIGURE 1.20 Window displayed by MATLAB for doc MATLAB command.

From MATLAB, we can get access to the MATLAB help functions by typing help tools which are used to solve doubts in complex problems. *Help* includes the information of MATLAB software version and its installation also.

```
>> help;
```

or

```
>> helpwin;
```

>> `help` will display 'functions' information in the second window whereas >> `helpwin` will display in separate window above HELP topics.

1.8   MOSTLY USED SYMBOLS IN MATLAB

Percentile (%) and semicolon (;) are mostly used symbols. The symbol '%' is used to indicate comments. A semicolon ';' at the end of a statement means that MATLAB will not display the result of the evaluated statement. If the ';' is omitted then MATLAB will display the result. This is also useful for printing the value of variables. Both the symbols need to be effectively used when one starts writing programs in MATLAB editor. Use of both the symbols is as shown in Figure 1.21.

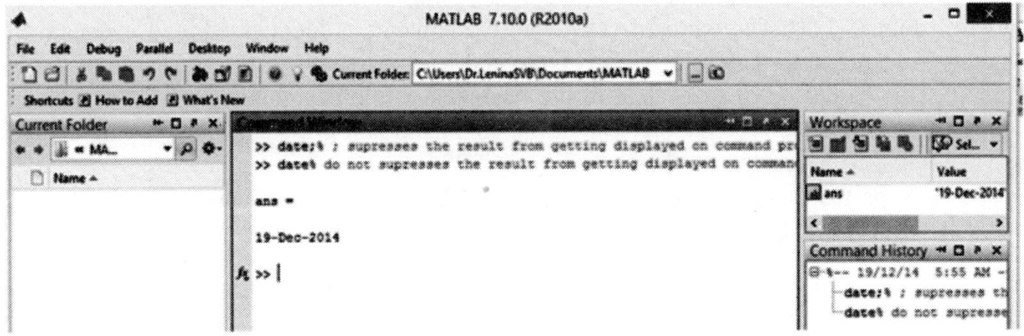

FIGURE 1.21   Window display illustrates symbols at MATLAB command prompt.

1.9   DEBUGGING IN THE MATLAB

In MATLAB, when our script fails, it will display the errors and also displays the reason. We will able to look at the data working with to see what went wrong. This is easy because after we run a script all of the data will be available at the MATLAB >> prompt. The following MATLAB commands are also useful for debugging:

who	lists presently active variables
whos	lists active variables and their sizes
what	lists.m files available in the current directory

This information is available in the workspace window on our screen.

1.10　ENDING A SESSION

The simplest way to conclude MATLAB session is to type 'quit' at the prompt. This can also be done by clicking on the 'X' symbol that closes our windows (in the upper right-hand corner). If more number of separate MATLAB windows are shown, then it is opened and closed separately. Do not close Desktop when MATLAB is generated windows around, this may be hazardous to our operating system.

Still another way to close the MATLAB is to type in the command window quit or click the Exit from the MATLAB File menu tab of the desktop. Before making an exit from MATLAB, make sure to save any variables, print any graphics or other files that are needed, and in general clean up before exit.

1.11　THE MATLAB PRODUCT FAMILY

The MATLAB product family is shown in Figure 1.22.

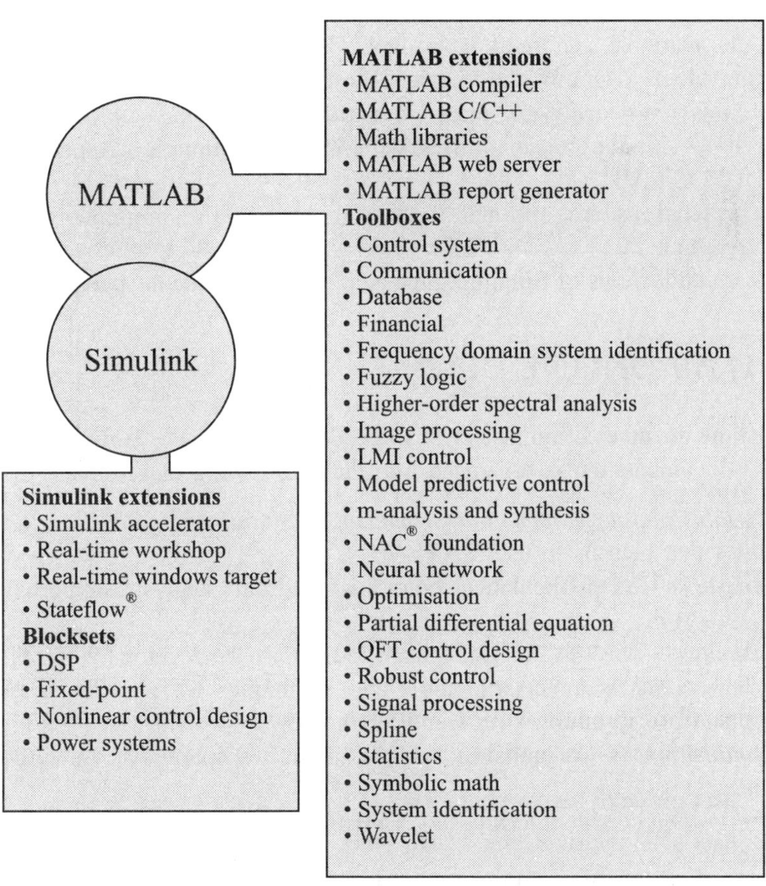

FIGURE 1.22　MATLAB product family.
Courtesy: The MathWorks or visit www.mathworks.com

MATLAB is the foundation for all the MathWorks products that combines numeric computation, 2D and 3D graphics,and language capabilities in a single, easy-to-use environment.

MATLAB extensions are optional tools that support the implementation of systems developed in MATLAB.

Toolboxes are libraries of MATLAB functions that are open and extensible; that customize for solving particular classes of problems. In toolboxes, we can view algorithms and add our own. It is very important for users to apply the toolbox for MATLAB applications. The toolboxes allow us to learn and apply specialised technology. Toolboxes are comprehensive collections of MATLAB functions (M-files) that extend the MATLAB environment in order to solve the particular classes of problems. During purchase of the software, we can opt for different toolboxes as per our needs from the MathWorks.

Simulink, developed by MathWorks, a scientific program in MATLAB, is an interactive system for simulating nonlinear dynamic systems. The MATLAB program allows us to model a system by drawing a block diagram on the screen and manipulating it dynamically. It is a data flow graphical programming language tool for modelling, simulating and analysing multidomain dynamic systems. Its primary interface is a graphical block diagramming tool and a customisable set of block libraries. It can work with linear, nonlinear, continuous-time, discrete-time, multivariable, and multirate systems. The Real-time program allows us to generate C code from our block diagrams and to run it on a variety of real-time systems.

So, Simulink is a system for nonlinear simulation that combines a block diagram interface. This can be 'live' simulation capabilities with the core numeric, graphics, and language functionality of MATLAB.

Simulink extensions are optional tools that support the implementation of systems developed in Simulink.

Blocksets are collections of Simulink blocks, designed for use in specific application areas.

1.12   MATLAB ONLINE HELP

To view the online documentation, select **MATLAB Help** from the **Help** menu in MATLAB. The MATLAB documentation is organised into these following main topics:

- *Desktop tools and development environment* — Startup and shutdown, the desktop, and other tools that help us to use MATLAB.
- *Mathematics* — All mathematical operations and data analysis support we can find in this.
- *Programming* — The MATLAB language that helps us to develop MATLAB applications.
- *Graphics* — This is a versatile tools and techniques for plotting, graph annotation, printing, and programming with Handle Graphics.
- *3D visualisation* — Visualising surface, data, transparency, viewing and lighting techniques.
- *Creating graphical user interfaces* — Helps to build GUI using tools and to write call back functions.
- *External interfaces/API* — MEX-files, the MATLAB engine, and interfacing to Java, Computer Object Model (COM) and the serial port.

SUMMARY

This chapter has been a very brief introduction to a few of the myriad functions and operations of MATLAB. It is meant to simply hone our appetite for using this wonderful tool. With this understanding, this would be a good time for us to get into the other chapters that cover all the basic functions and operations. By doing more exercises we will have better understanding and learning experience.

It is found that MATLAB is an invaluable tool for Matrix operations. Details of arrays to matrices will be discussed in details in Chapter 2. Also Chapter 2 shall put the reader into MATLAB script files.

REVIEW QUESTIONS

1. What are the key features of MATLAB that differentiates it from other software?
2. When was the MathWorks Inc. found?
3. On what operating system (OS) can MATAB be installed?
4. What version of MATLAB are we working on?
5. List out the steps involved in MATLAB installation.
6. How do we get help once we start with MATLAB?
7. Name the various windows we come across, when you start with MATLAB.
8. List various submenus in File menu of MATLAB.
9. Name the default variable which appears at the command prompt when we use MATLAB command prompt as a calculator (Example, 2+5 and press enter).
10. Write various ways to exit MATLAB.

PRACTICE EXERCISE

1. Display the following at the command window:

   "&&&&&&&&**** Hi! Enthusiastic to learn MATLAB*****&&&&&&&&&&"

2. Display the date at the command prompt.
3. Display clock at the command prompt.
4. Observe the difference between help and doc commands by typing the same at the command prompt.
5. What is the output, if we type word 'now' at the command prompt?
6. Recall at least one variable available in the history.

7. Load a variable from the workspace.

8. Display your name in the command window:

9. Compute the following at command prompt of MATLAB:

    (i) 2×3
    (ii) $2 + 3$
    (iii) $2/3$
    (iv) $3 - 2$

10. Exit MATLAB at least by three different ways.

CHAPTER 2

Building MATLAB Expression

<table>
<tr><td>

LEARNING OBJECTIVES

The aim of this chapter is to understand how to use different expression. By the end of this chapter, we should know:

- About the different types of variables.
- MATLAB concepts of character, variables and different precedence.
- Common mathematical functions and its use in algebraic functions and characters.
- The data types and the operators.
- The difference between relational and logical operators.
- MATLAB operators and its various examples.
- About MATLAB string, time and date concepts.

</td></tr>
</table>

INTRODUCTION

MATLAB is a powerful software package for computing numerical problems. Initially, this software was designed for solving linear algebra type problems using matrices. MATLAB has more features than other programming languages. Other programming languages mostly work with executing sequence of expression at a time, while MATLAB can operate on whole of matrix or array. Programming languages information consists of numbers, characters and strings. MATLAB has many built-in functions required for solving problems on data analysis, signal processing, optimisation and other scientific computations. MATLAB has its own library of vocabulary and grammar. It uses the vocabulary and grammar from its library to verify the syntax of words and symbols.

In this chapter, we will learn how to use MATLAB to do mathematics. Also, we will discuss the concept of MATLAB system commands, operator and different variables including the character set, data types, operators, constants and expressions. We will also learn various examples with MATLAB code in this chapter. Try the examples in a MATLAB Command Window as we go along the pages.

2.1   MATLAB DATA TYPES

There are different types of data that is recognised for various programming languages. In the same way, MATLAB, as a computing language, recognises different types of data. In MATLAB, data handling is much easier than in other languages like C, C++, Java, etc. Here we will understand the commonly used data types in MATLAB and their forms.

Scalars

Any number that represents magnitude (quantity or measure) is known as *scalar*. This includes integers, complex numbers and floating point numbers. For example, 5, –8, 9 + 2i, –67.19, etc.

Characters

The character constant is a representation of alphanumeric symbol enclosed in a single quote. For example, 'K', '6', '*', '+', etc. are character constants. The character that is not represented in single quote is numeric or sign.

Arrays

An array is a list of data placed in single row or column form. The elements of an array can be numeric or character or strings but not mixed up. However, array can be small or large array of similar types. There can be single or multidimensional arrays. An array is written using square brackets enclosing its elements separated by commas or spaces, e.g. [4, 8, 3, –5], [Cleve Moler], etc. which are also the examples of one-dimensional array.

Strings

Any two or more alphanumeric symbols enclosed in a single quote is known as *string data*. A string is an array of characters. For example, 'INDIA', 'MATLAB', '2015', etc. are all strings. Strings are basically the arrays of characters, such as 'INDIA' is equivalent to ['I', 'N', 'D', 'I', 'A']. The double quote is never used to write a character or string constants.

Cell arrays

A cell array is a special type of arrays, where the elements can be of different data types. This is distinguished from simple array by using braces, instead of square bracket for enclosing the elements. For example, {'KULIRMA', 'Kandalloor South', 'Kayamkulam', 'Kerala', 'PIN', '—', '690535'}. A cell array can incorporate other cell arrays as its elements.

Structures

A structure is a type of data that is having a meaningful field names. For example, ('Car', 'is', 'running', 'at', '70', 'KM', '/', 'Hrs'). Here the data is having a definite meaning.

2.2   COMMAND HANDLING

In this section, we will learn system commands that are required for getting familiar with MATLAB for command handling. In the command mode, we will write these commands name followed by inputs to observe their executions.

2.2.1   Common System Commands

In this section, we will learn commonly used system commands relating to files and directory management, that is, for proper handling of MATLAB. These commands are used to help the MATLAB during the change of the working directory from the Command window itself.

Clear command window (clc)

This function clears the Command window. This will clear window but nothing from Command History. All the variables will still appears in the workspace.

```
>> clc
```

Deleting file (delete)

It is used to delete any undesired files in the disk. This is represented as

```
delete filename or delete ('filename')
```

By typing this command, the file is deleted from the current directory.

Changing directory (cd)

This command is used to change the working directory as per Command window requirement. This is given as

```
cd pathname or cd('pathname')
```

Copy files (copyfile)

This command is used to copy a file from source to destination. In the absence of source file and destination file in the current directory, their respective full pathnames need to specify. Its form is represented as

```
copyfile('Source_file', 'Destination_file')
```

Directory listing (dir)

This command is used to list the name of subdirectories and files under a directory. It is represented in the following form:

```
dir directory_name      % Command mode
dir('directory_name')   % Functional mode
```

The first mode is not having argument variable name, whereas the second mode is having the argument variable written in a single quote and enclosed within a parenthesis.

Note: We will learn about parenthesis in next section.

Commands for working with the session

MATLAB provides various useful commands for working with the system, like saving the current work in the workspace as a file and loading the file later. It also provides various commands for other system-related activities like displaying date, listing files in the directory, displaying current directory, etc. Summarising in this topic, the list of commonly used general MATLAB commands. Table 2.1 displays some commonly used system-related commands.

TABLE 2.1   Command for working with the session

Command	Purpose
cd	Changes current directory
date	Displays current date
delete	Deletes a file
diary	Switches on/off diary file recording
dir	Lists all files in current directory
load	Loads workspace variables from a file
path	Displays search path
pwd	Displays current directory
save	Saves workspace variables in a file
type	Displays contents of a file
what	Lists all MATLAB files in the current directory
wk1read	Reads .wk1 spreadsheet file

2.2.2   Workspace Commands

Clear

It deletes all variables from the current workspace. If we want to specifically delete or remove variables form the workspace, their names are put after the clear command separated by space. It has form as

```
>> clear x y z
% will remove the variable x, y and z from the workspace.
```

Who

This command is used to list out variables used in the current workspace window. This also helps to identify the types of variable name for deciding further use of variable types.

```
>> who
```

Workspace

This command opens the Workspace browse displaying variable in the current workspace. The workspace displays the current variable that is used for operation having data placed in row or column arrays. We can view the variables in the workspace, to manipulate and clear as per needs.

Help

This function is used if any help is needed for MATLAB related function. Each main help topic corresponds to a folder name on the MATLAB search path. Help name displays the help text for the functionality, such as a function, method, class or toolbox.

Commands for managing a session

MATLAB provides various commands for managing a session. Summarising in this topic, the list of commonly used general MATLAB commands. Table 2.2 provides all such commands.

TABLE 2.2   Commands for managing session

Command	Purpose
Clc	Clears command window
clear	Removes variables from memory
exist	Checks for existence of file or variable
help	Searches for a help topic
lookfor	Searches help entries for a keyword
quit	Stops MATLAB
who	Lists current variables
whos	Lists current variables (long display)
global	Declares variables to be global

2.2.3   Command Line Editing

Various arrows and control keys on the keyboard allow us to edit, recall and reuse statements that we typed earlier. Suppose, e.g., we mistakenly type the value as shown in Example 2.1.

EXAMPLE 2.1

```
>> rho = (3 + sqt(64))/3
??? Undefined function or method 'sqt' for input arguments of type 'double'.
% MATLAB will respond with message      Type equation here.
Error: Unbalanced or unexpected parenthesis or bracket.
```

Here, instead of typing the entire line press the ↑, key, the statement typed earlier will be redisplayed. We can use the ← key to move the cursor over and insert the missing character. Even we can also copy the previously executed statement from the command history.

2.3   MATLAB BASICS

Using MATLAB, we can easily perform various mathematical operations as desire. MATLAB acts as a calculator, that is, by typing commands on a command window we can perform mathematical operations and view the results by pressing the enter key on the keyboard. The operations include exponentiation, division, multiplication, addition and subtraction. These mathematical calculations involving the mentioned operations can be directly carried out in a predefined order of sequence known as *order of precedence.*

2.3.1   Order of Precedence

In a mathematical expression, the order of precedence is very important for correct calculation. In general, the order of precedence is also called as *order of operation.* Each mathematical operator is assigned with precedence order; the operator having higher precedence is performed first. The following is the list of mathematical operations and their corresponding symbols arranged in descending order of precedence in Table 2.3.

TABLE 2.3   Precedence table for arithmetic operators

S No.	Description	Symbol
1.	Parentheses	(Bracket)...( )
2.	Exponentiation	(Order of)...^
3.	Multiplication, Division	*, /, \
4.	Addition, Subtraction	+, −
5.	Unary minus	−

We can start MATLAB to do certain calculations using some basic functions to display and finally to quit MATLAB. Arithmetic operators order is Multiplication, Division, Addition, and Subtraction (BODMAS). Initially, the command line >> from the command window is used to perform different arithmetic operations.

In Section 2.3.2, we will work through a simple example of this procedure. In beginning we can use MATLAB for simple arithmetic problem in which operators like plus (+), minus (−), multiply (*) and divide (/) are used. In addition to this, exponentiation (^) is also used.

Simple arithmetic operation

EXAMPLE 2.2

```
>> 100−25*2+10/5
ans =
    52
```

Enter all values and hit return (enter key). The result of the expression is calculated and displayed in the default variable ans as it is not assigned to any variable.

2.3.2 Operator Support

Some of the operator support commands are summarised as follows:

Format function

The format function controls the numeric display format of the value. It is only to display the value. The format function has the following forms used for numeric display as shown in Table 2.4.

TABLE 2.4 Format functions

Format function	Display up to	Example
Short	Scaled fixed point format, with 5 digits	3.1416
Long	Scaled fixed point format, with 15 digits for double; 7 digits for single	3.14159265358979
short e	Floating point format, with 5 digits	3.1416e + 000
long e	Floating point format, with 15 digits for double; 7 digits for single	3.141592653589793e + 000
short g	Best of fixed or floating point, with 5 digits	3.1416
long g	Engineering format that has at least 5 digits and a power that is a multiple of three	3.1416e + 000
long eng	Engineering format that has exactly 16 significant digits and a power that is a multiple of three	3.14159265358979e + 000

Table 2.5 shows the format types to switch between different output display formats for all numeric variables.

TABLE 2.5 Format output switching types

Format type	Display up to	Example
+	+, −, blank	+
Bank	Fixed dollars and cents	3.14
Hex	Hexadecimal (hexadecimal representation of a binary double-precision number)	400921fb54442d18
Rat	Ratio of small integers	355/113

Table 2.6 shows the format types used to affect the spacing in the display of all variables.

TABLE 2.6 Spacing variables format

Format type	Display up to	Example
Compact	Suppresses excess line feeds to show more output in a single screen. Contrast with loose.	theta = pi/2 theta = 1.5708
Loose	Adds linefeeds to make output more readable. Contrast with compact.	theta = pi/2 theta = 1.5708

The following examples show the change in resulting output, using different types of formats:

Here we are using Table 2.4 functions to manipulate the examples and observe results in the command window.

EXAMPLE 2.3

```
>> format short
```

EXAMPLE 2.4

```
>> 2/3   % Matlab works to 4 significant figures.
ans =
    0.6667
```

EXAMPLE 2.5

```
>> log 5    % Matlab works to 4 significant figures.
ans =
    0.6989
```

EXAMPLE 2.6

```
>> format long      % Matlab works to 15 significant figures.
>> 2/3
ans =
   0.666666666666667
```

EXAMPLE 2.7

```
>> format short   % Matlab works to 4 significant figures.
>> 2/3
ans =
    0.6667
```

By default, MATLAB displays numbers in short format, i.e., with four decimal place values. Next example illustrates the default condition.

If we want more precision, then use the format long command. The format long command displays 16 digits after decimal and 4 digits after the decimal point for short command.

EXAMPLE 2.8

```
>> format long
x =3+119/8+6^2
x =
   53.875000000000000
```

```
>> format short
>> x =3+119/8+6^2
x =
    53.8750
```

EXAMPLE 2.9

```
>> 2/3
ans =
    0.666666666666667
```

To double scaled fixed-point format with 14 to 15 digits after the decimal point refer to the Help menu.

Practice Exercise

```
>> format short up to 7 digit.
```

EXAMPLE 2.10   When the format is set to short, both pi and single(pi) will display 5-digit values as follows:

```
>> format short
>> pi
ans =
    3.1416
single(pi)
ans =
    3.1416
```

Now, set format to long, pi will display a 15-digit value while single(pi) will display an 8-digit value as follows:

```
>> format long
pi
ans =
    3.14159265358979
single(pi)
ans =
    3.1415927
```

EXAMPLE 2.11   When we use the following short format command and we will experience the display as follows:

```
>> format short
>> x= [7/2 3.2413-4]
```

```
x =

     3.5000    -0.7587
```

Also, we can set the format to short e   by typing
format short e
or use the function form of the syntax
format('short','e')

```
>> format short e
>> x= [7/2 3.2413-4]
x =

  3.5000e + 000 -7.5870e-001
```

```
>> format short g
>> x= [7/2 3.2413-4]
x =

          3.5        -0.7587
```

EXAMPLE 2.12   We can change the format to long by typing the following command:
format long

Now, view the result for the value of pi by typing the following command:

pi

ans =

3.14159265358979

View the current format by typing

get(0,'format')

ans =

long

EXAMPLE 2.13 Now, when we use the following long format command and we will experience the display as follows:

```
>> format long
>> x= [7/2 3.2413-4]
x =

   3.500000000000000          -0.758700000000000
```

```
>> format long e
```

```
>> x= [7/2 3.2413-4]
x =

      3.500000000000000e+000        -7.587000000000002e-001


>> format long g
>> x= [7/2 3.2413-4]
x =

                  3.5              -0.7587


>> format bank
>> x= [7/2 3.2413-4]
x =

                  3.50       -0.76


>> format rat
>> x= [7/2 3.2413-4]
x =

                  7/2            -327/431


>> format hex
>> x= [7/2 3.2413-4]
x =

    400c000000000000    bfe8474538ef34d8


>> format compact
>> x= [7/2 3.2413-4]
x =

    400c000000000000    bfe8474538ef34d8
```

In addition, the lines can also be suppressed using `compact` format.

EXAMPLE 2.14 When we set the format to its default, and display the maximum values for integers and real numbers in MATLAB then we will get the display as follows:

```
format
intmax('uint64')
ans =
18446744073709551615
realmax
ans =
1.7977e + 308
```

Now, change the format to hexadecimal, and display these same values:

```
format hex
intmax('uint64')
ans =
ffffffffffffffff
realmax
ans =
7fefffffffffffff
```

EXAMPLE 2.15   This example illustrates the short e and long e.

```
>> format   short e
>> d = 3.44 222444
   d =
        3.4422 e + 00
>> format long e
>> d = 3.44222444
d =
    3.44222444 0000000 e + 00
```

Common math functions

The common math functions has the following forms used for numeric display is shown in Table 2.7.

TABLE 2.7   Common math functions

Function	Description	Function	Description
abs (x)	$\|x\|$	sqrt(x)	$\sqrt{x}$
round (x)	nearest integer	fix (x)	nearest integer
floor (x)	nearest integer toward $-\infty$	ceil (x)	nearest integer toward ∞
sign (x)	$\begin{cases} -1, & x < 0 \\ 0, & x = 0 \\ 1, & x > 0 \end{cases}$	rem(x,y)	the remainder of x/y
exp (x)	e^x	log (x)	natural log ln x
log10 (x)	log base 10 $\log_{10}x$		

EXAMPLE 2.16

```
>> x = [-5.5 5.5]; % example of mathematical function
>> round(x)
```

```
ans = -6    6
>> fix(x)
ans = -5    5
>> floor(x)
ans = -6    5
>> ceil(x)
ans = -5    6
>> sign(x)
ans = -1    1
>> rem(23,6)
 ans = 5
```

Trigonometric and hyperbolic functions

Unlike pocket calculators, the trigonometric functions always assume the input argument in radians. The inverse trigonometric functions produce outputs that are in radians. The Trigonometric functions has the following forms used for numeric display is shown in Table 2.8.

TABLE 2.8   Trigonometric functions

Function	*Description*	*Function*	*Description*
sin (x)	$\sin(x)$	cos (x)	$\cos(x)$
tan (x)	$\tan(x)$	asin (x)	$\sin^{-1}(x)$
acos (x)	$\cos^{-1}(x)$	atan (x)	$\tan^{-1}(x)$
atan2 (y,x)	the inverse tangent of y/x including the correct quadrant		

EXAMPLE 2.17   Verify the trigonometric function on

$$\sin^2(x) + \cos^2(x) = 1$$

```
>> x = 0:pi/10:pi;
>> [x' sin(x)' cos(x)' (sin(x).^2+cos(x).^2)']
ans =
 0  0 1.0000 1.0000
 0.3142 0.3090 0.9511 1.0000
 0.6283 0.5878 0.8090 1.0000
 0.9425 0.8090 0.5878 1.0000
 1.2566 0.9511 0.3090 1.0000
 1.5708 1.0000 0.0000 1.0000
 1.8850 0.9511 -0.3090 1.0000
 2.1991 0.8090 -0.5878 1.0000
 2.5133 0.5878 -0.8090 1.0000
```

```
2.8274 0.3090 -0.9511 1.0000
3.1416 0.0000 -1.0000 1.0000
```

Example of commands in mathematics

We can use MATLAB as a calculator by typing at Commands Window at the command prompt to find the area of circle.

EXAMPLE 2.18

```
% to calculate area of circle
>> radius = 5;
>> area = pi*radius^2
% the latter part, in the Command Window is omitted if we had ended the expression
with a semicolon.
area =
78.5398
% the area is calculated by substituting the value of pi and radius.
```

Practice Exercise

Type the following commands and **TRY** them out.

```
>> 4+7
>> 6*9
>> 32/8
>> sin(5)
```

2.3.3   Operator and Special Characters

Some of the commonly used MATLAB operators and special characters are listed in Table 2.9. We can run these operators and experience the results and outputs.

TABLE 2.9   List of commonly used operators and special characters

Operator	Purpose	Example on operator or special character	Explanation
+	Plus; addition operator	>> 2 + 3 ans = 5	This adds numbers 2 and 3 and stores the result in variable ans.
−	Minus; subtraction operator	>> 8 - 2 ans = 6	This subtracts number 2 from 8 and stores the result in variable ans.

(Contd.)

TABLE 2.9 List of commonly used operators and special characters (*Contd.*)

Operator	Purpose	Example on operator or special character	Explanation

*	Scalar and matrix multiplication operator	`>> 2*3`
		`ans =`
		`      6`
			This multiplies numbers 2 and 3 and stores the result in variable ans.

.*	Array multiplication operator	`>> [2 3] .* [5 6]`
		`ans =`
		`     10    18`
			This may wonderus, how MATLAB made it possible! Two arrays were multiplied element to element and the result is stored in ans array. This would not have been possible for general multiplication because of inner dimension incompatibility.

*	Scalar and matrix multiplication operator	`>> [2 3] * [5 6]`
		`??? Error using ==>`
		`mtimes`
		`Inner matrix dimensions`
		`must agree.`
			This is not possible for general multiplication because of inner dimension incompatibility.

^	Scalar and matrix exponentiation operator	`>> 2^3`
		`ans =`
		`      8`
			Scalar exponentiation and result is stored in ans variable.

.^	Array exponentiation operator	`>> [2 3] ^ 5`
		`??? Error using ==>`
		`mpower`
		`Inputs must be a scalar`
		`and a square matrix.`
		`>> [2 3] .^ 5`
		`ans =`
		
		`     32   243`
			This example clearly shows that element wise exponentiation can be done only by using array exponentiation operator.

\	Left-division operator	`>> 8\4`
		`ans =`
		`      0.5000`
			Are you surprised with the result!

/	Right-division operator	`>> 8/4`
		`ans =`
		`      2`
			This performs general division.

.\	Array left-division operator	`>> [8 6] .\ [2 3]`
		`ans =`
		`0.2500 0.5000`
			Here 2 is divided by 8 and 3 is divided by 6. This shows the left division.

./	Array right-division operator	`>> [8 6] ./ [2 3]`
		`ans =`
		`   4     2`
			In this example, 8 is divided by 2 and 6 is divided by 3.

:	Colon; generates regularly spaced elements and represents an entire row or column	`>> 1:4`
		`ans =`
		`1  2   3     4`
			Colon, generates regularly spaced elements. Default spacing is 1.

(*Contd.*)

TABLE 2.9 List of commonly used operators and special characters (*Contd.*)

Operator	Purpose	Example on operator or special character	Explanation

( )	Parentheses; encloses function arguments and array indices; overrides precedence	`>> min(2,5)`
		`ans =`
		`    2`
		`>> max(2,5)`
		`ans =`
		`    5`
		`>>(10/5)+(2*6)`
		`ans =`
		`    14`
			Here function min and max finds minimum and maximum of two numbers enclosed in the bracket. Also, bracket overrides precedence by performing division and multiplication first and then addition.

[ ]	Brackets; enclosures array elements	`>> [1 2 3]`
		`ans =`
		`    1    2    3`
			Array elements are enclosed in the bracket.

.	Decimal point	`>> 3.5`
		`ans =`
		`    3.5000`
			Come of a number to a string with n decimal places.

...	Ellipsis; line-continuation operator	`>> 14 ...`
		`/2`
		
		`ans =`
		
		`    7`
			Provide the series of three consecutive periods.

,	Comma; separates statements and elements in a row	`>> a=[1,2,3;4,5,6]`
		`a =`
		`    1    2    3`
		`    4    5    6`
			Comma; separates statements and elements in a row.

;	Semicolon; separates columns and suppresses display	`>> a=[1,2,3;4,5,6]`
		`a =`
		`    1    2    3`
		`    4    5    6`
		`>> 12/6;`
			Semicolon; separates columns. It also suppresses the display of ans produced by dividing 12 with 6 here.

%	Percent sign; designates a comment and specifies formatting	`>> 12/6; %this is to`
		`illustrate suppression`
		`of result at command`
		`prompt`
			% sign suppress the comment of the row.

=	Assignment operator	`>> a=5`
		`a =`
		`    5`
			Assigns value 5 to variable a.

Other than these operators and special characters, MATLAB has several other operators and special characters. MATLAB operators can be classified as arithmetic, rational, logical, bit wise and set operators. All these are well explained in MATLAB documentation.

Examples on use of precedence with operators

% Once we type in the Command Window prompt (>>) and press <Enter>, MATLAB will calculates the value of the expression and respond with answer (ans).

EXAMPLE 2.19

```
>> 30/15/5
ans =
      0.4000
```

In above example, number 30 is divided by 15 and the result 2 is further divided by 5 giving result as 0.4000.

EXAMPLE 2.20

```
% first parenthesis (bracket) is solved and then division is carried out.
>> 30/ (15/5)
ans =
      10
```

Following example gives better understanding of precedence's rule.

EXAMPLE 2.21

```
% to solve example on more precedence's
>> 80-(10/2) + (5*3)
ans =
      90
% apply BODMAS to solve the expression
```

An expression becomes more complex when multiple parentheses are used for longer expression. Also see the following examples to understand the complexity of the order of precedence.

EXAMPLE 2.22

```
% Exponentiation of the number is read as 5 to the power of 2.
>> 5^2
ans =
      25
```

EXAMPLE 2.23

```
% First the expression inside parenthesis is evaluated and then apply arithmetical
operator for solving.
>> (2+5)/7*5+2-3
ans =
      4
```

EXAMPLE 2.24

% First the expression inside parenthesis is evaluated and then BODMAS operator for solving.

```
>> (2+5)/7*5+2-3^2

ans =

    -2
```

EXAMPLE 2.25

% First the expression inside parenthesis is evaluated and then applies BODMAS to solve the expression.

```
>> (2+5)^7/7*5+2-3

ans =

        588244
```

Practice Exercise

```
>> (2+5)^(7/7)*5+2-3
```

2.3.4 Common Mathematical Function

MATLAB provides an extensive set of mathematical functions, such as trigonometric, exponential, complex, and specialised functions. This algebraic function and characters are the fundamental operations involved in the creation and use of MATLAB variables. More detailed discussions of scalars, vectors, matrices, and strings are provided in separate sections.

MATLAB is having some inbuilt library that has following basic algebraic functions such as:

- sqrt(x) = Square root of x
- exp(x) = Exponentiation with base ()
- log(x) = Natural logarithm of x
- log10(x) = Natural logarithm of x, using base 10
- x^y = Exponentiation
- abs(-x) = Absolute value of –x
- round(1.74) = Round to the nearest integer
- floor(1.83) = Round to the smaller integer (towards minus infinity)
- ceil(1.25) = Round to the smaller integer (towards plus infinity)
- fix(1.9) = Round to the nearest integer towards zero
- sign(1) = The sign of 1:–1 if <0; and 0 if=0

The above functions calculation starts in the innermost pair of parenthesis and move outwards.

The following examples are related to above library functions.

EXAMPLE 2.26

```
% use mathematical function and try.
>> round(abs(-7)^4)     % If we want to calculate the absolute value of -7 to the
power of 4, and then round off to the nearest integer.
ans =
           2401
```

EXAMPLE 2.27

```
% use mathematical and parenthesis function.
>> exp(log(83))
ans =
    83.0000
```

EXAMPLE 2.28

```
% use mathematical and parenthesis function.
>> floor(abs(exp(log(83))))
ans =
       83
```

EXAMPLE 2.29

```
% consider the trigonometric equation
>> t=sin(x)*cos(x)
t =
      0.5000
```

The following commands can be written for the scalar x for a given angle of 45 degrees.

Practice Exercise

```
  (i)   >> x=45*pi/180;
 (ii)   >> ceil(1.25)
(iii)   >> sqrt(-1)
```

2.3.5 Relational and Logical Operators

In MATLAB, apart from arithmetic operators and functions, there are other operators that test whether certain relation or condition is true or false. There are two types of operators:

(i) Relational operators
(ii) Logical operators

Relational and logical operators are instrumental in program flow control. They are used in MATLAB M-files to test various conditions involving variables and expressions.

Relational operators

The operators which test the relation between two operands are known as *relational operators*. The relational operators are listed in Table 2.10.

TABLE 2.10   Relational operator description

Symbol	Description
<	less than
<=	less than or equal to
>	greater than
>=	greater than or equal to
==	equal to
~=	not equal to

The MATLAB relational operators compare corresponding elements of arrays with equal dimensions. The result of comparison if it is of identical size is array of 0s otherwise shown as array of 1s. Relational operators always operate element-by-element used to compare elements of a numerical array to a scalar.

EXAMPLE 2.30   The resulting matrix on comparing the elements of X to the corresponding elements of Y using the relation operator is as follows:

```
>> x = [5 6 2; 7 0.2 9; 0.6 0.2 8];
>> y = [0.5 6 4; 3 0.2 2; 9 0.7 3];
>> x==y  % Check locations where x and y are equal and store 1's in those locations
of logical array AB and 0's elsewhere
   ans =
        0      1      0
        0      1      0
        0      0      0
```

EXAMPLE 2.31

Refer to the Example 2.30 and using the relational operator verify z=2+3*ones (3), xy= x~=y and xy= x~=z.

```
>> z=2+3*ones (3)
   z =
        5      5      5
        5      5      5
        5      5      5
```

```
>> xy= x~=y   % verify locations elsewhere of logical array xy and star 0's when
equal otherwise 1's
   xy =
        1       0       1
        1       0       1
        1       1       1


>> xy= x~=z   % verify locations elsewhere of logical array xz and star 0's when
equal otherwise 1's
   xy =
        1       1       1
        1       1       1
        1       1       1
```

Logical operators

Logical operators are used to negate or combine relational expressions. The truth or falseness of compound expressions comprised of relational operators is possible with the use of logical operators. The standard logical operators are shown in Table 2.11.

TABLE 2.11   Logical operator description

Symbol	Description
&	AND
|	OR
~	NOT

EXAMPLE 2.32

```
% to verify the Logical operators
x = input ('Enter a value for x: ');
(x >= 0) && (x <= 15)
(x < 0) || (x > 15)
xor(x >= 0, x <= 15)


% result is shown as.
1   % ~true
0   % ~false
```

EXAMPLE 2.33

```
% to verify the Logical operators
>> x=3; y=-10; z=0;
```

```
>> a=x&y % x and y are True, then logical variable a is True
b=x&z % x is True and z is False, then logical variable b is False
c=x|y % x and y are True, therefore logical variable c is True
d=y|z % y is True and z is False, therefore logical variable d is True
e=~x % x is True, NOT x is False, therefore e is False
f=~z % z is False, NOT z is True, therefore f is True
% result is shown as.
a =

     1

b =

     0

c =

     1

d =

     1

e =

     0

f =

     1
```

Relational and logical functions

MATLAB provides several relational and logical functions which return logical arrays based on their argument(s) which can be either numerical or character string arrays. These relational and logical functions are shown in Table 2.12.

TABLE 2.12   Relational and logical function description

Function	*Description*
xor(x,y)	% Exclusive OR operation. Return True (1) for each element where either x or y is non-zero (True). Return False (0) where both x and y are zero (False) or both are non-zero.
any(x)	Return True (1) if any element in vector x is non-zero. Return True (1) for each column in a matrix x that has non-zero elements.
all(x)	Return True (1) if all elements in a vector x are non-zero. Return True (1) for each column in a matrix that has all non-zero elements.

EXAMPLE 2.34

```
% Apply relational and logical functions
>> x=0:10
>> y=-5:5
% when the program is execute the result will display as
```

```
>> x=0:10
x =
     0     1     2     3     4     5     6     7     8     9     10
>> y=-5:5
y =
    -5    -4    -3    -2    -1     0     1     2     3     4     5
>> xor(x,y)    % xor(x,y) % Perform exclusive OR on arrays x and y
ans =
     1     0     0     0     0     1     0     0     0     0     0
```

EXAMPLE 2.35

```
>> r=[1 2 3; 4 5 6; 7 8 9];
>> s=[1 2 3; 0 5 0; 0 8 9];
>> t=r-s
t =
     0     0     0
     4     0     6
     7     0     0
```

% Find columns in matrix C which are not all zeros and those which are all zeros using any(t)

```
>> any(t)
ans = 1 0 1
```

2.4 VARIABLE

We have learned about different data types used in MATLAB (Section 2.1). Handling data directly in computation is inconvenient due to repeated data at several places. To handle such situation, the name of the data need to represent. Such representation of data is known as *variable*. In programming, such variables denote the value in the workspace.

There are 100 different types of data in Maple; but in MATLAB generally, we have three types of data: the matrix, the string, and the cell array. All these three data types can be defined by variable name or function name consisting of string of letters, digits and underscores. MATLAB has certain rules to call a character or letters variable name as given below:

- Variable names begin with letter followed by letters, digits and underscore.
- Length of a variable should not be more than 32 characters.
- Variable name should not be assigned to keywords and program.
- Variables names are case sensitive.

Here are the illustrations that illustrate a variable name cannot start with a number. Similarly, variable name cannot start with a special character.

EXAMPLE 2.36

```
>> 1x
??? 1x
     |
Error: Unexpected MATLAB expression.
```

EXAMPLE 2.37

```
>> 1x=5
??? 1x=5
     |
Error: Unexpected MATLAB expression.
```

EXAMPLE 2.38

```
>> *X
??? *X
     |
Error: Unexpected MATLAB operator.
```

EXAMPLE 2.39

```
>> *X=5
??? *X=5
     |   % type by holding 'shift + button above enter'
Error: Unexpected MATLAB operator.
```

Now, let us see the command in MATLAB, that create variable and call functions. For example, create a variable named by typing the following statement at the command line.

```
>> x= 4;
```

The MATLAB add variable x to the workspace and displays the result in the Command Window.

```
x =
     4
```

Similarly, create few more variables,

```
>> y= 6;
y =
     6
```

EXAMPLE 2.40

```
>> x=5   % defined variable
x =
```

```
            5
>> y = 6 % defined another variable
% Combine the above two variables x and y in variable u
>> u= x + y  % defined variable
u =
        11
```

EXAMPLE 2.41

```
>> X=5
X =
        5
```

EXAMPLE 2.42

```
>> x1=5
x1 =
        5
```

EXAMPLE 2.43

```
>> X*=5 % variable is assigned with symbols
??? X*=5
        |
Error: The expression to the left of the equals sign is not a valid target for
an assignment.
```

EXAMPLE 2.44

```
>> X_=5
X_ =
        5
```

It is seen from the above illustrations that a variable name cannot be preceded by a number or a special character, but can be followed by a number or underscore.

A variable name can be of 63 characters long.

Following examples illustrate the fact, that a variable name cannot be more than 63 characters.

EXAMPLE 2.45

```
>> abcdefghijklmnopqrstuvwxyzabcdefghijklmnopqrstuvwxyzabcdefghijk=1
abcdefghijklmnopqrstuvwxyzabcdefghijklmnopqrstuvwxyzabcdefghijk =
        1
```

EXAMPLE 2.46

```
>> abcdefghijklmnopqrstuvwxyzabcdefghijklmnopqrstuvwxyzabcdefghijklmnopqrstuvwxyz=1
Warning:
'abcdefghijklmnopqrstuvwxyzabcdefghijklmnopqrstuvwxyzabcdefghijklmnopqrstuvwxyz'
% exceeds the MATLAB maximum name length of 63 characters and will be truncated to
 'abcdefghijklmnopqrstuvwxyzabcdefghijklmnopqrstuvwxyzabcdefghijk'.
abcdefghijklmnopqrstuvwxyzabcdefghijklmnopqrstuvwxyzabcdefghijk =

     1
```

2.4.1 MATLAB System Variables

MATLAB has certain variables that are recognised by MATLAB itself and not defined by users. Such variables are given below:

ans: This variable is automatically generated by MATLAB when there is no variable assigned to store the results of a statement for displaying it.

inf: It represents infinity, that is generated usually when a number is divided by zero.

eps: This is a constant value representing the floating-point relative accuracy uses in its calculations. Its value can be seen by typing *eps* in the command window.

NaN: It represents Not a Number is an invalid numeric value resulting from undefined operations like *0/0* and inf/inf.

pi: This represents the constant value of $\pi = 3.1415926535897$.

j: This is to represent a complex number in MATLAB. The data part is represented the complex number as x = i*y.

2.4.2 Numerical Variables

Variables are broadly classified in MATLAB as scalar, vector and arrays format. However, all the MATLAB variables are basically arrays itself. For example, the numerical variable command in MATLAB for instance simply represents a numeric value as shown in the following examples.

EXAMPLE 2.47

```
>> x=5
x =

     5
This shows the value of the variable as 5.
```

EXAMPLE 2.48

```
>> y= 4 * 20
y =
     80
```

We can determine whether input is scalar or not, using the isscalar command. This command reforms logic 1(true) and logic 0(false) otherwise.

Following examples illustrate the use of isscalar command.

EXAMPLE 2.49

```
>> a=20
a =
     20
>> isscalar(a)
ans =
     1
```

EXAMPLE 2.50

```
>> a=[20 2 3]
a =
     20     2     3
>> isscalar(a)
ans =
     0
```

Let us see another numerical variable expression with few more examples.

EXAMPLE 2.51

```
>> 40/10/8
ans =
     0.5000
```

The ans is the variable name and it directly displays the answer in the command window.

If, the variable is defined as *klm* = 40/10/8, then MATLAB creates the value as per the variable name.

EXAMPLE 2.52

```
>> klm=40/10/8
klm =
     0.5000
```

2.4.3 Logical Variable

In MATLAB, we test various conditions that involve variables and expressions. We create a logical variable to store the result of the expression involving logical operators, after execution. The logical variables are instrumental in program flow control. Such logical variable can be used to compare elements of a numerical array to a scalar. These variables are logically compared with identically sized array and indicate their results in 1s and 0s. This resulting array is called a array of logical variable.

Use the following function and manipulate the examples to observe form and results of the variables in the Command window.

EXAMPLE 2.53

In this example, we will discuss how the logical variable is used in the program.

```
clear    % it will delete all variables in the workspace
>> m=10;
>> k=1; n=7;
>> x=m+k*randn(1,n)         % Generate array x of n Normally distributed
% when the above code is executed, MATLAB produces the following logical variable result:
x =
      10.3426    13.5784    12.7694     8.6501    13.0349    10.7254     9.9369
>> Result_high=x>m    %  Find components of x which exceed m and store in logical
Result_high =
       0     1     1     1     1     1     0
>> Result_Low=x<m    %  Find components of x which go below m and store in logical
Result_Low =
       1     0     0     0     0     0     1
>> Result_high=x>m+k         %  Find components of x which exceed m+k and store
in logical
Result_high =
       0     0     1     0     1     0     0
>> Result_Low=x<m+k          %  Find components of x which go below m+k and store
in logical
Result_Low =
       1     1     0     1     0     1     1
% the logical variable verified with value of m is shown as logic 1 otherwise 0.
```

EXAMPLE 2.54

In this example we will discuss how matrix logical variable is used in the program.

```
clear    % it will delete all variables in the workspace
>> A=[7 5 2; 8 5 3; 1 5 9];
>> B=eye(3); % Create 3 ΄΄ 3 Identity matrix
>> AB=A==B % Check locations where A and B are equal and store 1s in
%   when the above code is executed, MATLAB produces the following logical variable
result:
AB =
```

```
         0         0         0
         0         0         0
         0         0         0
>> C=2+3*ones(3)
C =
         5         5         5
         5         5         5
         5         5         5
>> AC=A~=C    % Check locations where A and C are not equal and store 1s in
AC =
         1         0         1
         1         0         1
         1         0         1
```

2.4.4 Logical Values

In MATLAB, the vector elements are assigned with a value to a variable. The left-hand-side of the function must be a valid variable name, while the right-hand-side must be a valid expression. MATLAB is used to *evaluate the following expressions:*

EXAMPLE 2.55
```
>> pi
ans =
    3.1416
```

EXAMPLE 2.56   The value of pi as variable is added to 1 to save as variable u for future use.
```
>> u=pi+1
u =
    4.1416
```

EXAMPLE 2.57   In this example, the variable name is pi for arithmetic expression. This expression is evaluated and stored in the variable with name pi.
```
>> pi = 30/6
pi =
    5
```

EXAMPLE 2.58
```
>> j = pi + pi
j =
    10
```

Practice Exercise

  (i) The difference between the MATLAB constant pi and the variable *pio* is calculated and stored in the variable *yrt*.

```
>> pio = 15
>> yrt = pi + pio
```

 (ii) Try them out by substituting the variable value and solve the result for

     (a) `>> 4+6`
     (b) `>> 5*9`
     (c) `25/26`
     (d) `exp(-5)`

(iii) Similarly, when we type `cos(5)` in MATLAB then observe the result.

2.4.5 Workspace Variables

In MATLAB, the created and imported file variables appear in the workspace. Workspace display the 'workspace browser', a graphical interface that allow you to view the content and manage it of the MATLAB workspace. It provides a graphical representation of the display and perform equivalent functions. By typing the variable x, y, z values at appears in the Workspace pane of the desktop as shown in Figure 2.1.

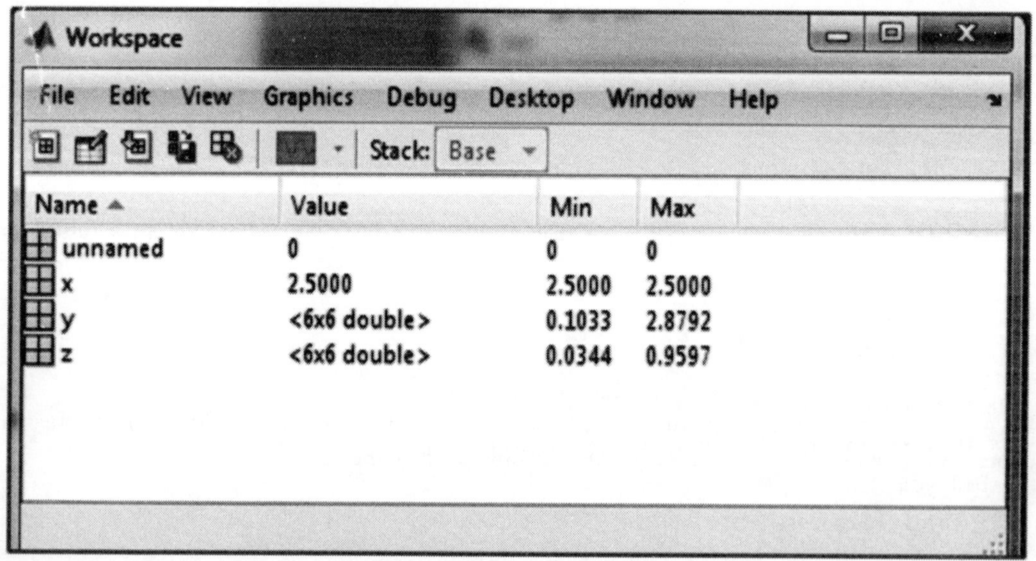

FIGURE 2.1 Workspace pane.

    The workspace browser also displays and automatically update statistical calculations for each variable.

2.5 MATLAB IS CASE SENSITIVE

A variable name shall start with an alphabet itself. As MATLAB is case sensitive (as in Linux, but in contrast to Windows), it considers lower and upper case alphabets uniquely. For example, MATLAB treats x and X differently. So lower case letters variables are different from uppercase letters variables. Thus, x and X are different variables. A variable name cannot start with a number or special character. For example, $1x$ or $*X$ is not allowed in MATLAB as a variable name. Following examples give the illustration of variable names.

EXAMPLE 2.59

```
>> x=2
x =
      2
```

EXAMPLE 2.60

```
>> y=X+2
Undefined function or variable 'X'         % X is uppercase but x is the lowercase
which is the input variable value of previous statement.
Did you mean:
>> y=x+2
```

Note: MATLAB will generate the error message and also enquire to identify the correct variables.

EXAMPLE 2.61

```
>> rupees = 100
rupees =
     100
```

EXAMPLE 2.62

```
>> Total = Rupees + 100
Undefined function or variable 'Rupees'
% This is an error for the value of shown variable.
 Did you mean:
>> Total = rupees + 100
Total =
     200
```

Note: MATLAB will generate the error message for undefined variable name and also enquire to identify the correct variable name.

Now, let us see another example.

Are 'tempsource1' and 'TempSource1' valid variable names? Do they refer to the same variable?

EXAMPLE 2.63

```
>> tempsource1 = 50
tempsource1 =
      50
```

EXAMPLE 2.64

```
>>  Temp = tempsource1 + 1
Temp =
      51
>> Temp = TempSource1 + 1
Undefined function or variable 'TempSource1'
 Did you mean:
>> Temp = tempsource1 + 1
```

Note: MATLAB produce error expression MATLAB converts special characters (like\ n and %d) in the error message string only when you specify more than one input arguments or wrong $2/\gamma$ arguments If it is valid name and has not been assigned a value, MATLAB produces a different error message.

Practice Exercise

Enter the variable name and its value for 'heatsource1' and 'HeatSource1'. Do they refer to the same variable for the following, verify it.

```
>> Heat = heatsource1 + 1
>> Heat = HeatSource1 + 1
>> Heat = heatSource1 + 1
```

Hint: Both are valid variable names, but refer to different variables in MATLAB.

```
>>  heatsource1 = 15
>>  HeatSource1 = 5
```

Caution
- MATLAB is case sensitive; m and M are different variables. If this is repeated, it is still one of the most common mistakes.
- We should not use a variable name that clashes with a constant, e.g., pi.
- Names cannot be MATLAB keywords, e.g., for, if, end, ...
- The maximum length of a variable name is given by namelengthmax, commonly 63 characters.

2.6   COMMA, SEMICOLON AND PERCENTAGE SIGN

There are various punctuation marks and special syntax we use in MATLAB. In MATLAB, we usually have to enter all instructions using some basic commands and syntax. A few characters have special meaning and are frequently used. Out of which comma, semicolon and percentage are often used.

[,] *Comma:*   This notation used to separate commands that are written on the same line. For example, type, `exp (4)`, `exp (9)` will enable MATLAB to calculate both the values at once.

[;] *Semicolon:*   This notation suppresses the output command to execute. Semicolon is used at-the-end of most of the executable statement in MATLAB. This suppresses output when commands are executed. If it is not used then the statement will be echoed on the command window. This is undesirable and difficult to trace in certain situation, when we execute a several statements of large size of data. Further, this also slows down the execution speed of a program.

For example, if we type 4 + 8; and press <Enter>, the expression is evaluated and saved in the ans variable. However, nothing is displayed in the Command Window. But if semicolon is not provided, then immediately ans variable will display 12. This is useful when we run the program and do not want intermediary calculation to be displayed.

[%] *Comments:* Any statement start after % string then; the end of the line is ignored. This is useful for adding comments in programs. It is seldom used in Command Window. In MATLAB program some basic syntax use as commands. A few characters are frequently used as follows:

EXAMPLE 2.65

```
>> 4 + 6;    % execute by ending with semicolon
% no result will be executed.
But,
>> 4 + 6     % execute by ending without semicolon
ans
   10
```

2.6.1 Suppressing Output

MATLAB prints the results of all calculations and operations as multiple intermediate results or the required results unless the expression on the right hand side is terminated with a semicolon. When we simply type a statement and press Return or Enter, MATLAB will automatically display the result on screen. If we end the line with semicolon, MATLAB performs the computation but do not display the output.

To see how the semicolon works enter the following statements exactly as shown in the following examples, ending each line with a carriage return.

EXAMPLE 2.66

```
>>  x = pi/3;         % execute by ending with semicolon
```

EXAMPLE 2.67

```
>> y = sin(x)/cos(x);        % execute by ending with semicolon
```

EXAMPLE 2.68

```
>> z = y - tan(x);      % execute by ending with semicolon
```

The values of z and y were assigned in the y = and z = statements.

EXAMPLE 2.69

```
>> z          % execute the variable
      0
```

EXAMPLE 2.70

```
>> y          % execute the variable
y =
    -10.3988
```

The last two examples 2.69 and 2.70 print the values of the expressions z and y. As they do not end with semicolon, so MATLAB prints the results after evaluating z and y.

2.7   CHARACTER AND STRINGS

A string is a set of sequence of characters enclosed in pair of single quotes. The character may contain alphabets, numbers, special characters or blank space.

A host of function and facilities are offered by MATLAB to deal with character and strings. A character text array create and concatenate strings. It store text in charater array and combine charater array. It also identify parts of strings, compare strings, find and replace substrings. A Character and Strings function is shown in Table 2.13.

TABLE 2.13   Character and strings

Function	Purpose
blanks	Create string of blank characters
cellstr	Convert to cell array of strings
char	Convert to character array (string)
iscellstr	Determine whether input is cell array of strings
ischar	Determine whether item is character array
sprintf	Format data into string
strcat	Concatenate strings horizontally
strjoin	Join strings in cell array into single string

We can type the following command for assigning a string to a variable.

```
>> message= 'Good Afternoon';
```

Further, use the two single quotes within the definition of variable.

```
>> nextmessage= 'Happy''Birthday'
% it will display as follows:
nextmessage =

Happy'Birthday
```

% message and nextmessage are arrays, like all MATLAB variables. Their class or data type is char, which is short for character.

Every variable we difine in MATLAB, as well as input and output forms, a command, or array of data it belongs to a class. When we type 'whos'(name) the expression displays the name, size, bytes, class and attribute. The set of variable difinitions showing by whos is called our workspace.

```
>> whos nextmessage
```

Name	Size	Bytes	Class	Attributes
message	1x14	28	char	

EXAMPLE 2.71   A string is a set of characters, like this

```
s='Mera Bharat Mahan'   % string on set of character
```

% if we just want to access part of a string, like the first 7 characters of s (defined above)

```
use
>> s(1:7)
ans =
Mera Bh
```

Some MATLAB commands require more options to be selected or set by using strings. We should make sure to enclose them in single quotes, as shown in this example. Even we can use `help` command to know more about how to handle strings.

Following examples are represented as set of string characters.

EXAMPLE 2.72

```
>> I='India'
I =
India
```

EXAMPLE 2.73

```
>> I='India is my country'
I =
India is my country
```

EXAMPLE 2.74

```
>> I='Everyone's growth'
% when an apostrophe is added to the character then the string is repeated double
in a single quote, like this:
I =
Everyone's growth
```

EXAMPLE 2.75   If we want to access part of a string, like the first 2 and 7 characters of 'Mahatma Gandhi' then write the command as follows:

```
>> I(1:2)
ans =
Ma
```

EXAMPLE 2.76

```
>> I(1:7)
ans =
Mahatma
```

EXAMPLE 2.77   We can try the following example to convert numeric value to strings, using functions such as num2str or int2str.

```
>> f= 93.2;
>> c= (f-32)/1.8;
>> tempText= ['Temperature is   ', num2str(c), 'C']
tempText =
Temperature is 34C
```

2.7.1   Identifying Characters in a String

We can use any of the following functions to identify a character or string, or certain characters in a string as shown in Table 2.14.

TABLE 2.14   Identify a character or string

Function name	*Function description*
Ischar	Determine whether the input is a character array
Isletter	Find all alphabetic letters in the input string
Isspace	Find all space characters in the input string
Isstrprop	Find all characters of a specific category.

EXAMPLE 2.78

```
str = 'This the space characters in this string';
%        |  |    |       |  |    |
%        5  9    15      26 29   34
% Applying linspace we will find.
find(isspace(str))
ans =
5    9    15    26    29    34
```

2.7.2   Concatenation of Strings

The joining of two or more strings to form a longer string is known as *concatenation of strings*. Strings can be concatenated horizontally or vertically just like two or more arrays row wise or column wise. The concatenation of strings is performed in various ways, by directly prepending or appending strings or using functions available in MATLAB, by writing them in cell arrays. Following are some concatenation methods.

Using direct methods

In this direct concatenation methods, strings are placed in a square bracket, that is, to be concatenated. The strings are placed in a row side-wise without any concern to the length of strings.

EXAMPLE 2.79   In this example of direct horizontal concatenation method, strings of array elements are placed in a square bracket.

```
>> s1= 'Abraham'; S2= 'Lincoln'
% by concatenation
>> s= [s1, s2]
S=
Abraham Lincoln
```

Using char Function

This is different from the direct concatenated methods. Here MATLAB also provides the manipulation of vertical concatenation. This is by using a char function with the string as its inputs.

EXAMPLE 2.80   Here extra space is padded to the right of shorter strings.

```
>> k= char('Hary', 'Shyam', 'Jesus', 'Ram')
% will produce the following results
k=
Hary
```

```
Shyam
Jesus
Ram
```

Concatenating strings vertically

In this case, concatenating strings vertically is done by using cell arrays. In a cell array, the length of elements in its cells need not be same. So, the strings of different element length of cell can be considered.

EXAMPLE 2.81

```
>> H= {'Wireless'; 'Sensor'; 'Nettworks'}
% executing this we will see
H=
    Wireless
    Sensor
    Networks
```

Using strcat arrays

In this case, MATLAB provides more powerful function called **strcat** for concatenating strings or arrays of strings horizontally. Its form is

```
S= strcat (s1, s2, ...)
```

where, s1, s2, etc., are simple strings or multi-line arrays of strings. All input arrays have the equal number of rows.

EXAMPLE 2.82   This function is to create concatenate strings. All input array must have the same number rows.

```
X= strcat('MAT', 'LAB')
X=
MatLab
```

EXAMPLE 2.83

```
>> name ='Dr. Sona';
>> position ='Practitioner';
>> worksAt ='Cancer Center';
>> profile =char(name, position, worksAt);
>> profile = cellstr(profile);
>> disp(profile)
    'Dr. Sona'
    'Practitioner'
    'Cancer Center'
```

Thus, a string is represented by using a series of character in single quotes. Some MATLAB commands require options to be selected or set by using strings.

There are many useful functions for string, can be reviewed by using help menu by typing strvcat.

2.8 DATE AND TIME

Date and time is represented as 'datetime' is the best date type of representing date and time. MATLAB works with three different types of date formats

   (i) Date strings
  (ii) Date vectors
 (iii) Serial date number

(i) Date string: The 'datenum' function is important for doing date string formats with 'dd-mmm-yyyy' or 'mn/dd/yyyy' or 'hh-mm:ssss' most commonly used.

EXAMPLE 2.84

```
Thursday, August 23, 2012  9:45:44.946 AM
```

(ii) Date vectors: It is a 1-by-6-numeric vector containing the year, month, day, hour, minute and second.

EXAMPLE 2.85

```
[2012   8   23   9   45   44.946]
```

(iii) Serial date number: A single number equal to number of days since January 0, 0000 in the proleptic ISO calander.

EXAMPLE 2.86

```
7.3510e + 005
```

Date strings, vectors and numbers can be stored as array of values.

2.8.1 Date Strings

A date string is a character string composed of fields related to a specific date and/or time. There are several ways to represent dates and times in character string format. For example, all of the following are date strings for **August 23, 2010 at 04:35:42 PM:**

```
'23-Aug-2010 04:35:06 PM'
'Wednesday, August 23'
'08/23/10 16:35'
'Aug 23 16:35:42.946'
```

We can represent time in a date string using either a 12-hour or 24-hour system. Even when we create a date string, include any characters to separate the fields, such as the hyphen, space, and colon as used here:

```
d = '23-Aug-2010 16:35:42'
```

Convert one or more date strings to a datetime array using the datetime function. For best performance, specify the format of the input date strings as an input to datetime.

```
t = datetime(d,'InputFormat','dd-MMM-yyyy HH:mm:ss:')
t =
   23-Aug-2010 16:35:42
```

To view the size and data type of each variable use the command as shown:

```
>> whos d t
  Name      Size        Bytes       Class           Attributes
  t         1x1         121         datetime
  d         1x20        40          char
```

To specify the dates outside of this range as a date vector, first convert the vector to a serial date number using the datenum function as shown in the following example.

EXAMPLE 2.87

```
>> datestr(datenum([1400 12 15 11 45 03]), 'mmm.dd,yyyy HH:MM:SS')
ans =
   Dec.15,1400 11:45:03
```

EXAMPLE 2.88   Return the current date and time in a string using the default format:

```
>> datestr(now)
ans =
   31-Jan-2015 09:19:57
```

EXAMPLE 2.89   Format the above result to show only the date in the mm/dd/yy format.

```
>> datestr(now, 2)
ans =
   01/31/15
```

EXAMPLE 2.90   Display the returned date string using our own format made up of symbols shown in the free-form Date Format Specifiers.

```
>> datestr(now, 'dd.mm.yyyy')
ans =
   31.01.2015
```

EXAMPLE 2.91   Convert a nonstandard date form into a standard MATLAB date form by first converting it to a date number and then to a string:

```
>> datestr(datenum('24.01.2015', 'dd.mm.yyyy'), 2)
ans =
    01/24/15
```

2.9 CALL FUNCTION

MATLAB provides a large number of functions that perform computational tasks. Such functions are equivalent to subroutines or methods like in other programming languages. Within the file, declare the function and add program statements:

```
function f = fact(n)
f = prod(1:n);
```

We can observe some of the call functions in the following examples.

EXAMPLE 2.92   To call a function using max function that encloses its input arguments in parentheses use the given command:

```
>> S= [4 9 2];
>> max(S)
ans =
    9
```

EXAMPLE 2.93   When there are multiple input arguments, it is separated with commas as shown:

```
>> T= [8 5 1];
>> max(S, T)
ans =
    8   9   2
```

EXAMPLE 2.94   The value of S is assigned to a variable as follows:

```
>> maxS= max(S)
maxS =
    9
```

EXAMPLE 2.95   When there are multiple output arguments, it is enclosed in square brackets as shown:

```
>> [maxS, location]= max(S)
maxS =
    9
```

```
location =

     2
```

2.10 SAVING AND LOADING DATA

In MATLAB, calculations need to be reused elsewhere, therefore, the values of such variables can be saved in a '.mat file'. This can be done with the command:

```
>> save filename
```

As a result all variables is being saved in the file with the name *'filename.mat'*. The extension '.mat' need not necessarily be given. In case, if only a few variables need to be saved, these variables should be specified after the file name, e.g., only the variables x and y are to be saved in the file *filename.mat* with the command:

```
>> save filename x y
```

A saved '.mat' file can be read into MATLAB with the command `load`

```
>> load filename
```

where, the extension '.mat' can be omitted. The saved variables and their values are stored in the workspace and can now be used again.

The `load` command requires that the data in the file is organised into a rectangular array as no column titles are permitted. Such load command is:

```
>> load measurements.txt
```

where 'measurements.txt' is the name of the file containing the data. The result of this operation is that the data in 'measurements.txt' is stored in a variable called 'measurements'. Files with various extension can be used. Note, that any extension except '.mat' indicates to MATLAB that the data is stored as plain ASCII text. A '.mat' extension is reserved for a file which has stored MATLAB variables.

Suppose we had a simple ASCII file named 'meas_xy.txt' that contained two columns of numbers. The following MATLAB statements will load this data into the variable 'meas_xy', and then copy it into two vectors x and y.

```
>> load meas_xy.txt;      %  read data into the meas_xy variable
>> x = meas_xy(:,1);      %  copy first column of my_xy into x
>> y = meas_xy(:,2);      %  and second column into y
```

Another option to import data in MATLAB is to select 'File \ Import Data'. In the window opening, we can select the desired data file. Selecting *next* in this window, various import options are accessible. On the right hand side of our window, we will see a preview of how MATLAB will import the data. If we are satisfied, select *finish*.

SUMMARY

This chapter has first discussed that a programming language has different data types and then followed by various system commands. The data types supported by MATLAB are constants and variables, have been discussed at length and illustrated with numerous examples in the chapter. Among variables the supported types are integer, floating point, character and string. The MATLAB basic operators are highlighted with workout examples. MATLAB supports an extensive number of operators like Arithmetic operators, Relational operators, Logical operators and Special operators.

Further, the discussion was also held with command mode and functional mode of parentheses pair. MATLAB supports character and string operations. This chapter has also discussed the arrays of characters and strings with various illustrated examples and functions available in MATLAB for string handling. The MATLAB functions for computing date and time were also discussed. Finally, the chapter concludes with how to save and load the file in the MATLAB.

REVIEW QUESTIONS

1. Mention the various data types used in MATLAB.

2. Which key displays the results in the command prompt when MATLAB is being used as a calculator?

3. List the various arithmetic operators used in MATLAB.

4. What is the order of precedence of MATLAB arithmetic operators?

5. What is the difference between `round`, `floor` and `ceil` functions in MATLAB?

6. What is the use of `clc` function?

7. What are the three basic datatypes of MATLAB?

8. Is MATLAB case sensitive?

9. What does a semicolon (;) do when used after a command at the command prompt of MATLAB?

10. List some of the trigonometric functions which MATLAB supports.

PRACTICE EXERCISE

1. Display the following results in the MATLAB command window by using various operators on the numbers 20 and 50

    (i) `ans =`

            `70`

    (ii) `ans =`

            `1000`

   (iii) ans =

$$2.500$$

   (iv) ans =

$$20$$

   (v) ans =

$$1.1259e+065$$

2. Evaluate the following:

   (i) 20/4

   (ii) 20\4

   (iii) 20:25

3. Generate table of 5 using colon (:) operator.

4. Find square root of 1089 using a function in MATLAB.

5. Display the output as follows:

   (i) X =

        your's lovingly

   (ii) ans =

        your's loving

   (iii) ans =

        I Love My Country: The India

6. Find the values for:

   (i) sin(0:pi/4:pi)

   (ii) cos(0:pi/4:pi)

   (iii) tan(0:pi/4:pi)

7. Find the values for:

   (i) sin(0:pi\4:pi)

   (ii) cos(0:pi\4:pi)

   (iii) tan(0:pi\4:pi)

8. Comment on the results obtained when you run the commands given in Examples 2.6 and 2.7.

9. What is the difference between clear and clc commands?

10. Display the following patterns using strvcat function.

```
x_new =
*********
*******
*****
****
**
*
```

11. If x=('**********'), then x_new=(strvcat(x(1:10),x(2:9),x(3:8),x(4:7),x(5:6), x(4:4)))'. Display x_new.

CHAPTER 3

MATLAB Vector and Matrix

LEARNING OBJECTIVES

This chapter intends to teach us the following:

- Different aspects of MATLAB scalar, vector and array.
- Understanding the concept of row and column vector.
- Formation of matrix and methods to replace data.
- About MATLAB use in arithmetic operations and matrix operations.
- Methods to assign a value to matrix and way to clear variables.
- Formation of more than one-dimensional array matrix.
- MATLAB operators and its various examples.

INTRODUCTION

MATLAB is a programming environment of arrays and matrices. The arrays and matrices form the fundamental mathematical entities that MATLAB handles effectively and straightforwardly. An array is a list of numbers arranged in rows and/or columns. A more complex array has more than one-dimension.

MATLAB was originally designed for solving the problem based on matrices, which was later adopted by scientific world. Matrix notation is chosen as a basic data element that simplifies the complex mathematical expression/equations to handle and manipulate problems. Matrices with only row elements and only column elements are called row and column vector, respectively. Scalar vector in matrices is having only one element. All variables used in single data element is a single matrix with one row and one column.

MATLAB numerical variables are typically defined as matrix, but not scalar. MATLAB can handle higher-dimensional arrays that help to store information and data. In science and engineering, one-dimensional array referred as vector, two-dimensional arrays as matrices and other higher-dimensional arrays as n-dimensional arrays.

3.1 SCALAR AND VECTOR

Quantity having magnitude only is called a *scalar*. For example, mass, temperature, volume and speed. Vectors have magnitude as well as direction. Examples of vectors are displacement, position, velocity, acceleration and force.

The basic data structure of MATLAB is the matrix. Even scalars (numbers) are considered to be 1×1 matrices (one row and one column).

EXAMPLE 3.1

```
>> x=7        % to create a scalar variable.
x =
7
```

EXAMPLE 3.2

```
>> whos('x')      % to find the assigned variable size details.
   Name      Size      Bytes     Class
   x         1x1       8         double array
```

Single element in a (1×1) matrix is a scalar. The increase in number of elements converts a scalar into vector, i.e., a scalar is no more a scalar. A column vector is a $(m \times 1)$ matrix that has m number of rows but a single column only. Similarly, a row vector is a $(1 \times n)$ matrix which has n number of columns and a single row only.

3.1.1 Creating Scalars

A scalar can be created by simply introducing it on the left hand side of an equal to sign or just typing it at the command prompt.

EXAMPLE 3.3

```
%   Define a scalar
>> x=1
x =
      1
%   Define a scalar
>> a=3; % is a scalar and it does not need to put in square bracket.
a =
      3
```

Look into another examples, where the single-element variables are representing the scalar quantities.

EXAMPLE 3.4   In this example, addition of two scalar variables is shown.

```
>> a = 4;
b = 6;
c = a + b
c =
     10
```

EXAMPLE 3.5   In this example, scalar is stored in default variable of MATLAB called ans.

```
>> 15
ans =
     15
```

EXAMPLE 3.6   In this example, scalar elements are displayed using a variable.

```
>> a=6
a =
      6
```

or, one could also define the scalar b as:

```
>> b=32;
```

Note that ending a command line with the semicolon suppresses the response that gives the value of the scalar. Of course, scalars can be thought of as vectors of length one.

3.1.2   Row Vectors

A row vector is expressed in the form

$$v = [v_1, v_2, \ldots, v_n]$$

where, $v_1, v_2, \ldots, v_n$ are usually scalars (either real or complex numbers). To enter a row vector in MATLAB, we can separate the individual elements with space or commas.

Also, MATLAB always treats arrays as vectors. There are two ways of representing vectors: row vectors and column vectors. Row vector elements are enclosed in a square bracket separated by comma (,) or separated by blank space is expressed in the following examples.

EXAMPLE 3.7

```
>> x= [2, 4, 9]        % a row vector using comma.
x =
      2     4     9
```

EXAMPLE 3.8

```
>> u= [2 3 5]          % a row vector using space.
```

```
u =

     2     3     5
```

This type of array is a row vector.

EXAMPLE 3.9

```
>> y= [3 5 8]     % a row vector using space.
y =

     3     5     8
```

MATLAB variables can also represent arrays or matrices. In row vector, the space can be either followed by colons or just space, is expressed in the following example.

EXAMPLE 3.10

```
>> x= 1:5     % array of equal distribution
x =

     1     2     3     4     5
```

EXAMPLE 3.11   This example uses the arithmetic function to the row arrays.

```
>> a = [4 2 6 3];
b = [2 5 8 7];
c = a + b
c =

     6     7     14     10
```

3.1.3   Column Vectors

The element of an array can also be termed as column vector. An array whose elements are arranged in the form of a column is known as *column array*. A column array is assigned by list of elements enclosed in a square bracket form in the command window.

A column vector is expressed in the form:

$$v = \begin{bmatrix} v_1 \\ v_2 \\ \vdots \\ v_n \end{bmatrix}$$

where, $v_1, v_2, ..., v_n$ are usually scalars (either real or complex numbers). To enter a column vector in MATLAB, we can separate the individual elements with semicolon. This is useful in building column vectors.

When all the elements enclosed by square bracket are separated by semicolons then such quantities represent a column vector. Here listed the examples of a column vector.

EXAMPLE 3.12

```
>> z= [4; 5; 6]   % Define a column vector
z =
        4
        5
        6
```

EXAMPLE 3.13

```
>> y= [1; 2; 3]    % Define a column vector
y =
        1
        2
        3
```

MATLAB variables have been already discussed in previous Chapter 2. The following is a brief introduction to a few of the elementary features and functions of MATLAB designed for us to get started along the learning path.

3.1.4 Row and Column Variables

Variables are broadly classified in MATLAB as scalars (with a single numerical value), vectors (with more than one value organised in one dimension) and arrays (with multiple numerical values organised in more than one dimension). The following examples cover the row and column vectors.

EXAMPLE 3.14

```
>> r= [45, 33, 27, 48]     % Row vector of arrays
r =
      45    33    27    48
```

EXAMPLE 3.15

```
>> c= [45; 33; 27; 48]     % Column vector of arrays
c =
      45
      33
      27
      48
```

Note the use of the comma to separate elements in the definition of the row vector and the semicolon to separate elements in the definition of the column vector. The row vector can also be defined using a space between each element instead of the comma.

EXAMPLE 3.16   Row and column vectors can be combined to generate a matrix. The matrix *A* is defined as:

```
>> A= [11 12 13; 21 22 23; 31 32 33; 41 42 43]
A =
      11      12      13
      21      22      23
      31      32      33
      41      42      43
```

Thus, matrices are 4 rows and 3 columns dimensional arrays.

Note the elements of a given row are separated from those of the next row by a semicolon. Also, note the use of lower case alphabet for scalars and vectors, and upper case alphabet for matrices. This is not a necessary syntax, but some convention is helpful to distinguish arrays of more than one dimension. The general notion of arrays continues to be three or more dimensions.

3.2   ELEMENTARY FEATURES IN VECTOR ARRAY

The array of an element formed by a listing of individual elements arranged in row or column array. Here are listed various way of accessing the elements of an array.

3.2.1   Selected Array Element

In MATLAB, every element of an array can be accessed by referring to the name and position of the element in the array. There are different methods to access a particular element of an array such as subscript indexing and linear indexing. In the former, we can specify the column and row information of an element in the array and in the later you refer the position of the particular index. For example, to access the *k*th element of an array *A* using subscript indexing, we write:

- $A(1, k)$ for the row array accessing
- $A(k, 1)$ for the column array accessing

The following examples are explained how to access the row and the column elements.

EXAMPLE 3.17   Accessing a particular element of row vector, using the given command:

```
>> D= [4, 6, 2, 9, 5, 8, 1];
>> D(1,4)     % gives the 4th element of D
ans=
    9
```

EXAMPLE 3.18   Accessing a particular element of column vector, using the given command:

```
>> E= [1; 6; 7; 9; 5; 8; 3];
>> E(5, 1)    % access the 5th element of 1st column
ans=
    5
```

EXAMPLE 3.19   The command to access last element of an array with predefined index end is given below.

```
>> D (end)    % gives the last element of the array
ans=
    1
>> E (end)    % gives the last element of the array
ans=
    3
```

3.2.2 Accessing More Array Elements

MATLAB also supports to access two or more elements or a range of elements of an array. This can be done by using the subscript or linear indexing. To access two or more elements, initially, the array is formed and then specifies the indices of the corresponding elements. Let us consider the following examples of row elements and the corresponding desired indices formed to get the required result.

EXAMPLE 3.20

```
>> X= [6, 1.7, 2, 1.5, 10, 4.1, 1.4, 7.4, 2.4, 3]; % array of row element
>> I= [1, 3, 6, 7];    % to create the array of indices.
>> X(I)
ans=
    6.0002.0004.1001.400
```

These are the elements corresponding to the indices of X.

EXAMPLE 3.21   To access the first and last element of the array X, use the following command:

```
>> X([1, end])
ans=
    6    3
```

3.2.3 Vector Length Function

MATLAB has two functions that can be used to determine the length and the size of an array.

The length of an array means the total number of elements in an array. The size of an array determines the dimensions of an array that finds the number of rows and columns of an array.

Length

The length function gives the number of elements in a row and column of an array.

L = length(y) returns the length of the largest array dimension in y. For vectors, the length is simply the number of elements.

For arrays with more dimensions, the length is max(size(y)). The length of an empty array is zero.

EXAMPLE 3.22   The length function gives the number of elements in row and column array as shown in this example.

```
>> y= [5    4    8.9    2    6.8    3.5    7    1.4    8    2.1];
>> length (y)      % gives the number of elements of y
ans=
    10
```

EXAMPLE 3.23   In this example to identify the last element of y use the given command:

```
>> y (length(y))   % gives the last element of y.
ans=
    2.1
```

Size

This function gives the number of row and column in an array.

d = size(y) returns the size of each dimension of an array y in a vector, d, with n dims(y) elements.

[m,n] = size(y) returns the size of matrix y in separate variables m and n.

EXAMPLE 3.24

```
>> S= size (y)
ans=
    10
```

EXAMPLE 3.25

```
>> N=2
N =
        2
>> size(N)        % to find the size of variable N in an array
ans =
    1        1
```

EXAMPLE 3.26

```
>> a= [1, 2, 3, 4]      % Array of variables
size (a)
a =
        1       2       3       4
ans =
    4
```

This is a 1×4 matrix (row vectors are built with commas).

EXAMPLE 3.27

```
The array
>> b=[1;2;3;4]
b =
        1
        2
        3
        4
>> size (b)
ans =
        4       1
```

This is a 4×1 matrix (column vectors are built with semicolons).

3.2.4 Sorting Arrays

MATLAB use the sort function to arrange the element of an array in ascending order. The sort function returns two outputs as sorted array and variable generation.

EXAMPLE 3.28   In this example, we learn to find the sorted array in ascending order.

```
>> S = [ 2, 3, 4, 7, 8, 5]      % row array vector
>> sort(S)    % sorting S
ans =

   Columns 1 through 4


        2       3       4       5


   Columns 5 through 6


        7       8
```

EXAMPLE 3.29   In this example, we create a matrix and sort each of its rows and columns in ascending order using the given commands form:

```
>> m = [2 6 4; 5 3 9; 2 0 1]; % two dimensional array
>> sort(m, 1)    % sorting m along the row
ans =
        2      0      1
        2      3      4
        5      6      9


>> sort(m, 2)    % sorting m along the column
ans =
        2      4      6
        3      5      9
        0      1      2
```

3.2.5   Vector Increment Notation

MATLAB can create vector with constant increment arrays. We can easily create vectors with a constant increment between start and end entries. That is, default increment is one. To denote such increment the MATLAB general command format is represented as

```
>> start: increment: finish
```

In case, no increment is supplied, it is understood to be 1.

EXAMPLE 3.30

```
>> 6:12
ans =
        6      7      8      9     10     11     12
```

An increment in the order of 1 step each.

EXAMPLE 3.31

```
>> x=1:7
% elements of x forms an arithmetic progression with common difference of 1.
x =
        1      2      3      4      5      6      7
```

Here, the increment is fixed by steps of 1 each.

3.2.6   Increment Steps Size

A row vector with evenly spaced elements can be written with the following notation.

$$\text{Variable name = e: f: g}$$

where, e is the initial value of the row vector.

f is the step size increment value.

g is the final value of the row vector.

EXAMPLE 3.32

```
>> x=1:2:7    % increment in the interval of 2.
x =
        1       3       5       7
```

EXAMPLE 3.33

```
>> 6:2:12     % increment in the interval of 2.
ans =
        6       8      10      12
```

EXAMPLE 3.34

```
>> x=1:0.5:7 % increment in the interval of 0.5.
x =
    Columns 1 through 4
      1.0000      1.5000      2.0000      2.5000
    Columns 5 through 8
      3.0000      3.5000      4.0000      4.5000
    Columns 9 through 12
      5.0000      5.5000      6.0000      6.5000
    Column 13
      7.0000
```

EXAMPLE 3.35

```
>> g=100:-10:10    % to decrement in the interval of -10.
g =
    Columns 1 through 7
      100      90      80      70      60      50      40
    Columns 8 through 10
       30      20      10
```

We can even access entry starting from the 4th entry and extending to the last entry in the vector with the following notation.

EXAMPLE 3.36

```
>> g (4: end)% to access the element from 4 till end.
```

```
ans  =
70        60        50        40        30        20        10
```

Even, we can access the entry in the even or odd positions of the vector as follows. Here the even position in the vector is shown with the following notation.

EXAMPLE 3.37   g(x: y: z) means the indices of x to z with interval of y elements.

```
>> g (2: 2: end)  % to arrange element of interval
ans  =
90        70        50        30        10
```

3.3 MATRICES

In MATLAB, a matrix is a rectangular array of numbers. MATLAB is able to generate matrix for a given numbers to identify the row and column elements. Special meaning is sometimes attached to 1-by-1 matrices, which are scalars, and to matrices with only one row or column, which are vectors. MATLAB has other ways of storing both numeric and non-numeric data, but in the beginning, it is usually best to think of everything as a matrix.

The size of the matrix is measured by the number of rows and columns. This is pronounced as 'row-by-column'. When a scalar is 1×1 matrix, this means one column and one row vector. A scalar matrix can be added, subtracted, multiplied, etc. This is called matrix algebra. Furthermore, a matrix with equal number of rows and columns is often called a square matrix. In this section, we will learn how to create and change matrices.

3.3.1 Matrices Formation

The MATLAB can perform various operations on matrices. To understand how to create matrix, type the command as explained in the discussed examples. There are different ways to enter matrices into MATLAB:

- We can enter an explicit list of elements.
- Load matrices from external data files.
- Generate matrices using built-in functions.
- Create matrices with our own functions in M-files.

Magic squares

In the MATLAB, 1-by-1 matrices are scalars and the matrices with only one row or column, are vectors. In this environment, a magic square as shown in Figure 3.1 is an arrangement of distinct numbers usually integers, in a square grid. The grid when add in each row, in each column, and diagonals results in the same number.

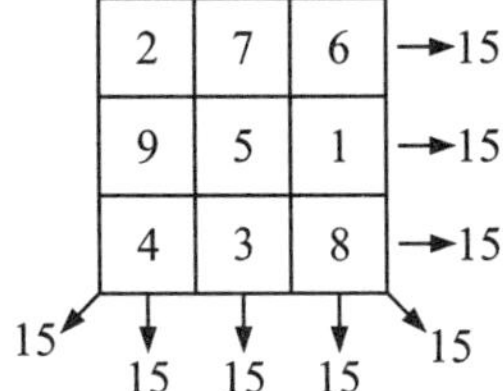

FIGURE 3.1 Magic square.

To observe such matrix example, it will appears in the Figure 3.2, the Renaissance engraving Melencolia I by the German artist and amateur mathematician Albrecht Dürer.

FIGURE 3.2 The Renaissance engraving Melencolia.

The image is filled with mathematical symbolism, matrix as appear in the upper-right corner like a magic square as shown in Figure 3.3. During the Dürer's time many believed that such genuinely magical properties have some worth full fascinating characteristics.

FIGURE 3.3 Engraved magic square.

Hence, in the **magic square** when the elements are added row-wise, column-wise or diagonal-wise produce the same sum.

The **magic ()** function command is to form a magic square array.

M = magic (n) returns an *n*-by-*n* matrix constructed to form a magic square array of equal row and column sums. The order of *n* must be a scalar and it should be greater than or equal to 3.

EXAMPLE 3.38 In this example, we use the Dürer's matrix, function to create a magic matrix square of order 4.

Solution: In the matrix of order n = 4 is applied to function M = magic(n)

```
>> n=4;
>> M = magic(n)
% By running the code
M =

    16     2     3    13
     5    11    10     8
     9     7     6    12
     4    14    15     1

% the magic square of equal sum of the elements in each row, column and diagonal
is same.


% calculating the sum of elements in the magic square of row elements
>> sum(M)
```

```
ans =
      34      34      34      34
% the sum of the elements in the magic square of row elements is the same.


% calculating the sum of elements in the magic square of column elements
>> sum(M')'
ans =
      34
      34
      34
      34
% the sum of the elements in the magic square of column elements is the same.


% calculating the sum of elements in the magic square of diagonal elements
>> sum(diag(M))
ans =
      34
% calculating the sum of elements in the magic square of diagonal elements have
the same sum.


% to evaluate the characteristic sum for a magic square of order n
>> n=4;
>> sum(1:n^2)/n
ans =
      34
% the characteristic sum for a magic square of order 4 appears to be 34.
```

Dürer's matrix as a list of its elements can also follow the following methods for creating matrix:

- Separate the elements of a row with blanks or commas.
- Use a semicolon ' ; ' to indicate the end of each row.
- Surround the entire list of elements with square brackets, [ ].

EXAMPLE 3.39

```
% enter Dürer's matrix, in the Command Window
>> A = [16 3 2 13; 5 10 11 8; 9 6 7 12; 4 15 14 1]
```

MATLAB displays the matrix we just entered:
```
A =
16  3    2    13
5   10   11   8
```

```
9    6    7    12
4    15   14   1
```

EXAMPLE 3.40

```
>> A(4, 5)= 20
% in this the size of the array increase to accommodate the newcomers.
A =
    16   2    3    13   0
    5    11   10   8    0
    9    7    6    12   0
    4    14   15   1    20
```

Practice Exercise

Find the size of this matrix
```
c= [1, 2, 3; 4, 5, 6; 7, 8, 9]
size(c)
```

When the elements of a matrix need to access then use the syntax A (row, column). For example, to get the element of c in the 2nd row, 5th column use c (2, 5).

And if we have a matrix or an array to access the last element in a row or column, we can use the following MATLAB end commands:

```
>> c (end)
>> c (3, end)
>> c(3,end)
```

3.3.2   Matrix Sum, Transpose and Random Function

Let us create a matrix and sum its row and column to verify that using MATLAB. Try the following statement.

EXAMPLE 3.41

```
>> U = [4 11 5 9; 1 8 15 5; 14 8 3 9; 7 13 9 16]
U =
    4    11   5    9
    1    8    15   5
    14   8    3    9
    7    13   9    16
>> sum(U)
% MATLAB replies with
```

```
ans =
     26   40   32   39
```

When we do not specify an output variable, MATLAB uses the variable ans, to store the results of a calculation.

EXAMPLE 3.42

```
>> % 3 x 3 matrix
>> z=[2 3 4; 5 2 6; 5 4 9]
z =
     2      3      4
     5      2      6
     5      4      9
```

EXAMPLE 3.43

```
>> % transpose of z
>> Z=z'
Z =
     2      5      5
     3      2      4
     4      6      9
```

EXAMPLE 3.44

```
>> % access ith row and jth column
>> Z(3,2)
ans =
     6
```

EXAMPLE 3.45

```
>> % matrix modify
>> Z(2,2)=7
Z =
     2      5      5
     3      7      4
     4      6      9
```

EXAMPLE 3.46

```
Z (3 , 3)     % addressing row and column number.
ans
     3
```

EXAMPLE 3.47

```
>> % Scalar multiplication
>> 2*z
ans =
     4     6     8
    10     4    12
    10     8    18
```

Practice Exercise

```
>> z/3
>> z+1
```

EXAMPLE 3.48

```
>> % Variable new assigned
>> k=z+2
k =
     4     5     6
     7     4     8
     7     6    11
```

EXAMPLE 3.49

```
>> % square of matrix
>> k^2
ans =
    93    76   130
   112    99   162
   147   125   211
```

EXAMPLE 3.50

```
>> % element by element operator
>> k.^2
ans =
    16    25    36
    49    16    64
    49    36   121
```

'rand' stands for random number. The 'rand' is a sequence of number produced by the internal setting of the uniform pseudorandom number generator. Every time 'rand' command is called different output value will be displayed.

EXAMPLE 3.51

```
>> % random matrix
>> S=rand(3,4)
S =
      0.8147      0.9134      0.2785      0.9649
      0.9058      0.6324      0.5469      0.1576
      0.1270      0.0975      0.9575      0.9706
```

EXAMPLE 3.52

```
>> % random matrix repeat on same variable
>> S=rand(3,4)
S =
      0.9572      0.1419      0.7922      0.0357
      0.4854      0.4218      0.9595      0.8491
      0.8003      0.9157      0.6557      0.9340
```

Practice Exercise

Identify different variables we have so far used

Hint:

```
>> who
% by typing this command we can see all the variables that we have used so far.
```

3.3.3 Matrix Data Element

The matrix data elements of different row and column vector consist of real or complex numbers are represented in the given examples.

EXAMPLE 3.53

```
>> x= [2 4 7; 5 1 9; 7 2 8]        % is a real vector element
X =
      2      4      7
      5      1      9
      7      2      8
```

EXAMPLE 3.54

```
>> y= [3+5i 9+2i 8+3i; 7+3i 6+9i 5+4i; 3+7i 8+6i 3+4i]        % is a complex vector
element
```

```
y =

    3.0000 + 5.0000i    9.0000 + 2.0000i    8.0000 + 3.0000i
    7.0000 + 3.0000i    6.0000 + 9.0000i    5.0000 + 4.0000i
    3.0000 + 0.0000i    8.0000 + 6.0000i    3.0000 + 4.0000i
```

3.3.4 Accessing Matrix Element

The matrix elements specify their respective row and column numbers can be made in to sub-matrices. The subset of subscript array can be selected by using colon operator. The index refers to identify element of row or column from matrices.

Sub-matrices or Sub-arrays: The sub-matrix $M(i, j)$ represents the element in ith row and in jth column of the matrix element.

EXAMPLE 3.55 Matrix representation of (2×2) matrix is given as:

```
>> x (1:2, 2:3)          % x(ith row, jth column)
ans =

    4       7
    1       9
```

EXAMPLE 3.56 This example represents the sub-matrix of 2nd and 3rd row with 1st and 2nd column elements.

```
>> x (2:3, 1:2)          % (ith row, jth column)
ans =

    5       1
    7       2
```

EXAMPLE 3.57 This example represents the sub-matrix of 2nd and 3rd row with 1st to 3rd column elements.

```
>> x (2:3, 1:3)
ans =

    5       1       9
    7       2       8
```

Array of column vector: The sub-matrix $M(1{:}k, j)$ represent the element in ith row of jth column.

EXAMPLE 3.58 This example represents the (3×3) matrix.

```
>> x= [2 4 7; 5 1 9; 7 2 8]
x =

    2       4       7
    5       1       9
    7       2       8
```

EXAMPLE 3.59 The sub-matrix of the matrix x is executed for 1st and 2nd row with 3rd column expression as:

```
>> x (1:2, 3)
ans =
        7
        9
```

EXAMPLE 3.60 The sub-matrix of the matrix x is executed for 2nd and 3rd row with 2nd column expression as:

```
>> x (2:3, 2)
ans =
        1
        2
```

EXAMPLE 3.61 The sub-matrix of the matrix x is executed for 1st to 3rd row with 3rd column expression as:

```
>> x (1:3, 3)
ans =
        7
        9
        8
```

Multi-dimensional matrices and arrays dimensions can be found using command, size(x) as follows:

EXAMPLE 3.62

```
>> size(x)
ans =
        3      3
```

This function is used for single dimension matrix size identification.

The command format used for the two-dimensional matrix $[m, n]$ where, the number of rows represented by variable m and the column by variable n, is as follows:

EXAMPLE 3.63

```
>> [m,n]= size(x)
m =
        3
n =
        3
```

3.3.5   Special Matrix Arrangement

In the following commands of MATLAB function, the special matrices are often used for computation. They are listed as follows:

zeros (x, y):   It represents a matrix of all zeros element.

EXAMPLE 3.64

```
>> x=3;
>> y=5;
>> z=zeros(x, y)   % will generate (3 rows x 5 columns) matrix with zero elements.
z =
        0      0      0      0      0
        0      0      0      0      0
        0      0      0      0      0
```

ones (x, y):   It represents the matrix where all elements equal to one.

EXAMPLE 3.65

```
>> z=ones(x, y)    % will generate (3 rows x 5 columns) matrix with ones elements.
z =
        1      1      1      1      1
        1      1      1      1      1
        1      1      1      1      1
```

eye (x, y):   It represents the matrix with ones on the main diagonal and zero elsewhere.

EXAMPLE 3.66

```
>> z=eye(x, y)           % will generate (3 rows x 5 columns) matrix with diagonal
                         ones elements and remaining zero.
z =
        1      0      0      0      0
        0      1      0      0      0
        0      0      1      0      0
```

EXAMPLE 3.67   To produce an identity matrix use the given command:

```
>> M= eye(3)
M =
        1      0      0
        0      1      0
        0      0      1
```

rand(n):   This generates matrix of random numbers where entries are uniformly distributed in the interval (0, 1).

EXAMPLE 3.68

```
>> z=rand(4)  % will generate (4 rows x 4 columns) matrix with random elements.
z =
    0.9649    0.4854    0.9157    0.0357
    0.1576    0.8003    0.7922    0.8491
    0.9706    0.1419    0.9595    0.9340
    0.9572    0.4218    0.6557    0.6787
```

z=rand(m, n):   It is another command used to generate 'm' number of rows and 'n' number of columns having random entries.

EXAMPLE 3.69

```
>> z=rand(3, 2)
z =
    0.0971    0.3171
    0.8235    0.9502
    0.6948    0.0344
```

z=rands(m, n):   Similarly, to generate 'm' number of rows and 'n' number of columns having random entries of uniform distribution in the interval $(-1, +1)$, the `z=rands(m, n)` command is used.

EXAMPLE 3.70

```
>> z=rands(3, 2)
z =
    0.1705    -0.4898
   -0.5524     0.0119
    0.5025     0.3982
```

diag(x):   By this command, the vector is created with the elements of main diagonal of the matrix.

EXAMPLE 3.71

```
>> x=[3 6 2 7];
>> s=diag(x)  % the components are placed on the main diagonal of matrix x.
s =
    3    0    0    0
    0    6    0    0
    0    0    2    0
    0    0    0    7
```

3.3.6   Useful Matrix Commands

With the help of following examples, we will see the special MATLAB function commands, used for computation:

EXAMPLE 3.72   Let us create a square matrix x use the given command:

```
>> x=[4   5; 8   2]
x =
        4       5
        8       2
```

det(x):   It calculates the determinant of square matrix x.

EXAMPLE 3.73

```
>> det(x)
ans =
    -32
```

rank(x):   It calculates the rank of rectangular matrix x.

EXAMPLE 3.74

```
>> rank(x)
ans =
      2
```

trace(x):   It returns the sum of the diagonal elements of rectangular matrix x.

EXAMPLE 3.75

```
>> trace(x)
ans =
      6
```

inv(x):   It computes the inverse of a non-singular matrix x.

EXAMPLE 3.76

```
>> inv(x)
ans =
    -0.0625     0.1563
     0.2500    -0.1250
```

norms(x):   It evaluates the Euclidean norms of the given rectangular matrix x.

EXAMPLE 3.77

```
>> norm(x)
ans =
    9.9306
```

Transpose(x'): It is denoted by apostrophy (') and used to interchange the row and column.

EXAMPLE 3.78

```
>> x'
ans =
    4    8
    5    2
```

poly(x): It evaluates coefficient of polynomial with specified root (x).

EXAMPLE 3.79

```
>> poly(x)
ans =
1.0000  -6.0000  -32.000
```

eig(x): It evaluates the eigenvalue norms of the given rectangular matrix x.

EXAMPLE 3.80

```
>> eig(x)
ans =
    9.4031
   -3.4031
```

3.4 EIGENVALUES AND EIGENVECTORS

In this section, we will learn the concept of eigenvalue and eigenvector. The eigenvalue problem is a problem of considerable theoretical interest and has wide-ranging application. For example to solve crucial system of differential equation we focus our attention on eigenvalue and eigenvector for the computation.

So, eigenvalues and eigenvectors play a prominent role in the study of ordinary differential equations and in many applications of the engineering. We can use them in a variety of contexts.

Let us consider, A be an $n \times n$ matrix, then

$$AV = \lambda V$$

where, λ is an eigenvalue of A and

V is called an **eigenvector** of A corresponding to λ.

Typically, if a matrix change the length of a vector, but not its direction, the vector is called an eigenvector of the matrix. The scaling factor of eigenvalue is also called eigenvector.

Matlab function for eigenvalue and eigenvector

e= eig(X) is a column vector containing the eigenvalue of square matrix 'X'.

One of the many useful linear algebra and matrix functions is eig which operates on a square matrix X with the following syntax:

$$[V,D] = eig(X)$$

This function returns diagonal matrix D of eigenvalue and matrix V whose columns corresponds to eigenvector. So that

$$AV = VD$$

$$[V,D, W] = eig(A)$$

This function returns   full matrix W whose columns are the corresponding left eigenvector; so that

$$W' * A = D * W'$$

3.4.1   Eigenvalue Decomposition

An eigenvalue and eigenvector of a square matrix A are denoted as a scalar λ and a non-zero vector v represented as:

$$AV = \lambda V$$

With the eigenvalue on the diagonal matrix A and the corresponding eigenvector of the columns of a matrix V is given as:

$$AV = VA$$

If V is non-singular matrix this becomes the eigenvalue decomposition

$$A = VAV^{-1}$$

Consider the following examples that will provide us to understand the coefficient matrix of the ordinary differential equation.

EXAMPLE 3.81

```
>> M = [1 0 6; 2 8 4; 9 5 6]
M =

        1       0       6
        2       8       4
        9       5       6
```

The command
```
>> lambda = eig(M)
```

```
% produce a column vector containing the eigenvalues.
lambda =
    14.1255
    -4.5170
    5.3915
```

To compute the eigenvectors and store the eigenvalues in a diagonal matrix, use the command:

```
>> [V, D] = eig(M)
V =
    -0.3359    -0.7326     0.4426
    -0.5894    -0.0982    -0.8361
    -0.7347     0.6736     0.3240


D =
    14.1255        0           0
        0      -4.5170         0
        0          0        5.3915
```

The matix can be written within round-off error of and

```
>> V*D*inv(V)
ans =
    1.0000    -0.0000     6.0000
    2.0000     8.0000     4.0000
    9.0000     5.0000     6.0000

>> inv(V)*M*V
ans =
    14.1255     0.0000     0.0000
    -0.0000    -4.5170     0.0000
    0.0000    -0.0000     5.3915
```

EXAMPLE 3.82

```
>> M = [0 2 -6; -2 8 -4; -9 5 6];
>> lambda = eig(M)
% produce a column vector containing the eigenvalues.
lambda =
    -3.4910
    8.7455 + 1.6053i
    8.7455 - 1.6053i
```

The matrix eigenvalues are complex. The real part of each of the eigenvalue are positive and negative. The non-zero imaginary part of two of the eigenvalues is $\pm\omega$ contributing to oscillation.

To compute the eigenvectors and store the eigenvalues in a diagonal matrix, use the command:

```
>> [V, D] = eig(M)
V =

    -0.7657    -0.4378 - 0.1775i    -0.4378 + 0.1775i
    -0.3262    -0.7153                         -0.7153
    -0.5543     0.3522 + 0.3758i     0.3522 - 0.3758i


D =

    -3.4910           0                    0
          0     8.7455 + 1.6053i           0
          0           0            8.7455 - 1.6053i
```

The first eigenvector is real and the other two vectors are complex conjugates of each other.

EXAMPLE 3.83   To find the eigenvalue and eigenvectors of a matrix refer the following example.

```
>> A=[2 2 1; 1 3 1; 1 2 2];
>> [v,e]=eig(A)
  v =
    -0.5774    -0.9045     0.8253
    -0.5774     0.3015    -0.5213
    -0.5774     0.3015     0.2172
e =
     5.0000          0          0
          0     1.0000          0
          0          0     1.0000
```

The matrix v is a matrix whose columns are the eigenvectors of A and corresponding eigenvalues given as the diagonal elements of the matrix e.

EXAMPLE 3.84

```
>> [v,e]=eig(A,'nobalance')
  v =

    -1.0000    -1.0000     1.0000
    -1.0000     0.3333    -0.6316
    -1.0000     0.3333     0.2632
```

```
e =
    5.0000    0          0
    0         1.0000     0
    0         0          1.0000
```

Sometimes, the unbalanced version looks more like the numbers, we can extract the eigenvalues from the matrix and store them in a vector using the command:

```
>> evalues=diag(e)
        evalues =
                5.0000
                1.0000
                1.0000
```

Suppose, we are given the six independent components of a stress tensor in Cartesian coordinates. The principal values and directions are found as follows:

EXAMPLE 3.85

```
>> sxx = 2; syy = 1; szz = .5; sxy = .75; syz = .5;   szx = .25;
>> S = [sxx sxy szx; sxy syy syz; szx syz szz]
S =

        2.0000      0.7500      0.2500
        0.7500      1.0000      0.5000
        0.2500      0.5000      0.5000
```

EXAMPLE 3.86

```
>> [V,D] = eig(S)
V =
        -0.1361      0.5256      -0.8398
         0.5965     -0.6333      -0.4930
        -0.7909     -0.5681      -0.2273

D =
         0.1659      0           0
         0           0.8261      0
         0           0           2.5080
```

3.5 MATRIX OPERATION

MATLAB supports two types of operations between array of elements, i.e., Matrices operations and Array operations.

Arithmetic operation on matrices

In the matrix operations follow the rules of linear algebra when using the arithmetic operations. Some of the arithmetic operation notations are listed below:

+ (Addition), − (Subtraction), * (Multiplication), / (Right division), \ (Left division), ^ (Exponentiation)

EXAMPLE 3.87

```
>> x= [3 5; 8 2];
>> y= [5 6; 5 2];
```

Addition: Use the command for addition of two equal matrices.

```
>> z=x+y

z =

         8      11
        13       4
```

Subtraction: Use the command for subtraction of two equal matrices.

```
>> z=x-y

z =

        -2      -1
         3       0
```

Multiplication: Use the command for multiplying of two equal matrices.

```
>> z=x*y

z =

        40      28
        50      52
```

Exponentiation: Use the command for raising the power of matrices.

```
>> z=x^2

z =

        49      25
        40      44
```

Right division: Use the command for multiplying the matrix with the inverse of another matrix, i.e., z=x*y^-1.

```
>> z=x/y

z =

        0.9500     -0.3500
       -0.3000      1.9000
```

Left division: Use the command for multiplying the matrix with the inverse of another matrix, i.e., z=x^-1*y.

```
>> z=x\y
z =
     0.4412     -0.0588
     0.7353      1.2353
```

Arithmetic operation on arrays

In the matrices, Array operations are done on element-by-element basis. The matrices should have identical numbers of rows and columns arrays for these operations. The addition and substraction are same for matrices and arrays, but multiplication operation are different.

MATLAB use a period/decimal point on left of arithmetic operator as part of the notation for arithmetic operations except for addition and substraction. Some of the operand notations are listed below:

+ (Addition), − (Subtraction), .* (Multiplication), ./ (Right division), .\ (Left division), .^ (Exponentiation)

EXAMPLE 3.88

```
>> x= [3 5; 8 2];
>> y= [5 6; 5 2];
```

Multiplication: Use the command for multiplying element-by-element of the matrices.

```
>> z=x.*y
z =
     15       30
     40        4
```

Right division: Use the command for dividing element-by-element of the matrices.

```
>> z=x./y
z =
     0.6000     0.8333
     1.6000     1.0000
```

Left division: Use the command for dividing element-by-element of the matrices but inverse mode. The array of inverse matrix is divided by next matrices.

```
>> z=x.\y
z =
     1.6667     1.2000
     0.6250     1.0000
```

Exponentiation: Use the command for squaring element-by-element of the matrices.

```
>> z=x.^2
z =

     9    25
    64     4
```

3.6 MATRIX OPERATORS

MATLAB support two types of operators used with array and matrices which are as follows:

1. Relational operators
2. Logical operators

3.6.1 Relational Operators Matrices

In the matrices the corresponding elements of arrays, are compared using relational operators having equal dimension. The vector and matrices of the corresponding operator must be of the same size, unless one of them is scalar. The operator compute using element-to-element computation. Some of the relational operators notations are listed below:

< (Less than), <= (Less than or equal to), > (Greater than), >= (Greater than or equal to), = =(Equal to), ~ = (Not equal to).

If the relational operator is *True* indicate a value 1 or if *False* indicate a value 0.

```
>> x=[2 6 9];
>> y=[7 4 6];
```

< (Less than): Statement verifies if satisfy then it is 1 otherwise 0.

EXAMPLE 3.89

```
>> k= x<y
k =

     1     0     0
```

<= (Less than or equal to): Statement verifies if satisfy then it is 1 otherwise 0.

EXAMPLE 3.90

```
>> k= x<=y
k =

     1     0     0
```

> (Greater than): Statement verifies if satisfy then it is 1 otherwise 0.

EXAMPLE 3.91

```
>> k= x>y
k =
     0     1     1
```

>= (Greater than or equal to):   Statement verifies if satisfy then it is 1 otherwise 0.

EXAMPLE 3.92

```
>> k=x>=y
k =
     0     1     1
```

= = (Equal to):   Statement verifies if false then it is 0 otherwise 1.

EXAMPLE 3.93

```
>> k=x==y
k =
     0     0     0
```

~= (Not equal to):   Statement verifies if satisfy then it is 1 otherwise 0.

EXAMPLE 3.94

```
>> k=x~=y
k =
     1     1     1
```

3.6.2   Logical Operators Matrices

In the matrices the corresponding elements of arrays, are compared using logical operators having equal dimension. The vector and matrices of the corresponding operator must be of the same size, unless one of them is scalar. The operator computes using element-to-element computation. Some of the logical operators notations are listed below:

    & (Logical AND), |(Logical OR), ~(Logical complement), **xor** (Logical exclusive-OR)

The logical operator is *True* indicate a value 1 or if *False* indicate a value 0.

```
>> x= [4  6  9];
>> y= [5  4  8];
```

& (Logical AND):   The logical AND operation corresponding to vector x and y. When both elements are non-zero the result is consider as *true* (1), otherwise *false* (0).

EXAMPLE 3.95

```
>> x&y
ans =
        1     1     1
```

| (Logical OR):   The logical OR operation corresponding to vector x and y. When both elements are non-zero the result is considered as *true* (1), otherwise *false* (0) will display.

Note: Typing operator | depends on what kind of keyboard we have, to type OR sign (|) normally it is above the backslash (\), which is near to enter key. Sometimes it is displayed on keyboard as two smaller vertical stripes. Type by holding shift key and press |.

EXAMPLE 3.96

```
>> k= x|y
k =
        1     1     1
```

~ (Logical Complement):   The logical complement operation corresponding to vector x and y. When elements are non-zero, the result is consider as *false* (0), otherwise *true* (1).

Example 3.97

```
>> k= ~x
k =
        0     0     0
```

xor (Logical Exclusive-OR):   The logical Exclusive-OR operation corresponding to vector x and y. When elements are unequal, the result is consider as *false* (0), otherwise *true* (1).

EXAMPLE 3.98

```
>> m=xor(x, y)
m =
        0     0     0
```

3.7   CREATING MATRIX ARRANGEMENT

Matrix arrangement reshapes the elements and matrices in different format based on commands used.

3.7.1   Matrix Reshape to Vector

Matrix shape and size can be altered by using MATLAB commands. Matrix x can be grouped into a single column vector by a command z=x(:).

EXAMPLE 3.99

```
>>    x= [2  4  7;  5  1  9;  7  2  8]
x =
        2       4       7
        5       1       9
        7       2       8
```

By applying the matrix reshape command as:

```
>> z=x(:)
z =
        2
        5
        7
        4
        1
        2
        7
        9
        8
```

Hence, matrix x is stored in column format.

3.7.2 Matrix Reshape to Different Vector

Matrices can be reshaped by changing the position of rows and columns. If a given matrix X is (a × b), it can be reshaped into a Y (c × d) matrix. The reshaping command is given by:

```
Y = reshape (X, c, d)
```

EXAMPLE 3.100

```
>> X= [2  4  7  8;  5  1  9  3;  7  2  8  1]
X =
        2       4       7       8
        5       1       9       3
        7       2       8       1
```

The elements of matrix Y are taken column wise from the matrix X.

EXAMPLE 3.101

```
>> Y = reshape (X, 6, 2)
Y =
        2       7
        5       9
```

```
         7        8
         4        8
         1        3
         2        1
```

The reshape of matrix Y has six rows and two columns.

3.7.3 Expanding Matrix Size

In a matrix, the element can be accommodated into proper size. The specified element can be represented in the matrix of proper dimension. And the remaining unspecified elements are denoted as zero.

EXAMPLE 3.102

```
>> c (2,2)=10
c =
        0        0
        0       10
```

This is a matrix of (2×2) dimension.

EXAMPLE 3.103

```
>> d (2,1:2)=10
d =
        0        0
       10       10
```

In this example, matrix is (2×2) size and the value of 1st and 2nd column of 2nd row is 10.

EXAMPLE 3.104

```
>> d (2,1:2)=[7 3]
d =
        0        0
        7        3
```

In this example, matrix is (2×2) size and the value of 1st and 2nd column of 2nd row is 7 and 3.

EXAMPLE 3.105

```
>> d (3,1:2)=[7 3]
d =
        0        0
        7        3
        7        3
```

In this example, matrix is (3 × 2) size and the value of 1st and 2nd column of 2nd and 3rd row is 7 and 3.

3.7.4 Appending Matrix Array

In the matrix, the variable is appended in a row or column to expand the size of the matrix. To append column in a given matrix, following command is used:

```
G = [k   x]
```

And, to append row in a given matrix, semicolon has been used in the following command:

```
H = [k : y]
```

EXAMPLE 3.106

```
>> k=[6 3; 9 3]    % Append column vector.
k =
        6        3
        9        3

>> x=[4;8]
x =
        4
        8
```

When executed the append column command, we get following result:

```
>> G = [k  x]
G =
        6        3        4
        9        3        8
```

EXAMPLE 3.107

```
>> y= [6 7]   % to append row vector.
y =
        6        7
```

When executed the append row command, we get following result:

```
>> H = [k; y]
H =
        6        3
        9        3
        6        7
```

3.7.5   Matrix Array Deletion

In a matrix, a row or a column can be deleted by setting the corresponding row or column equal to a null vector. The required row or column pair to delete is represented by colon, and equate them to square bracket [] without any element as shown in the following example.

EXAMPLE 3.108   To delete row vector consider the following vectors:

```
>> g= [2 4; 5 7; 9 2]       % is the column vector
g =
        2       4
        5       7
        9       2


>> k= [2 5 3; 9 7 1; 5 2 8]     % is the 3x3 matrix
k =
        2       5       3
        9       7       1
        5       2       8


>> g (1, :) = []        % is the command to reduce row vector array
g =
        5       7
        9       2


>> k (:, 1:2)= []       % is the command to reduce column vector array
k =
        3
        1
        8
```

3.7.6   Concatenation of Matrix Array

Concatenation is the process of joining arrays to make larger ones. In the form of matrices, the row or column vectors are combined or joined together to make larger or bigger matrices.

EXAMPLE 3.109

```
>> a= [1 2 3; 4 5 6; 7 8 9];
>> A= [a, a]
```

Concatenating arrays next to one another using commas is called *horizontal concatenation*.

```
A =
     1     2     3     1     2     3
     4     5     6     4     5     6
     7     8     9     7     8     9
```

EXAMPLE 3.110

```
>> A= [a; a]
```

Concatenating arrays next to one another using semicolon is called *vertical concatenation.*

```
A =
     1     2     3
     4     5     6
     7     8     9
     1     2     3
     4     5     6
     7     8     9
```

EXAMPLE 3.111   The two matrix expressions are combined together to expand as shown in this example.

```
>> g=[2 4; 5 9];
>> s= [g g+3 g+7 g+9]
s =
     2     4     5     7     9    11    11    13
     5     9     8    12    12    16    14     1
```

The result is obtained by adding the row vector of g with s in a consecutive way.

Use the matrix s and create a (4 × 4) matrix as shown below:

```
s =
      2     4     5     7
      5     9     8    12
      9    11    11    13
     12    16    14    18
```

3.8 INDEXING ARRAY VALUE

Indexing into MATLAB arrays is actually a powerful and fast technique. These can be done by just indexing into a MATLAB array to avoid 'for' loops and in vectorizing code.

Repmat is a powerful and commonly used function as it can be used to 'vectorize' code. The reasoning for this is that Matlab has traditionally been very slow in executing code with loops, but is quite fast with matrix operations. This function is used to create an array whose size and value is given, use the following command form:

```
X = repmat (val, siz);
```

Many times it is important to find out the dimensions of an array, use the following command from:

```
Size [mn pq...]
```

We will discuss these in detail in the following section.

3.8.1 Size of an Array

B = repmat(A,n) returns an array containing n copies of A in the row and column dimensions.

EXAMPLE 3.112   In this example, we will create a matrix into a 2-by-2 block arrangement, using the following commands:

```
A = diag([100 200 300])
A =
```

```
    100       0       0
      0     200       0
      0       0     300
```

```
B = repmat(A,2)
B =
```

```
    100       0       0     100       0       0
      0     200       0       0     200       0
      0       0     300       0       0     300
    100       0       0     100       0       0
      0     200       0       0     200       0
      0       0     300       0       0     300
```

B = repmat(A,r1,...,rN) specifies a list of scalars, r1, ..., rN, that describes how copies of A are arranged in each dimension.

EXAMPLE 3.113   In this example, we will create a matrix into a 2-by-3 block arrangement, using the following commands:

```
A = diag([100 200 300])
A =
```

```
    100       0       0
      0     200       0
      0       0     300
```

```
B = repmat(A,2,3)
B =
```

```
   100      0      0    100      0      0    100      0      0
     0    200      0      0    200      0      0    200      0
     0      0    300      0      0    300      0      0    300
   100      0      0    100      0      0    100      0      0
     0    200      0      0    200      0      0    200      0
     0      0    300      0      0    300      0      0    300
```

`B = repmat(A,r)` specifies the repetition scheme with row vector r.

EXAMPLE 3.114   Consider a matrix into a 2-by-3-by-2 block arrangement.

```
A = [1 2; 3 4]
A =
```

```
   1      2
   3      4
```

```
B = repmat(A,[2 3 2])
B(:,:,1) =
```

```
   1      2      1      2      1      2
   3      4      3      4      3      4
   1      2      1      2      1      2
   3      4      3      4      3      4
```

```
B(:,:,2) =
```

```
   1      2      1      2      1      2
   3      4      3      4      3      4
   1      2      1      2      1      2
   3      4      3      4      3      4
```

Further let us use *size* function for the following sample of arrays and vectors to find out their dimension

```
VectorValue1 = [1; 5; 2; 9; 4; 5];
VectorValue2 = [1 5 2 9 4 5];
```

```
MatrixValue1 = [1 5 2; 9 4 5];
MatrixValue2 = [1 5; 2 9; 4 5];
```

EXAMPLE 3.115   In the case of dimensions of an array. The function `size` returns a vector of dimensions:

```
>> MatrixValue1 = [1 5 2; 9 4 5];
>> size(MatrixValue1)
ans =
      2      3


>> MatrixValue2 = [1 5; 2 9; 4 5];
>> size(MatrixValue2)
ans =
      3      2
```

EXAMPLE 3.116   In order save the numbers for future use, type the command:

```
>> [RowNumber, ColNumber] = size(MatrixValue1)
RowNumber =
      2
ColNumber =
      3
```

or use a vector to save the information by the command:

```
>> SizeNumber = size(MatrixValue1)
SizeNumber =
      2      3
```

3.8.2   Length of a Vector

In MATLAB, a vector is basically a $1 \times N$ (or $N \times 1$) array. Therefore, we do not really need the size; all we need is the `length` (i.e., the value of N).

EXAMPLE 3.117

```
>> length(VectorValue1)
ans =
      6


>> length(VectorValue2)
```

```
ans =
     6
```

3.8.3 Length of an Array

Sometimes, we are not interested in all the dimensions, but just the longest one (as with $1 \times N$ arrays). MATLAB provides the handy function `length` to obtain that number.

EXAMPLE 3.118
```
>> length(MatrixValue1)
ans =
     3

>> length(MatrixValue2)
ans =
     3
```

Note that the length of the two matrices are same.

3.8.4 Subscripts

Subscripts are the intuitive mathematical representation for accessing data that has more than one dimension. Let us say the subscripts have these sample arrays and vectors as refered in the following examples.

EXAMPLE 3.119
```
>> VectorValue2(3)
ans =
     2

>> VectorValue1(3)
ans =
     2
```

This refers to the third element of the vector `VectorValue1`, and
```
>> MatrixValue2(3)
ans =
     4

>> MatrixValue1(3)
ans =
     5
```

EXAMPLE 3.120

```
>> MatrixValue1(1,2)
ans =
        5
```

This refers to the element in the first row, second column of the array MatrixValue1.

The following is the discussion of an element in row i and column j in $A(i,j)$. We can understand this in the following examples.

EXAMPLE 3.121

```
>> MatrixValue1 (2,2)
ans =
        4
```

When we sum this matrix of desired row and column, observe the result.

```
>> MatrixValue1 (2,2)+  MatrixValue1 (1,2)+ MatrixValue1 (2,1)+ MatrixValue1 (1,1)
ans =
        19
```

Create a magic square using following example.

EXAMPLE 3.122

```
M = [2 7 3 4; 6 9 7 1; 3 2 6 5; 9 8 5 2];
```

For the magic square, compute the sum of elements in the fourth column of M.

```
>> M = [2 7 3 4; 6 9 7 1; 3 2 6 5; 9 8 5 2];
>> M (1,4) + M (2,4) + M (3,4) + M (4,4)
```

This subscript produce the answer as

```
ans =
        12
```

Conversely, if we store a value in an element outside the matrix, then the size need to be increased. As these values can be used in different variables. The following example explain more.

EXAMPLE 3.123

```
>> M = [2 7 3 4 1; 6 9 7 6 1; 3 2 4 6 5; 9 1 8 5 2; 7 4 7 9 8];
>> Y= M (1,4) + M (2,4) + M (3,4) + M (4,4) + M (5,5);
>> X = Y
```

This subscript produce the answer as

```
X =
        30
```

3.8.5   Colon Operator as Subscript

In the MATLAB, the colon (:) is the operator that constitute several different forms. The interval is distributed in equal range from initial to final value by the colon operator. If we want to see a range of values, use the colon operator.

Following examples show the use of colon operator as a subscript.

EXAMPLE 3.124   This is a row vector containing the integer from 1 to 10.

```
>> 1:10
ans =
     1    2    3    4    5    6    7    8    9    10
```

If we want to obtain non-unit spacing with specific increment use the command given in the following example.

EXAMPLE 3.125

```
>> 20:-2:5
ans =
    20    18    16    14    12    10    8    6
```

EXAMPLE 3.126

```
>> M = [2 7 3 4 1; 6 9 7 6 1; 3 2 4 6 5; 9 1 8 5 2; 7 4 7 9 8];
>> sum(M(1:5,5))
% this will compute the sum of all fifth column and display the value.
ans =
    17
```

EXAMPLE 3.127

```
>> sum(M(:,end))
% this expression compute the sum of the elements in the last column of M.
ans =
    17
```

EXAMPLE 3.128

```
>> sum(1:9)/5
% this is the expression to add all the integers of 1 to 9 and the sum is divided
by 5.
ans =
    9
```

EXAMPLE 3.129

```
>> A = [1:5; zeros(1,3),ones(1,2); 10:-1:6];
S = size(A);
Q = S(1) + length(A) - A(2,5) + length(zeros(1,3));
>> A = [1:5; zeros(1,3),ones(1,2); 10:-1:6]

A =

     1     2     3     4     5
     0     0     0     1     1
    10     9     8     7     6

>> S = size(A)

S =

     3     5

>> Q = S(1) + length(A) - A(2,5) + length(zeros(1,3))

Q =

    10
```

3.8.6   Concatenation Matrix

Matrix concatenation is the process of joining one or more matrices to make a new matrix. The brackets [ ] operator serves not only as a matrix constructor, but also as the MATLAB concatenation operator. The expression C = [A B] horizontally concatenates matrices A and B. The expression C = [A; B] vertically concatenates them.

We can try these examples to construct a new matrix C by concatenating matrices A and B in a vertical direction.

EXAMPLE 3.130

```
>> A = ones(2, 5) * 4        % 2-by-5 matrix of 4s

A =

     4     4     4     4     4
     4     4     4     4     4
```

```
>> B = rand(3, 5)        % 3-by-5 matrix of random values

B =

    0.8147      0.9134      0.2785      0.9649      0.9572
    0.9058      0.6324      0.5469      0.1576      0.4854
    0.1270      0.0975      0.9575      0.9706      0.8003

>> C = [A; B]

C =

    4.0000      4.0000      4.0000      4.0000      4.0000
    4.0000      4.0000      4.0000      4.0000      4.0000
    0.8147      0.9134      0.2785      0.9649      0.9572
    0.9058      0.6324      0.5469      0.1576      0.4854
    0.1270      0.0975      0.9575      0.9706      0.8003
```

EXAMPLE 3.131   In this example, to create a magic square of 4-by-4 matrix use the given commands:

```
>> A = ones(4, 4) * 4
A =
     4      4      4      4
     4      4      4      4
     4      4      4      4
     4      4      4      4
>> A = ones(4, 4) * 4;
>> B = [A A+10; A+12 A+15]
```

The result is an 8-by-8 matrix, obtained by joining the four submatrices.

```
B =
     4    4    4    4   14   14   14   14
     4    4    4    4   14   14   14   14
     4    4    4    4   14   14   14   14
     4    4    4    4   14   14   14   14
    16   16   16   16   19   19   19   19
    16   16   16   16   19   19   19   19
    16   16   16   16   19   19   19   19
    16   16   16   16   19   19   19   19
```

EXAMPLE 3.132   The following command use in this example will sum all the column.

```
>> sum(B)
ans =
    80      80      80      80      132     132     132     132
```

3.8.7   Concatenating Matrices and Arrays

The alternatives of the [ ] operator for concatenation are the three functions cat, horzcat, and vertcat. With these functions, we can construct matrices (or multidimensional arrays) along a specified dimension.

C = [A; B] used in the section 3.8.7 for Concatenating Matrices, we can also use the following functions to get the similar results.

```
C = cat(1, A, B);          % Concatenate along the first dimension
C = vertcat(A, B);         % Concatenate vertically
```

EXAMPLE 3.133

```
>> A = ones(4, 4) * 4;
>> B = ones(4, 4) * 5;
>> C = cat(1, A, B);
>> C = cat(1, A, B)
```

By applying, we will find the result of C.

```
C =
     4      4      4      4
     4      4      4      4
     4      4      4      4
     4      4      4      4
     5      5      5      5
     5      5      5      5
     5      5      5      5
     5      5      5      5
```

Similarly, we can also look for the result of D.

```
>> D = vertcat(A, B)
D =
     4      4      4      4
     4      4      4      4
     4      4      4      4
     4      4      4      4
     5      5      5      5
```

```
5   5   5   5
5   5   5   5
5   5   5   5
```

3.8.8 Scalar Expansion

In this expansion, the matrices and scalar are combined in several different ways. We can refer to the following example for understanding.

EXAMPLE 3.134

```
>> M = [2 7 3 4 1; 6 9 7 6 1; 3 2 4 6 5; 9 1 8 5 2; 7 4 7 9 8];
>> Y = M - 2.5
% the scalar is subtracted from each element of the matrix.
Y =
  -0.5000    4.5000    0.5000    1.5000   -1.5000
   3.5000    6.5000    4.5000    3.5000   -1.5000
   0.5000   -0.5000    1.5000    3.5000    2.5000
   6.5000   -1.5000    5.5000    2.5000   -0.5000
   4.5000    1.5000    4.5000    6.5000    5.5000


>> sum(Y)
% the sum of column vector elements are shown in row vector
ans =
   14.5000   10.5000   16.5000   17.5000    4.5000


>> Y(1:3, 2:4) = 0
% the 1 to 3 rows and 2 to 4 columns range elements are turned to zero.
Y =
   -0.5000         0         0         0   -1.5000
    3.5000         0         0         0   -1.5000
    0.5000         0         0         0    2.5000
    6.5000   -1.5000    5.5000    2.5000   -0.5000
    4.5000    1.5000    4.5000    6.5000    5.5000
```

3.9 OTHER OPERATIONS

3.9.1 Row to Column

In this case, the distribution is spread in the form of row vector and this can be wraped in the form of column vector. Columns 1 through 13 indicate the entire row array elements with the following notation in the given example.

EXAMPLE 3.135

```
>> x= (1:0.5:7)   % Increments in column wise at the rate of 0.5
x =
    1.0000
    1.5000
    2.0000
    2.5000
    3.0000
    3.5000
    4.0000
    4.5000
    5.0000
    5.5000
    6.0000
    6.5000
    7.0000
```

3.9.2 Linspace

MATLAB has another function called linspace that generates linearly increasing or decreasing array like colon operators. Linspace not specify the step-size between two successive elements. The linspace function generates linearly spaced vectors. It is similar to the colon operator ':' but gives direct control over the number of points and always includes the endpoints.

Intact, linspace is generalised form and specify the variable step-size forms between two successive elements. In general, linspace function is evenly spaced row vector can be created using following general syntax as:

```
linspace(r, s, t)
```

The order of array generates t value between r and s at regular intervals. If $r > s$, then it generates an array whose elements are in decreasing order. If $r < s$, it will generate an array whose elements are in increasing order. If $r = s$, then it will generate t times of r.

Here, the linearly spaced vector of length t is equally spaced between r and s.

```
y = linspace(x1,x2)
% y = linspace(x1,x2) returns a row vector with 100 linearly spaced points in
the interval [x1,x2].
y = linspace(x1,x2,N)
% y = linspace(x1,x2,N) returns N linearly spaced points.
```

EXAMPLE 3.136

```
>> A=linspace(0,10,5)
A =

         0    2.5000    5.0000    7.5000   10.0000
```

We can see it has started from 0 and ended at 10 and we have 5 elements.

EXAMPLE: 3.137   Similarly, to create a logarithmic spaced vector of length n in the interval 10^a and 10^f, the command window can be expressed as:

```
logspace (a, f, n)
>> A=logspace (0,4,3)
A =

         1        100      10000
```

We can see it has started from 0 and ended at 4 and we have 3 elements.

EXAMPLE 3.138

```
>> linspace (2,2,8)        % 8 nos. of linspace element
ans=

    2 2 2 2 2 2 2 2
```

We can see it has started from 2 and ended at 2 and we have 8 elements.

EXAMPLE 3.139

```
>> linspace(0,18,5)        % 8 nos. of linspace element
ans

         0    4.5000    9.0000   13.5000   18.0000
```

We can see it has started from 0 and ended at 18 and we have 5 elements.

EXAMPLE 3.140   We can assign `linspace` to variable a, using the given command:

```
>> a=linspace(0,18,5)
a =

         0    4.5000    9.0000   13.5000   18.0000
```

EXAMPLE 3.141   Here, if we want to create a vector from 0 to 0.001 in 5 steps, use the following command then we will get the last number as 1.0000.

```
>> b=linspace(0,0.001,5)
b =

    1.0e-003*

         0    0.2500    0.5000    0.7500    1.0000
```

EXAMPLE 3.142 For the vector x_i with n = 4 uniformly spaced values from 0 to *pi*, given function is evaluated as follows:

```
>> X=linspace(0,pi,n);
>> T=sin(X).*cos(X)
T =
```

```
         0     0.4330    -0.4330    -0.0000
```

In contrast, the multiplication operator * is used to multiply a matrix by a vector, or a matrix by a matrix, using the rules of linear algebra, as we will see in Chapter 4.

3.9.3 Index Colon Operator

Most of the data used in MATLAB consists of vectors and an array has the importance of indexing. One of the most useful operators in this context is the colon. For example, to create a row vector containing the integers need to be listed out then *xsub*, may be defined using the colon operator:

EXAMPLE 3.143

```
>> x=[21 76 93 44 57 25 11 98];
>> xsub=x(1:4)
xsub =
     21     76     93     44
```

In the following example, the matrix A use the colon by itself to specify all of the elements in column 2:

EXAMPLE 3.144 Generate a 4 × 3 matrix using the command:

```
>> A = [11:13; 21:23; 31:33; 41:43]
>> A =
     11     12     13
     21     22     23
     31     32     33
     41     42     43
```

To identify the second column elements, write the following command.

```
>> A(:,2)
ans =
     12
     22
     32
     42
```

> **Practice Exercise**
> What would we expect as a result for A (:,:)?

If only the values in rows 2 through 3 and in columns 1 through 2 are needed from the matrix *A* that has 4 rows and 3 columns, the subset, *ASUB*, is defined:

EXAMPLE 3.145

```
>> ASUB=A (2:3, 1:2)
ASUB =
      21      22
      31      32
```

To select an interval through the last value in the rows and in the columns, we can use end as shown in the example for matrix *A* defined in Example 3.144, we can execute the following command.

EXAMPLE 3.146

```
>> ASUB2=A(2:end,3:end)
ASUB2 =
      23
      33
      43
```

3.9.4 Linear Index Identification

MATLAB is able to identify the location of element in the vector. Some useful commands or functions related to identifying the position in the z vectors are explained as follows:

EXAMPLE 3.147

```
>> z= [4.5 8.7 -3.3 5.6]
z =
      4.5000      8.7000      -3.3000      5.6000
```

ceil(z): It rounds the elements of a vector z integers towards positive infinity representing the command as:

EXAMPLE 3.148

```
>> ceil(z)
ans =
      5      9      -4      6
```

floor(z):   It rounds the elements of a vector z integers towards negative infinity representing the command as:

EXAMPLE 3.149

```
>> floor(z)
ans =
     4      8      -3      5
```

fix(z):   It rounds the elements of a vector z integers near to zero representing the command as:

EXAMPLE 3.150

```
>> fix(z)
ans =
     4      8      -3      5
```

round(z):   This command rounds the elements of z nearest integer representing as:

EXAMPLE 3.151

```
>> round(z)
ans =
     5      9      -3      6
```

sort(z):   It list the elements of a vector z integers in the ascending order representing the command as:

EXAMPLE 3.152

```
>> sort(z)
ans =
    -3.3000     4.5000     5.6000     8.7000
```

mod(x, z):   The function of the mod(x,z) when analysed the resultant vector will have same sign as z. This mod command is expressed as:

EXAMPLE 3.153

```
>> mod(x,z)
ans =
   2.0000     4.0000    -2.9000     3.4000
```

rem(x, z):   The function of rem(x,z) is similar to *mod* function except the quotient is rounded to zero. The resultant vector will have same sign as x. This is represented as:

EXAMPLE 3.154

```
>> rem(x,z)
ans =
     2.0000    4.0000    0.4000    3.4000
```

3.10 MATHEMATICAL OPERATIONS ON ARRAY

Mathematical operation of array can have different lengths and types are applied with rules for performing arithmetic operations on scalar and vector. Some useful commands/functions related to vectors are explained as follows.

Consider a statistical function 'x' as an array contains observations of a few variables as,

```
>> x = [2 4 7 9];
```

The command function examples are explained by using array 'x' are as follows:

sum(x):   This function represents the sum of all elements in a row or column vector representing command as:

EXAMPLE 3.155

```
>> a=sum(x)
a =
    22
```

mean(x):   It gives average of the row and column vector representing command as:

EXAMPLE 3.156

```
>> a=mean(x)
a =
    5.5000
```

length(x):   It gives the number of elements in a row/column vector representing command as:

EXAMPLE 3.157

```
>> a=length(x)
a =
    4
```

max(x):   It gives the maximum value in a row/column vector representing command as:

EXAMPLE 3.158

```
>> a=max(x)
a =
    9
```

min(x): It gives the minimum value in a row/column vector representing command as:

EXAMPLE 3.159

```
>> a=min(x)
a =
     2
```

prod(x): It gives the product of elements in a row/column vector representing command as:

EXAMPLE 3.160

```
>> a=prod(x)
a =
   504
```

sign(x): It returns 1 for positive and −1 for negative sign element of a vector representing as:

EXAMPLE 3.161

```
>> a=sign(x)
a =
     1     1     1     1
```

find(x): It shows the non-zero entries of the array vector representing command as:

EXAMPLE 3.162

```
>> a=find(x)
a =
     1     2     3     4
```

3.10.1 Vector Product

MATLAB is designed to operate primarily on whole matrices and arrays. A row or column vector can be used for elementary operations. Such operations in MATLAB works for both scalar and non-scalar data.

EXAMPLE 3.163

```
>> x= [5; 7; 2];
y= [5, 7, 4];
z=y*x
The answer will appear as
z =
82
```

EXAMPLE 3.164

```
>> B= [11 12 13; 21 22 23; 31 32 33];
>> x= [1; 2; 3];
>> y=B*x
y =
        74
       134
       194
```

EXAMPLE 3.165

```
>> x= [5; 7; 2];
y= [5, 7, 4];
z=x*y
```

The answer will appear in z. Note that for matrix multiplication, inner dimension should be same, that is, number of rows of one matrix should be equal to number of columns of other matrix.

```
z =
       25        35        20
       35        49        28
       10        14         8
```

Another useful linear algebra function is meshgrid which has the following syntax:

```
[X,Y] = meshgrid(x,y)
```

This function transforms the domain specified by vectors x and y into arrays X and Y that can be used for the evaluation of functions of two variables and the construction of 3-D surface plots. The rows of the output array X are copies of the vector x and the columns of the output array Y are copies of the vector y.

EXAMPLE 3.166

```
>> x=[0 1 2 3];
>> y=[0 1 2 3];
>> [X,Y]=meshgrid(x,y)
X =
        0        1        2        3
        0        1        2        3
        0        1        2        3
        0        1        2        3
Y =
        0        0        0        0
        1        1        1        1
```

```
    2        2        2        2
    3        3        3        3
```

Taking the corresponding elements in the first rows of X and Y as pairs, defines the coordinates of points along the x-axis with X values of 0, 1, 2, and 3 along the line Y = 0, respectively. The second row defines coordinates with the same X values along the line Y = 1, so on and so forth.

3.10.2   Vector Transpose

MATLAB support the operation of turning the row vector into column vector and vice-versa. For this operation, MATLAB uses the *apostrophe* or *single quote* to denote transpose. Mathematically, we use the following symbolism to denote the transpose of a vector.

$$\begin{bmatrix} v_1 \\ v_2 \\ \vdots \\ v_n \end{bmatrix}^T = [v_1, v_2, \ldots, v_n]$$

The command of transpose is represented as follows:

EXAMPLE 3.167

```
>> x= [2 3 4]
x =
        2        3        4
>> xt=x'
xt =
        2
        3
        4
```

Similarly, for converting the column vector into row vector refer to following example.

EXAMPLE 3.168

```
>> y= [5; 6; 7]
y =
        5
        6
        7
>> yt=y'
yt =
        5        6        7
```

If a vector is complex, its conjugate can be obtained by using conj(x) command and the transpose can be made by applying apostrophe to the variable.

EXAMPLE 3.169

```
>> s= [3+5i, 4+9i, 7+2i];
t=conj(s)
t =
        3.0000 - 5.0000i   4.0000 - 9.0000i   7.0000 - 2.0000i
```

To find the transpose of t, the command is written as:

EXAMPLE 3.170

```
>> xt=t'
xt =
   3.0000 + 5.0000i
   4.0000 + 9.0000i
   7.0000 + 2.0000i
```

The transpose of t is the transpose conjugate of t.

3.10.3　Deleting Rows and Columns

In MATLAB, we can try to delete rows and columns from a matrix using just a pair of square brackets as shown in the following examples.

EXAMPLE 3.171　Create a 5×5 matrix of M.

```
>> M = [2 7 3 4 1; 6 9 7 6 1; 3 2 4 6 5; 9 1 8 5 2; 7 4 7 9 8]
M =
     2     7     3     4     1
     6     9     7     6     1
     3     2     4     6     5
     9     1     8     5     2
     7     4     7     9     8
```

Apply the function of row and column deletion.

```
>> X = M;
>> X(:,3) = []
```

% this command will delete 3rd column of M and replace the 5x5 matrix of M as follows:

```
X =
     2     7     4     1
     6     9     6     1
```

```
        3       2       6       5
        9       1       5       2
        7       4       9       8
```

If we are using a single subscript then it deletes a single element, or a sequence of elements to reshape the remaining elements into a row vector. See the following example.

EXAMPLE 3.172

```
>> X(1:2:10) = []
X =
   Columns 1 through 10
        6       9       7       2       4       4       6       6       5       9
   Columns 11 through 15
        1       1       5       2       8
```

EXAMPLE 3.173

```
   X =
       16       2      13
        5      11       8
        9       7      12
        4      14       1
```

If we delete a single element from a matrix, the result is not a matrix anymore. So, expressions like

$$X(1,2) = [\,]$$

result in an error.

However, using a single subscript deletes a single element, or sequence of elements, and reshapes the remaining elements into a row vector. So

$$X(2:2:10) = [\,]$$

results in

```
   X =
       16   9   2   7   13   12   1
```

3.11 ARRAY TYPES

In MATLAB, the arrays are categorised into the following four types:

1. Multidimensional Array
2. Cell Array
3. Character and Text
4. Structure

3.11.1 Multidimensional Array

Multidimensional arrays in the MATLAB environment are arrays with more than two subscripts. An array having more than two dimensions is called a multidimensional array in MATLAB. Multidimensional arrays in MATLAB are an extension of the normal two-dimensional matrix.

One way of creating a multidimensional array is by calling *zeros, ones, rand* or *randn* with more than two arguments. Let us use *rand* function to create a multidimensional array in the following example.

EXAMPLE 3.174

```
>> R = rand(1,4,7)
R(:,:,1) =
      0.6277     1.0933     1.1093    -0.8637
R(:,:,2) =
      0.0774    -1.2141    -1.1135    -0.0068
R(:,:,3) =
      1.5326    -0.7697     0.3714    -0.2256
R(:,:,4) =
      1.1174    -1.0891     0.0326     0.5525
R(:,:,5) =
      1.1006     1.5442     0.0859    -1.4916
R(:,:,6) =
     -0.7423    -1.0616     2.3505    -0.6156
R(:,:,7) =
      0.7481    -0.1924     0.8886    -0.7648
```

In MATLAB, multidimensional arrays are an extension of the normal two-dimensional matrix. Generally to generate a multidimensional array, we first create a two-dimensional array and extend it. This is represented in matrices that have two dimensions: the row and the column dimension as shown in Figure 3.4.

	Column →			
Row	(1, 1)	(1, 2)	(1, 3)	(1, 4)
	(2, 1)	(2, 2)	(2, 3)	(2, 4)
	(3, 1)	(3, 2)	(3, 3)	(3, 4)
	(4, 1)	(4, 2)	(4, 3)	(4, 4)

FIGURE 3.4 Matrix dimension.

We can access a two-dimensional matrix element with two subscripts: the first representing the row index, and the second representing the column index.

EXAMPLE 3.175   In this example, we will try to create a two-dimensional array *a*.

```
a = [7 9 5; 6 1 9; 4 3 2]
```

Solution: MATLAB will execute the given statement and return the following result:

```
a =

    7        9        5
    6        1        9
    4        3        2
```

The array a is a 3-by-3 array; we can add a third dimension to a, by providing the values like

```
a(:, :, 2)= [ 1 2 3; 4 5 6; 7 8 9]
```

Multidimensional arrays use additional subscripts for indexing. For example, a three-dimensional array is shown in Figure 3.5 uses the following three subscripts:

- The first reference dimension 1, the row.
- The second reference dimension 2, the column.
- The third reference dimension 3. This uses the concept of a page to represent dimension 3 and higher.

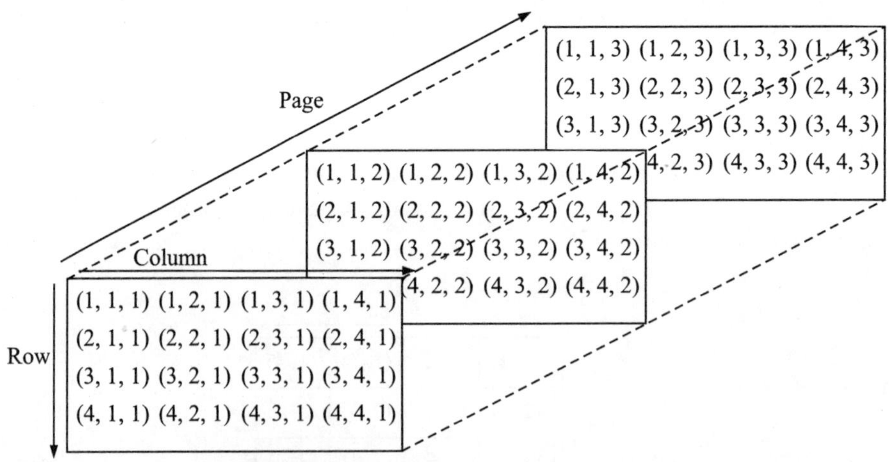

FIGURE 3.5   Three dimension array matrix.

Further, we can see the following example.

EXAMPLE 3.176   From Example 3.175 of MATLAB execute the following statements and show the results.

Solution: MATLAB will execute the given statements and return the following results:

```
a(:,:,1)  =
        7       9       5
        6       1       9
        4       3       2

a(:,:,2)  =
        1       2       3
        4       5       6
        7       8       9
```

EXAMPLE 3.177   To access the element in the second row, third column of page 2, we can use the subscripts $(2, 3, 2)$.

```
A(2, 3, 2)
        6   8
        4   3
        5   9   2
    1   0   3
    4  -1   2
    8   2   1
```

```
A(:,:,1)  =
        1       0       3
        4      -1       2
        8       2       1

A(:,:,2)  =
        6       8       3
        4       3       6
        5       9       2
```

Remember as we add dimensions to an array, we also add subscripts. Now, we can learn to create a four-dimensional array that has four subscripts. The first two reference a row-column pair; the second two access the third and fourth dimensions of data.

We can use this techniques to create multidimensional arrays for N-dimensional matrices. Following are the two ways to create a multidimensional array:

Generating arrays using indexing

EXAMPLE 3.178

```
>> B = [5 7 8; 0 1 9; 4 3 6];
```

B is a 3-by-3 array, that is, its row dimension is 3 and its column dimension is 3. We can add a five dimension to B, using the following commands:

```
>> B(:,:,2) = [9 3 1; 2 8 3; 7 5 6];
>> B(:,:,3) = [1 6 1; 9 8 5; 1 7 3];
>> B(:,:,4) = [8 1 4; 9 5 7; 4 2 6];
```

When we run the given MATLAB commands respond with the following results:

```
B(:,:,1) =
      5      7      8
      0      1      9
      4      3      6


B(:,:,2) =
      9      3      1
      2      8      3
      7      5      6


B(:,:,3) =
      1      6      1
      9      8      5
      1      7      3


B(:,:,4) =
      8      1      4
      9      5      7
      4      2      6
```

Generating arrays using MATLAB functions

We can use MATLAB functions such as randn, ones, and zeros to generate multidimensional arrays. Each argument represents the size of the corresponding dimension in the resulting array that we apply.

EXAMPLE 3.179   To create a 4-by-3-by-2 array of normally distributed random numbers, use the command:

```
>> X = randn(4,3,3);
```

When we run the given MATLAB commands respond with the following results:

```
X(:,:,1) =

   -0.2779    -0.8236     0.0335
    0.7015    -1.5771    -1.3337
   -2.0518     0.5080     1.1275
   -0.3538     0.2820     0.3502
```

```
X(:,:,2) =

    -0.2991    -0.2857    -0.5336
     0.0229    -0.8314    -2.0026
    -0.2620    -0.9792     0.9642
    -1.7502    -1.1564     0.5201


X(:,:,3) =

    -0.0200    -0.1332    -0.5890
    -0.0348    -0.7145    -0.2938
    -0.7982     1.3514    -0.8479
     1.0187    -0.2248    -1.1201
```

To generate an array filled with a single constant value, we can use the repmat function through a vector of array dimensions.

EXAMPLE 3.180

```
>> Y = repmat(9,[3 4 3])
```

When we run the given commands MATLAB responds with the following results:

```
Y(:,:,1) =

     9     9     9     9
     9     9     9     9
     9     9     9     9


Y(:,:,2) =

     9     9     9     9
     9     9     9     9
     9     9     9     9


Y(:,:,3) =

     9     9     9     9
     9     9     9     9
     9     9     9     9
```

3.11.2 Cell Arrays

In MATLAB, a cell array contains the elements in cells, that can hold other MATLAB arrays. The curly braces, '{}', are cell array constructors, just as square brackets are numeric array constructors. Curly braces behave similarly as square brackets, except that we can nest curly braces to denote nesting of cells. A cell array of empty matrices can be created with the cell function.

For example, one cell of a cell array might contain a real matrix, another an array of text strings, and another a vector of complex values as shown in Figure 3.6.

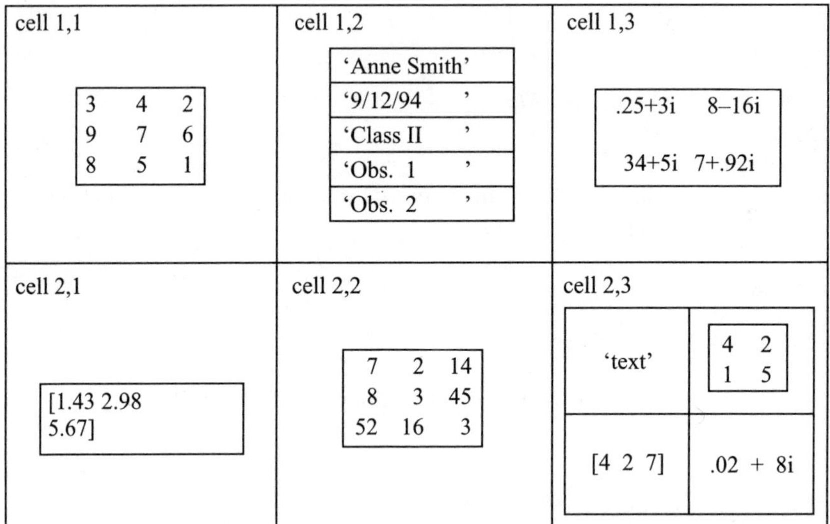

FIGURE 3.6   Cell array dimension.

We can build cell arrays of any valid size or shape, including multidimensional structure arrays.

EXAMPLE 3.181

```
>> C = {[1 2], [3 4]; [5 6], [7 8]}
```

When we run the given command MATLAB responds with the following results:

```
C =
    [1x2 double]    [1x2 double]
    [1x2 double]    [1x2 double]
```

This is represented in Figure 3.7.

cell 1,1	cell 1,2
[1 2]	[3 4]
cell 2,1	cell 2,2
[5 6]	[7 8]

FIGURE 3.7 Cell array dimension.

We can use square brackets to concatenate cell arrays, just as for numeric arrays.

We can use the cell function to pre-allocate empty cell arrays of the specified size. The command use to create an empty 3-by-4 cell array as shown in the following example.

EXAMPLE 3.182

```
>> C = cell(3,4)
```

Use assignment statements to fill the cells of C.

```
C =

    []      []      []      []
    []      []      []      []
    []      []      []      []
```

Multidimensional cell arrays

Like numeric arrays, the framework for multidimensional cell arrays in MATLAB can be extended to different dimensional cell array model. We can use the cat function to build multidimensional cell arrays, similar to the way you use for numeric arrays.

EXAMPLE 3.183 To create a simple three-dimensional cell array use the given command:

```
>> A = {[1 2], [3 4]; [5 6], [7 8]};
>> B = {[5 3], [9 2]; [7 1], [4 5]};
>> A{1,1} = [1 2;4 5]
```

Use the given assignment statements to fill the cells.

```
A =

    [2x2 double]    [1x2 double]
    [1x2 double]    [1x2 double]


>> A{1,2} = 'Name'
A =

    [2x2 double]    'Name'
    [1x2 double]    [1x2 double]
```

```
>> A{2,1} = 2-4i
A =

          [2x2  double]          'Name'
    [2.0000 - 4.0000i]          [1x2  double]


>> A{2,2} = 7
A =

          [2x2  double]          'Name'
    [2.0000 - 4.0000i]          [     7]
```

Similarly, we use the following assignment statements to fill the cells of cell array B.

```
>> B{1,1} = 'Name2';
>> B{1,2} = 3;
>> B{2,1} = 0:1:3;
>> B{2,2} = [4 5]';
```

To build multidimensional cell arrays use the command:

```
C = cat(3,A,B);
```

The subscripts for the cells of *C* look like in Figure 3.8.

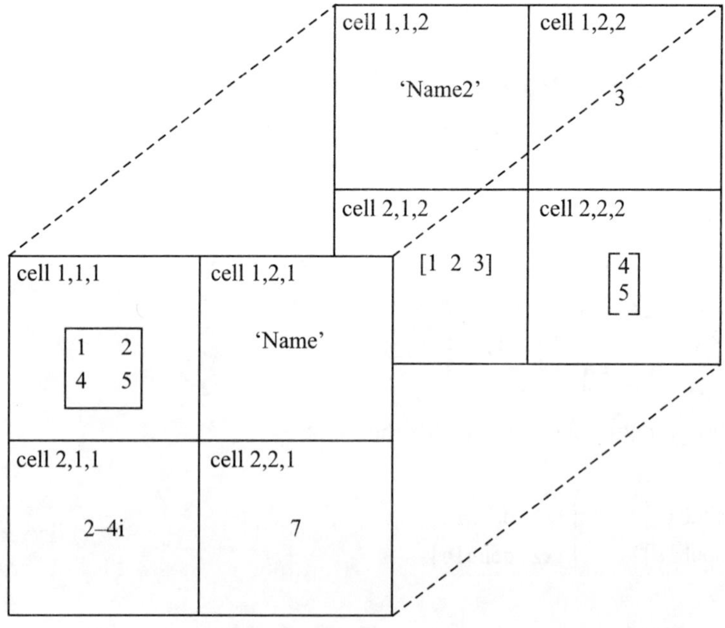

FIGURE 3.8   Multidimensional cell array.

Multidimensional structure arrays are composed of structure arrays. Like other types of multidimensional arrays, we can build them textual field designators. To apply functions to multidimensional structure arrays, operate on fields and field elements using indexing.

EXAMPLE 3.184   In this example, we learn to find the sum of the columns of the test array in patient (3, 1, 2), by using the given command:

```
sum((patient(3,1,2).test));
```

Similarly, add all the billing fields in the patient array, use the given command:

```
total = sum([patient.billing]);
```

Solution: We can create a simple three-dimensional cell array by typing the given commands as follows:

```
>>patient(1,1,1).name = 'Ram';
patient(1,1,1).billing = 18.00;
patient(1,1,1).test = [54 43 28; 87 25 64; 85 28 49];
patient(1,2,1).name = 'Sita';
patient(1,2,1).billing = 28.50;
patient(1,2,1).test = [58 12 84; 67 38 55; 38 87 92];
patient(1,1,2).name = 'Sara';
patient(1,1,2).billing = 504.70;
patient(1,1,2).test = [28 82 185; 58 35 24; 14 175 77];
patient(1,2,2).name = 'Rahim';
patient(1,2,2).billing = 1173.90;
patient(1,2,2).test = [46 38 28; 58 76 17; 57 154 321];

Executing the required function
>> sum((patient(1,1,2).test))
ans =
   100   292   286

>> total = sum([patient.billing])
total =
   1.7251e+03
```

Conclusion: A cell array is a data type with indexed data containers called cells. Each cell contains different type of data like lists of text strings, combinations of text and numbers from spreadsheets or text files, or numeric arrays of different sizes.

SUMMARY

In this chapter, we focussed on the concept of scalar and vector in MATLAB with wide-range of examples. Different types of vector elements and their product and transpose were explained. Wide variety of matrix operations were carried out and discussed. You have learnt different vector operations of matrix which was explained with examples. Generation of special matrices with all zeros, ones, identity and diagonal matrix, matrix operation for deletion and appending of matrix row or column were also explained with examples. Arithmetic, logical and rational operations on vectors and matrices have been discussed. You have also understood about matrix eigenvalue, eigenvector, sorting, rank, trace, inverse, etc. Finally, we discussed different types of multidimensional arrays in detail for your easy understanding.

REVIEW QUESTIONS

1. Define scalar and vector quantity.
2. What is the use of the comma in the definition of the row vector and the semicolon in the definition of the column vector?
3. Write syntax to create evenly spaced row vector.
4. Row vector elements are separated by using what special characters.
5. What special character is used to separate elements in column vector?
6. What special character is used to convert row vector to column vector and vice-a-versa?
7. What is the use of end keyword in MATLAB row vector notation?
8. What MATLAB function gives review of matrix functions?
9. How do you create and display a matrix in the MATLAB?
10. Write relational and logical operators of MATLAB.

PRACTICE EXERCISE

1. Create 1×6 row vector.
2. Create 6×1 column vector.
3. Use transpose to convert row to column vector and vice-a-versa for the vectors created in Examples 3.1 and 3.2, respectively.
4. Create a 5×5 matrix and apply the following function on the matrix:

    ```
    Inv
    Det
    Rank
    ```

```
Eig
Svd
Norm
```

5. For the given matrix *A*:

```
A =
       1       2       3       4       5
       8       9      10      11      12
      14      15      16      17      18
      19      20      21      22      23
      24      25      26      27      28
```

Determine the output of the following commands:

```
>> A(2,1)
>> A(5,1:5)
>> A(:,end)
>> A([7 12;9 14])
```

6. Create the following matrix from the matrix *A* given in the previous problem.

```
S =

       1    2    3    4    5    2    3    4    5    6
       8    9   10   11   12    9   10   11   12   13
      14   15   16   17   18   15   16   17   18   19
      19   20   21   22   23   20   21   22   23   24
      24   25   26   27   28   25   26   27   28   29
```

Algebra and Polynomials

LEARNING OBJECTIVES

This chapter aims to provide the basic ideas on algebraic expression and related polynomial equations in MATLAB. At the end of this chapter, we should able to understand:

- Methods to write the algebraic expression using MATLAB.
- How to perform different operation on polynomial expression to evaluate the values of variables and roots.
- Apply different mathematical operations to solve polynomial equations.
- Compute the derivative and integration of a polynomial.
- Evaluate the polynomials with matrix arguments.
- Estimate the Fourier series and its transform.

INTRODUCTION

Polynomial functions occur frequently in mathematics and engineering. MATLAB provides a number of functions for manipulating polynomials. MATLAB works with these collections of very useful functions.

General form of an nth degree polynomial function is given as:

$$f(x) = a_0 x^n + a_1 x^{n-1} + a_2 x^{n-2} + \cdots + a_{N-2} x^2 + a_{N-1} x + a_N$$

where, degree denotes the highest power of x present and the polynomial coefficients are a_0, a_1, ..., a_N in the equation.

Polynomial is a precisely defined term. It is constructed from constants and variables. Algebraic expression is not a precisely defined term that includes many things that are not polynomials. In MATLAB, addition and multiplication commands can be used to solve the linear algebra expressions.

There are three different ways in which we can define a polynomial in MATLAB. We will learn to define a polynomial in this introduction. A polynomial is an expression of finite number of constants and variables. These variables are combined using different operations like addition, subtraction, multiplication and non-negative power of whole numbers. Polynomials are easily differentiated and integated to find the polynomial root. However, the higher-order polynomials pose numerical difficulties in a number of situations and need to apply appropriately.

In MATLAB, the expression x^5 is interpreted as multiplication of a matrix named x by itself five times i.e., $x^5 = x.x.x.x.x$. In this context, the variable x is the name of the set of x coordinates to the fifth power.

A polynomial is considered to be an algebraic expression, but an algebraic expression does not always be a polynomial. An algebraic expression is an expression with a variable in it. For example, a function denoted by $y = f$ is algebraic if it can be expressed in the form:

$$f_n y^n + f_{n-1} y^{n-1} + \cdots + f_1 y + f_{n0} = 0$$

where, f_i = an ith order polynomial in x.

A polynomial is an expression with multiple terms and variables in it. They are a simple class of algebraic expressions that are generally represented as:

$$f_n(x) = a_0 + a_1 x + a_2 x^2 + \cdots + a_n x^n$$

where n = the order of polynomial in and $a's$ = constants.

Let us consider the following examples which show the difference:

Algebraic expression but not a polynomial: $3b$
Algebraic expression and a polynomial: $7x^2 + 8x - 5$.

Some other examples of such polynomial expressions are as follows:

$$x^2 + 2x - 5, \quad x^3 + 4x^2, \quad x^5$$

These polynomial expressions can be evaluated using MATLAB for evaluation of roots, differentiation, integration and so on. MATLAB includes the polynomial function in *polyfun* library. Transcendental functions like exponential, logarithmic and other less familiar functions are also called non-algebraic. MATLAB can be used as a capable tool for finding roots of both algebraic and transcendental equations. It can also locate roots of polynomials.

4.1 LINEAR EQUATION

To solve the linear system equation the matrix equation $[A * X = B]$ expression can be used. Where, A is a square matrix, B is a column vector and X is a set of unknowns represented as a column vector. For instance, the expression of the system equations as defined below can be solved by the following representation:

$$\begin{cases} x_1 + 2x_2 + 3x_3 = 15 \\ x_1 + 2x_2 + x_3 = 13 \\ -2x_1 + 5x_2 - 2x_3 = 19 \end{cases}$$

Logically, the expression can be equated by inverse of matrix A as

$$A^{-1} * A * X = A^{-1} * Y$$
$$I * X = A^{-1} * Y$$
$$X = A^{-1} * Y$$

In Example 4.1, if matrix A is formed by taking the coefficients of the given algebraic equations. Similarly, vector Y is also formed from RHS (right hand side) values of the equations.

EXAMPLE 4.1

```
>> A= [1 2 3; 1 2 1; -2 5 -2];%A is composed by taking coefficients of x1 x2 and x3
Y= [15 13 19]';%Y is composed by taking values on RHS of equations
A * X=Y % here are A and Y corresponding to the equations above
X=A\Y,   % now solve it by rewriting as
X=inv (A)*Y
X =

        2

        5

        1
```

where, $x_1 = 2$, $x_2 = 5$ and $x_3 = 1$.

This can be verified as follows:

```
>> A*X
ans =
       15

       13

       19
```

It is same as Y which is vector generated from original RHS values of equations. There are number of algebraic functions in MATLAB that can be summarised in Table 4.1.

TABLE 4.1   Summary of algebraic functions in MATLAB

Category	Function	Description
Matrix analysis	norm	Matrix or vector norm
	normest	Estimate the matrix 2-norm
	rank	Matrix rank
	det	Determinant
	trace	Sum of diagonal elements
	null	Null space
	orth	Orthogonalisation
	rref	Reduced row echelon form
	subspace	Angle between two subspaces

(Contd.)

TABLE 4.1 Summary of algebraic functions in MATLAB (*Contd.*)

Category	Function	Description
Linear equations	\ and /	Linear equation solution
	inv	Matrix inverse
	cond	Condition number for inversion
	condest	1-norm condition number estimate
	chol	Cholesky factorisation
	cholinc	Incomplete Cholesky factorisation
	linsolve	Solve a system of linear equations
	lu	LU factorisation
	ilu	Incomplete LU factorisation
	luinc	Incomplete LU factorisation
	qr	Orthogonal-triangular decomposition
	lsqnonneg	Non-negative least-squares
	pinv	Pseudoinverse
	lscov	Least squares with known covariance
Eigenvalues and singular values	e	Eigenvalues and eigenvectors
	svd	Singular value decomposition
	eigs	A few eigenvalues
	svds	A few singular values
	poly	Characteristic polynomial
	polyeig	Polynomial eigenvalue problem
	condeig	Condition number for eigenvalues
	hess	Hessenberg form
	qz	QZ factorisation
	schur	Schur decomposition
Matrix functions	Expm	Matrix exponential
	Logm	Matrix logarithm
	Sqrtm	Matrix square root
	Funm	Evaluate general matrix function

4.2 REPRESENTATION OF POLYNOMIALS

In MATLAB, a polynomial function is represented as row vector where the variable terms are entered in descending order of its power. If the polynomial has degree n, the corresponding representing vector has length $n + 1$ and contains the coefficients associated with decreasing powers from left to right. Zero coefficients must be marked as zero entries. For example, [6 4 1] represents as $P(r) = 6s^2 + 4s + 1$. whereas [1 0 1] represents as $P(r) = s^2$.

Polyval function command is used for such evaluation.

The command polyval(vector,arg) interprets vector as polynomial and evaluates it at *arg*, which can be a number, a vector or even a matrix. Common syntax of this command:

$$\text{polyval(c, s) ;}$$

where, c is a vector whose elements are the coefficients of a polynomial in descending order of power of variable s.

EXAMPLE 4.2

```
>> p=[1 2 1];
>> polyval(p,1)
ans =

        4
```

Note: Here $P(r) = s^2 + 2s + 1$, is evaluated for $s = 1$, i.e., $4 = (1)^2 + 2(1) + 1$.

```
polyval(p,[1 2])
ans =

        4      9
```

Note: Here $P(r) = s^2 + 2s + 1$, is evaluated for $s = 1$ and also at $s = 2$, i.e., $4 = (1)^2 + 2(1) + 1$ and $9 = (2)^2 + 2(2) + 1$.

EXAMPLE 4.3   In this example, we evaluate the polynomial $p(x) = 5x^2 + x + 4$ at $x = 2$, 4, and 3.

```
>> p = [5 1 4];
>> polyval(p,[2 4 3])
% which results in
ans =
      26     88     52
```

EXAMPLE 4.4   In this example, we find the value of $p(x) = 4x^2 + 9x + 2$ at $s = -6$.

```
>> y= [4 9 2];
>> s=-6;
>> z=polyval(y, s)
% The solution obtained is
z =
92
```

EXAMPLE 4.5

```
>> r=linspace(-2,0,100);plot(r,polyval([1 2 1],r))
```

Note: A plot of $P(r) = s^2 + 2s + 1$ in the range $-2 < r < 0$ is created using 100 supporting points and is plotted as shown in Figure 4.1.

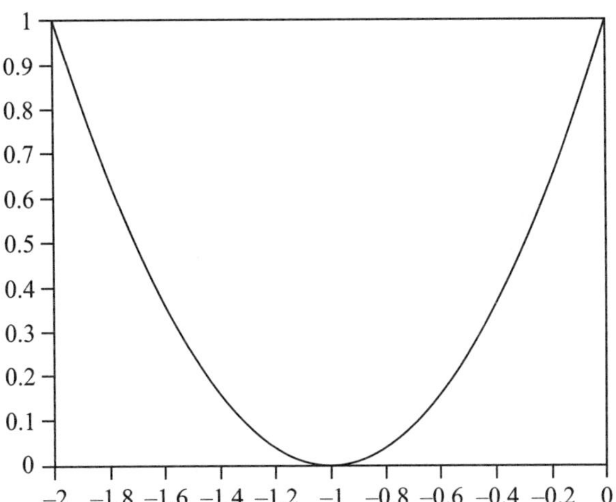

FIGURE 4.1   Plot plotted using linspace.

Practice Exercise

Create a polynomial matrix using the values of the polynomial equation $y = s^4 - 4s^3 + 10$ and evaluate at $s = [-2, 5]$, using a s increment of 0.1. Also plot y.

 Note the use of a semicolon at the end of each line to suppress the output as shown:

```
s= [2: 0.1: 5];
y= s.^4-4*s.^3+10;
```

4.3 POLYNOMIAL ROOTS

In MATLAB to find the roots of a polynomial, associated argument command is rootes(vector). MATLAB represents polynomials as row vectors containing coefficients ordered by descending powers. For example, the polynomial or equation $P(x) = x^4 + 7x^3 - 5x + 9$ can be represented as: p = [1 7 0 -5 9].

 In MATLAB, the roots of a polynomial function can be determined by roots (x) function. The syntax for finding roots is as follows:

```
p= roots(x)
```

where, x is a row vector containing the coefficient of a polynomial and p is the column vector whose elements are the roots of polynomial.

 So, the roots function calculates the roots of a polynomial.

EXAMPLE 4.6   In this example, we learn to calculate the roots of our polynomial p, typing the following at the command prompt:

```
>> p =[1 7 0 -5 9];
>> r = roots(p)
```

MATLAB executes the above statements and returns the following result:

```
r =
-6.8661 + 0.0000i
-1.4247 + 0.0000i
0.6454 + 0.7095i
0.6454 - 0.7095i
```

Here the polynomial has four roots of which two are real and other two are complex.

The function poly is an inverse of the roots function and returns the polynomial coefficients. For example,

```
>> p2 = poly(r)
```

MATLAB executes the above statement and returns the following result as coefficient vector whose power is in descending order:

```
p2 =
    1.0000   7.0000   0.0000   -5.0000   9.0000
```

EXAMPLE 4.7   This example is used to define a polynomial of degree six with random coefficients and compute its roots as shown below:

```
>> p=rand([1 7]),roots(p)
p =
    0.9169    0.4103    0.8936    0.0579    0.3529    0.8132    0.0099

ans =
    -0.4043+1.0987i
    -0.4043-1.0987i
    0.5809+0.6921i
    0.5809-0.6921i
    -0.7883-0.0122
```

The first output shows seven random numbers between 0 and 1 to which a polynomial of degree six is associated. The second output contains numerical approximations of the six roots of this polynomial which are stored in a column vector.

EXAMPLE 4.8   In this example, we find the roots of the polynomial $s^2 + 3s + 2$.

The expression is represented by coefficient in terms of vector x and its roots are computed as follows:

```
>> x= [1 3 2];
p=roots(x);
>> p
```

The solution obtained is

```
p =
      -2
      -1
```

The value of p represent root $r_1 = -2$ and root $r_2 = -1$.

EXAMPLE 4.9   In this example, we find the roots of the polynomial $s^4 - 7s^3 + 2s^2 + 3s + 56$.

The polynomial is represented by a row vector p of its coefficient in descending order and its roots are computed as follows.

```
>> p = [1 -7 2 3 56] % polynomial is represented by a row vector
p =
        1      -7      2      3     56
>> r = roots(p) % to find polynomial root vector
r =
    6.4008
    2.5998
   -1.0003 + 1.5378i
   -1.0003 - 1.5378i

% polynomial are row vector and roots are column vector
>> pp = poly(r)   % to construct the polynomial
pp =
      1.0000    -7.0000    2.0000    3.0000    56.0000

>> pp(abs(pp)<1e-12) =0 % change small element to zero
pp =
      1.0000    -7.0000    2.0000    3.0000    56.0000
```

4.3.1 Multiple Roots

When there are more than one roots for a polynomial such a polynomial is known as *multi-root polynomial*. There are some complexities involved with the multiple roots. For second degree polynomials these are usually recognised, but not necessarily recognised for polynomials of higher degree.

EXAMPLE 4.10   The polynomials $s^2 + 2s + 1$ have just one root $s = -1$, but in the cubic case $s^2 + 3s^2 + 3s + 1$ three different (though close) values are returned as shown:

```
>> roots([1 2 1]),roots([1 3 3 1])
ans =
    -1 -1
ans =
  -1.00000913968880
  -0.99999543015560 + 0.00000791513186i
  -0.99999543015560 - 0.00000791513186i
```

4.4 POLYNOMIAL ARITHMETIC OPERATION

In MATLAB, mathematical operations like addition, subtraction, multiplication and division can be performed on polynomials.

EXAMPLE 4.11   In this example, we carry out arithmetic operations like addition, subtraction, multiplication and division on polynomials $8s^2 + 4s + 2$ and $5s^2 + 2s + 1$.
Row vectors to the polynomials are represented as:

```
>> x= [8 4 2];
>> y= [5 2 1];
```

The execution of these arithmetic operations and their results are computed as follows:

Addition

```
>> z= x + y
```

The solution obtained is

```
z =
    13    6    3
```

Subtraction

```
>> z= (x - y)
```

The solution obtained is

```
z =
    3    2    1
```

Multiplication: Polynomial multiplication is supported by the function conv, that performs the convolution of two arrays.

```
>> z= conv(x, y)
```

The solution obtained is

```
z =
    40    36    26    8    2
```

Division

```
>> [z,r]=deconv(x, y)
```

The solution obtained with resultant quotient z and reminder r.

```
z =
    1.6000
r =
        0    0.8000    0.4000
```

Here, the quotient is 1.6 and the remainder is $0.8s + 0.4$.

EXAMPLE 4.12   In this example we use the arithmetic operations with polynomials $(a)s = s^3 + 5s^2 + 4s + 8$ and $b(s) = 5s^3 + 8s^2 + 3s + 9$.

The polynomials are represented as:

```
>> a = [1 5 4 8];
>> b= [5 8 3 9];
```

Multiplication

```
>> c = conv(a,b)
c =
    5    33    63    96    121    60    72
```

Addition

```
>> d = a + b
d =
    6    13    7    17
```

We can also perform the addition of two different order polynomials as shown:

```
>> e = c + [0 0 0 d]     % two different polynomials are added using null value
to increase the order.
e =
    5    33    63    102    134    67    89
```

Division

```
>> [q, r] = deconv(c,b)   % polynomial division
q =
    1.0000    5.0000    4.0000    8.0000
```

```
r =
   1.0e-013 *
   Columns 1 through 6
          0          0          0          0     0.0888     0.0444
   Column 7
      0.1776
```

4.4.1 Complex Arithmetic

MATLAB does most of its computation using complex number of the form $a + bi$, where $i = \sqrt{-1}$ and a and b are real numbers. The complex number is represented with i in MATLAB. Many polynomials with real coefficients have a complex roots.

EXAMPLE 4.13

```
>> solve x^2+2*x+2
```

The solution obtained is

```
ans =
  [- 1 + i]
  [- 1 - i]
```

Here, both roots of this quadratic equation are complex numbers, expressed in the form of $a + bi$.

4.5 POLYNOMIAL EQUATION FORMULATION

In MATLAB, if the roots of a polynomial column vector are known then the corresponding polynomial can be obtained by command *poly*.

EXAMPLE 4.14

```
>> r= [3; -7];
>> p= poly(r)
```

The solution obtained is

```
p =
        1       4     -21
```

Hence, the polynomial equation is $s^2 + 4s - 21 = C$.

4.6 RATIONAL POLYNOMIAL

In MATLAB, the polynomial numerator and denominator can be treated separately to find the roots, derivative and residue function.

EXAMPLE 4.15　In this example, we find the roots of the rational polynimal.

```
>> n = [2 -9 71]        % a numerator
n =
      2      -9      71


>> d = [5 14 36]        % a denominator
d =
      5      14      36


>> z = roots(n)         % the zeros of n(x)/d(x)
z =
    2.2500 + 5.5170i
    2.2500 - 5.5170i


>> p = roots(d)         % the zeros of n(x)/d(x)
p =
   -1.4000 + 2.2891i
   -1.4000 - 2.2891i
```

EXAMPLE 4.16　In this example, we find the derivative of this rational polynomial with respect to x, using polyder which gives the numerator and denominator polynomials of the derivative as shown:

```
>> [nd, dd] = polyder(n, d)
nd =
          73         -566        -1318
dd =
       25        140        556       1008       1296
```

EXAMPLE 4.17　In this example, we find the residue partial-function expansion to coefficient r, pole p and direct term polynomial k, use the commands as follows:

```
>> [r, p, k] = residue(n, d)
r =
   -1.4600 - 3.3655i
   -1.4600 + 3.3655i


p =
   -1.4000 + 2.2891i
   -1.4000 - 2.2891i


k =
    0.4000
```

4.7 CHARACTERISTIC POLYNOMIAL OF A MATRIX

In MATLAB, the characteristics polynomial or equation of a matrix is obtained by using the command:

```
>> p= poly (x)
```

Where, x is the matrix characteristic equation, p is the row vector whose coefficient equation is in descending order of power.

EXAMPLE 4.18

```
>> x= [3  7;  2  3]
x =

        3       7
        2       3
```

Applying the command to obtain the characteristic polynomial or equation of a matrix as;

```
>> p= poly(x)
```

The solution obtained is

```
p =
        1.0000     -6.0000     -5.0000
```


4.8 DIFFERENTIATION AND INTEGRATION

Integration and differentiation are the fundamental tools in calculus. Integration is used to compute the area under a function, and differentiation describes the slope or gradient of a function. MATLAB provides functions for numerically approximating the integral and slope of a function.

4.8.1 Integration in Polynomial

In MATLAB, to compute the integration of a polynomial a command *polyint* is used. The command function is:

```
polyint (y, h)
```

Where, y represents the coefficient of polynomial and h represents the scalar constant of the integration to compute the result.

EXAMPLE 4.19 In this example, we compute integration of the polynomial $y = 3s^4 + 7s^3 + 5s^2 + 4s + 5$, using the given commands as follows:

```
>> y= [3 7 5 4 5];
>> x= polyint(y, 4)
```

The solution obtained is

```
X =
   Columns 1 through 5
      0.6000      1.7500      1.6667      2.0000      5.0000
   Column 6
   4.0000
```

Hence, the resultant polynomial is $x = 0.6s^5 + 1.75s^4 - 1.667s^3 + 2s^2 + 5s^1 + 4$ with a constant 4.

Humps function

'humps' is a function used by QUADDEMO, ZERODEMO and FPLOTDEMO.

```
    Y = humps(X) is a function with strong maxima near x = .3 and x = .9.


    [X,Y] = humps(X) also returns X.  With no input arguments,
humps uses X = 0:.05:1.


    %   Copyright 1984-2014 TheMathWorks, Inc.
```

For example, if we type the following function it will plot the maxima and minima value as shown in Figure 4.2.

```
    fplot(@humps,[0,2]);          % This function shows a plot of HUMPS in the domain
[0,2] using FPLOT.
```

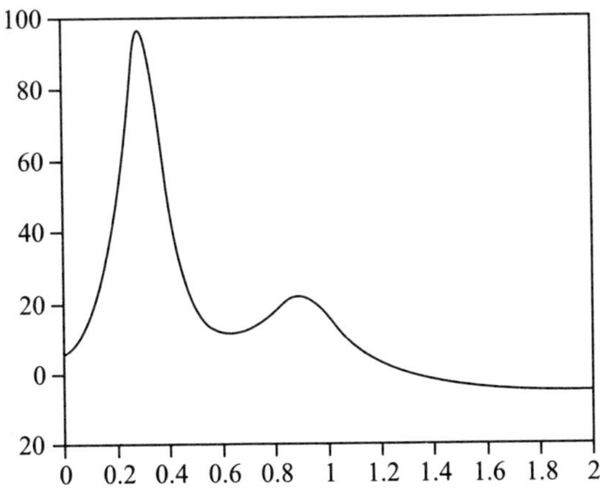

FIGURE 4.2 Humps function plot.

EXAMPLE 4.20 In this example, we show the integration of function using humps(x) command as follows:

```
>> x = -1:10:6;
>> x = -1:.10:6;
```

```
>> y = humps(x);
>> area = trapz(x,y)
area =
      3.5770
```

EXAMPLE 4.21   If we illustrate the integration of function using humps(x) with more accuracy.

```
>> x = linspace(-1,8,47);
>> y = humps(x);
>> format long
>> area = trapz(x,y)
area =
  -10.035100738619255
```

4.8.2 Differentiation in Polynomial

In MATLAB, one can compute the derivative of a polynomial by using a command *polyder*. The syntax for this command is,

dydx = polyder (y)

Where, y represents the coefficient of polynomial and *dydx* represents the vector of the coefficient of the derivative.

Another useful command is polyder(vector). Here, again the vector argument is interpreted as polynomial and the output is the vector representing the derivative of this polynomial. For example, the derivative of $P(r) = s^2 + 2s + 1$ (vector [1 2 1]) is $P'(r) = 2s + 2$ (vector [2 2]) which we can find by executing the following command:

```
>> polyder([1 2 1])
ans =
      2     2
```

EXAMPLE 4.22   This equation $y = 2s^5 + 4s^4 - 3s^3 + 9s^2 + 5s + 7$, is represented by using its coefficients as

```
>> y= [2 4 -3 9 5 7];
```

Using the command of *polyder*, we get

```
>> dydx= polyder (y)
```

The solution obtained is

```
dydx =
   10     16     -9     18      5
```

Hence, $\dfrac{dy}{dx} = 10s^4 + 16s^3 - 9s^2 + 18s^1 + 5.$

4.9 POLYNOMIAL CURVE EQUATION

The MATLAB function polyfit is used to find the coefficients of a polynomial p of degree n. In MATLAB, the vector x and y can be formed into polynomial that can fit in descending order.

$p= polyfit\ (x,\ y,\ n)$

where, x and y represent the vector of the points for curve fitting and n represent the order of the desired polynomial.

EXAMPLE 4.24

```
>> x= [3 7 9 2];
>> y= [1 4 5 8];
```

The polynomial of degree

```
>> C= polyfit(x, y, 2)
```

The solution obtained is

```
C =
0.3593    -3.9848    12.5751
```

Hence, $0.3593s^2 - 3.98484s + 12.5751$ is a fitting polynomial.

EXAMPLE 4.25 In order to find a third degree polynomial that fits the points (1, 5.5), (2, 43.1), (3, 128), (4, 290.7), (5, 498.4), we can write the expression as follows.

Define matrices X and Y containing the x and y coordinates, respectively, of the points given

```
>> X= [1:5]
>> Y= [5.5 43.1 128 290.7 4]
% we can try to apply p= polyfit(x,y,n) with n= 3, to find the coefficients of the
third degree polynomial.
>> polyfit(X, Y, 3)
% observe the result.
Ans =
    -41.3917    331.7536    -707.7548    430.8600
```

4.10 POLYNOMIAL MATRIX EVALUATION

In MATLAB, the polynomial evaluate for the square matrix can be solved using the commands as follow:

>> polyval(p xvalue)

Having defined the polynomial as the coefficient matrix p, we can use the MATLAB command polyval to evaluate the polynomial for a specific value of x or for a range of x values.

The general syntax for this command is polyval(p xvalue), where *p* is the name of the coefficient and xvalue is the value of *x* or a matrix of *x* values.

p= polyvalm (a, m)

Where, *a* is a row vector element the coefficient of the matrix polynomial and *m* specifies the square matrix.

EXAMPLE 4.26   For $p(x) = x^4 + 7x^3 - 5x + 9$

```
>> p = [1 7 0 -5 9];
```

The polyval function is used to evaluate our previous polynomial p, at $x = 4$,

```
p =[1 7 0 -5 9];
>> polyval(p,4)
```

MATLAB executes the above statements and returns the following result:

```
ans =
693
```

MATLAB also provides the *polyvalm* function for evaluating a matrix polynomial. A matrix polynomial is a polynomial with matrices as variables.

EXAMPLE 4.27   In this example, in order to create a square matrix, we can evaluate the polynomial *p* at *x* as follows:

```
>> p = [1 7 0 -5 9];
X = [1 2 -3 4; 2 -5 6 3; 3 1 0 2; 5 -7 3 8];
polyvalm(p, X)
```

MATLAB executes the above statements and returns the following result:

```
ans =
   2307      -1769      -939      4499
   2314      -2376      -249      4695
   2256      -1892      -549      4310
   4570      -4532     -1062      9269
```

EXAMPLE 4.28

```
>> a= [3 5 9];    % Represent the matrix polynomial 3s² + 5s + 9.
>> m= [5 1; 8 3];
>> z=polyvalm(a, m)
```

The solution obtained is

```
z =
       7      1
       8      5
```

EXAMPLE 4.29

```
>> x = [0 .1 .2 .3 .4 .5 .6 .7 .8 .9 1];
y = [-.12 2.4 3.5 4.2 5.9 6.2 6.8 7.3 7.9 8.5 9.8];
n = 2;
p = polyfit(x,y,n) % to find polynomial coefficients
p =
    -5.3730    13.9457    0.5786
>> xi = linspace(0,2,50);
>> yi = polyval(p,xi)
yi =
  Columns 1 through 12
    0.5786    1.1389    1.6812    2.2057    2.7122    3.2009    3.6716    4.1245    4.5594
4.9765    5.3756    5.7568
  Columns 13 through 24
    6.1202    6.4656    6.7931    7.1028    7.3945    7.6683    7.9242    8.1622    8.3824
8.5846    8.7689    8.9353
  Columns 25 through 36
    9.0838    9.2144    9.3271    9.4219    9.4988    9.5578    9.5989    9.6221    9.6273
9.6147    9.5842    9.5358
  Columns 37 through 48
    9.4695    9.3852    9.2831    9.1631    9.0251    8.8693    8.6956    8.5039    8.2944
8.0669    7.8216    7.5583
  Columns 49 through 50
    7.2772    6.978
```

EXAMPLE 4.30

```
>> x = [0 .1 .2 .3 .4 .5 .6 .7 .8 .9 1];
>> y = [-.12 2.4 3.5 4.2 5.9 6.2 6.8 7.3 7.9 8.5 9.8];
>> n = 2;
>> p = polyfit(x,y,n)   % to find polynomial coefficients
p =
    -5.372960372960372   13.945687645687647    0.578601398601397

>> xi = linspace(0,2,50);
>> yi = polyval(p,xi); % to evaluate polynomial
>> plot(x,y,'-*',xi,yi,'o')
>> xlabel('x'), ylabel('y=f(x)')
>> title('Second Order Curve Fitting')
```

```
>> pd = polyder(p)        % polynomial derivative function
pd =
  -10.745920745920744   13.945687645687647
```

By running the MATLAB code the second order derivative curve is shown in Figure 4.3.

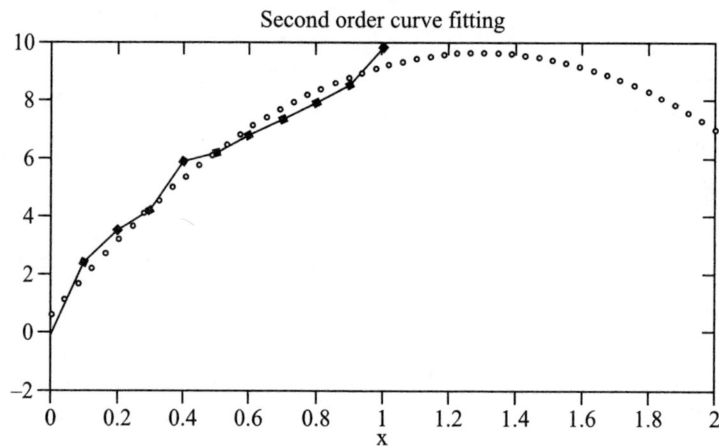

FIGURE 4.3   Second order curve.

> **Practice Exercise**
>
> ```
> Xval= [- 2 : 5]    % The semicolons have been omitted so we can see the output.
> Polyval= (p, xval
> ```

Polynomial functions in MATLAB can be as summarised in Table 4.2.

TABLE 4.2   Summary of polynomial functions in MATLAB

Function Name	Description
Roots	Polynomial roots
Residue	Convert between partial fraction expansion and polynomial coefficients
Polyvalm	Matrix polynomial evaluation
Polyval	Polynomial evaluation
Polyint	Integrate polynomial analytically
Polyfit	Polynomial curve fitting
Polyeig	Polynomial eigenvalue problem
Polyder	Polynomial derivative
Poly	Polynomial with specified roots
Deconv	Deconvolution and polynomial division
Conv	Convolution and polynomial multiplication

4.11 FOURIER ANALYSIS

Fourier analysis is a term named after the French mathematician Joseph Fourier, is the process of breaking down a complex function and expressing it as a combination of simpler functions. In the MATLAB the frequency-domain tools such as Fourier series and Fourier transforms form a part of signal processing for discrete time counterpart. These transform decompose a signal into a sequence or continuous sinusoidal components to identify the frequency-domain content of the signal. MATLAB provides the Fourier analysis functions such as *fft, ifft, fft2, ifft2, fftn, ifftn, fftshift* and *ifftshift*. These functions perform the discrete Fourier transform and the inverse.

We can go between the time domain and the frequency domain by using a tool called **Fourier Transform**. This can be understood as follows:

- A Fourier transform converts a signal in the 'time domain' to the 'frequency domain' spectrum.
- An inverse Fourier transform converts the 'frequency domain' components back into the original 'time domain' signal.

The Fast Fourier Transform does not refer to a new or different type of Fourier transform. It refers to a very efficient algorithm for computing the **Discrete Fourier Transform** (DFT).

The *fft* function approximates the Fourier series of a periodic continuous time signal. Following examples are used Fourier series for such periodic continuous time signal.

EXAMPLE 4.31   Using MATLAB function plot the continuous sine wave.

```
>> Fs = 100; % sampling frequency
t = 0:1/Fs:1; % Time vector of 1 second
f = 10; % Create a sine wave of f Hz.
x = sin(2*pi*t*f);
nfft = 1024; % Length of FFT

% Take fft for the lenth(x) to be equal to nfft by padding with zeros
X = fft(x, nfft);
% FFT is symmetric, throw away second half
X = X(1:nfft/2);
% Take the magnitude of fft of x
mx = abs(X);
% Frequency vector
f = (0:nfft/2-1)*Fs/nfft;
% Generate the plot, title and labels.
figure(1);
plot(t,x);
title('Sine wave signal');
xlabel('Time(s)');
```

```
ylabel('Amplitude');
figure(2);
plot(f, mx);
title('Power spectrum of a sine wave');
xlabel('Frequency (Hz)');
ylabel('Power');
```

By running the MATLAB code, output is shown in Figure 4.4.

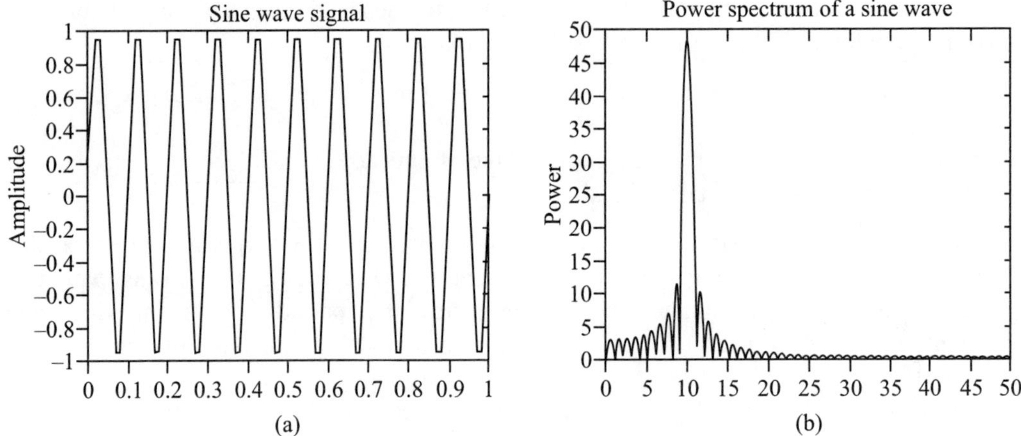

FIGURE 4.4   (a) Sine wave signal and (b) Power spectrum of sine wave signal.

4.11.1 Discrete Fourier Transform

In MATLAB, the function `fft` computes the discrete Fourier transform of a signal. The fast Fourier transform implementation in MATLAB is represented as:

$$F(k) = FFT\{f(n)\} = \sum_{n=0}^{N-1} f(n)e^{-\frac{j2\pi nk}{N}} \qquad k = 0, 1, ..., N-1$$

When the index value is shifted by one then $F(k)$ is represented as follows:

$$F(k) = FFT\{f(n)\} = \sum_{n=1}^{N} f(n)e^{-\frac{j2\pi(n-1)(k-1)}{N}} \qquad k = 0, 1, ..., N-1$$

The inverse transform is represented accordingly as follows:

$$F(n) = FFT^{-1}\{F(k)\} = \frac{1}{N}\sum_{k=1}^{N} F(k)e^{-\frac{j2\pi(n-1)(k-1)}{N}} \qquad n = 0, 1, ..., N-1$$

In MATLAB, we can type help *fft* to read more about fast Fourier transform.

```
>> help fft
```

```
FFT Discrete Fourier transform.
    FFT(X) is the discrete Fourier transform (DFT) of vector X.  For
    matrices, the FFT operation is applied to each column. For N-D
    arrays, the FFT operation operates on the first non-singleton
    dimension.

    FFT(X,N) is the N-point FFT, padded with zeros if X has less
    than N points and truncated if it has more.

    FFT(X,[],DIM) or FFT(X,N,DIM) applies the FFT operation across the
    dimension DIM.

    For length N input vector x, the DFT is a length N vector X,
    with elements
                      N
        X(k) =       sum   x(n)*exp(-j*2*pi*(k-1)*(n-1)/N), 1 <= k <= N.
                     n=1
    The inverse DFT (computed by IFFT) is given by
                      N
        x(n) = (1/N) sum   X(k)*exp( j*2*pi*(k-1)*(n-1)/N), 1 <= n <= N.
                     k=1

    See also fft2, fftn, fftshift, fftw, ifft, ifft2, ifftn.
```

EXAMPLE 4.32   Estimate the continuous Fourier transform of the signal $f(t) = 2e^{-3t}$; $t \geq 0$

We can analytically find the Fourier transform of $f(t)$ given as $F(w) = 2/3 + jw$

```
>> N = 64;     % choose the power of 2
>> t = linspace(0,3,N);      % time points for function evaluation
>> f = 2*exp(-2*t);          % minimise aliasing by evaluating function
>> Ts = t(2)-t(1);           % sampling period
>> Ws = 2*pi/Ts;             % sampling function in rad/sec
>> F = fft(f);               % compute the fft
>> Fc = fftshift(F)*Ts; % shift and scale
>>
>> W = Ws+(-N/2:(N/2)-1)/N;             % frequency axis
>> Fa = 2./(2+j*W);                     % analytical Fourier transform
>> subplot(1,2,1);                      % two plots in single figure
>> plot(W,abs(Fa),W,abs(Fc),'.')       % generate plot, 'o' mark fft
>> xlabel('Frequency, Rad/s')
```

```
>> ylabel('|F(\omega)|')
>> title('Fourier Trasform Approximation')
>>
>> N = 128;
>> t = linspace(0,3,N);
>> f = 3*exp(-2*t);
>> Ts = t(2)-t(1);
>> Ws = 3*pi/Ts;
>> F = fft(f);
>> Fc = fftshift(F)*Ts;
>>
>> W = Ws+(-N/2:(N/2)-1)/N;
>> Fa = 2./(2+j*W);
>> subplot(1,2,2);
>> plot(W,abs(Fa),W,abs(Fc),'.')
>> xlabel('Frequency, Rad/s')
>> ylabel('|F(\omega)|')
>> title('Fourier Trasform Approximation')
```

By running the code the following Figure 4.5 is displayed.

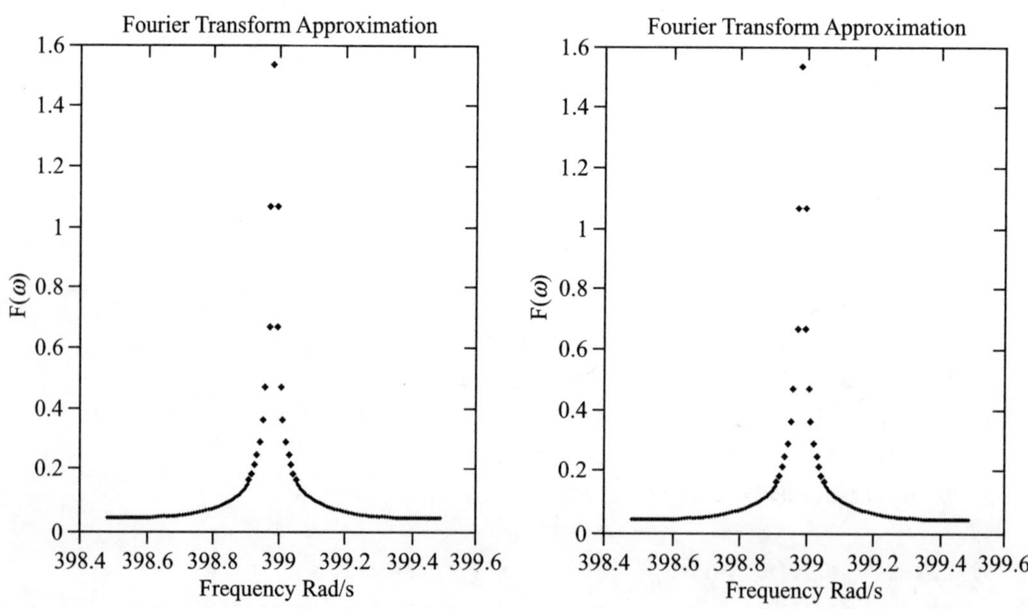

FIGURE 4.5 Fourier transform analysis.

4.11.2   Fourier Series

In MATLAB, the Fourier series analysis cannot be easily manipulated. Such Fourier series can be transformed by understanding the relation between Fourier transform of signal and its Fourier series.

The Fourier series representation of a real-valued periodic signal $f(t)$ is as follows:

$$f(t) = \sum_{n=-\infty}^{n=\infty} F_n e^{j\omega_0 t}$$

where the Fourier series coefficient is given by

$$F_n = \frac{1}{T_0} \int_t^{t+T_0} f(t) e^{-j\omega_0 t} dt$$

where, ω_0 is the fundamental frequency.

EXAMPLE 4.33

```
>> N = 40;
To = 0.35;
n = 2*N;
t = linspace(0, To, n+1);
t(end)= [];
f = sawtooth(t,To);
Fn = fft(f);
Fn = [conj(Fn(N+1)) Fn(N+2:end) Fn(1:N+1)];
Fn = Fn/n;
AO = Fn(N+1);
An = 2*real(Fn(N+2: end));
Bn = -2*imag(Fn(N+2: end));
idx = -N:N;
Fna = 10j./(idx*pi);
Fna(N+1) = 5;
Bna = -4*imag(Fna(N+2: end));
Bn_error = (Bn-Bna)./Bna;
stem(idx, abs(Fn))
xlabel('Harmonics Index')
title('Sawtooth Harmonic Content')
axis tight
```

By running the MATLAB code the following Figure 4.6 is displayed.

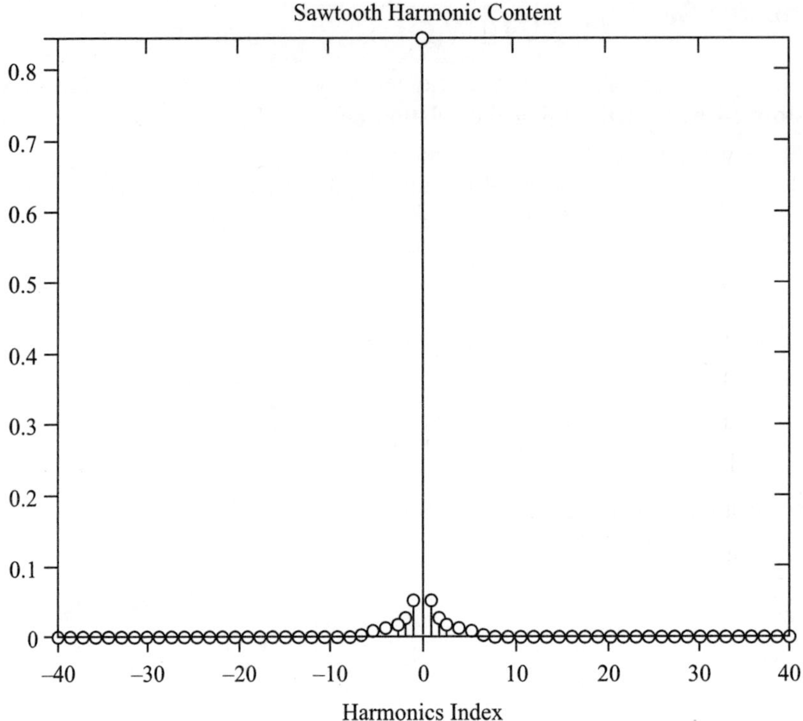

FIGURE 4.6   Fourier series of sawtooth.

SUMMARY

In this chapter, we have seen a very brief introduction to a few of the polynomial functions and operations of MATLAB. In MATLAB, the linear algebra solves the matrix equation using Ax = B. The polynomial is represented in row vector in MATLAB with polynomial coefficients of variables are arranged in descending order. In a polynomial different functions are used. The function *polyval* is to evaluate the given value of variable. The polynomial root is evaluated using *roots (p)* where, *p* is a row vector coefficient. Polynomials are used for arithmetic operations such as addition, subtraction, multiplication and division. We have learnt about the integration and differentiation of the polynomial. The function *polyder* and *polyint* are used to compute the derivative and integration of polynomial. Polynomial function like *polyfit* is used to fit the set of vectors and *polyvalm* is used for evaluating matrix. The list of commands and its description are also shown. Several worked out examples covered in the entire chapter are self-explanatory. In the last section, we have also learn about Fourier functions such as FFL (x) and get an idea of FFT computation.

REVIEW QUESTIONS

1. Define algebraic function and give example.
2. What do we mean by the degree of a polynomial?
3. Give examples of transcendental functions.
4. How do we represent linear expressions in MATLAB?
5. How do we write polynomials in MATLAB?
6. When a polynomial is said to have multiple roots?
7. What is the significance of solutions or roots of a polynomial?
8. What is the significance of derivative of a polynomial?
9. What is the significance of integration of a polynomial?
10. Can we use `polyvalm` function/command for rectangular matrices?
11. Is every matrix have inverse?

PRACTICE EXERCISE

1. Compute and Display exponential for matrix A.

   $$A = \begin{matrix} 2 & 2 & 0 \\ 0 & 1 & 2 \\ 0 & 1 & -1 \end{matrix}$$

2. Find logarithm of matrix A in question 1.
3. For x = [2 4 6] and y = [1 2 3], compute x′, y′, x + y, x − y, x/y, x\y.
4. Find inverse of matrix B = [1 2 3;4 5 6;7 8 9].
5. Analyse the given code and plot the output.
```
subplot(1,2,1)
cc = [-1/4 1 0];
pp1 = mkpp([-8 -4],cc);
xx1 = -8:0.1:-4;
plot(xx1,ppval(pp1,xx1),'k-')
subplot(1,2,2)
pp2 = mkpp([-4 0],-cc);
xx2 = -4:0.1:0;
plot(xx2,ppval(pp2,xx2),'k-')
```

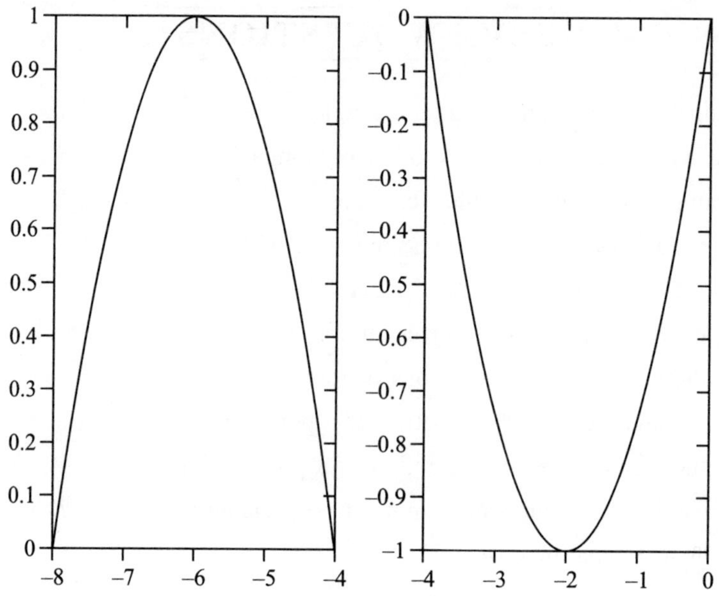

FIGURE 4.7   Output of commands.

6. Explore the function conv for a polynomial.

7. Explore the function deconv for a polynomial.

8. For $f(x) = 12x^{3/2} + 1$ find derivative of $f(x)$ using MATLAB.

9. For $f(x) = 12x^{3/2} + 1$ find integration of $f(x)$ using MATLAB.

CHAPTER 5

Input-Output

LEARNING OBJECTIVES

This chapter aims to provide the understanding of input and output functions. At the end of this chapter, we should learn:

- About the concept of data input using assignment statement.
- Some of the basic input and output statements used in MATLAB.
- Study of different interactive input statements.
- Different types of functions to display the formatted data.
- Opening and closing of a file.

INTRODUCTION

In MATLAB, the data processing commands or functions are used to process raw data into desired format with the use of computer system. Data is processed as input data using command on the command window and represented as output on the command window as vectors, matrix, statements, pictorial format or graphical display. In addition, it has powerful file-handling feature and it is also able to interface with other programming environments.

5.1   INPUT AND OUTPUT FUNCTIONS

In MATLAB, the data is expressed in the form of arrays. MATLAB extensively and effectively supports input and output of data of all types. Data can be in the form of objects shown as integers, real numbers, matrices, character strings, structure and cells. MATLAB library automatically generates the real or complex, when the data is processed from inputs or execute from memory. Some of the basic input-output statements used in the MATLAB are as listed below:

input()
disp()
fprintf()
fopen()
fclose()
fread()
fwrite()
fscanf() ...etc.

5.1.1   Low-Level File Input/Output in MATLAB

A low-level file I/O function is used to control reading or writing data to a file. These functions require by us to specify more detailed information from the file that is easier-to-use for *high-level functions*, such as importdata. In the high-level functions use one of the following:

- *fscanf*, which reads formatted data in a text or ASCII file; i.e., a file we can view in a text editor.
- *fgetl* and *fgets*, which read one line of a file at a time, where a newline character separates each line.
- *fread*, which reads a stream of data at the byte or bit level.

Similarly, few file input-output functions are as listed below:

fclose	:	Close one or all open files
feof	:	Test for end-of-file
ferror	:	Information about file Input/Output errors
fgetl	:	Read line from file, removing newline characters
fgets	:	Read line from file, keeping newline characters
fopen	:	Open file, or obtain information about open files
fprintf	:	Write data to text file
fread	:	Read data from binary file
frewind	:	Move file position indicator in beginning of the open file
fscanf	:	Read data from a text file
fseek	:	Move to specified position in file
ftell	:	Position in open file
fwrite	:	Write data to binary file

A brief description of the above functions or commands is given. They are used for the interactive inputs using input from keyboard, and menu or pause commands.

5.1.2 The Input Function

The input function is used to input data from a standard input unit using keyboard. The INPUT function enables us to explicitly convert character data values to numeric values.

To enter into a script request and assign a value to the variable using input built-in function, the user needs to provide some inputs.

```
x= input ('read the values....')
% displays the values to read with prompt on the screen.
```

The syntax is

INPUT(*source,informat*)

where

- *source* indicates the character variable, constant, or expression to be converted to a numeric value.
- a numeric *informat* must also be specified.

   For example,

```
input(payrate,2.)
```

EXAMPLE 5.1

```
>> reply = input('Do you really want to learn MATLAB? \n {Y/N}', 's');
Do you really want to learn MATLAB?
 {Y/N}Y
% here it is not really necessary to provide Y or N as input from keyboard!! Even
if input from key board is just an enter key, we return to the command prompt again.
>> age = input('How old are you: ');
   % Left side will contain  variable as: age
   % the variable value is given on right side
How old are you: 15
% if only enter key is pressed then age variable stores empty string!!!
>> age = input('How old are you: ');
How old are you:
>> age
age =
     []
```

EXAMPLE 5.2

```
>> N=input(' Enter a value for N = ')
 Enter a value for N = 109
N =
   109
```

EXAMPLE 5.3

```
% The command window will display the value that user needs to feed.
>> N=input (' Enter a value for resistor R = ')
  Enter a value for resistor R =
```

When the above command is executed following character string is displayed on the monitor.

```
N =
   5
```

EXAMPLE 5.4

```
>> N=input (' Enter a voltage across resistor R = ')
  Enter a voltage across resistor R = 5
```

The value of the variable 'R' when entered will displayed as

```
N =
   5
```

5.1.3   Max and Min Functions

In the MATLAB program, the **max** and **min** functions shows the largest and smallest values in a vector. Following example refer to the series.

The *min* function returns the minimum value of the elements along an array dimension. The *max* function returns the maximum value of the elements along an array dimension. Syntax and diagram representation of min function is as shown in Figure 5.1.

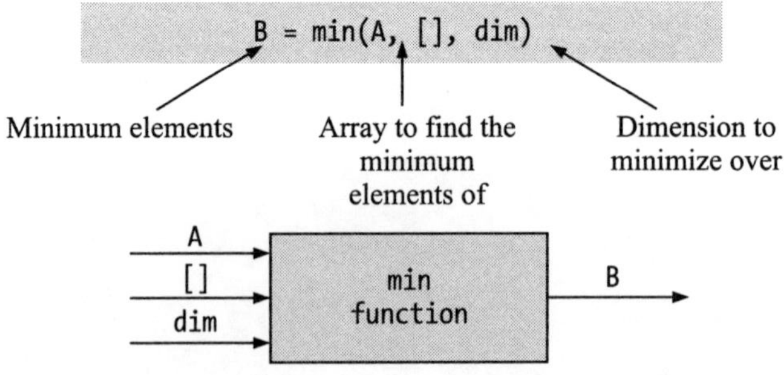

FIGURE 5.1   Minimum function.

EXAMPLE 5.5   In this example, we find the different ways to apply *min* to array *A*.

```
>> A = [1, 2, 6; 4, -7, 0];
B = min(A, [], 1);
C = min(A, [], 2);
```

$$A = \begin{bmatrix} 1 & 2 & 6 \\ 4 & -7 & 0 \end{bmatrix}$$

```
>> B = min(A, [], 1)
B =
        1      -7        0
>> C = min(A, [], 2)
C =
        1
       -7
```

Non-singleton dimension

When we call *min* with only one argument, minimum elements can be representing as single row or column. The function is represented as follows:

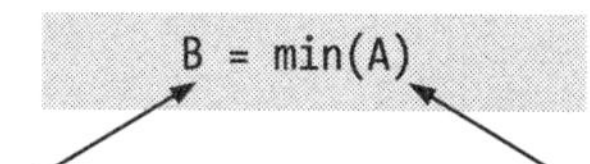

EXAMPLE 5.6   Find the first non-singleton dimension of A.

```
>> A = [5, -3, 9; 3, -6, 8]
A =
5-39
3       -68
>> B = min(A)
B =
-3       -63

>> C = min(A(:))
C =
      -3
```

EXAMPLE 5.7   Find the one row dimension of A.

```
>> A = [3, 5, 7];
>> B = min(A);
```

The first non-singleton dimension is 2

```
>> B = min(A)
B =
    3
```

EXAMPLE 5.8   Find the one columns dimension of A.

```
>> A = [4; 9];
B = min(A);
```

The first non-singleton dimension is 1

```
B = min(A)
B =
   4
```

EXAMPLE 5.9

```
>> G = [5 -3 -8 -4 -3 -5]
G =
      5     -3     -8     -4     -3     -5
>> max(G)    % max value compute
ans =
      5
>> C = min(G)      % min value compute
C =
   -8
```

Now, let us learn about max function. If we called **max** function with a matrix as its argument, **max** returns a row vector in which each element is the maximum value of each column of the input matrix. The **max** function can also return a second value: the index of the maximum value in the vector. To get this, assign the result of the call to **max** to a two element vector instead of just a single variable. The following examples help us to understand the concept in a better way.

EXAMPLE 5.10

```
>> [a b] = max(G)
a =
   5
b =
   1

>> C = min(a,b)         % minimum value of a and b
C =
   1
```

EXAMPLE 5.11   We can learn how to call a function, such as max, enclosed the parentheses of input arguments.

```
>> C= [2 6 7];
>> max(C)
ans =
        7
```

If there are multiple input arguments, we can separate with commas in shown in the following example.

EXAMPLE 5.12

```
>> D= [8 1 5];
>> max(C,D)   % verifying the two input arguments to observe the maximum three
numbers.
ans =
        8    6    7
```

EXAMPLE 5.13   We can see how to return output from a function by assigning it to a variable, using the given command:

```
>> maxC= max(C)
maxC =
        7
```

When there are multiple output arguments, enclose them in square brackets as shown below:

EXAMPLE 5.14

```
>> [maxC, location] = max(C)
maxC =
        7
location =
        3
```

EXAMPLE 5.15   Create a matrix and compute the largest element in each column.

```
>> A = [6  5  9; 3  8  1]
A =
        6    5    9
        3    8    1

>> M = max(A)          % to compute the maximum column value
M =
        6    8    9
```

```
>> M = max(A,[],2)              % compute two largest element and placed in column.
M =

        9
        8


>> M = min(A)                   % to compute the minimum column value


M =


        3       5       1


>> C = min(A,[],2)              % compute two smallest element and placed in column.
C =


        5
        1
>> C = min(M,[],2)             % compute min element and placed in column.
C =
        1
```

5.1.4 MATLAB String Handling

In MATLAB program by default, the input function expects to read a number, and if we really want the string 'hello' then type **'hello'** (within tick marks or single cotes). The string is actually a vector whose components are the numeric codes for the characters (the first 127 codes are ASCII). The actual characters displayed, depending on the character set encoding for a given font.

S =char(X) command is used to converts array X into a MATLAB character array of positive numeric integers. The length of S number of characters given as S = [S1 S2 ...] arrays into a new character array.

A row of a character array in the cell array of strings is put inside the curly braces. Further, a collection of strings can be created in the following ways:

- Convert character array and cell array of strings using char and cellstr.
- ischar(S) indicates whether S is a string variable.
- iscellstr(S) indicates whether S is a cell array of strings.

To read a string of characters directly without having to type the tick marks, we must use the 's' syntax. The syntax is as shown here:

```
y= input ('read the values….','s')
```

The command returns the entered string as a text variable rather than as a variable name of numerical value. Following example help us to understand how to use these functions.

EXAMPLE 5.16

```
>> name = input('what is your name:', 's');
what is your name: Ardra S Kumar % we type Ardra without tick marks
```

Remember at this point, the variable: name, will contain and whatever value the user types (as a string of characters), in this case 'Ardra S Kumar'

EXAMPLE 5.17   In this example, we create a simple string that includes in a single quote.

```
>> msg = 'My name is AdarshRoshan'

msg =

    My name is AdarshRoshan
```

Now, let us create the string, name, using two methods of concatenation as follows:

```
>> name = ['Thomas' 'Alva' 'Edison']
>> name = strcat('Thomas','Alva','Edison')
```

Following command will create a vertical array of strings:

```
C = strvcat('Good','Morning','How','are','You')

C =
Good
Morning
How
Are
You
```

We use following command to create a cell array of strings:

```
S = {'Good','Morning','How','are','You'}

S =
'Good' 'Morning' 'How' 'are' 'You'}
```

5.2 OTHER INPUT OPERATIONS IN MATLAB

5.2.1 Keyboard

We use keyboard to enter into a script request and assign a value to the variable. Reading from the keyboard can be accomplished by using the input function. The syntax of the function call is:

```
A = input('prompt_string')
```

Where *A* is the variable to be loaded, and 'prompt_string' is a message to be included to inform the user about the variable being loaded.

EXAMPLE 5.18

```
>> z = input('Enter the value of z:')
% press  <return> the MATLAB responds with the prompt
Enter the value of z:
```

% once this operation is completed, the value entered by the user is assigned to variable x.

It is possible to enter strings as input by adding a second argument 's' to the function call, e.g.,

```
>> name = input('Enter filename: ','s')
```

At the prompt enter filename: ADARSH % Type a string of characters.

```
% press  <return> the MATLAB responds with the prompt
name =
ADARSH
```

EXAMPLE 5.19

```
>> a=10;
>> b=28;
>> x=a+b;
>> y=2*x;
>> keyboard   % The keyboard command will change the Command Window prompt, i.e.,
K >>
K>> ans=2*y
ans =
    152
```

5.2.2 Menu

Menu is used to select the scalar value of the stored variables. When executed, it will display a small menu window with the list on the options. The choice when selected using mouse will display the corresponding order value. The syntax of menu is written for user input is:

```
k = menu('mtitle','opt1','opt2',...,'optn')
```

where k displays the menu whose title is in the string variable *'mtitle'* and whose choices are string variables *'opt1'*, *'opt2'*, and so on. Menu returns the number of the selected menu item.

EXAMPLE 5.20   Type the following code to see the execution of menu function:

```
>> K = menu('Do you really want to learn and excel MATLAB','Yes','Yes I Do','Not
really!!!!')
```

When MATLB runs this code, will display the output as in Figure 5.2

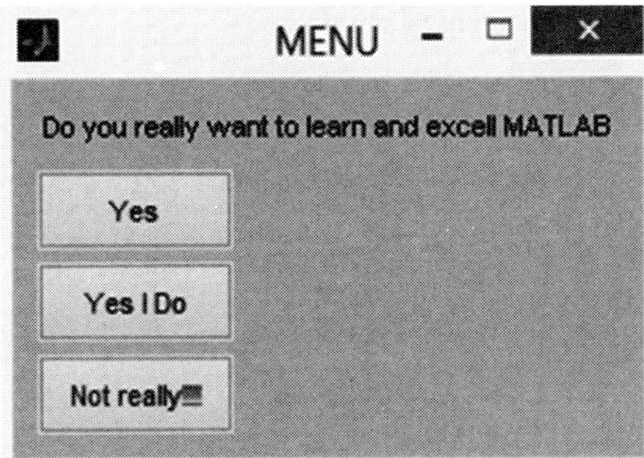

FIGURE 5.2   Output displayed on use of menu command.

EXAMPLE 5.21

```
>> S= menu('Select the state', 'Bengal', 'Goa', 'Kashmir', 'Kerala', 'Karnataka')
```

When MATLB runs this code, will display the output as shown in Figure 5.3.

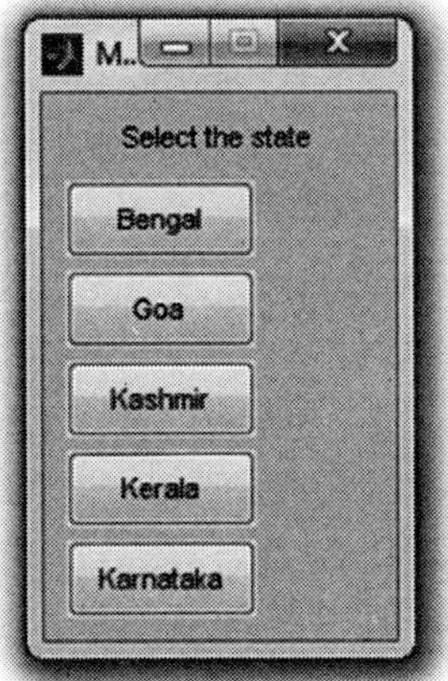

FIGURE 5.3   MATLAB command window demonstrating menu command execution.

When the Kerala menu button shown in Figure 5.2, is pressed using the mouse, it will display the value as:

```
S =
    4
```

5.2.3 Pause

In MATLAB, pause command causes stop and wait of the execution till any key is further pressed before continuing. This command is used to temporarily halt the current computation and wait for a while until the next command is executed. Pause(n) command delays the execution for n seconds before continuing, where n can be any real number. This is normally useful interactive scripts to run unattended applications.

EXAMPLE 5.22

```
>> p= [3 5; 2 9];
>> q=[6 3; 8 5];
>> disp('The matrix p is given as:');
>> disp(p)
>> disp 'Program is paused, press any key to display matrix q'
>> pause
>> disp('The matrix q is given as:');
>> disp(p)
>> z=p+q;
>> disp('Program is paused')% Press any key to display matrix sum p and q')
>> pause
>> disp(z)
When program is executed, it will show the following:
>> disp(p)    % Matrix p is displayed.
    3    5
    2    9
```

Program is paused, press any key to display matrix q.

```
>> disp(q)    % Matrix q is displayed.
    6    3
    8    5
```

Program is paused, press any key to display matrix sum p and q.

```
>> disp(z)        % Matrix p and q sum is displayed.
    9    8
    10   14
```

Pause syntax

Pause, by itself, causes the currently executing function to stop and wait for you to press any key before continuing. There are different types of pause syntax used for pause command as follows:

```
pause
pause(n)
pause on
pause off
```

The following are the outlines about the above pause syntax:

pause, causes M-files to stop and wait for us to press any key before continuing.
pause(n), pauses execution for *n* seconds before continuing.
pause on, allows subsequent pause commands to pause execution.
pause off, ensures that any subsequent pause or pause(n) statements do not pause execution. This allows normally interactive scripts to run unattended.

5.3   THE OUTPUT FUNCTION

In MATLAB, when value is assigned to a variable, output commands produce results. Even when MATLAB suppresses the output by putting a semicolon after the command, output data can be displayed in the command window by writing it by skipping the semicolon (;) at the end of the statement.

EXAMPLE 5.23

```
>> a = 43 + 21 % The output statement when executed will display the value on
command window directly.
a =
64
```

EXAMPLE 5.24

```
>> syms x                % Shortcut for creating symbolic variable and function.
>> y = x + 4
y =
x + 4
```

In above example, MATLAB processes the command internally, to produce the response to the command *y*.

```
>> z = x + 4;
>> z
z =
x + 4
```

However, the use of semicolons separates a string of commands without suppressing output. If semicolon is used after a graphics command, it will not suppress the graphic.

Another object that suppress MATLAB label for the output is disp(x), which will print the value of the variable *x* without printing the label and the equal to sign.

Following examples help us to understand the concept in a better way.

EXAMPLE 5.25

```
>> x = 7;
>> disp(x)
      7
```

Similarly, to display matrix the following command is used:

```
>> x= [5 9; 3 8];
>> disp(x);
```

The result obtained is as:

```
   5    9
   3    8
```

To display printed results use the `fprintf` command.

EXAMPLE 5.26

```
>> fprintf(' N =%g \n',500)
 N =500
```

Most frequently used output commands in MATLAB are `display` and `fprintf`. Here \n prints the output on newline.

5.3.1   Saving and Loading Variables

MATLAB has the functions/commands to store the files that are currently used, for the future needs. Very often, results of MATLAB calculations need to be reused elsewhere.

Load

In MATLAB, the saved '.mat' file can be obtained back by using the command 'load'. Load command loads the file that is already saved. The saved variables and their values are stored in the workspace and can now be used again with the help of the command:

```
>> load filename
```

where, the extension '.mat' can be omitted.

Besides loading data stored in '.mat' files, MATLAB is also useful for processing data.

Let us clear the variables in MATLAB and reload the values of *A* and *b* using the load command:

```
clear<enter>
who<enter>
load 'DataAb.mat' <enter>
```

```
A <enter>
b <enter>
```

Function saves all current active variables in MATLAB with the file name. Function load will load the variables in a mat file with the appropriate names.

Load syntax: In MATLAB, the load function is used to load variables or data in workspace from the storage location disk file. The syntax for such load function is as follows:

```
load
load ('filename')
load filename ('á', 'b', 'c')
load filename a, b, c
```

Description of the above functions are as follows:

The load ('filename'), loads all the variables named filename.mat from the MAT-file. It loads only if it exists, and returns an error if it does not exist.

The load filename ('á', 'b', 'c') loads only the variable specified in the statement, that is *a*, *b* and *c*.

The load filename a, b, c, loads just the specified variables from the MAT-file.

EXAMPLE 5.27   Let us consider the data file *abc.txt* saved in two rows having equal separation in the current directory is shown below:

```
4  6  8  2  3
2  4  7  3  6
```

The following command is used load data in workspace:

```
>> load abc.txt
```

This will load the file and the result will be obtained as:

```
abc =

4   6   8   2   3
2   4   7   3   6
```

Save

The values of variables can be saved in a '.mat' using the command save. The save command is used in the form:

```
>> save filename
```

The file results in all variables in use being saved in the file with the name *'filename.mat'*. The extension '.mat' is not necessary to be given. Consider the variables that are saved in the file filename.mat with the use of save command

```
>> save filename a b
```

Save syntax: The save function saves the current workspace data or variable in the storage disk file. It operates similar to load function. The only difference is that save function saves the file. The syntax for such save function is as follow:

```
save
save ('filename')
save filename ('á', 'b', 'c')
save filename a, b, c
```

Where, filename is the name of the file saved as *a, b, c* variables in the file.

Table 5.1 gives summary of the functions used in MATLAB for file opening, loading and saving.

TABLE 5.1   File Opening, Loading, and Saving

Function name	Description
winopen	Open file in appropriate application (Windows)
uisave	Open standard dialog box for saving workspace variables
uiputfile	Open standard dialog box for saving files
uiimport	Open import wizard to import data
uigetfile	Open standard dialog box for retrieving files
uigetdir	Open standard dialog box for selecting directory
save	Save workspace variables to file
open	Open file in appropriate application
load	Load data from MAT-file into workspace
importdata	Load data from file
daqread	Read Data Acquisition Toolbox (.daq) file

5.3.2   Opening and Closing Files

Files can be opened and closed by using funtions called fopen and fclose respectively. Use of fopen and fclose as is illustrated by the example below.

```
>> Months=fopen('MonthsInAYear.txt','w+');
>> fprintf(Months,'Jan\nFeb\nMar\nApr\nMay\nJun\nJul\nAug\nSep\nOct\nNov\nDec');
>> fclose(Months);
```

First command here creates a file named MonthsInAYear.txt. w+ here indicates this file has read-write permission, i.e., we can read the contents in this file as well as we can also make the desired changes to it contents. Second command here writes names of months in the file. \n here denotes a new line for every month name. Third line closes the file called Months which in turn has the contents of MonthsInAYear.txt. This file MonthsInAYear.txt can be opened with any program that can read .txt file. For example, it can be opened with MATLAB editor or with simple notepad editor. Figure 5.4 illustrates the output of file opening and closing commands.

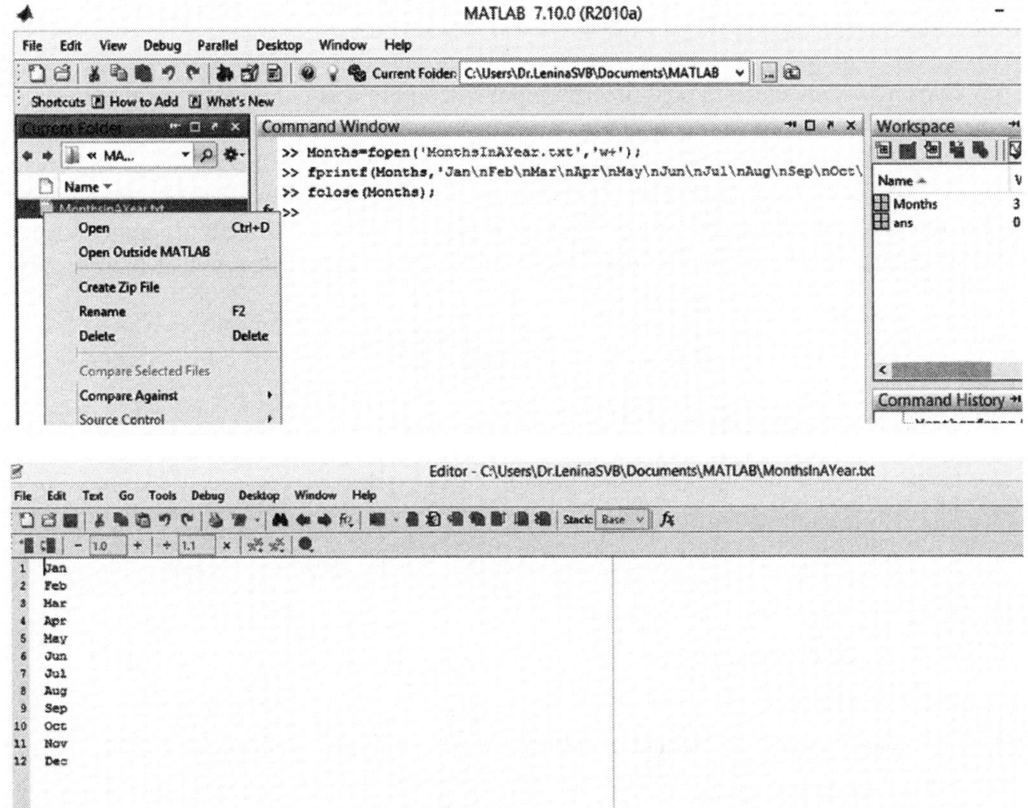

FIGURE 5.4   MATLAB command window and editor window demonstrating open command execution.

Various types of permissions to a file are as listed below. Strings that are used to describe the type of access for the file: read, write, append, or update. Also, specifies whether to open files in binary or text mode.

For opening files in binary mode, you should specify one of the following:

'r' : Open file for reading (default).
'w' : Open or create new file for writing. Discard existing contents, if any.
'a' : Open or create new file for writing. Append data to the end of the file.
'r+' : Open file for reading and writing.
'w+' : Open or create new file for reading and writing. Discard existing contents, if any.
'a+' : Open or create new file for reading and writing. Append data to the end of the file.
'A' : Append without automatic flushing. (used with tape drives)
'W' : Write without automatic flushing. (used with tape drives)

For more details of fopen and fclose, type at the command prompt of MATLAB as doc fopen or help fopen or doc fclose or help fclose.

SUMMARY

In this chapter, we have learnt about the data input and output was fed through assigned variable statement in the Command Window. There were different input-output functions, such as *save, load, textread, dimread, textscan, dimwrite* function are explained with examples. The special commands such as *keyboard* and *pause* were also discussed for input function execution. Further, the *disp* function was discussed to represent data output. Various formatting output functions were also discussed. Permissions to open file were also seen in the last part of the chapter.

REVIEW QUESTIONS

1. What is the purpose of data processing commands?
2. Enlist any five input output commands in MATLAB.
3. List any ten low level file I/O commands.
4. State the command/s which asks or waits the user to enter input from keyboard.
5. What does the command keyboard do?
6. What is use of menu command in MATLAB?
7. Write syntax for pause command.
8. State the functions in MATLAB which are used to save and load files.
9. What does fopen do?
10. State the command which displays the output or answer even after the use of a semicolon.
11. List any five low level file I/O functions in MATLAB.
12. Differentiate between load and save functions.

PRACTICE EXERCISE

1. Calculate your average marks in six subjects of your choice. Use input functions to enter your marks.
2. Execute: >> K = menu('Choose a color','Red','Blue','Green')
3. What is the output of following: >> pause; disp('A pause to learn MATLAB')
4. Suppress output of sum of two numbers using semicolon and display it using display command.
5. Display your percentage marks with percent sign (%) and an alarm (use *fprintf*).
6. Create save and load a .mat file containing english vowels.
7. Use fopen,fclose,fprintf to write names of your five close friends in a text file.
8. Use >> doc frintf and read MATLAB documentation.

CHAPTER 6

Graphics in MATLAB

LEARNING OBJECTIVES

This chapter aims to provide the basic ideas on plotting in MATLAB. At the end of this chapter, one should be able to understand:

- Various methods to plot functions using MATLAB.
- The power of plots to analyse mathematical functions.
- Complex mathematical equations with visual plots.
- Different mathematical functions and data using 2D and 3D (two-dimensional and three-dimensional) plots.
- The use of special graphics in MATLAB related to animation and movie functions.

INTRODUCTION

It is rightly said that a picture speaks thousand words. This chapter gives insight to understand the graphics in MATLAB. These can be used for various data interpretations and presentation of results. MATLAB provides tools for two-dimensional (2D), three-dimensional (3D), 3D volume visualisation functions and various graphic formats. It also provides the functions for visualising 2D matrices, 3D scalar and 3D vector data. In MATLAB, graphics is one of the most powerful features. This chapter describes the MATLAB graphics commands to annotate (edit) and customise them. The graphics commands in MATLAB are simple and easily understandable.

MATLAB graphics commands can be obtained by typing *help graphics* (for general graphics commands), *helpgraph2d* (for two-dimensional graphing), *helpgraph3d* (for three-dimensional graphing), or *help specgraph* (for specialised graphing) commands. In this chapter we will discuss some techniques for customising and manipulating graphics.

6.1 TWO-DIMENSIONAL PLOTS

When we want to draw a curve in the x-y plane, then there is a need of two variables that generate a display based on commands. To plot the two-dimensional graph of a function, following syntax needs to be followed:

- Define x, by specifying the range of values for the variable x, for which the function is to be plotted
- Define the function, $y = f(x)$
- Call the plot command, as *plot(x, y)*

where, x is a row or column vector containing the x-co-ordinates of the plot and y is a row or column vector containing the y-co-ordinates of the plot. When executed, the command will create a plot in the MATLAB figure window with data in vector x-axis and y-axis. It is required that x and y arrays should be of same form, i.e., either row or column vectors of same size. If this is not taken care then MATLAB plot function gives an error.

EXAMPLE 6.1 Let us plot the simple function $y = x$ for the range of values for x from 0 to 100, with an increment of 5.

```
>> x = [0:5:100];
>> y = x;
>> plot(x, y)
```

Executing the command file, MATLAB will display the graphic plot as shown in Figure 6.1.

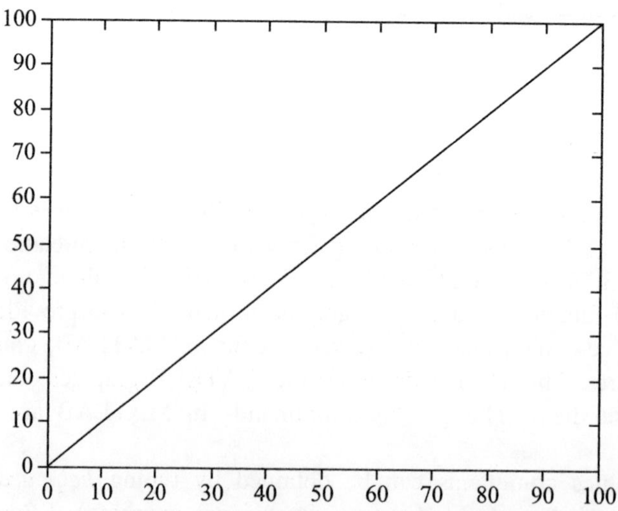

FIGURE 6.1 Plot of function $y = x$ as in Example 6.1.

Now, let us plot the function $y = x^2$. To further smooth the curve, same function in Example 6.2 is plotted in Example 6.3 using different range. Both examples are written to observe two different types smoothened graphs for the same function.

EXAMPLE 6.2

```
>> x=1:1:10;
>> x = [-100:20:100];
>> y = x.^2;
>> plot(x, y)
```

Executing the command file, MATLAB will display the graphic plot as shown in Figure 6.2.

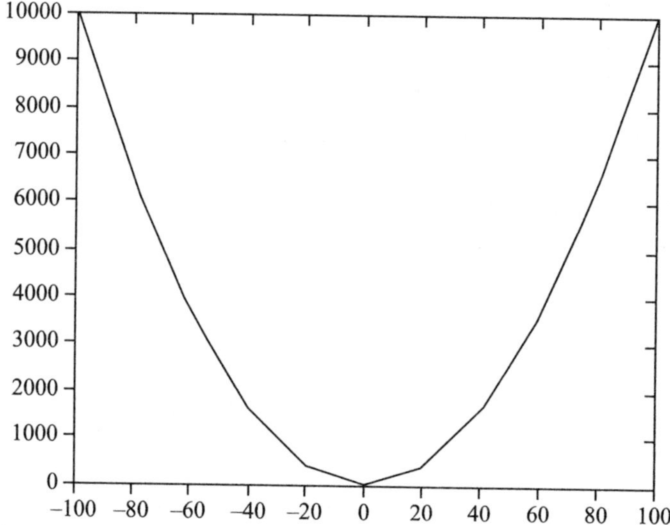

FIGURE 6.2   Plot of function $y = x^2$ as in Example 6.2.

In this example, we can observe the changes, if the code is changed to reduce the increment by 5.

EXAMPLE 6.3

```
>> x=1:1:10;
>> x = [-100:5:100];
>> y = x.^2;
>> plot(x, y)
```

Executing the command file, MATLAB will display smoother graphic plot as shown in Figure 6.3.

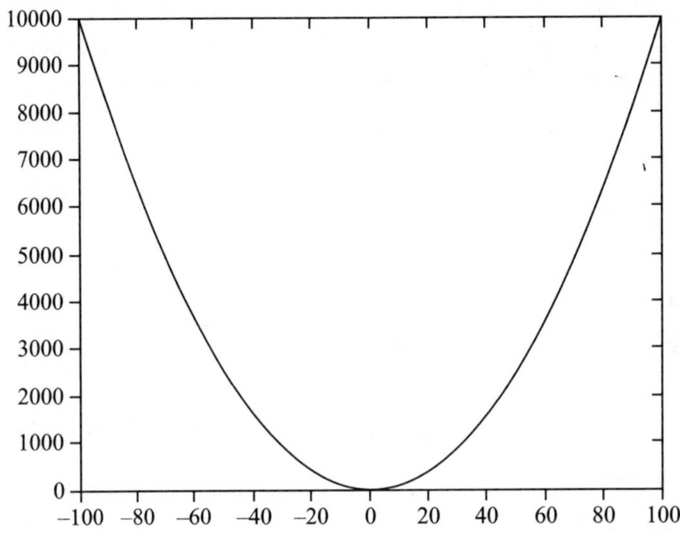

FIGURE 6.3   Plot of function $y = x^2$ as in Example 6.3.

The two graphs displayed in Figures 6.2 and 6.3 plots with the same function, show that by reducing the value of increment, the graph becomes smoother.

6.1.1 Line Plots

In the following example, we learn to create two-dimensional line plots using the plot function.

EXAMPLE 6.4 Let us plot the values of the *sine* function from 0 to 3π

```
>> x=0:pi/50:3*pi;
>> y=sin(x);
>> plot(x,y)
```

Runing the program, MATLAB will display smoother graphic plot as shown in Figure 6.4.

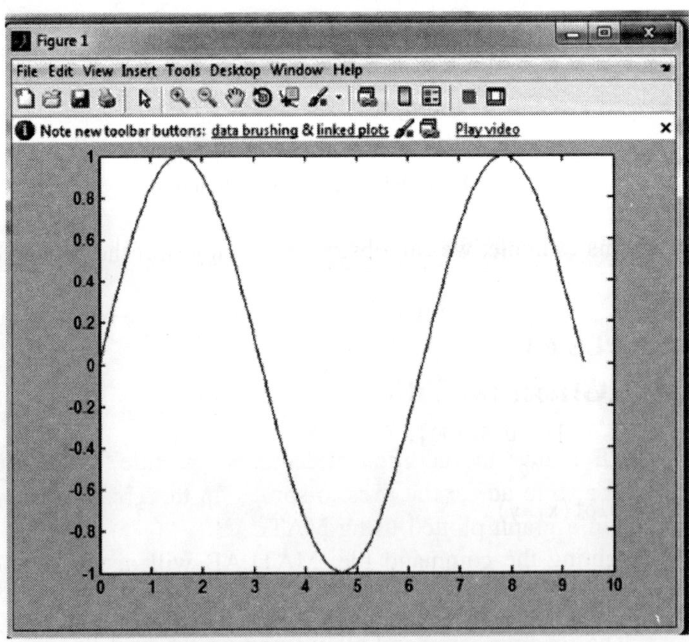

FIGURE 6.4   Plot of sine function.

6.2 PARAMETRIC PLOT

Parametric plot is another type of plot where two functions are given. Following example shows the plot where, x and y represent the parameter. The circle of radius 4 centered at (0, 0) can be expressed in parametric form as $x = \cos(2\pi t)$, $y = \sin(2\pi t)$ where t varies from 0 to 4. The code to this graph is represented by using *axis square* function as follows:

EXAMPLE 6.5

```
>> t = 0:0.01:4;
>> plot (cos(2*pi*t), sin(2*pi*t));
>> axis square
```

Executing the command file, MATLAB will display the graphic plot as shown in Figure 6.5.

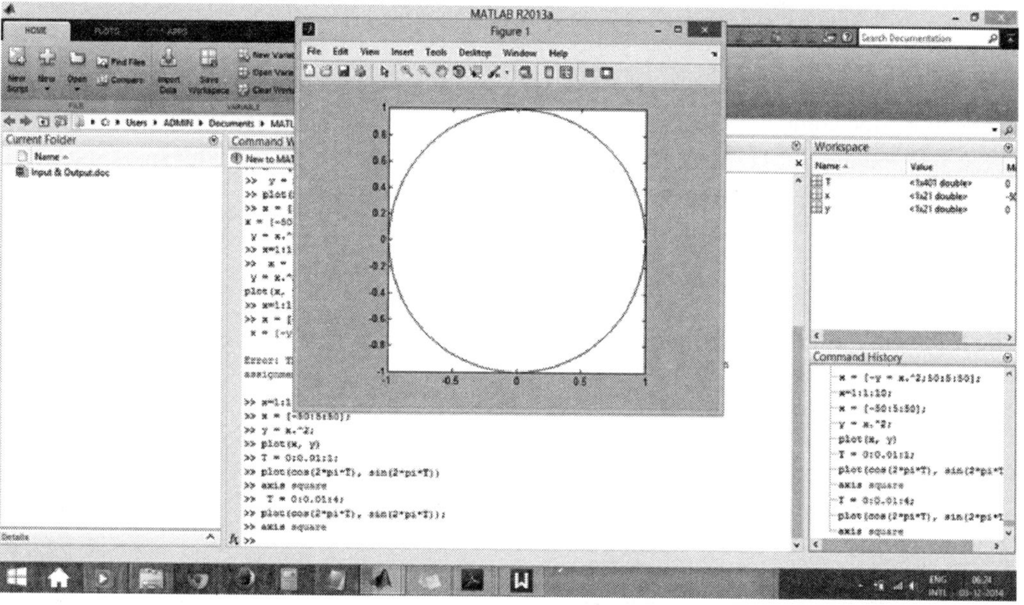

FIGURE 6.5 Plot to illustrate axis square function.

6.2.1 Graphical Title, Printing Labels, Grid Lines and Scaling

MATLAB allows the addition of features like title, labels along the x-axis and y-axis, grid lines and also to adjust the axes to spruce up the graph. Following are the commands that can features in a graph plotted using MATLAB:

- The *x-label* and *y-label* commands generate labels along x-axis and y-axis.
- The *title* command allows putting a title on the graph.
- The *grid on* command allows putting the grid lines on the graph.

- The *axis equal* command allows generating the plot with the same scale factors and the spaces on both axes.
- The *axis square* command generates a square plot.

Following examples are created to demonstrate xlabel, ylabel, title, grid on, and axis equal commands in codes at command prompt:

EXAMPLE 6.6 In this example, we create two-dimensional line plots using the plot function for the values of the *sine* function from 0 to 3π. Also, label the *x* and *y* co-ordinate with the title of the plot.

```
>> x=0:pi/50:3*pi;
>> y=sin(x);
>> plot(x,y)
>> xlabel('Time axis')
>> ylabel('Amplitude axis')
>> title('Plot of the Sine Function')
```

Executing the command file, MATLAB will display the graphic plot as shown in Figure 6.6.

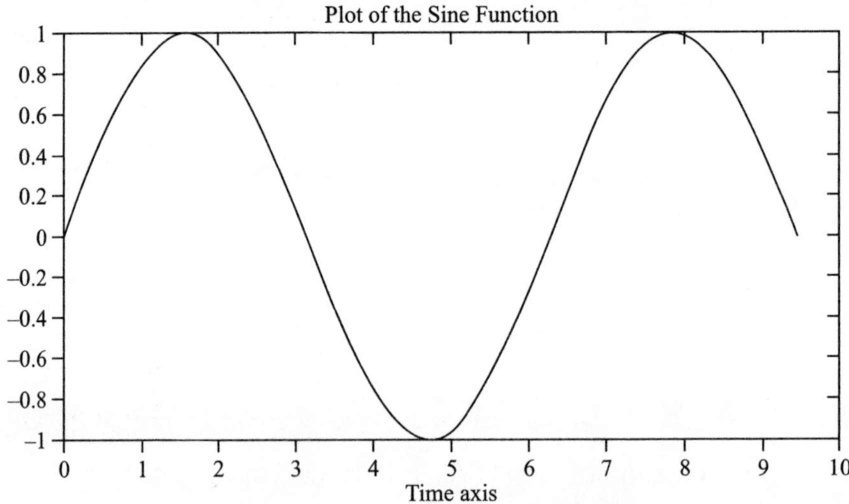

FIGURE 6.6 Plot to illustrate Example 6.6.

EXAMPLE 6.7

```
>> x = [0:0.01:10];
>> y = sin(x);
>> plot(x, y);
>> xlabel('x'), ylabel('Sin(x)'), title('Sin(x) Graph'), grid on, axis equal
```

Executing the command file, MATLAB will display the graphic plot as shown in Figure 6.7.

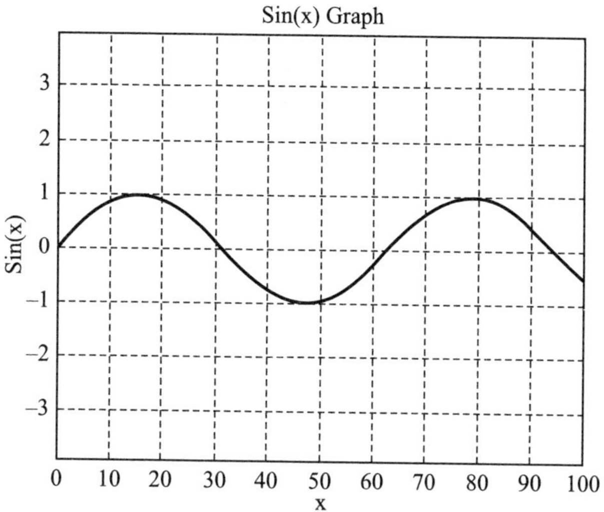

FIGURE 6.7   Plot to illustrate Example 6.7.

EXAMPLE 6.8

```
>> x = [0:0.01:10];
>> y = cos(x);
>> plot(x, y);
>> xlabel('x','FontSize',16), ylabel('Cos(x)','FontSize',16), title('Cos(x)
Graph','FontSize',36), grid on, axis equal
>> text(pi,0,' \rightarrow Cos(\pi)','FontSize',28)
```

Executing the commands above, MATLAB will display the graphic plot as shown in Figure 6.8.

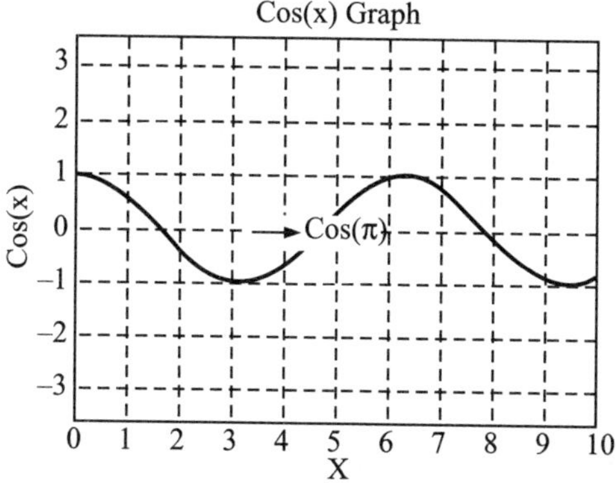

FIGURE 6.8   Plot to illustrate Example 6.8.

6.3 CONTOUR PLOTS AND IMPLICIT PLOTS

A contour plot of the level function are curves of two variables, i.e., sets of points in the *x-y* plane where the function assumes a constant value. For example, the level curves of $x^2 + y^2$ are radii of the circles centered at the origin, and these levels get distributed in the square. The contour plots are produced in MATLAB with the command called *meshgrid* in the specified region. The following example code for the script file is written to make a contour plot of $x^2 + y^2$.

EXAMPLE 6.9

```
>> [X Y] = meshgrid(-3:0.1:3, -3:0.1:3);
>> contour(X, Y, X.^2 + Y.^2);
axis square
```

Executing the command, MATLAB will display the graphic plot as in Figure 6.9.

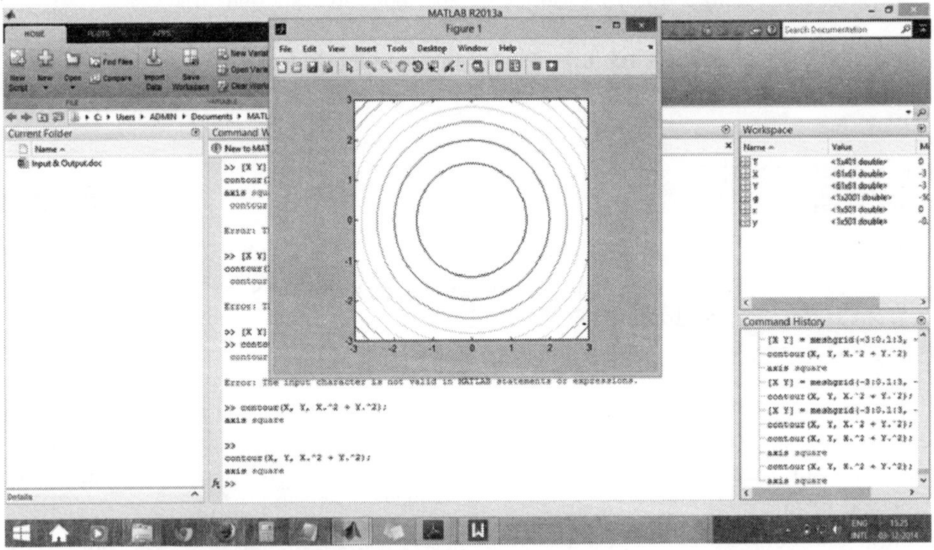

FIGURE 6.9   Plot to illustrate Example 6.9 on contours.

We have used MATLAB vector notation to produce a grid with spacing 0.1 on both directions. Also we have used axiss quare to force the same scale on both axes.

6.4 FIELD PLOTS

In MATLAB, library 'quiver' function is used to plot vector fields or arrays of arrows. The arrows can be spaced equally in the plane or at specified locations. The following Example 6.10 code plots a vector field with a 'saddle point' corresponding to a combination of an attractive force pointing towards *x*-axis and repulsive force pointing away from the *y*-axis.

EXAMPLE 6.10

```
>> [x, y] = meshgrid(-1.1:.2:1.1, -1.1:.2:1.1);
quiver(x, -y); axis equal; axis off
```

Executing the command file, MATLAB will display the graphic plot as shown in Figure 6.10.

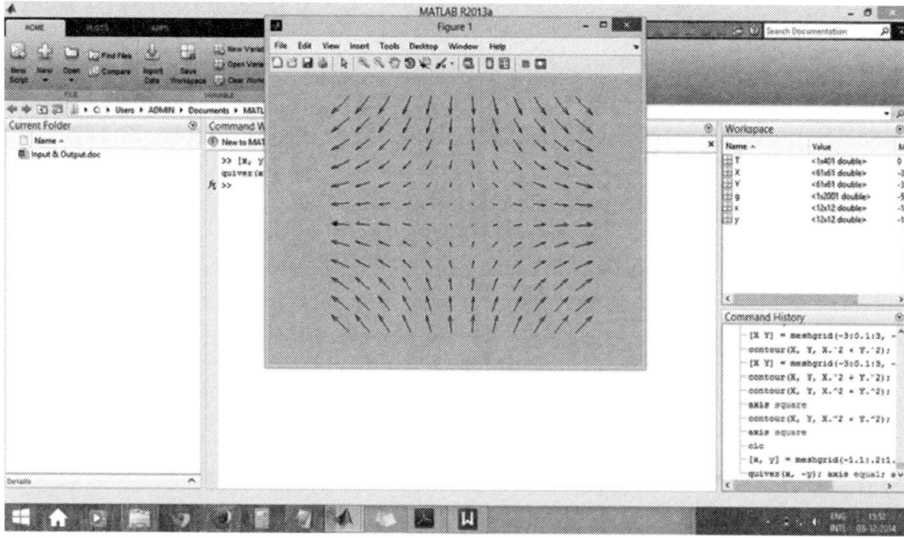

FIGURE 6.10 Plot to illustrate quiver function.

6.5 MULTIPLE GRAPHICAL DISPLAY FUNCTIONS

MATLAB has numerous techniques for graphics that allow simple, easy visualisation of functions and data. The interactive tools provide a wide variety of techniques to display data graphically. Also, manipulate graphs to find results information about our data. We can also interpret and print graphs for presentations, or export graphs for further use.

In this chapter, we are discussed the basic of 2D and 3D plotting capabilities. The MATLAB Graphics Window has the typical menu and shortcut icons associated with Window™ applications. MATLAB contains a multiple graphics toolbox called *Handle Graphics*. The multiple graphic display function allows us to have control over any graphics display. This includes font type and font sizefor text, location of text on the screen, embedding graphs within other graphs, etc.

MATLAB Handle Graphics refers to a system of graphics objects has afixed set of properties. We can use these properties to control the behaviour and appearance of our graph. When we call a plotting function, MATLAB creates the graph using variousgraphics objects, such as a figure window, axes, lines, text, and so on. MATLAB enables us to query and set the values of most properties.

For example, the following statement creates a figure with a white background colour and without displaying the figure toolbar:

figure('Colour','white','Toolbar','none')

6.5.1   Setting Colours on Graph

MATLAB use the default option for setting colours on Graph. A line-style is defined by choosing an entry from each column of the line-style options table. The stringis optional when the plotting command is invoked.

MATLAB provides eight basic colour options for drawing graphs. Line-style options of colour, symbol and line type selectors are the part of 2D plots in MATLAB. The colour selection and symbols types are summarised in Table 6.1.

TABLE 6.1   Line-style options of colour, symbol and line type selectors for 2D plots.

Line-style Options					
	Line colour		*Line symbol*		*Line type*
y	yellow	.	point	-	solid
m	magenta	o	circle	:	dotted
c	cyan	x	x-mark	-.	dash dot
r	red	+	plus	--	dashed
g	green blue	-	star		
b	blue	s	square		
w	white	d	diamond		
k	black	v	triangle (down)		
		^	triangle (up)		
		<	triangle (left)		
		>	triangle (right)		
		p	pentagram		
		h	hexagram		

The symbol or line type for the data can be changed by an optional third argument of the plot command. The third argument of the plot command is a one, two or three character string of the form 'cs', where 'c' is a single character indicating the colour and 's' is a one or two character string indicating the type of symbol or line.

In MATLAB, there is a facility to draw multiple graphs on the same plot. Following examples demonstrate the concept using the *plot* code. Various plot commands and their respective descriptions are as follows:

```
>> plot(x,y);  plots x vs y with default line specifications
>> plot(x,y,'m<');  plots x vs y with magenta left-triangles (no line)
>> plot(x,y,'d-.b');  plots x vs y with blue diamonds and blue dash-dot line
```

`>> plot(x,y,'o');`   plots data in the *x* and *y* vectors using circles drawn in the default colour (yellow)

`>> plot(x,y,'r:');`   plots data in the *x* and *y* vectors by connecting each pair of points with a red dashed line

These types of plot are appropriate when connecting data points with various impression of sampled data points. Following are the examples that will show us how to plot data with symbols using the script file code.

EXAMPLE 6.11   In this example, we learn to create two-dimensional line plots using the plot function for the value of the *sine* function from 0 to 3π. Also, title and label the *x* and *y* co-ordinate using colour.

```
>> x=0:pi/50:3*pi;
>> y=sin(x);
>> plot(x,y,'r')   % 'r' string is a line specification.
>> xlabel('Time axis')
>> ylabel('Amplitude axis')
>> title('Plot of the sine function using color')
```

Executing the command file, MATLAB will display the graphic plot as shown in Figure 6.11.

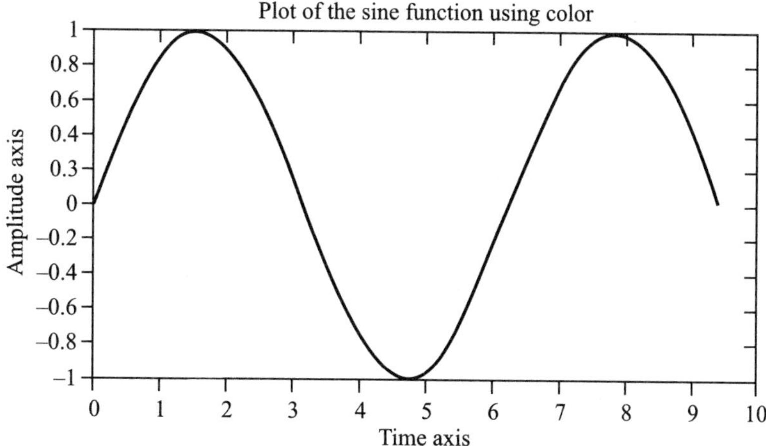

FIGURE 6.11   Plot to illustrate Example 6.11.

Further, specification can include characters for the line colour, style and marker. The marker is a symbol +, *, -, o, etc.

For example, `plot(x,y,'r:o')` means dotted red lines with round markers.

EXAMPLE 6.12   In this example, we use the `plot(x,y,'r:o')` command for Example 6.11 and plot the function. Executing the command file, MATLAB will display the graphic plot as shown in Figure 6.12.

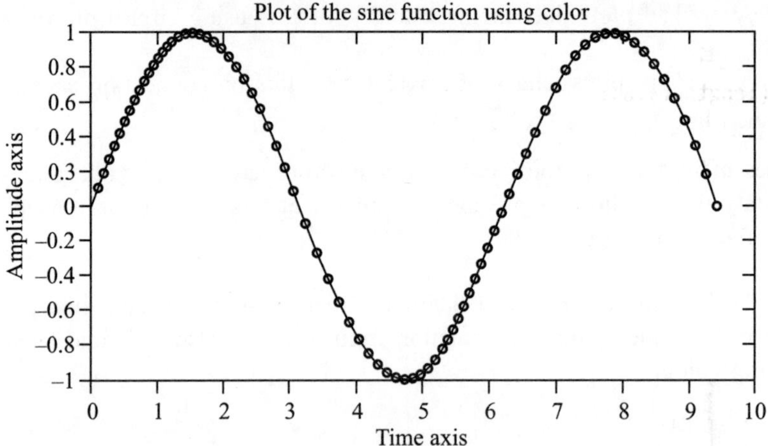

FIGURE 6.12   Plot to illustrate Example 6.12.

In MATLAB, there is a facility to draw multiple graphs on the same plot. Following examples demonstrate the concept using *tegend* function.

EXAMPLE 6.13

```
>> x = [0 : 0.01: 10];
>> y = sin(x);
>> g = cos(x);
>> plot(x, y, x, g, '.-'),
>> legend('Sin(x)', 'Cos(x)')
```

Executing the command file, MATLAB will display the graphic plot in Figure 6.13.

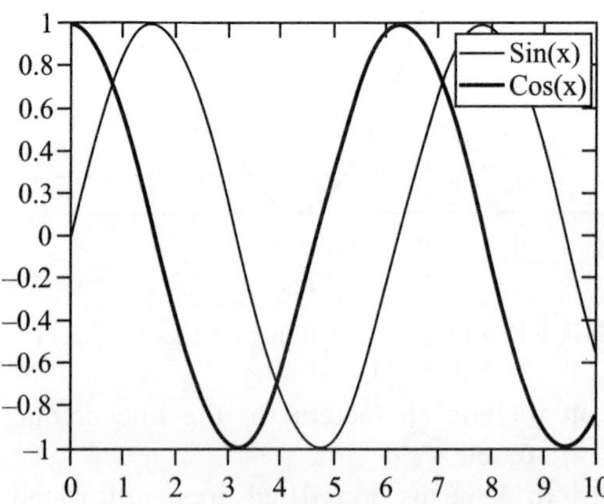

FIGURE 6.13   Plot to illustrate Example 6.13.

EXAMPLE 6.14   In this example, we draw a multiple plots using following functions.

```
>> t = 0:pi/12:2*pi;
a = ones(length(t),8);
for i = 1:8
a(:,i) = sin(t-i/5);
end
plot(t,a)
```

Executing the command file, MATLAB will display the graphic plot as shown in Figure 6.14.

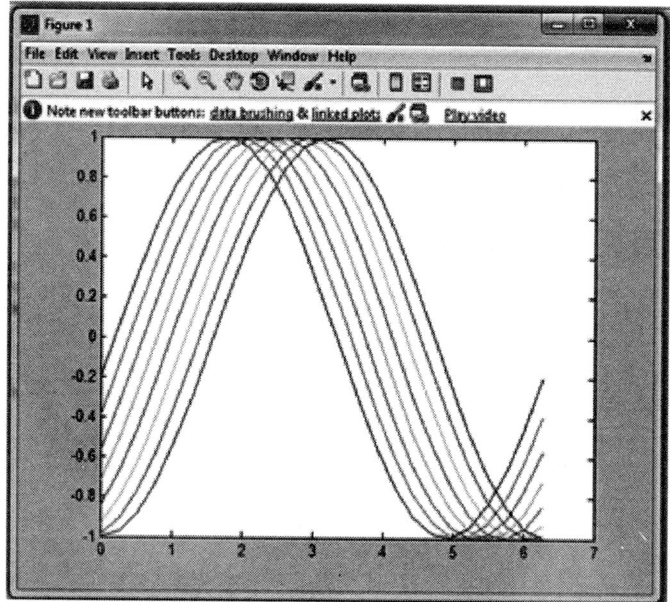

FIGURE 6.14   Plot to illustrate Example 6.14 of multiple plots.

EXAMPLE 6.15   In this example, we demonstrate the concept to draw the graph of two polynomials $f(x)$ and $g(x)$.

$$f(x) = 3x^4 + 2x^3 + 7x^2 + 2x + 9 \text{ and } g(x) = 5x^3 + 9x + 2$$

The script file is created by typing the following code:

```
>> x = [-10 : 0.01: 10];
>> y = 3*x.^4 + 2 * x.^3 + 7 * x.^2 + 2 * x + 9;
>> g = 5 * x.^3 + 9 * x + 2;
>> plot(x, y, 'r', x, g, 'g')
```

Executing the command file, MATLAB will display the graphic plot as shown in Figure 6.15.

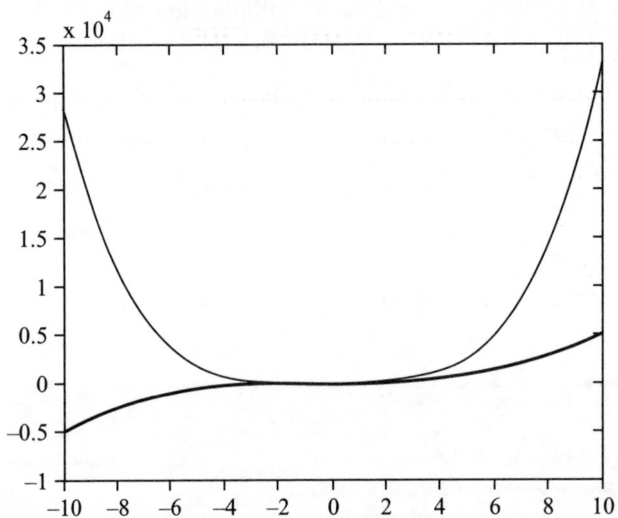

FIGURE 6.15   Plot to illustrate Example 6.15 of multiple plots.

EXAMPLE 6.16   In this example, we demonstrate the experimental graph plot.

The script file is created by typing the following code:

```
>> x = [0 : 0.01: 10];
>> y = exp(-x).* sin(2*x + 3);
>> plot(x, y), axis([0 10 -1 1])
```

Executing the command file, MATLAB will display the graphic plot as shown in Figure 6.16.

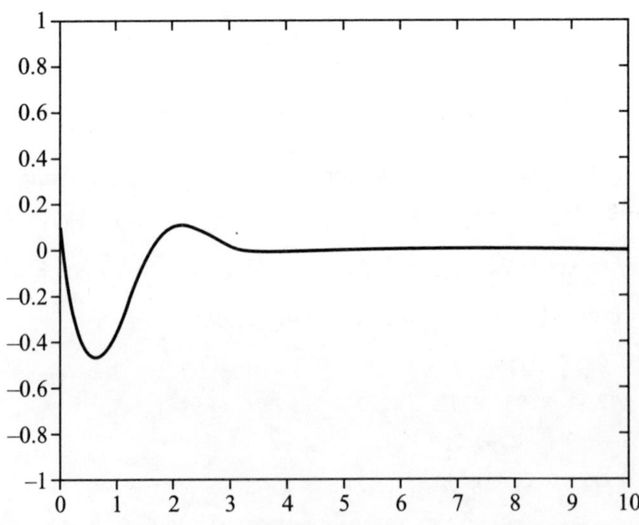

FIGURE 6.16   Plot to illustrate Example 6.16.

6.5.2   Methods for Drawing Multiple Plots

MATLAB generally supports for multiple plot displays in a separate window or in a same window page. There are three different methods of drawing multiple plots which are as follows:

1. Using *plot* command
2. Using *hold* command
3. Using *line* command

1. The *plot* command is used to provide arguments to generate more plots in the same graphic windows. The syntax for the command:

    ```
    plot(x¹, y¹, x², y²);
    ```

    where, (x^1, y^1) and (x^2, y^2) are two data sets for two plots.

2. The *hold* command is used to freeze the current plot in graphic window. The syntax for the command:

    ```
    hold on;  % Commands holds the cursor on the current plot in the graphic window.
    hold off; % Commands is used to clear the hold on command.
    ```

3. The *line* command is used along with the *plot* command to generate multiple plots. Once plot is generated in the graphic windows. More plots can be added in the graphic window, using the *line* command. The syntax for the command:

    ```
    line(xdata, ydata, parameter_name, parameter_value)
    ```

    Where, *xdata* and *ydata* are vectors containing x and y co-ordinates of point on the graph and parameters name or value are used to represent line style options. All these three functions are illustrated by Example 6.17 and Figure 6.17.

EXAMPLE 6.17

```
>> hold on
t = 0:pi/20:2*pi;
hline1 = plot(t,sin(t),'r');
hline2 = line(t+.06,sin(t),'LineWidth',6,'Color',[.5 .5 .5]);
hline3 = plot(t,cos(t),'k');
title('Example to illustrate 'hold on', 'line' and 'plot' functions','FontSize',16)
```

The *plot* command is used to draw the sine curve. The *line* command is used to add more curves to the exiting plot. Out of these more frequently used is the *plot* command.

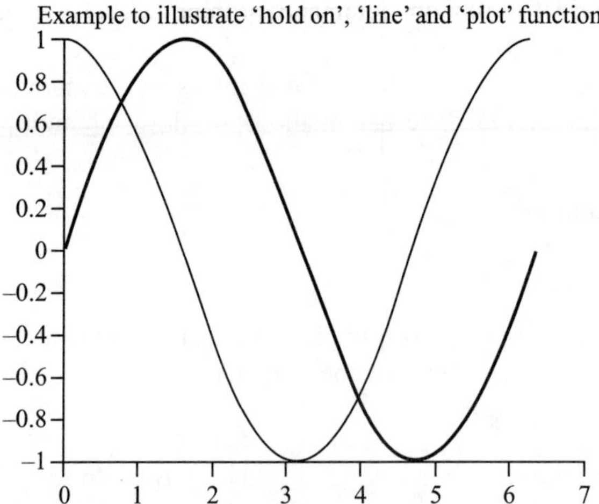

FIGURE 6.17   Plot to illustrate Example 6.17.

6.5.3   Generating Subplots

In MATLAB, there is a provision of creating an array of plots in the same figure. A graphical window can be subdivided into many subgraphs or subplots in common window using *subplot* command. Such plots split the figure window into $m \times n$ parts and it is treated as subplot. The *subplot* command select pth area of the current plot for creating subplots. The syntax used for this command is

```
subplot(m, n, p)
```

where, m and n are the number of rows and columns of the plot array and p specifies where to put a particular plot. Each plot created with the subplot is numbered starting from top row left to right and then towards next row and so on. Example 6.18 demonstrates the use of *subplot* command.

subplot displays multiple plots in the same window. This is represented by subplot (nrows, ncols, plot_number). We can see the following examples.

EXAMPLE 6.18

```
>> x=0:.2:3*pi;
>> subplot(2,2,1);
>> plot(x,sin(x));
>> subplot(2,2,2);
>> plot(x,cos(x));
>> subplot(2,2,3)
>> plot(x,exp(-x));
>> subplot(2,2,4);
>> plot(peaks);
```

When the above code is run on command prompt, MATLAB generates the graphical displays as shown in Figure 6.18 plot.

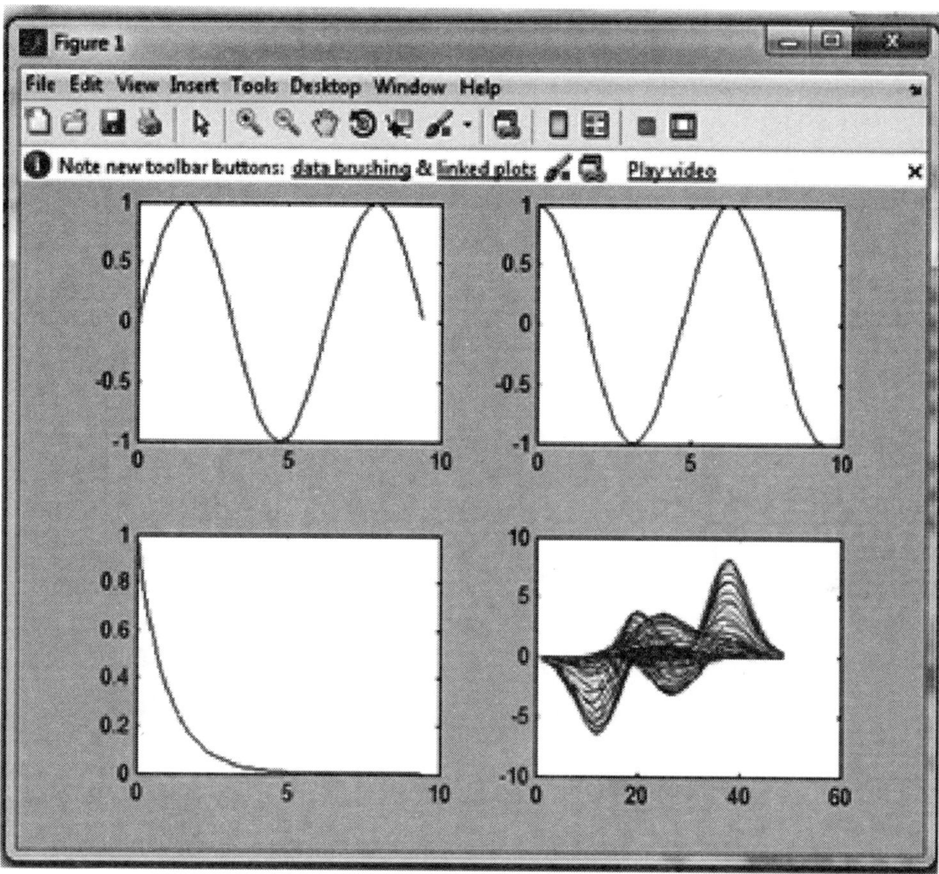

FIGURE 6.18   Plot to illustrate subplot.

EXAMPLE 6.19   Let us first generate two plots and then combine these plots using *subplot* command:

1. $y = e^{-1.5x}\ \sin(10x)$ and
2. $y = e^{-2x}\ \sin(10x)$

The script file is created to generate first function by typing the following code:

```
>>  x = [0:0.01:5];
>>  y = exp(-1.5*x).*sin(10*x);
>>  plot(x,y)
```

When the above code is run on command prompt, MATLAB generates the graphical displays as shown in Figure 6.19 plot.

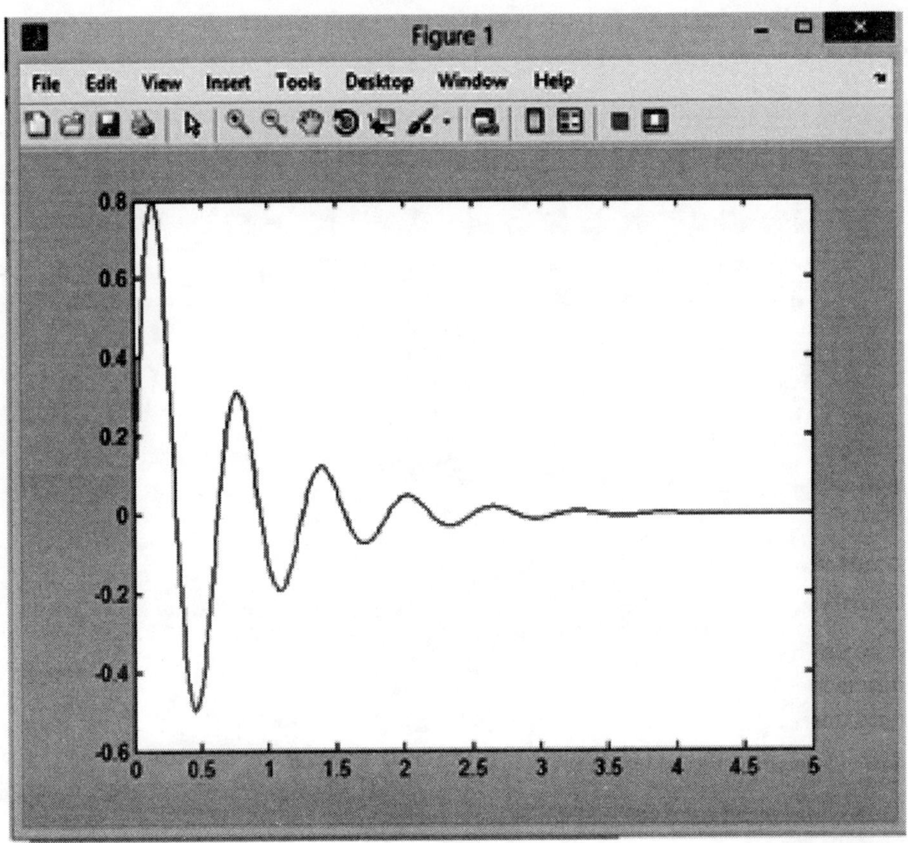

FIGURE 6.19   Plot to illustrate Example 6.19.

Further, the subplot file is created to generate second function with first ffunction by typing the following code:

EXAMPLE 6.20

```
>> subplot(1,2,1)
>> plot(x,y)
>> xlabel('x'),ylabel('exp(-1.5x)*sin(10x)'),axis([0 5 -1 1])
>> y = exp(-2*x).*sin(10*x);
>> subplot(1,2,2)
>> plot(x,y)
>> xlabel('x'),ylabel('exp(-2x)*sin(10x)'),axis([0 5 -1 1])
```

When the above commands are executed, MATLAB generates the graphical displays as shown in Figure 6.20 plot.

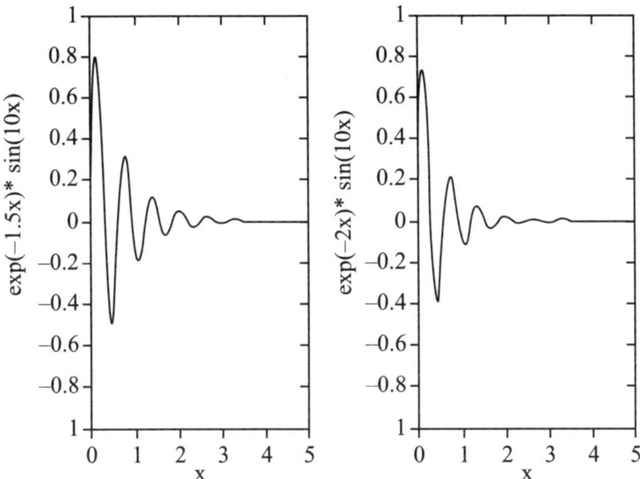

FIGURE 6.20   Plot to illustrate Example 6.20.

The following example is illustrate 2×2 array of plots of the first four Bessel functions. It produces the four subplot file created by typing the following code:

EXAMPLE 6.21

```
>> x = 0:0.05:40;
for j = 1:4, subplot(2,2,j)
plot(x, besselj(j*ones(size(x)), x))
end
```

When we run the above commands, MATLAB generates the graphical displays as shown in Figure 6.21 plot.

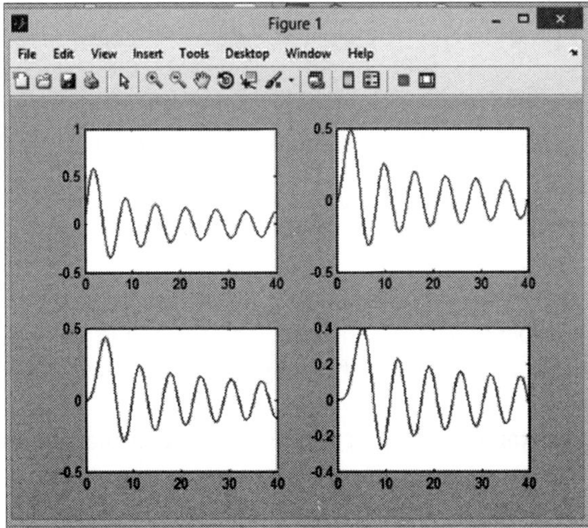

FIGURE 6.21   Plot to illustrate Example 6.20.

In MATLAB, the *subplot* command also enable us to display multiple plots in the single same window. There will be one region over which multiple plots can be drawn.

EXAMPLE 6.22   In this example, we plot two different functions and their convolute result in single figure.

```
>> x= 0: pi/10:2*pi;
>> subplot(3,1,1); plot(sin(x));
>> subplot(3,1,2); plot(cos(x));
>> subplot(3,1,3); plot(sin(x).*cos(x));
```

When we run the above commands, MATLAB generates the graphical displays as shown in Figure 6.22 plot.

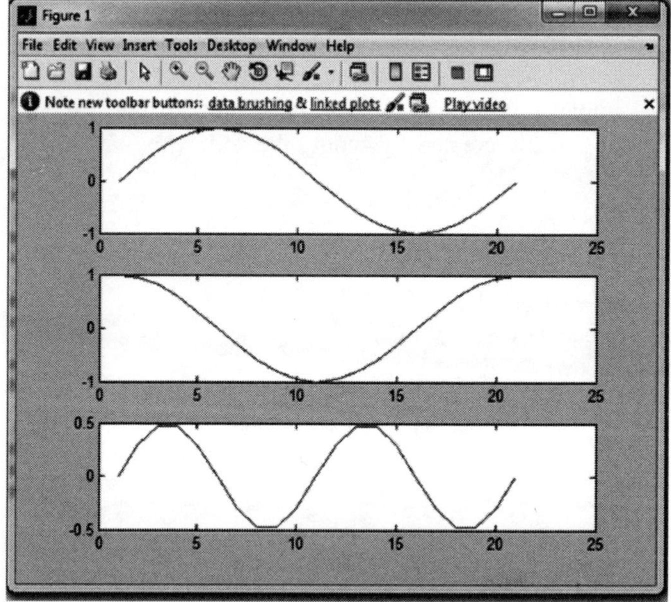

FIGURE 6.22   Shows the multiple plots on single figure.

6.5.4   Create Subplots and Add Subplot Titles

The syntax, *subplot(m,n,p)*, divides the figure into an *m*-by-*n* grid with an axes in the *pth* grid location. The grids are numbered along each row. The following example shows how to create a figure containing multiple graphs using the subplot function with subplot titles.

EXAMPLE 6.23   In this example, we plot a sine wave using the subplot command with titles.

```
x = linspace(-5,5); % define x
y1 = sin(x); % define y1
```

```
figure % create new figure
subplot(2,2,1) % first subplot
plot(x,y1)
title('First subplot')
```

Now, plot another sine wave in the second subplot, executing the following codes:

```
y2 = sin(2*x); % define y2
subplot(2,2,2) % second subplot
plot(x,y2)
title('Second subplot')
```

Further, plot two more sine waves in the third and fourth subplots, executing the following codes:

```
y3 = sin(4*x); % define y3
y4 = sin(6*x); % define y4


subplot(2,2,3) % third subplot
plot(x,y3)
title('Third subplot')


subplot(2,2,4) % fourth subplot
plot(x,y4)
title('Fourth subplot')
```

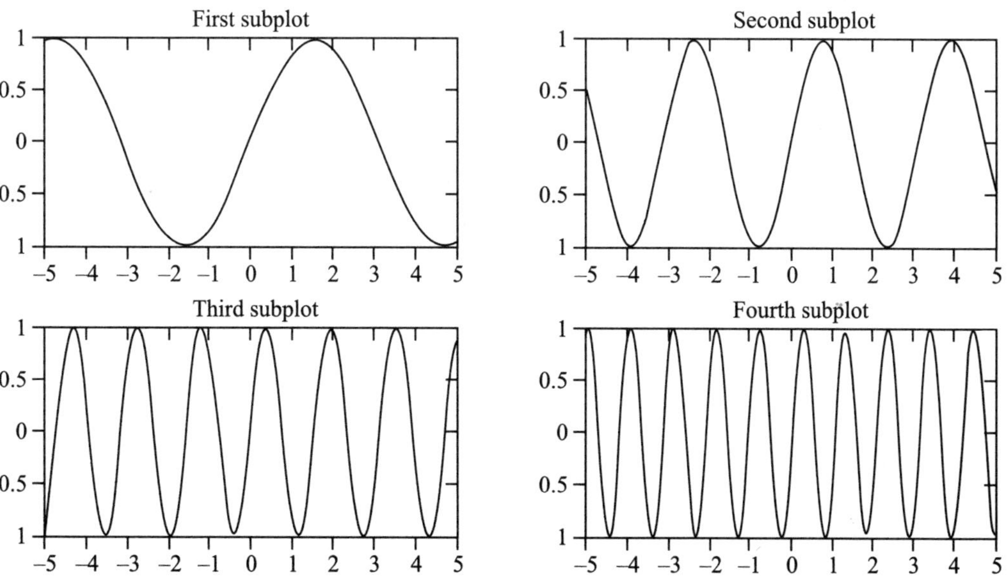

FIGURE 6.23   Multiple subplot.

6.5.5 Controlling the Axes

In MATLAB, plenty of options are available for setting the scaling, orientation and aspect ratio of plots using axis commands. In the graphical plots using MATLAB axes, the functions can be controlled as per the desired axis dimensions. The plot default axis length depends automatically upon the maximum and minimum values of x and y vectors. However, axis length can be changed based on axis command. The syntax of the command is in the form:

```
axis([xmin,xmax,ymin,ymax])
```

where,

 xmin and xmax: represent the minimum and maximum limits of x-axis respectively.

 ymin and ymax: represent the minimum and maximum limits of y-axis respectively.

EXAMPLE 6.24

```
>> axis ( [-5 1 3 8] )
```

When above command is executed, it will set the x limits from -5 to 1 and y limits from 3 to 8. When the above commands are run at command prompt, MATLAB generates the graphical displays as shown in Figure 6.24 plot.

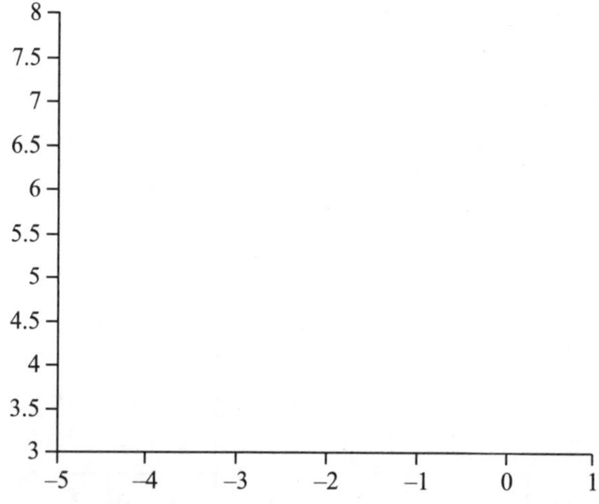

FIGURE 6.24   Plot to illustrate Example 6.24.

The axis command contains the x and y minimum and maximum values.
Further, the following Example 6.25 presents a scripted code for axis control.

EXAMPLE 6.25

```
>> x=.01:.02:40;
>> close all;
x=.01:.02:40;
```

```
y=cos(x);
plot(x,y)
axis([0 30 -10 10])
```

When the above commands are run at command prompt, MATLAB generates the graphical displays as shown in Figure 6.25 plot.

6.5.6   xlim, ylim and zlim

In the MATLAB, the axis limit modes are fixed in the default state. MATLAB uses limits that spans the range of the data being displayed in round numbers. Setting a value for any of the limits also

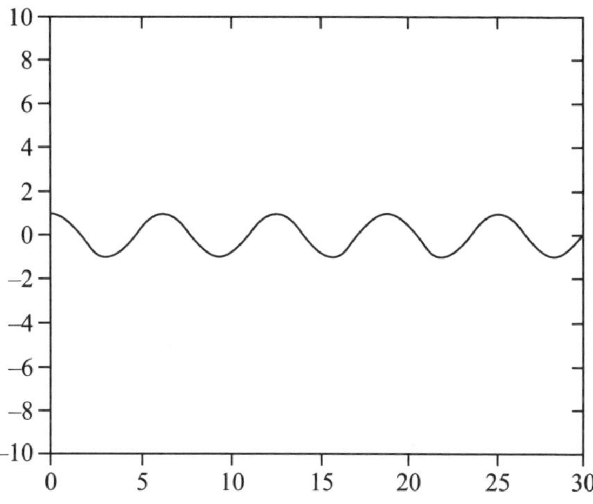

FIGURE 6.25   Plot to illustrate Example 6.25.

sets the corresponding mode to manual. If we want to set the limits on an existing graph, use xlim, ylim, and zlim commands to set the axes object.

EXAMPLE 6.26   In this example, we will learn to create desired limit of x-axis.

```
>> plot(x,y)
xlim([ 0 25])
```

When the above commands are executed, MATLAB generates the graphical displays as shown in Figure 6.26 plot.

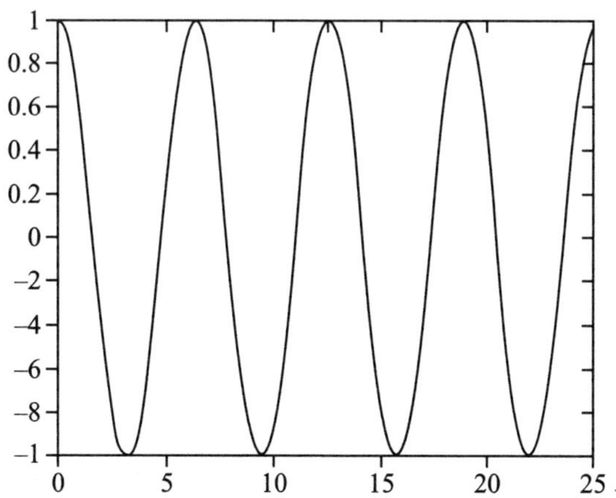

FIGURE 6.26   Plot to illustrate Example 6.26.

EXAMPLE 6.27   In this example, we will learn to create desired limit of y-axis.

```
>> plot(x,y)
ylim([-5 5])
```

When the above commands are executed, MATLAB generates the graphical displays as shown in Figure 6.27 plot.

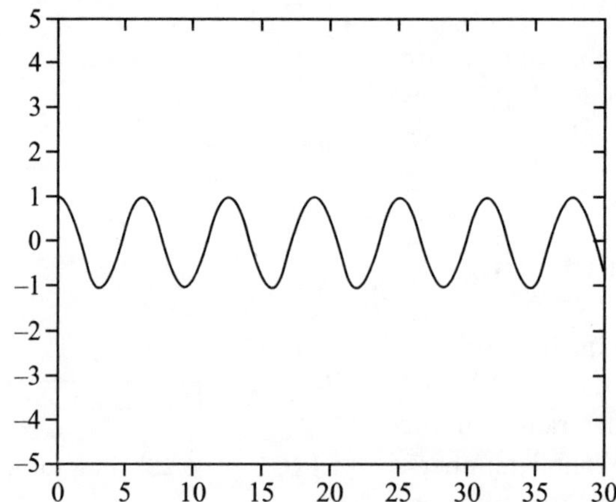

FIGURE 6.27   Plot to illustrate Example 6.27.

EXAMPLE 6.28   In this example, we will learn to create equal distribution of axis.

```
>> axis equal
```

On executing the above command, MATLAB generates the graphical displays as shown in Figure 6.28 plot.

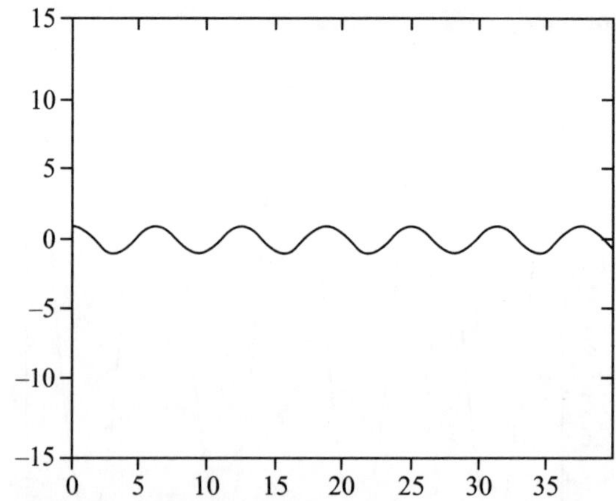

FIGURE 6.28   Plot to illustrate Example 6.28.

Referring to the graph it shows the *x*-axis and *y*-axis is distributed to almost equal value.

EXAMPLE 6.29   Create a figure with two subplots and plot the same data in each subplot. Set the x-axis limits for the bottom subplot.

```
>> x = linspace(0,2.5,500);
>> y = sin(200*x)./exp(x);
>> ax1 = subplot(2,1,1);
>> plot(x,y)
>> ax2 = subplot(2,1,2);
>> plot(x,y)
>> xlim(ax2,[0 1])
```

When the above commands are executed, MATLAB generates the graphical displays as shown in Figure 6.29 plot.

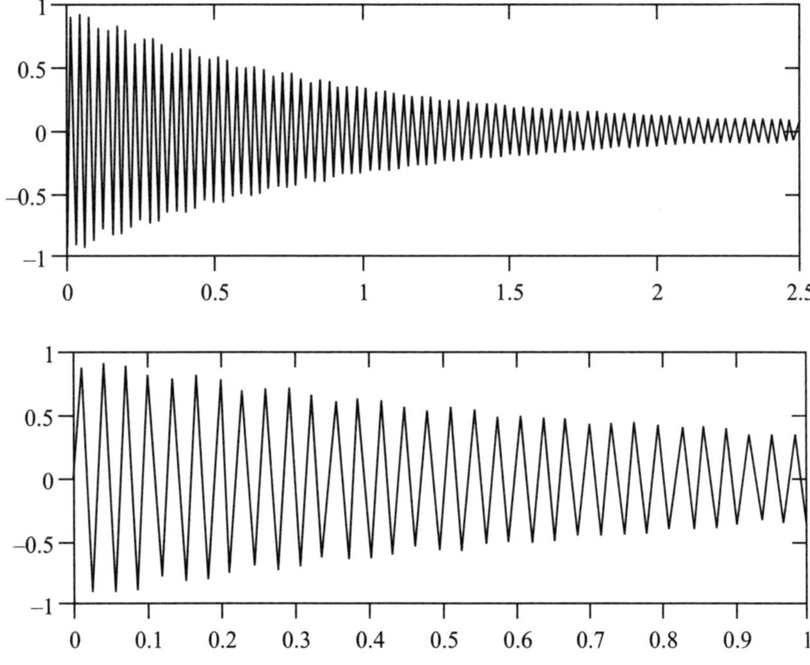

Figure 6.29   Plot to illustrate Example 6.29

6.5.7   Axis Aspect Ratio

Axis Aspect Ratio in MATLAB stretches the axis to fill the window. In many cases, the aspect ratio character is the relative length or scaling of axis. MATLAB provides control over the aspect ratio with the axis command. The axis command provides we a number of useful options for adjusting the aspect ratio of graphs. The aspect ratio of on image describes the proportional relationships between its width and its height.

There are some predefined arguments for setting the axis aspect ratio using axis command. They are as listed in Table 6.2.

TABLE 6.2   Axis commands and their functions

Command	Function
axis off	It turns off all axis lines, mark ticks and labels.
axis equal	It represents equal scale on both axes. This sets the aspect ratio so that the data units are the same in every direction. This makes the surface displayed by sphere look like a sphere instead of an ellipsoid.
axis normal	It is the default window that sets the axis limits to span the data range along each axis and stretches the plot to fit the figure window. It also resets the axis to default values.
axis square	It used to set the rectangular frame to a square frame. This makes the current axes region square and overrides stretch-to-fill behaviour.
axis axis	It freezes the current axes limits.
axis equal tight	It sets the aspect ratio so that the data units are the same in every direction and then sets the axis limits to the minimum and maximum values of the data.

Note: These axis commands need to be used after the plot command.

By default, MATLAB displays graphs in rectangular axes that have the same aspect ratio as the figure window. This makes optimum use of space available for plotting.

EXAMPLE 6.30   In this example, we will learn to use *axis normal* command.

```
>> t = 0:pi/20:2*pi;
>> plot(sin(t),2*cos(t));
>> title('axis normal');
>> axis normal
>> grid on
```

When run, the above command in MATLAB generates the graphical displays as shown in Figure 6.30 plot.

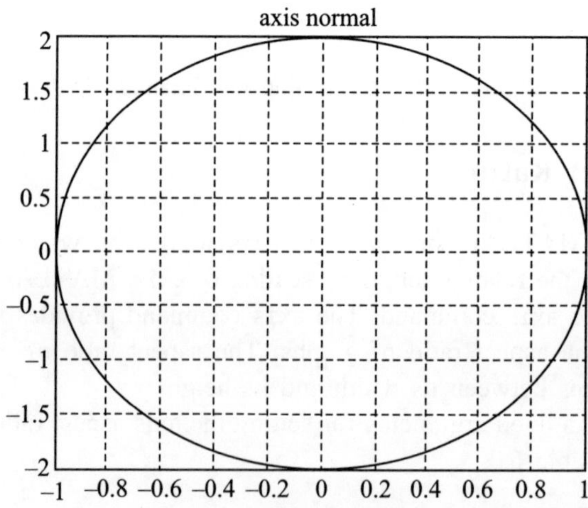

FIGURE 6.30   Axis normal command execution result.

EXAMPLE 6.31   In this example we will learn to use *axis square* command.

```
>> title('axis square');
>> axis square
```

When run, the above command in MATLAB generates the graphical displays as shown in Figure 6.31 plot.

The square axes have one data unit in x to equal two data units in y.

EXAMPLE 6.32   In this example, we will learn to use axis x and y data units to be equal.

```
>> title('axis equal');
>> axis equal
```

When run, the above command in MATLAB generates the graphical displays as shown in Figure 6.32 plot.

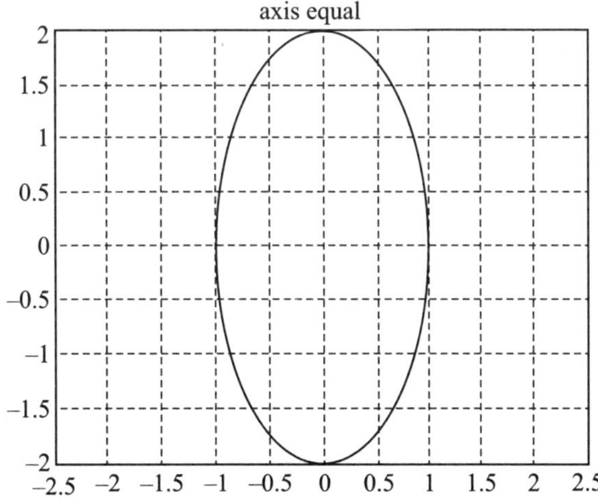

FIGURE 6.31   Axis square command execution result.

FIGURE 6.32   Axis equal command execution result.

This produces axes that is rectangular in shape, but has equal scaling along each axis.

EXAMPLE 6.33   In this example, we will learn to make the axes shape to conform to the plotted data by using the `tight` option in conjunction with `equal`.

```
>> title('axis equal tight');
>> axis equal tight
```

When run, the above command in MATLAB generates the graphical displays as shown in Figure 6.33 plot.

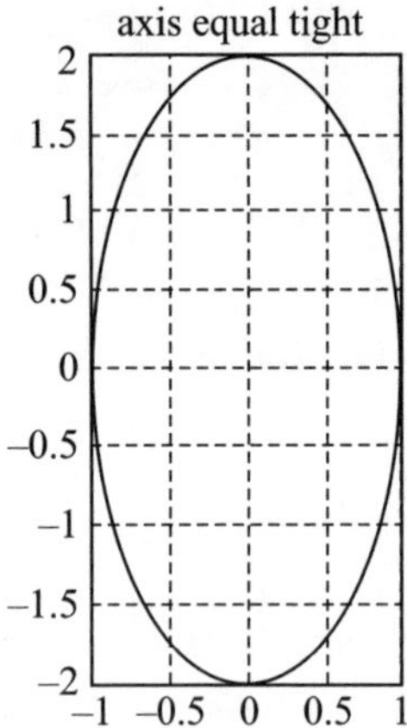

FIGURE 6.33   Axis equal tight command execution result.

Additional commands for setting aspect ratio

We can control the aspect ratio of our graph in three ways:

- Specifying the relative scales of the x, y, and z axes (data aspect ratio).
- Specifying the shape of the space defined by the axes (plot box aspect ratio).
- Specifying the axis limits.

The following commands enable us to set these values as shown in Table 6.3.

TABLE 6.3   Additional commands for setting aspect ratio

Command	*Purpose*
daspect	Set or query the data aspect ratio
pbaspect	Set or query the plot box aspect ratio
xlim	Set or query x-axis limits
ylim	Set or query y-axis limits
zlim	Set or query z-axis limits

Practice Exercise

We can try using the above command and experience the outputs by using code in column A to produce plots in column B. [given in question 6 of practice exercise at the end of the chapter].

6.6   THREE-DIMENSIONAL PLOTS

In the MATLAB for the effectiveness of data visualisation, there are several functions that are commonly used. Most of the functions are the extension of 2D functions that hav several routines for producing three-dimensional plots. The three-dimensional (3D) graphs are generally used to display two types of display, i.e., 2D variables is a function of single independent variable and in 3D variables is a single variable function of two independent variables. The lists of independent variables are *surface*, *mesh* and *contour* plots.

6.6.1   plot3

The three-dimensional plots, the basic command of *plot3*, takes three vectors such as, x-co-ordinates, y-co-ordinates and z-co-ordinates to generate 3D graphs. The syntax for this function is as follows:

```
plot3(x, y, t, 'style_options')
```

where,

x, y, and t are array of location points and
'style_options' specifies the style option.

EXAMPLE 6.34   In this example, we show the use of *plot3* command to generate 3D plots.

```
>> t=-3:0.2:10;
>> x=t.^2;
>> y=4*t;
>> plot3(x,y,t);
grid on;
>> xlabel ('x-axis');
>> ylabel ('y-axis');
>> zlabel ('z-axis');
>> title('plo3 function plot');
```

When run the above command, MATLAB generates the graphical displays as shown in Figure 6.34 plot.

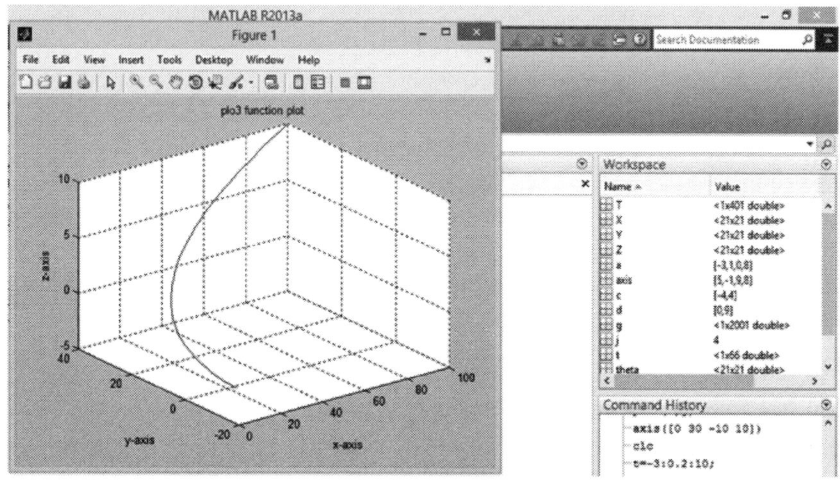

FIGURE 6.34   Plot to illustrate Example 6.25.

In Example 6.35 we show the *plot3* command use to generate a helix.

EXAMPLE 6.35

```
>> T = -2:0.01:2;
plot3(cos(2*pi*T), sin(2*pi*T), T)
```

On execution of the above command, MATLAB generates the graphical displays as shown in Figure 6.35 plot.

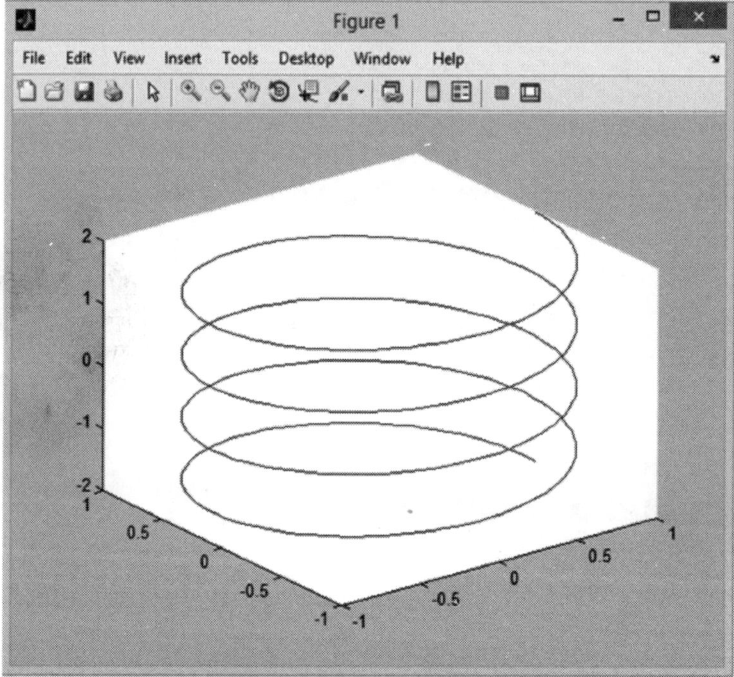

FIGURE 6.35   Plot to illustrate Example 6.35.

6.6.2   Mesh Function

In three-dimensional space we use two basic commands for plotting surfaces. They are *mesh* and *surf*. The 'mesh' surface is transparent and an 'opaque' is a shaded one. These commands are used in two different ways; one in which the z-co-ordinate is a function of x and y for plotting surfaces, and other in which x, y, and z are given as functions for related surface of plot to draw. The syntax of the command is given as:

```
>> mesh(x, y, z, c)
```

where,

    x is an array containing x-value.

    y is an array containing y-value.

z is an array containing z-value.

c is a argument determines the colour scaling.

Following Example 6.36 illustrates the plot $z = f\ (x,\ y)$, one begins with a `meshgrid` command as in the case of contour.

EXAMPLE 6.36

```
% The "saddle surface" z = x² + y² plots.
>> [X,Y] = meshgrid(-2:.1:2, -2:.1:2);
>> Z = X.^2 - Y.^2;
>> mesh(X, Y, Z)
```

When run, the above commands, MATLAB generates the graphical displays as shown in Figure 6.36 plot.

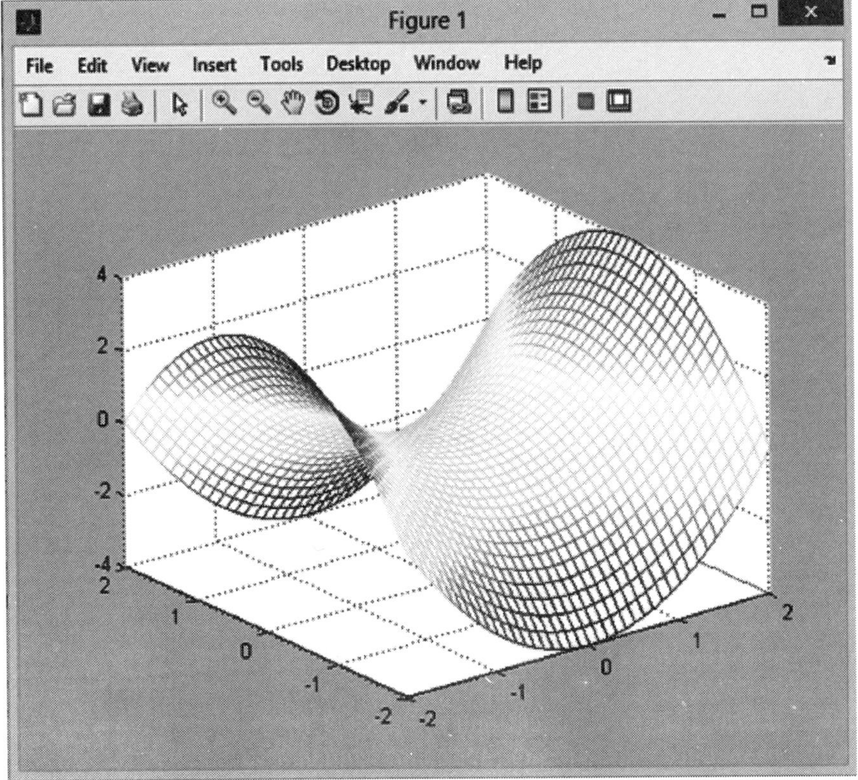

FIGURE 6.36   Plot to illustrate Example 6.36.

The result is shown in Figure 6.36, shades the surface with a colour scheme of x, y and z axes in an opaque grid surface.

6.6.3 Surf Function

surf is a function similar to *mesh* function. The only difference is instead of wire-frame plot it is used to display surface plot. The syntax given as

```
>> surf (x, y, z, c)
```

where,

x is an array containing x-value
y is an array containing y-value
z is an array containing z-value
c is a argument determines the colour scaling.

In case c is not mentioned, z is considered to be default value for c.

surf(Z) creates a three-dimensional shaded surface from the z components in matrix Z, using x = 1:n and y = 1:m, where [m,n] = size(Z). The height Z, is a single-valued function defined over a geometrically rectangular grid. Z specifies the colour data, as well as surface height, so colour is proportional to surface height.

EXAMPLE 6.37

```
>> [x, y, z] = peaks(20);   % create a peaks plot of 20-by-20
>> surf(x,y,z)
>> xlabel('x-axis'), ylabel('y-axis'), zlabel('z-axis')
>> title('Surface Plot of Peaks')
```

When run, the above command in MATLAB generates the graphical displays as shown in Figure 6.37 plot.

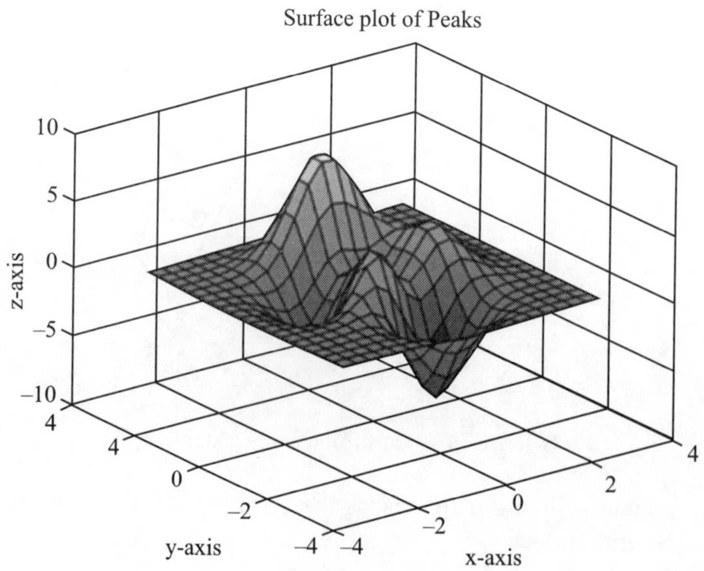

FIGURE 6.37 Plot to illustrate surf function.

EXAMPLE 6.38

```
>> [theta, Z] = meshgrid((0:0.1:2)*pi, (-1:0.1:1));
>> X = sqrt(1 - Z.^2).*cos(theta);
>> Y = sqrt(1 - Z.^2).*sin(theta);
>> surf(X, Y, Z);
```

When run, the above command in MATLAB generates the graphical displays as shown in Figure 6.38 plot.

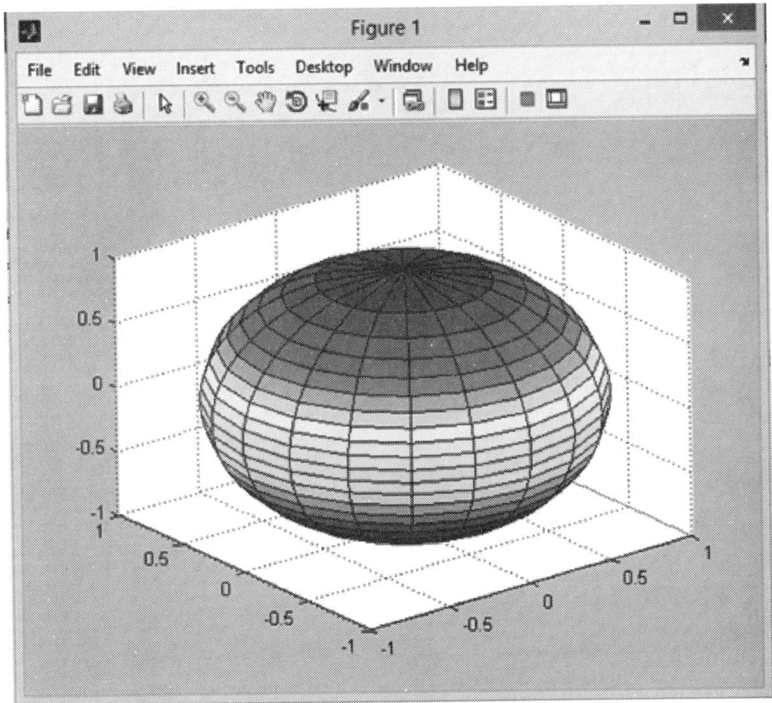

FIGURE 6.38   Plot to illustrate Example 6.38.

EXAMPLE 6.39   In this example, we illustrates how to set the x-axis and y-axis limits to match the actual range of the data, rather than the rounded values of [–2 3] for the x-axis and [–2 4] for the y-axis originally selected by MATLAB.

```
>> [x,y] = meshgrid([-1.50:.2:3.50]);
>> z = x.*exp(-x.^2-y.^2);
>> surf(x,y,z)
>> ylim([-1.50 3.50])
>> ylim([-1.50 3.50])
```

When the above commands are executed, MATLAB generates the graphical displays as shown in Figure 6.39 plot.

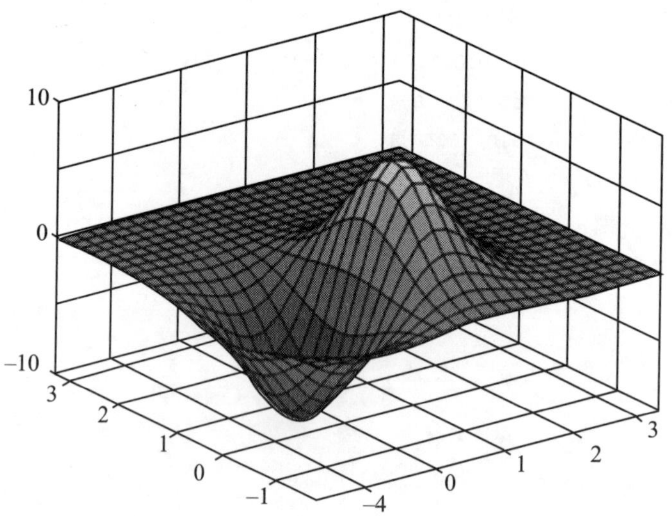

FIGURE 6.39   Plot to illustrate Example 6.39.

Three-dimensional plots typically display a surface defined by a function in two variables, $z = f(x, y)$.

We evaluate the value of z by creating a set of (x, y) points over the domain in the following example using `meshgrid`.

EXAMPLE 6.40

```
>> [X, Y]=meshgrid(-5:.4:5);
>> Z= X.*exp(-X.^2-Y.^2);
>> surf(X,Y,Z)          % to create a surface plot
```

Here, by running, the above commands, MATLAB generates the graphical displays as shown in Figure 6.40 plot.

The 3D plot in Figure 6.40 is the combination of `surf` function and look like `mesh` display surfaces. `Surf` displays both the connecting lines and the faces of the surface in colour. On the other hand, `mesh` produces wireframe surfaces that colour only the lines connecting the defining points.

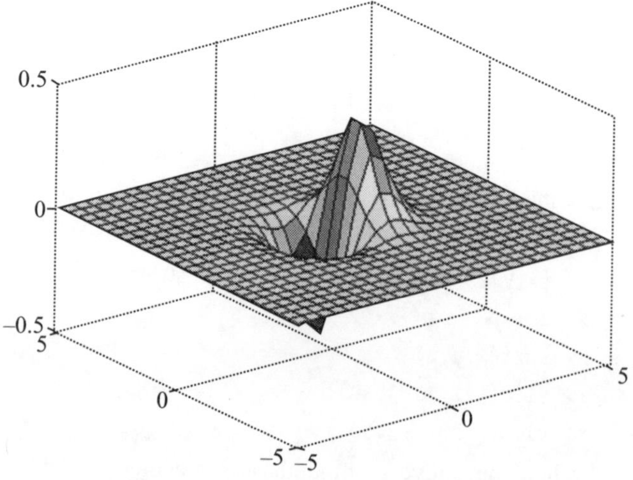

FIGURE 6.40   Surface plot.

EXAMPLE 6.41   In this example, we generate the X and Y matrices consisting of repeated rows and columns.

```
>> subplot(2,2,1); surf(X,Y,Z); title('Fig 1');
>> subplot(2,2,2); mesh(X,Y,Z); title('Fig 2');
>> [X,Y]= meshgrid(-4:.2:4);
>> R= sqrt(X.^2+2*Y.^2)+eps;
>> Z=sin(2*R)./R;
>> mesh(X,Y,Z)
>> subplot(2,2,1); surf(X,Y,Z); title('Fig 1');
>> subplot(2,2,2); mesh(X,Y,Z); title('Fig 2');
```

When run, the above commands, in MATLAB generates the graphical displays as shown in Figure 6.41 plot.

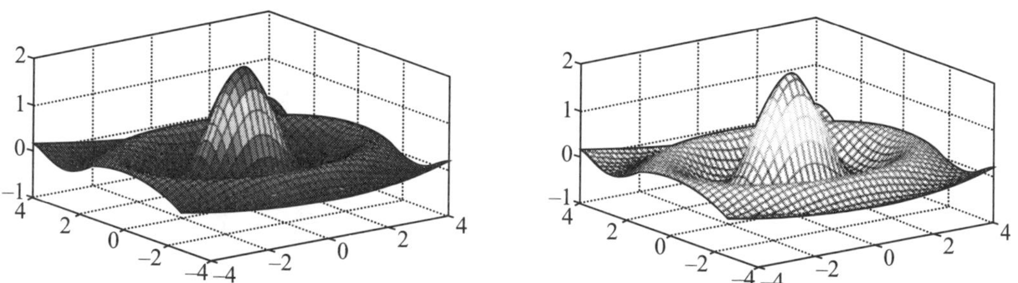

FIGURE 6.41   Plot to illustrate function.

Surfc function

Contour plot under a 3D shaded surface plot command is `surfc`. `surfc(Z)` creates a contour plot under the three-dimensional shaded surface from the Z components in matrix Z, using `x = 1:n` and `y = 1:m`, where `[m,n] = size(Z)`. The height, Z, is a single-valued function defined over a geometrically rectangular grid.

Z specifies the colour data, as well as surface height, so colour is proportional to surface height.

Surface Plot of Peaks use the `peaks` function to define X, Y, and Z as value-by-value matrices. Then, it will create a surface plot.

EXAMPLE 6.42   In this example, we will display a contour plot under a surface plot of the peaks function.

```
[X,Y,Z] = peaks(30);% create a peaks plot of 30-by-30
figure
surfc(X,Y,Z)
```

When run, the above command in MATLAB generates the graphical displays as shown in Figure 6.42 plot.

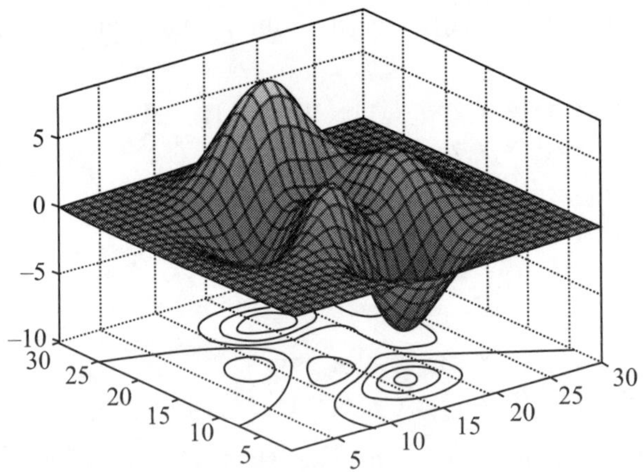

FIGURE 6.42   Plot to illustrate Example 6.42.

6.6.4   Contour Function

The contour(z) is a function that gives the contour plot. The *contour(x, y, z)* plot co-ordinate the surface. Similarly, *contour3(x, y, z)* plot co-ordinate for the *z*-level. Contour function is illustrated by Example 6.43.

EXAMPLE 6.43

```
>> xlabel ('x-axis');
>> ylabel ('y-axis');
>> zlabel ('z-axis');
>> title('plo3 function plot');
>> [x,y]= meshgrid(-6:0.3:6,
-6:0.3:6);
>> z=sqrt(y.^2-x.^2);
>> contour(x,y,z);
```

When run, the above commands, MATLAB generates the graphical displays as shown in Figure 6.43 plot.

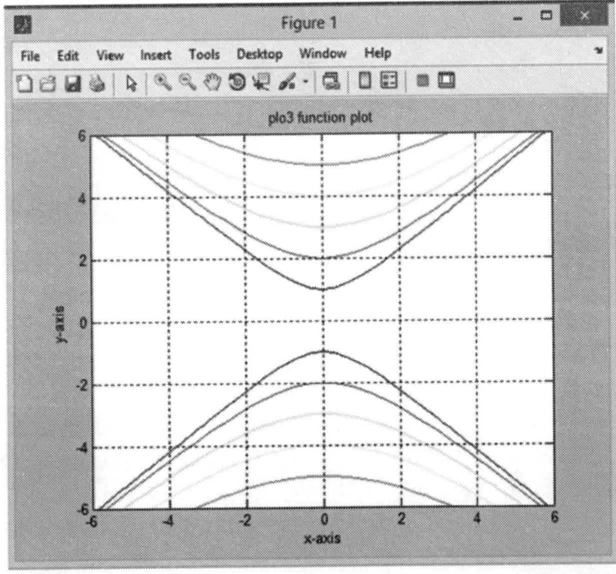

FIGURE 6.43   Plot to illustrate contour function.

6.6.5   Subplots of 3D Plots

In MATLAB, we can display multiple plots in different subregions within the same window using the subplot function.

EXAMPLE 6.44

```
>> [X,Y,Z] = cylinder(5*cos(t);
??? [X,Y,Z] = cylinder(5*cos(t);
%  Error: Unbalanced or unexpected parenthesis or bracket.
>> [X,Y,Z] = cylinder(5*cos(t));
>> subplot(2,2,1); mesh(X); title('X');
>> subplot(2,2,2); mesh(Y); title('Y');
>> subplot(2,2,3); mesh(Z); title('Z');
>> subplot(2,2,4); mesh(X,Y,Z); title('X,Y,Z');
```

Here, the first two inputs to subplot argument indicate the number of plots in each row and column. The third input specifies the active plots. On running, the above commands MATLAB generates the graphical displays as shown in Figure 6.44 plot.

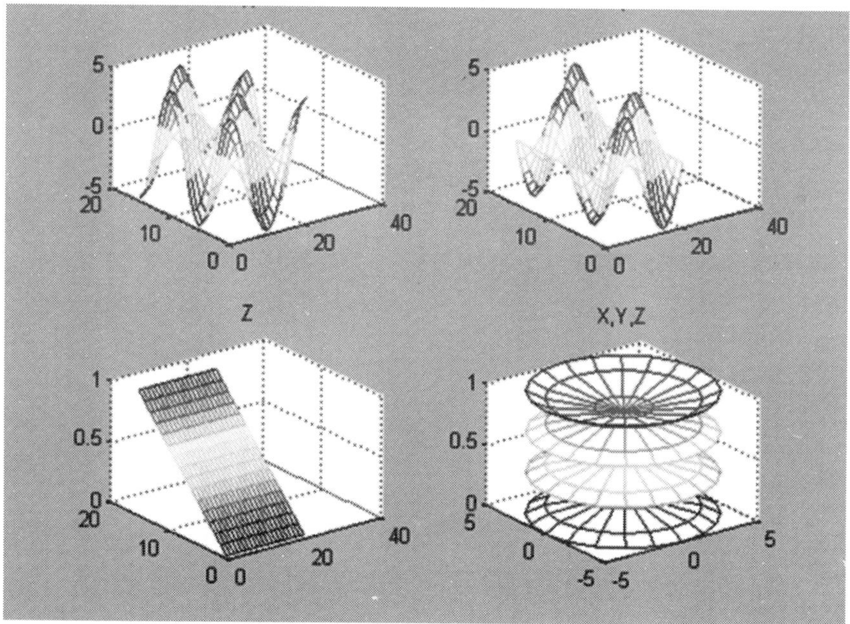

FIGURE 6.44　Example of Subplot..

Here we see hot to draw the subplot of modulation using the following example.

EXAMPLE 6.45

```
% Calculate the data for the plots
fm = 10e3;
fc = 110e3;
```

```matlab
tstep = 110e-9;
tmax  = 220e-6;
t = 0:tstep:tmax;
xam = (1 + cos(2*pi*fm*t)).*cos(2*pi*fc*t);


T = 1e-6;
N = 220;
nT = 0:T:N*T;
xn = (1 + cos(2*pi*fm*nT)).*cos(2*pi*fc*nT);


% Create the stem plot for the Sampled Signal spanning positions 1 & 3 of a 2x2 grid
fig = figure;
subplot(2, 2, [1 3]);
stem(nT,xn);
xlabel('t');
ylabel('x[n]');
title('Sampled Every T=1e-6 ');


% Create the xy plot for the AM Modulated signal in position 2 of a 2x2 grid
subplot(2, 2, 2);
plot(t, xam);
axis([0 220e-6 -2 2]);
xlabel('t');
ylabel('xam(t) ');
title('AM Modulated Signal');


% Create the xy plot for the reconstructed signal in position 4 of a 2x2 grid
subplot(2, 2, 4);
plot(nT, xn);
xlabel('t');
ylabel('x_zoh(t)');
title('Reconstruction at T=4e-6 ');
```

Here, by running, the above commands MATLAB generates the graphical displays as shown in Figure 6.45.

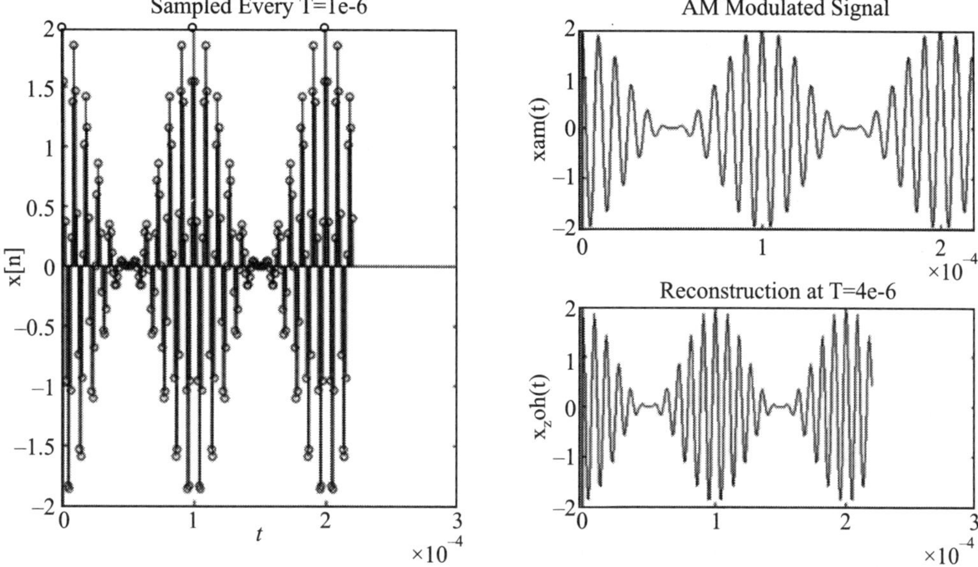

FIGURE 6.45 Subplot of modulation.

6.7 MULTIVARIATE DATA

In MATLAB, the multivariatore statistical data is analysed using a column oriented data structure. The matrix of each column in the data set represents a variable and each row an observation. The row and column consider as (i, j) element. The (i, j)th element is the ith variable.

EXAMPLE 6.46 Consider a data set example with the following three variables:

- Heart rate
- Weight
- Exercise in hours/week

In this example, we create a resulting array for the given observation values as follows:

```
>> X = [12 656 49; 82 44 12; 25 34 56; 89 74 85; 15 26 25; 14 1 8]
X =
        12    656    49
        82     44    12
        25     34    56
        89     74    85
        15     26    25
        14      1     8
```

We can note that first row contain *heart rate, weight* and *exercise hours* for 1st patient, the second row for 2nd patient and so on.

We can apply MATLAB functions for data analysis to obtain the mean and standard deviation of each column by using the following commands:

```
>> mu = mean(X), sigma = std(X)
```

On running the commands, we can get the following results:

```
mu =
39.5000    139.1667    39.1667
sigma =
35.9819    254.3135    29.6339
```

6.8   DATA ANALYSIS

The analysis of data is a process of inspecting, cleaning, transforming, and modelling data to discovering useful information, suggesting conclusions, and supporting decision making goal. Data analysis has multiple facets and approaches that encircling diverse techniques under a variety of names, class, or group domains. In other words, data analysis technique focuses on modelling and knowledge discovery for predictive rather than purely descriptive purposes.

Every data analysis has the following standard components:

1. Pre-processing data
2. Summarising
3. Visualising
4. Modelling

These components are used to describe the patterns in the data with simple models for accurate predictions and to understand the relationship among variables of the model. Following are the explanation of these standard components with the help of common example.

6.8.1   Pre-processing Data

Pre-process data is used to analyse the possible model. This model considers outliers and missing values to smooth data. Using the data analysis, MATLAB identify the good and weak data that assures meaningful conclusions in future.

Loading the data

To load the data in count.data, the load command is used. Let us consider the count contain 24-by-3 array hourly traffic counts (the rows) at three intersections (the column) for a single day.

```
>> load count.dat
```

Loss of data

In the MATLAB, the *NaN* (Not a Number) value is normally used to represent missing data of the structure. We can check the third intersection for *NaN* value using the *isnan* function.

```
>> c3 = count (:,3);
>> x3NaNCount = sum(isnan(c3))
```

By running the commands will display the result as:
```
c3NaNCount =
      0
```

EXAMPLE 6.47   Further, in this example, we draw the plot based on the mean and standard deviation commands for c3.

```
>> bin_counts = hist(c3);
>> N = max(bin_counts);
>> mu3 = mean(c3);
>> sigma3 = std(c3);
>> mu3 = mean(c3);

% create a plot as shown in Figure 6.46.
>> hist(c3)
>> hold on
>> plot([mu3 mu3], [0 N], 'r', 'LineWidth', 2)
>> X = repmat(mu3+(1:2)*sigma3,2,1);
>> Y = repmat([0;N], 1,2);
>> plot(X,Y,'g','LineWidth',2)
>> legend('Data', 'Mean', 'Stds')
>> hold off
```

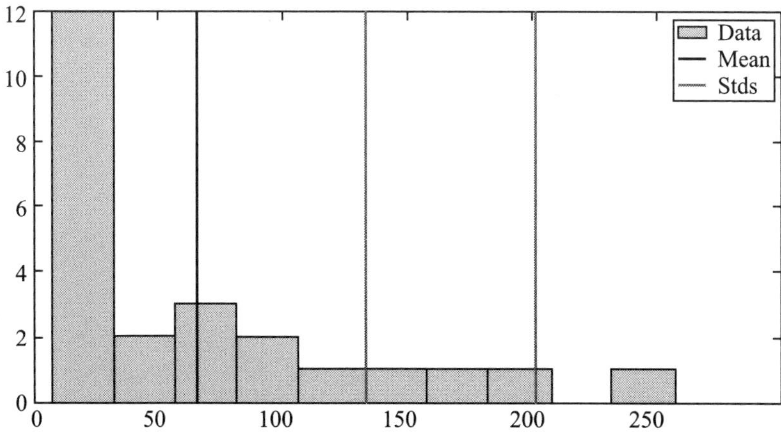

FIGURE 6.46   Histogram plot.

The plot in Figure 6.47 shows the data that have more than two standard deviations are above the mean.

```
>> plot(x3, 'o-')
>> hold on
```

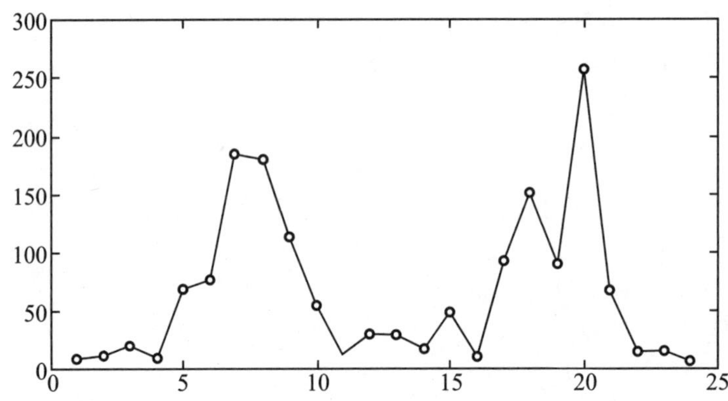

FIGURE 6.47 Time-series plot.

6.8.2 Summarising Data

This is to summarise the data of the plot. In MATLAB, many functions enable us to compute the basic statistics to describe the overall location, scale and shape of the data. The advantage is that function operates on array of data.

Measurement of the location of a data

The following example summarise the measure of the location of data by computing the functions mean, median and mode.

EXAMPLE 6.48

```
>> load count.dat
>> x1 = mean(count)
x1 =
    32.0000    46.5417    65.5833


>> x2 = median(count)
x2 =
    23.5000    36.0000    39.0000


>> x3 = mode(count)
x3 =
    11      9      9
```

The plot is drawn for the above code is shown in Figure 6.48.

```
>> figure
>> hist(count)
>> legend ('Intersection 1', 'Intersection 2','Intersection 3')
```

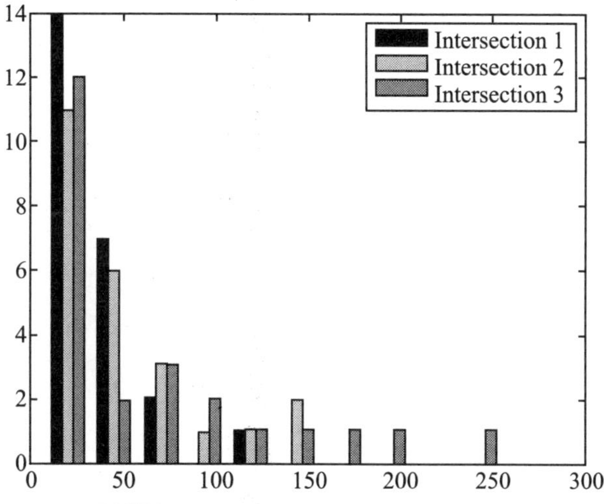

FIGURE 6.48   Summarising data plot.

6.8.3   Visualising

This is used to identify the data plot for pattern and trend. The 2D and 3D plots visualise the data pattern at different intersections. In order to explain this concept, we use two functions *scatter* and *scatter3*. The scatter function generates a scatter plot, i.e., a plot of circle of data points, colour the circle size or colour can vary, point by point. Scatter3 (x, y, z) displays circles at the locations specified by the vector **x**, **y** and **z**.

EXAMPLE 6.49

```
>> load count.dat
>> c1 = count(:,1); % first data at intersection
>> c2 = count(:,2); % second data at intersection
>> subplot(2,2,1)% for c1 and c2
>> scatter(c1, c2, 'filled')
>> xlabel('Intersection 1')
>> ylabel('Intersection 2')
>> legend ('figure 1')
>>
>> c3 = count(:,3); % second data at intersection
```

```
>> subplot(2,2,2)% for c1, c2 and c3
>> scatter3(c1, c2, c3, 'filled')
>> xlabel('Intersection 1')
>> ylabel('Intersection 2')
>> zlabel('Intersection 3')
>> legend ('figure 2')
```

By running the above commands the two subplot is drawn in single plot as shown in Figure 6.49.

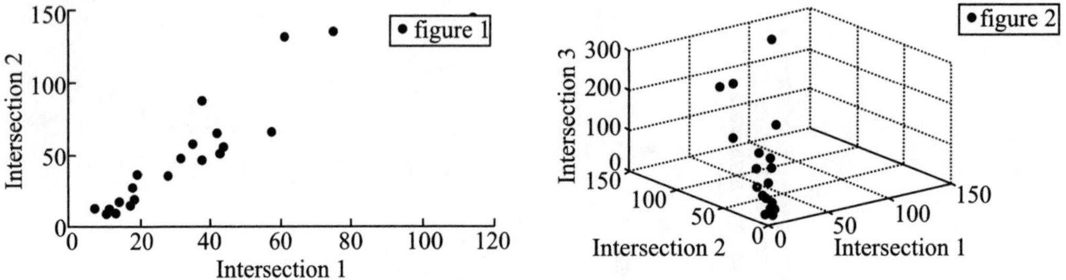

FIGURE 6.49   Visualisation plot.

6.8.4 Modelling

This provides the trend of data that gives full description suitable for predicting new values. Parametric models translate an understanding of data relationships into analytic tools.

EXAMPLE 5.60 We can understand the following traffic data at the third intersection with a polynomial model of degree six using the following commands:

```
>> load count.dat
>> c3 = count(:,3); % data at intersection 3
>> tdata = (1:24)';
>> p_coeffs = polyfit(tdata,c3,6);
```

Use the polyfit function to estimate coefficient of polynomial model at arbitrary values of the predictor.

```
>> figure
>> plot(c3,'*-')
>> hold on
>> tfit=(1:0.01:24)';
>> yfit= polyval(p_coeffs, tfit);
>> plot(tfit, yfit, 'r-', 'LineWidth', 2)
>> legend('Data', 'Polynomial Fit', 'Location', 'NW')
```

By running the code the accuracy can be predicted by observing up and down trend as shown in Figure 6.50.

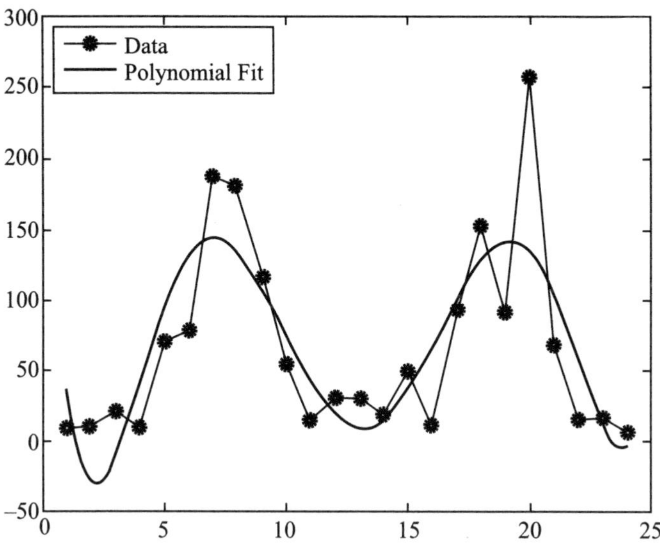

FIGURE 6.50   Predictive plot of modelling data.

SUMMARY

In this chapter, the focus was on the plots of 2D and 3D graphics. Thus, we have seen a simple *plot* can be drawn using the plot command and the methods to use the *labels*, *title*, grids and axis commands were also illustrated in the chapter. Multiple plots using the *plot*, *hold* and *line* commands for the single window graphical display were also discussed. We have seen 2D plotting of MATLAB allows various plots like line, area, bar and pie charts, direction and velocity plots, histograms, polygons and surfaces, scatter or bubble plots and animations too. The way to use *subplot* command to display many plots at the same time was discussed in detail. The 3D plot functions discussed were mesh, *surf* and *contour3*. Specialised plotting tools like bar graphs we have also seen, horizontal bar graphs, histograms, area plots, 3D pie charts and polar histograms were also supported by MATLAB. Definitely this chapter has equipped us with better visualisation tools as all the graphics features that are required to visualise engineering and scientific data are available in MATLAB.

REVIEW QUESTIONS

1. List any three MATLAB graphics commands.

2. What should you do with the step size to increase the smoothness of the plot?

3. Write syntax for *plot* function.

4. What is significance of *axis square* command?

5. How do you insert labels and titles in a plot?

6. Write syntax for *subplot* function and explain the terms involved in it.

7. What does *axis off* function do?

8. Write syntax for *plot3*, surf and contour functions.

9. How and when do you use *meshgrid* function?

10. Differentiate between *plot3*, *surf* and *contour* functions.

11. Do you think graphics add value to visualisation? If yes illustrate with an example of your choice.

PRACTICE EXERCISE

1. Use the following code and list various fonts present by your MATLAB
```
h = uicontrol('Style','text','String','My Font','FontName','MyFont');
list = listfonts(h)
```

2. Execute the following command and observe the result
```
x=0:pi/100:2*pi;y1=cos(x);y2=2*cos(x);y3=3*cos(x);y4=4*cos(x);y5=5*cos(x);
plot(x,y1,'+',x,y2,'o',x,y3,'--',x,y4,'-.',x,y5,'');legend('y1','y2','y3',
'y4','y5')
```

3. Use appropriate plot commands and plot the plot shown in Figure 6.51:

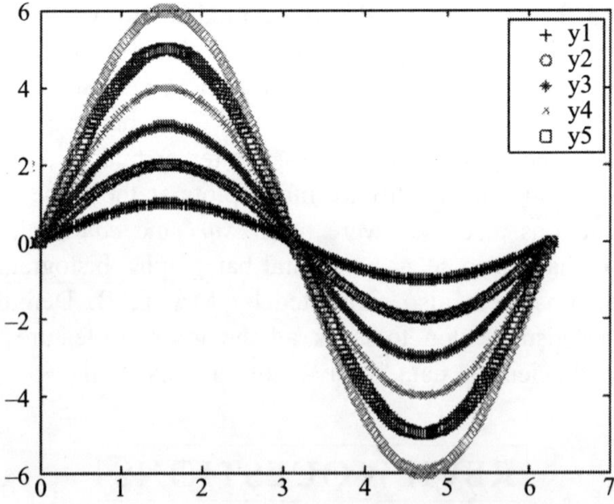

FIGURE 6.51   Appropriate plot command result.

4. Use surfc(peaks(30)) and colourbar to produce following plot shown in Figure 6.52.

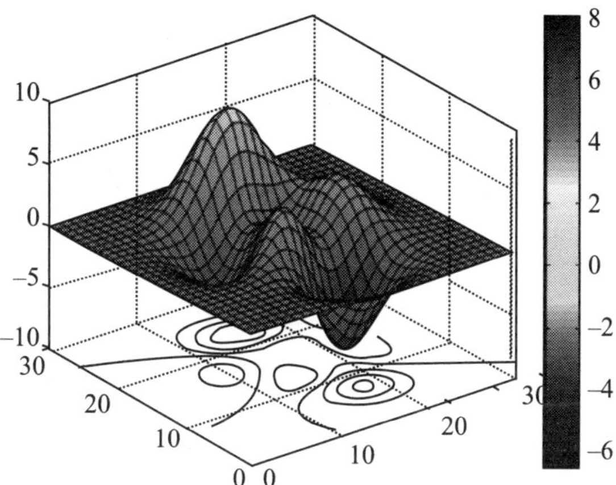

FIGURE 6.52   Plot using surface function.

5. Use MATLAB doc functions and plot at least one plot using slice, stream and cone commands.

6. Use code in column A and write on command window to observe the plots shown in column B.

Note: Select the command and press 'F1' key to observe the detail of function.

Column A	Column B

(i) `[x,y,z,v] = flow;`
`p = patch(isosurface(x,y,z,v,-3));`
`isonormals(x,y,z,v,p)`
`set(p,'FaceColour','red','EdgeColour','none');`
`daspect([1 1 1])`
`view(3); axis tight`
`camlight`
`lighting gouraud`	

(ii) `h = worldmap('India');`
`landareas=shaperead('landareas.shp','UseGeoCoords',true);`
`geoshow (landareas, 'FaceColour', [1 1 .5]);`	

(Contd.)

Column A	Column B

(iii)
 	
``matlab
t = 0:pi/10:2*pi;
[X,Y,Z] = cylinder(2+cos(t));
surf(X,Y,Z)
axis square
``
	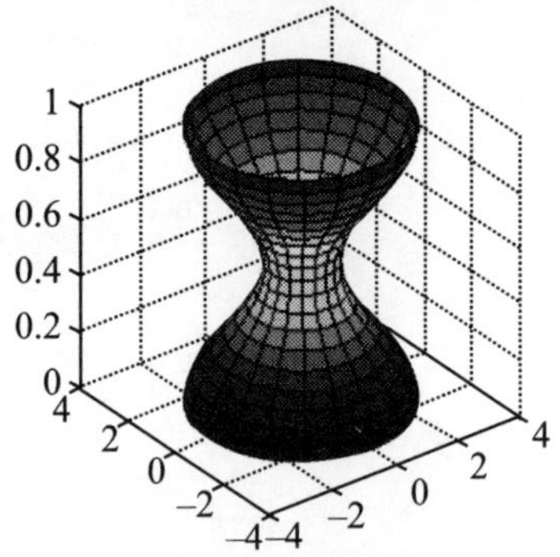

(iv)
 	
``matlab
k = 5;
n = 2^k-1;
theta = pi*(-n:2:n)/n;
phi = (pi/2)*(-n:2:n)'/n;
X = cos(phi)*cos(theta);
Y = cos(phi)*sin(theta);
Z = sin(phi)*ones(size(theta));
colormap([0 0 0;1 1 1])
C = hadamard(2^k);
surf(X,Y,Z,C)
axis square
``
	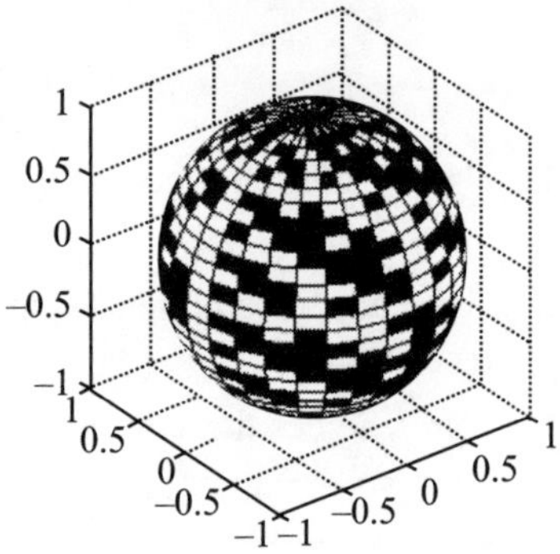

(v)
 	
``matlab
[X,Y,Z] = peaks(30);
waterfall(X,Y,Z)
``
	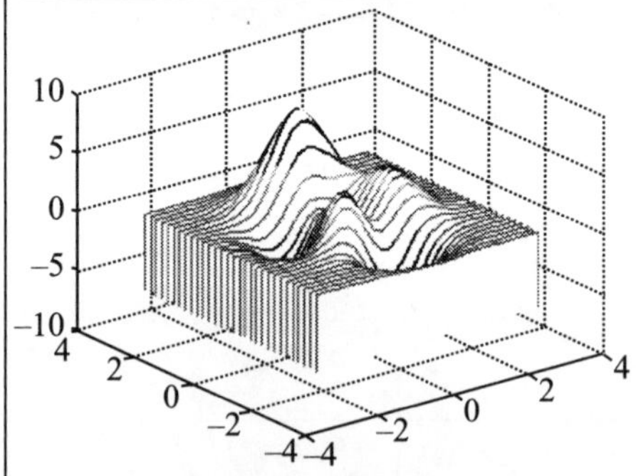

(vi)
 	
``matlab
theta = 2*pi*rand(1,50);
rose(theta)
``
	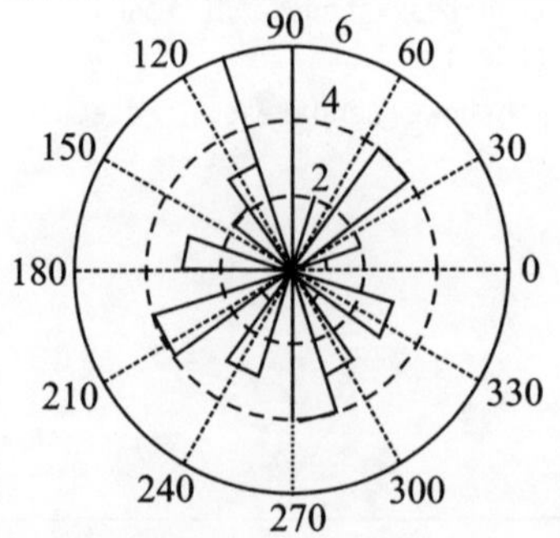

7. Use following code to understand movie function of MATLAB:

```
Z = peaks; surf(Z);
axis tight
set(gca,'nextplot','replacechildren');
% Record the movie
for j = 1:20
surf(sin(2*pi*j/20)*Z,Z)
F(j) = getframe;
end
% Play the movie ten times
movie(F,10)
```

CHAPTER 7

Flow Logic

<table><tr><td>

LEARNING OBJECTIVES

This chapter aims to provide the basic ideas on flow control. At the end of the chapter, we will be able to:

- Write the programs using programming language called MATLAB.
- Understand how the flow of a program can be controlled by using various control logics available in MATLAB.
- Understand the power of MATLAB programming with different control functions.
- Make MATLAB program user friendly by having the flow and control of the program logics with the programmers to achieve desired task.

</td></tr></table>

INTRODUCTION

MATLAB provides a friendly interactive environment for the scientific programming and visualisation purpose. Though, MATLAB is not intended as a substitute for programming languages like Fortran and C, it is still very helpful for developing and testing of models, as well as, obtaining immediate feedback for solving problems.

In MATLAB, the programs are executed as per the instructions given through commands and executed in the sequence. Sometimes, it is likely to happen that these instructions need to be repeatedly executed before the final result is generated. So for this, the instruction needs to be arranged accordingly. This instruction may be single execution command or multiple execution commands. MATLAB program structure takes care of such needs using conditional statement instructions to decide the execution steps.

The conditional statement (in simple terms like true or false) when met the condition based on the loop syntax will produce the next set of activities or terminate the current activity. Such types of repeated logical instructions are called *conditional looping* where, the condition is checked and the action is taken when the condition is met. There is another type of instructions where group of instructions that are executed repeatedly for specified number of times and this is called *unconditional looping*. In such cases, repetition is already defined.

In this section, we will be introduced to many useful constructs used over and over again in MATLAB programming.

In MATLAB, we can use different forms of control flow logic for group of instructions for execution. Executions are broadly based on two categories.

1. *Looping structure:* It is the repetition process of the groups of instructions until the condition is met. For example, for, while, etc.
2. *Branching structure:* It specifies the condition of the execution program when a group of instructions attains the given condition. For example, if, if-else, switch, etc.

Apart from the above instructions, there are some other commands like break, error and continue for the program flow logic execution.

7.1　LOOPS

We use MATLAB to solve many physics problems, so it is essential to know the way to write loops and how to use flow logic for execution of these loops. A loop is a way of repeatedly executing a section of code of a program. Here, different kinds of loops are used such as the for loop, the *nested* loop and the *while* loop.

7.1.1　For Loop

We will look *for* loop in this logic section. The *for* loop structure is an unconditional looping. In case of *for* loop, the number of repetitions is already defined where, a group of instructions are executed repeatedly for a fixed and specified number of times. Let us consider '*n=1: N . . . end*' in number of instructions are executed repeatedly for a fixed specified number of times that is known before the start of loop and it is decided by an index. The *for* loop which tells MATLAB to start *n* at 1, then increment it by 1 over and over until it counts up to *N*, executing the code between *for* and *end* for each new value of *n*. The syntax of *for* loop with multiple statements is given as follows:

```
forindex = initial value : increment : last value
statement 1;
statement 2;
.
.
.
statement n;
end;
next statement
```

Initially, the index is assigned with starting value say, 1 and the group of statement is executed till end statement is reached. After completion of loop instruction the index keeps on incrementing. This step keeps on repecting until the index last value is reached, after this, the *for* loop is terminated.

EXAMPLE 7.1   In this example, we crate a rogram to obtain the sum of integers from 0 to 15.

```
>> sum=0;
>> for j=0:15
sum=sum+j;
end;
```

When the coded script is run, the results displayed in MATLAB command window as follows:

```
>> sum

sum =

    120
```

The beauty of MATLAB is it allows observing the intermediate output values just by not using semicolon (;) at the output statement. The execution of Example 7.2 makes Example 7.1 self explanatory. In the following example, we give step wise output of the program:

EXAMPLE 7.2

```
>> sum=0;
for j=0:15
sum=sum+j
end;
sum =

      0
sum =

      1
sum =

      3
sum =

      6
sum =

     10
sum =

     15
sum =

     21
sum =
```

```
        28
sum =
        36
sum =
        45
sum =
        55
sum =
        66
sum =
        78
sum =
        91
sum =
        105
sum =
        120
```

'For' loop repeats a calculation a certain number of times. For example, let us multiply 2 times the 8 elements of the vector x. The 'For' loop begins by setting a counter, I, that varies over the required range, here 1 to 8, and ends with the statement end. Between *for* statement and *end* statement, we write the calculations with the particular value of x designated as x (i) .

EXAMPLE 7.3

```
>> for i=1 : length (x)
X(i) = 2*x(i);
End
>> x
X =
42  152  186  88   114  50   22   196
```

EXAMPLE 7.4   In this example, we learn create a program to obtain the sum of squares integers from 0 to 50 using the *for* loop command.

```
>> Sum = 0; %initialise sum
for n = 1:50
Sum = Sum + n^2;
end
```

When the coded script is run, MATLAB will display the following result in the command window:

```
Sum      %     this will display the final sum
Sum =
        42925
```

EXAMPLE 7.5   In this example, we are referring to the summing a series coded in different way as follows:

```
>> n=1:10000;        % integers from 1 to 10,000
sum(1./n.^2)  % calculate the sum of the squares of the reciprocals.
```

When the coded script is run, MATLAB will display in the command window the result by entering the variables as follows:

```
ans =
     1.6448
```

Actually, the summing with a loop takes a lot longer than the colon (:) operator way of doing it. Therefore, it is suggested to use colon operator rather than using *for* loop whenever possible.

EXAMPLE 7.6   In this example, we learn a program to add the decrement value of the loop statement using the *for* loop command.

```
>> result=0;
>> for s = 15:-3:0
result= result + s;
end;
```

When the coded script is run, MATLAB will display result in the command window which is as follows:

```
>> result
result =
      45
```

EXAMPLE 7.7   In this example, we learn program for processing each elements of an array using the loop for add 2 to each elements of the vector.

```
>>  Vector = [8 5 1 3 4 7 2 3 5 9];
for Index = 1:length(Vector)
Vector(Index) = Vector(Index) + 2;
end
```

When the coded script is run, MATLAB will display the result in the command window which is as follows:

```
>> disp (Vector);
    10      7      3      5      6      9      4      5      7     11
```

7.1.2 While Loop

The 'while' loop is used to repeat a specific group of code for an unknown number of times until a condition is met. That means in case of a *while* loop execution is repeated until the condition is satisfied. In this flow logic, the group of statements associated with the *while* statement are executed repeatedly or indefinitely until the given condition(true or false) is attained. The generic syntax of *while* loop for statement is given as follows:

```
whileexpression
statements
end
```

EXAMPLE 7.8   This example illustrates the short eng and long eng formats.

The value assigned to variable A increases by a multiple of 8 each time through the for loop.

```
A = 5.123456789;
for k=1:10
disp(A)
A = A * 10;
end
```

The values displayed for A is choosen and compute the short eng format, and in exactly 15 digits for long eng:

```
>> format short eng
>> A = 3.8167492536;
for k=1:8
disp(A)
A = A * 8;
end
      3.8167e+000
     30.5340e+000
    244.2720e+000
      1.9542e+003
     15.6334e+003
    125.0672e+003
      1.0005e+006
      8.0043e+006
```

Similarly, the format long is computed.

```
>> format long eng
>> A = 3.8167492536;
```

```
for k=1:8
disp(A)
A = A * 8;
end
```

```
      3.81674925360000e+000
     30.5339940288000e+000
    244.271952230400e+000
      1.95417561784320e+003
     15.6334049427456e+003
    125.067239541965e+003
      1.00053791633572e+006
      8.00430333068575e+006
```

Note that the group of statements may alter the result of the condition. When the condition becomes false, i.e., 0, the program will exit from the loop and shift to next statement. This process will continue until the end of the statement in the program is reached. The generic syntax of *while* loop is given as:

```
while ( condition is true )
do something
    % Note: the "something" should eventually result
    % in the condition being false
end
```

If the action inside the loop does not modify the variables being tested in the loop's condition, the loop will 'run' forever. The generic syntax is given as:

```
While (y<n)x=x+1;   end
```

The advantage of a *while* loop is that it will go (repeat) as often as necessary to accomplish its goal.

EXAMPLE 7.9   In this example, we create a program for processing *while* loop for finding a number that falls between the range and if not then terminated.

```
>> n=0;
>> sum=0;
>> while n < 20
sum = sum + n;
n = n + 1;
end;
```

When the coded script is run, MATLAB will display in the command window the result which is as follows:

```
>> fprintf ('The sum of series of number is = \t %d .\n', sum);
The sum of series of number is =190.
```

Here, \t %d .\n are used to display the output in more presentable form. Reader can use *help* command to know more about them.

EXAMPLE 7.10   In this example, we learn another program for processing *while* loop for finding a number that falls between the range and if not then terminate.

```
>> value = input ('Please Enter a Number between 1 and 10 (1-10) = ');
>> while ( value< 1 || value > 10)
fprintf('Incorrect input, please try again.\n');
value = input ('Enter a Number between 1 and 10 (1-10) = ');
fprintf ('Within range, terminate.\n');
end % while
```

When the coded script is run, MATLAB will display in the command window the result as which is follows:

```
Please Enter a Number between 1 and 10 (1-10) = 33
Incorrect input, please try again.
Enter a Number between 1 and 10 (1-10)= 22
Incorrect input, please try again.
Enter a Number between 1 and 10 (1-10)= 5
Within range, terminate.
```

EXAMPLE 7.11   In this example, we learn a program for processing *while* loop for finding a number of years to attain the amount close to maximum limits of amount desired.

```
>> Balance = 100; %initialise Balance
>> year = 0; %initialise year counter
>> while Balance < 1000
>> Balance = (1)*Balance + 100;
year = year + 1; %update year counter
end
>> year, Balance %This will display the year and the corresponding balance.
```

When the coded script is run, MATLAB will display in the command window the results which are as follows:

```
year =
     9
Balance =
     1000
```

Differentiate between **for** *loop and* **while** *loop*

In a flow logic, the 'for' loops and the 'while' loops allows to run through a series of commands, repeatedly until and unless the condition is met. In case of a 'for' loop, the commands are executed a fixed number of times, whereas in a while loop the commands are executed until some specified condition is attained. In both loops, the variables can change values from one iteration (cycle through the commands of the loop) to the next. Table 7.1 shows the basic structure of each type of loop:

TABLE 7.1   Basic structure of each type of loop

For loop	*While loop*
for n = vector	while <<condition>>
...MATLAB Commands...	...MATLAB Commands...
End	End

In the 'for' loop, *n* is the counter, and the 'MATLAB Commands', constituting the body of the loop get executed (in order) each time the counter runs through a different element of vector, a list of numbers.

In the 'while' loop, counter may, or may not appear in the body of the loop. Notice that both 'for' and 'while' loops require an end after the body of the loops (to complete the loop). Also, note that if the condition inside the looping structure of the condition in a *while* statement is not well defined then such loops will continue indefinitely. We can stop the execution in such cases by pressing *Ctrl+C* from the keyboard.

7.1.3   Nested For Loop

In MATLAB, when one *for* loop is embedded within another *for* loop, then the integrated two loops are termed as *nested for loops*. The necessary condition is that one loop is completely nested within the other loop.

EXAMPLE 7.12   In this example, we write a program for illustrating *nested for loop* structure.

```
>> x = 0: 2: 4;
>> y = 0;
>> value= 0;
>> for y= 1:3;
value= value+x+y;
fprintf('Inner loop:\n');
fprintf('x=%d\t y=%d\t value=%d\n',x,y);
end;
fprintf('Outer loop:\n');
fprintf('x=%d\t y=%d\t value=%d\n\n',x,y,vlaue);
```

```
end;
fprintf('Outer loop:\n');
fprintf('x=%d\t y=%d\t value=%d\n\n',x,y,vlaue);
end;
```

When the coded script is run, MATLAB will display the results as follows in the command window:

```
Inner loop:
x=0   y=3   value=6
Inner loop:
x=2   y=3   value=12
Outer loop:
x=4   y=3   value=18
```

7.2 BRANCH CONTROL STRUCTURE

The branch control structure is a statement that allows selection or execution of specific blocks of statement out of many statements depending upon condition. There are different types of branche statement structures such as if structure statement, break structure statement, continue structure statement, switch structure statement, error structure statement and try-catch structure statement.

7.2.1 Structures Types

The *if* structure is a conditional structure that controls some group of statements to be executed when certain condition is true. The following are the different forms of *if* control structures:

- 'if' structure
- 'if-else' structure
- 'if-elseif-else' structure
- 'nested if' structure

if structure

This *if* structure command has one group of statements that is executed when the condition is true, otherwise the program exists. The syntax of *if* structures command is given as:

```
if expression
statement 1
statement 2
   .
                 Group of statements
   .
```

```
statement n
end
next statement
```

The most basic structure for an 'if' statement is illustrated in Example 7.13.

EXAMPLE 7.13   In this example, while running the following code will set the variable j to be −1.

```
>> a = 4;
   b = 7;
if (a<b)
    j = -1;
end
```

EXAMPLE 7.14   In this is the example when both of the given conditions are satisfied, then the student passes the course.

```
>> attendance = input('Enter attendance number = ');
>> grade_average = input ('Inputgrade_averag = ');
>> if ((attendance >= 0.90) & (grade_average>= 60)),
disp('pass');
end
```

When the coded script is run, MATLAB will display the results in the command window as follows:

```
Enter attendance number = .99
Inputgrade_averag = 80
% The result will display as:
pass
```

Where, the statement is a logical expression, i.e., true or false. If the statement is true then follows the next statement and if false then statement on group is skipped and control goes to the next statement as appears after the end statement.

if-else structure

This *if-else* structure has two groups of statements, i.e., one for true and the other for false condition. The syntax of the *if-else* structure is given as:

```
if expression
statement 1
statement 2
    .
    .
    .
```

Group 1 statements

```
else
statement 1
statement 2
    .
    .                    } Group 2 statements
    .

end
next statement
```

Note, if the statement is true, then group 1 statement or statements are executed and group 2 statement or statements are skipped. The program shifts to next executable statement or statements after end statement.

If the statement is false, then group 1 statement or statements are skipped and group 2 statement or statements are executed. The program shifts to next executable statement or statements after end statement. It is illustrated by Example 7.15.

EXAMPLE 7.15   In this example, addition of two statements added for more refined decision making. Also, The following code when run will set the variable j to be 2.

```
>> a = 5;
b = 4;
if (a<b)
    j = -1;
elseif (a>b)
    j = 2;
end
```

if-elseif-else structure

This *if-elseif-else* structure is suitable for the condition when there are large number of different conditions of statements, i.e., one for true and the other for false condition. The syntax of the structure is given as:

```
if expression
statement 1
statement 2
    .
    .                    } Group 1 statements
    .

else
```

```
statement 1
statement 2
    .
    .
    .
else
                        Group 2 statements

    .
    .
    .
    .
statement 1
statement 2
                        Group n statements
    .
    .
    .

end
next statement
```

Note, if the statement is true, then group 1 statements are executed and group 2 statements are skipped. The program shifts to next executable statement after the end statement.

If the statement is false, then group 1 statements are skipped and group 2 statements are executed. The program shifts to next executable statement after the end statement.

If the statement is true, then group 2 statements are executed and group 3 statements are skipped. If the statement is false, then group 2 statements are skipped and group 3 statements are executed.

The program continues to shifts to next executable statement after the end statement.

EXAMPLE 7.16   In this example, *if-elseif*-else statement will be executed if no other condition is met. Also, the following code when run will set the variable j to be 3.

```
>>    a = 4;
   b = 4;
if (a<b)
        j = -1;
elseif (a>b)
        j = 2;
else
        j = 3;
end
```

EXAMPLE 7.17   In this example, *if-elseif-else* part of the loop is run. When the variable is bigger than 4, it would specify outcomes depending on whether *a* is smaller than 1, between 1 and 4 or greater than 4.

```
>> a=exp(3);
>> if a<1
a=3*a,
elseif 1<a<4
a=a-0.5,
else
a=a/2
end
```

When the coded script is run, MATLAB will display the results in the command window as follows:

```
a =
    19.5855
```

EXAMPLE 7.18   In this example, *if-elseif-else* part of the loop is executed to identify the largest number.

```
>> x1= input ('Enter first number = ');
>> x2= input ('Enter second number = ');
>> x3= input ('Enter third number = ');
>> if (x1 > x2),
if (x1 > x3),
fprintf('The largest number is %d\n', x1);
end;
elseif (x2 > x3),
fprintf('The largest number is %d\n', x2);
else
fprintf('The largest number is %d\n', x3);
end
```

When the coded script is run, MATLAB will display the result in the command window as follows:

```
Enter first number = 78
Enter second number = 53
Enter third number = 23
```

Finally the result will be displayed as follows:

```
The largest number is 78
```

Nested *if* structure

The nested *if* structure command has one group of statements within other structure. The syntax of nested *if* structure command is given as:

```
if (conditional)
statement 1
statement 2
```
⎫ Group of statements

```
if (conditional)
statement 1
statement 2
    .
end
statement 3
statement 4
    .

    .

    .

statement n
end
```

Where, the statement is a logical expression, i.e., true or false. If the statement is true then follows the next statement and if false then statement on group is skipped and control goes to the next statement that appears after the end statement.

7.2.2 Break Structure Statement

This *break* structure statement is suitable for the inside loop, when the condition is true or terminate then the loop is executed and transfer the control to the next statement of the loop. The break command terminates the execution of a *for* or *while* loop. Statements in the loop that appear after the break statement are not executed.

EXAMPLE 7.19   This example illustrates that the sum of numbers when exceed the limit the loop stops.

```
>> sum = 0;
>> for k = 1 : 20;
sum = sum + k;
if (sum > 30)
break;   % Use the break statement to terminate the 'for'loop instruction.
end;
fprintf('sum = %d\n', sum);
end;
```

When the coded script is run, MATLAB will display in the command window the results which are as follows:

```
sum = 1
sum = 3
sum = 6
sum = 10
sum = 15
sum = 21
sum = 28
```

The program stops in-between as the sum becomes more than 30.

7.2.3 Continue Structure Statement

The *continue* structure statement is used to skip the loop statement from the current structure only. It will not exit from the loop. The remaining iteration will continue for remaining values of the index or decision variables. The continue command control shifts to the next iteration of the *for* or *while* loop and skip any remaining statements in the body of the loop.

EXAMPLE 7.20   This example illustrates the display of variable values between 1 to 20 and skip off the range between 11 and 16 by using *continue* structure statement.

```
>>   for k=1:20,
if ((k>11)&(k<16)),
continue;
end;
fprintf('k = %d\n', k);
end
```

When the coded script is run, MATLAB will display the results in the command window as follows:

```
k = 1
k = 2
k = 3
k = 4
k = 5
k = 6
k = 7
k = 8
k = 9
k = 10
k = 11
k = 16
k = 17
```

```
k = 18
k = 19
k = 20
```

7.2.4 Switch Structure Statement

The *switch* structure statement is suitable for the multiway branching where the selection of block of statement exists. When the desired condition is reached and flag is initiated then the particular block of statements is selected. The integer, character or expression is the condition of flag. This structure is suitable for logical branching. The syntax of nested *switch* structures command is given as:

```
switch flag,
case value1,
block1 statements;
...........
switch flag,
case value2,
block2 statements;
...........
switch flag,
casevalueN,
blockN statements;
end
next statement
```

Note, if the flag (vlaue1) condition is reached then block1 statements are executed and program will exit the switch structure. If the flag condition does not attain all the statements of the blocks are finally transfer the control to the next statement of the loop.

The switch statement syntax is a means of conditionally executing code statements selected from an arbitrary number of alternatives. Each alternative is called a case, and consists of the following:

- The case statement
- One or more case expressions
- One or more statements

EXAMPLE 7.21 In this example the switch part of the loop is used to identify the branch from code.

```
code = input('Select the (E,S,C,M):','s');
switch code
case 'E'
```

```
fprintf('Electronics and Communication Engineering \n');
case 'S'
fprintf('Computer Engineering \n');
case 'C'
fprintf('Civil Engineering \n');
case 'M'
fprintf('Mechanical Engineering \n');
otherwise
fprintf('No department \n');
end;
```

When the coded script is run, MATLAB will display in the command window the result which is as follows:

```
Select the (E,S,C,M): E
Electronics and Communication Engineering
```

Further the result of wrong entry will be displayed as follows:

```
Select the (E,S,C,M):u
No department
```

7.2.5   Error Structure Statement

The *error* structure is to identify the incorrect error input value. The program will terminate when desired message is to display. The syntax for such *error* command is as follows:

```
error ('error message to be displayed')
```

EXAMPLE 7.22   In this example, we illustrate a program which displays the 'error' for wrong entry.

```
>> x = input ('Enter the value of pen = ');
Enter the value of pen = [8 63]
>>  y = input ('Enter the value of pencil = ');
Enter the value of pencil = [9 4]
>> sum = x + y
```

When the coded script is run, MATLAB will display in the command window the result which is as follows:

```
Error using +
Matrix dimensions must agree.
```

7.2.6   Try-catch Structure Statement

In MATLAB, the *try-catch* structure statement is to capture and to handle the errors without stopping the program. The syntax for *try-catch* error command is as follows:

```
try
statement 1
statement 2        } Group 1 statements


catch
statement 1
statement 2        } Group 2 statements
.                  .

end
```

Note, initially the try block of statements are executed. If no error occurs, the statements in the catch block are skipped and program control shift after *try-catch* structure. In case an error occurs, program stops executing the try block statemenst and execute the catch block statements. Finally, exits *try-catch* structure.

EXAMPLE 7.23   In this example, we illustrate a program to display the 'error' for wrong entry using *try-catch* structure.

```
>> x = input ('Enter the value of pen = ');
>> y = input ('Enter the value of pencil = ');
try
sum = x + y
catch
disp('Error: Both vector should be of same length')
end
```

When the coded script is run, MATLAB will display the results in the command window as follows:

```
Enter the value of pen = [9 6 8]
Enter the value of pencil = [9 6]
Error: Both vector should be of same length
```

The control flow functions along with their use can be summarised in Table 7.2.

TABLE 7.2   Control flow functions and their uses in MATLAB

Function	Use
break	Terminate execution of for or *while* loop
case	Execute block of code *if* condition is true

(Contd.)

TABLE 7.2   Control flow functions and their uses in MATLAB (*Contd.*)

Function	Use
catch	Handle error detected in *try-catch* statement
continue	Pass control to next iteration of *for* or *while* loop
else	Execute statements if condition is false
elseif	Execute statements if additional condition is true
end	Terminate block of code, or indicate last array index
error	Display message and abort function
If	Execute statements if condition is true
otherwise	Default part of switch statement
parfor	Parallel *for* loop
for	Execute statements, specified number of times
return	Return to invoking function
switch	Switch among several cases, based on expression
try	Execute statements and catch resulting errors
while	Repeatedly execute statements while condition is true

SUMMARY

In this chapter we have discussed different types of loop instructions. We have also seen the conditional and unconditional loop instructions were used where repetition of loops was known and unknown.

There are different types of branch structure statements such as, 'if structure statement', 'break structure statement', 'continue structure statement', 'switch structure statement', 'error structure statement' and 'try-catch structure statement' which were discussed in detailed manner. There are special statements that are used to change the sequence of looping such as 'break', 'continue', 'error' were also discussed and illustrated in this chapter.

REVIEW QUESTIONS

1. What do we understand by a condition?

2. What do we perceive by a branch?

3. Define a loop.

4. Write general syntax for 'for', 'while' and 'nested' loops.

5. How do we come out of an indefinite while loop via keyboard?

6. What is the MATLAB command to get documentation regarding any of the loop commands?

7. List all the control flow functions available in our MATLAB version.

8. What is difference between if and elseif structures?

9. How does try-catch structure help as error control function?

10. List all other error handling functions in our version of MATLAB?

PRACTICE EXERCISE

1. Write a MATLAB program to find sum of all odd numbers less than 50 using for loop.

2. Observe the output of the following code:

```
n=0;
chapter=0
while n < 12
n= n + 1;
chapter = chapter + 1
display('I am Learning MATLAB from the book "EASY WAYS TO LEARN MATLAB AND
ITS APPLICATIONS"')
end;
```

3. Write a short MATLAB program to find your friends grade if he has studied six subjects and not scored marks less than 40 in each of the subjects. (**Hint:** Use if structure)

4. Write a program to advice the Big Bazar mall owner to increase the number of counters if the rush at present counter is greater than 10.

5. Write a code to find compound interest our on your saving saved for a period of 10 years.

6. Execute the following code to evaluate your performance:

```
code = input('Select the Score grade you obtained(A,B,C,D,F):','s');
switch code
case 'A'
fprintf('I really need to work smart to get A+ \n');
case 'B'
fprintf('I really need to work hard and smart to get A+ \n');
case 'C'
fprintf('I really need to concentrate on my work to get atleast A \n');
case 'D'
fprintf('Was it really a difficult task or my Laziness!!! \n');
otherwise
fprintf('I really need introspection \n');
end;
```

7. Write a MATLAB program to illustrate the use of error structure.

8. Write a code to get the following output.

```
>> x = input ('Enter the value of pen = ');
y = input ('Enter the value of pencil = ');
total=x+y
Enter the value of pen = 1 2
??? 1 2
    |
Error: Unexpected MATLAB expression.
```

9. Write a program to find largest of three input numbers.

10. Write a program to sort given 10 (1, 78, 56, 22, 9, 0, 10, 7, 3, 6) numbers in to ascending and descending order.

CHAPTER 8

MATLAB Programming
Introduction to M-files

LEARNING OBJECTIVES

This chapter aims to provide the basic ideas on m-files. At the end of the chapter we are able to:

- Write a program and execute it as m-files.
- Understand how to execute a MATLAB program step by step and see the results.
- Understand how to navigate between editor, command window and the help window.

INTRODUCTION

MATLAB provides a friendly interactive environment for the scientific programming and visualisation purpose. MATLAB allows the user to write programs and execute them as per the instructions or commands and execute them in the sequence written in the script file. Sometimes, it is needed to have longer codes, in such cases it is not possible to execute everything at the command prompt. Therefore, MATLAB script files comes to our rescue. Thousands of line codes can be written and executed using MATLAB editor. It is not necessary to run the entire code when it is not needed. MATLAB allows us to be selective because we can use CTRL+F9 to run only the selected specific part of the code.

MATLAB is not only a powerful language, but also it features an excellent integrated development environment, including a powerful editor, debugger, profiler, compiler, etc. In this chapter, we will discuss the editor, which is the recommended way to interact with MATLAB using a number of examples in different sections. The MATLAB editor, programs, functions and debugging tools are discussed subsequently in this chapter. This will provide the necessary background to write programs to solve the different problems.

In this chapter, we will also discuss the methods by which MATLAB function is used for writing and running the code written in MATLAB editor for finding the results. Further, the discussion on some of the features of the MATLAB interface and script M-files, function M-files, and error code for debugging M-files shall also be discussed.

8.1 NAVIGATION AND TOOLS

MATLAB platform consists of variety of different windows for displaying different types of information and to perform specific tasks. Each window can generally be opened or closed, docked or popped out, and repositioned or resized in the main window depending on need or preference of the user. The Window menu helps to navigate between the currently open or new windows, even from desktop menu.

As we have already seen that, **Command Window** is the window where the commands and non-graphic output is displayed. A '>>' prompt is flashed on the screen from where the input is fed. Previous commands can be accessed using arrow, to save and reduce errors.

Command History record shows the sessions activities using commands. This can be used for reference or to copy or paste commands for future use.

Workspace is space where all the variables are defined for creating, saving, deleting, plotting, etc. All the variables can be saved as '.mat' files, 'which can be loaded and used as and when required.

This chapter gives us the detailed description of another window called the *editor window* or *script editor*.

8.2 MATLAB EDITOR

In MATLAB, the user is able to edit and debug the basic text using certain tool features such as editor and debugger that provides the user interface in programming. It allows the user to observe the values of the variable or variables in the program. A program is simply a list of commands written using the text editor, for instance notepad. In MATLAB, while writing programs, the usual method is to use separate window, called the *editor*. MATLAB editor allows editing m-file that holds script and functions using standard word processing options. The program when run, the commands are executed from beginning to end. The editor is integrated in MATLAB and has many features like program code writing patterns and debugger that provides tips for correction and improvement of the program.

8.2.1 Operating the Editor

The editor can be opened in a number of ways. To open the editor, initially select the File menu and choose either the 'New...M-file' or 'Open' option. The 'New...M-file' is to create a new program and 'Open' to open an old document that is already saved. In the first option, Editor is opened by typing the command edit from the command window. And in the second option, the new script can be opened by choosing File $\rightarrow$ New $\rightarrow$ Script. It can also be opened by just pressing Ctrl+N key on the keyboard. Steps to open MATLAB editor which we have discussed are as shown in Figure 8.1.

The saved file can be opened by typing *edit* in the command window and even typing *edit myfile* will open 'myfile.m' for editing. Multiple files can also be opened as tab in the same editor window like setting or clearing and executing program line by line by debugging the program.

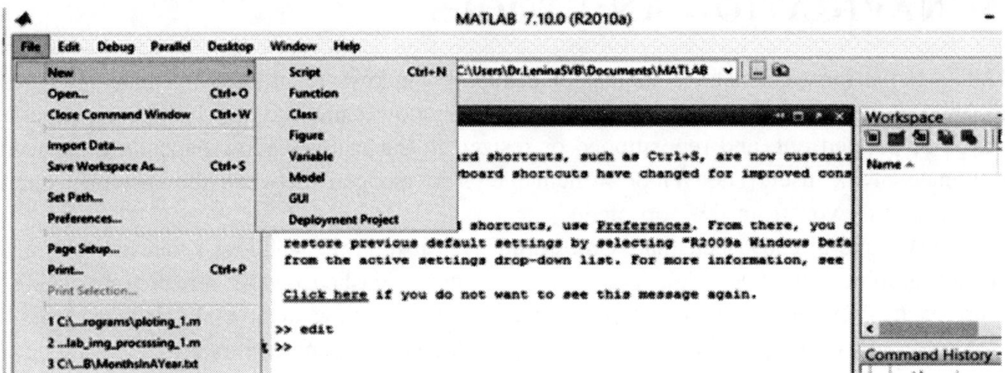

FIGURE 8.1   Editor window displayed after typing edit at command prompt.

8.2.2   Editor Toolbar

The MATLAB editor can be used to create new file using its toolbar.

Figure 8.2 shows the editor toolbar for creating the New file for first time. For creating a file with extension '.m', file from the main MATLAB window (MATLAB 2013), go up to following tabs and press the Home → New → Function. This should open the editor window and after writing on it the file can be saved as '.m File'. In other words, the code is saved as '<filename>.m', where <filename> is the name of the file. We should not get confused with the '<' '>' symbols used as they are used as convention that the part enclosed in them is the name of the file. They need not be included in the file name while naming and saving any file. It is important to add '.m' at the end of our file name. Otherwise, MATLAB may not understand our program.

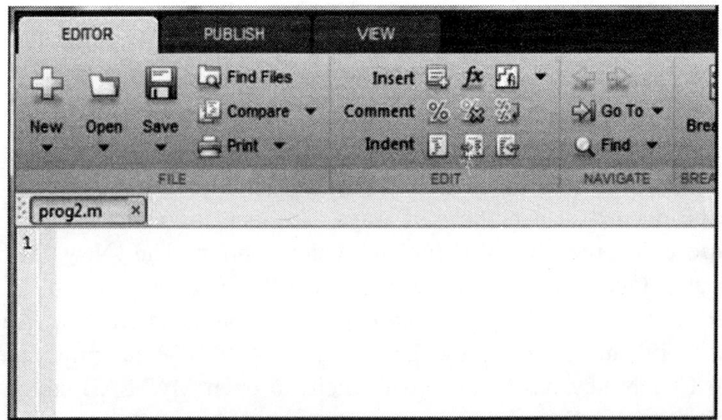

FIGURE 8.2   Editor window displayed after typing edit at command prompt.

Typing the command edit or edit <filename> in the command window at the command prompt will display the editor window.

8.2.3   Editor Main Menu

In the MATLAB window (MATLAB 2013), by pressing the tabs such as the Home $\rightarrow$ New $\rightarrow$ Function, the editor window will appear. The program is written in the editor window and saved. In the editor, we can now type our code, in a similar way as in a word processor. There are menus for editing the text, just like word processor. While typing our program code in the editor, no commands will be executed at the command prompt. Figure 8.3 shows the editor window main menu bar.

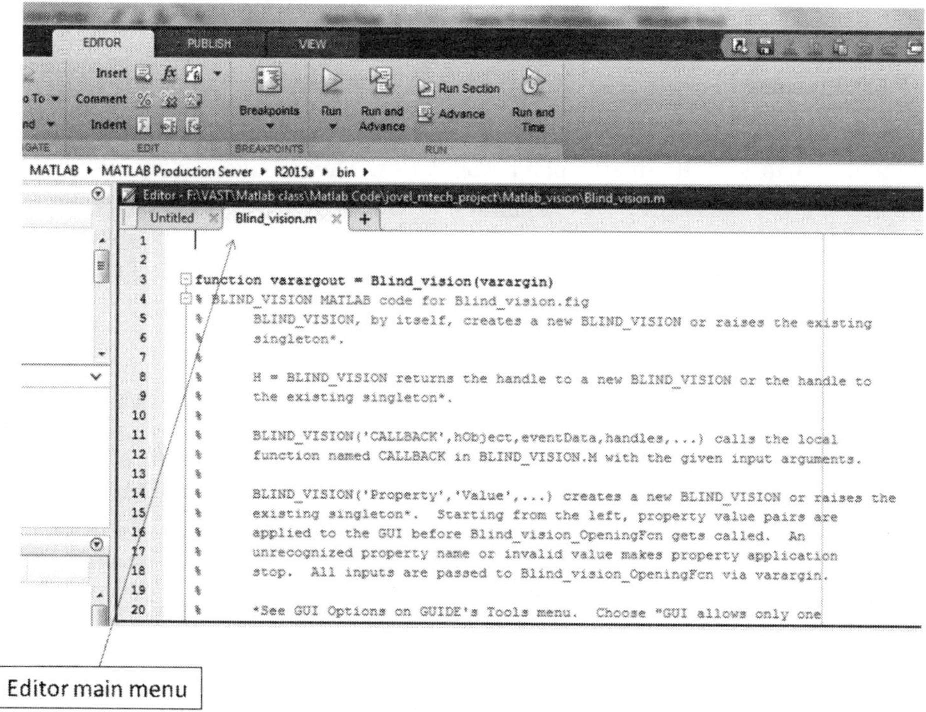

FIGURE 8.3   Editor window main menu bar.

8.3   M-FILES

In MATLAB, there are different methods to solve the problems. If the problem is of small type, it is solved by typing the code of program on Command Window itself. However, when there are situations in which writing a problem involves repeating of same operation many times, it could be solved by writing a program using m-file.

M-file is ordinary text file that contains the MATLAB commands. M-file can be created using any text editor whether it is Notepad, Wordpad or MATLAB Editor program. The editor can be invoked in a number of ways as discussed in Section 8.2.1, can be summarised as follows.

- Choosing a New file or Open file from the File submenu in MATLAB desktop as seen in Figure 8.1.
- Click on the icons for new file or open file on the toolbar available in the MATLAB desktop.
- Enter the command edit or edit filename at the command prompt in the MATLAB Command Window as shown in Figure 8.2.

In MATLAB to provide the solution of the complicated problems, the simple editing tools of command window and its history window are of sufficient. In order to have an easy approach, it is better to create an m-file. There are two different types of M-file such as:

1. Script files
2. Functions files

M-file can be created and modified using any text editor that includes notepad in window or word processor to save the file as plain ASCII text. More conveniently, the Editor or the Debugger is used for the new file by typing edit or followed by typing the existing M-file in the current working directory. By double-clicking on an M-file in the current directory browser, if will open in the Editor or the Debugger. MATLAB allows writing two kinds of program m-files as discussed earlier. We will see each of them in detail in Sections 8.4 and 8.5.

8.4   SCRIPTS

The Script files are the simplest program files with '.m' extension. In these files, we write series of commands, which can be executed together. Scripts do not accept input arguments and do not return any output arguments. They operate on data in the workspace.

The variables that get created remain in the same workspace and can be used for further computation. A script file contains multiple sequential lines of MATLAB commands and function calls.

MATLAB Editor or any other text editor (notepad) creates '.m file'. We can run a script by typing its name at the command line.

8.4.1   Creating and Running Script File

To create scripts files, the text editor is used. We can open the MATLAB editor in the following two ways:

1. Using the command prompt
2. Using the IDE (Independent Development Environment)

Using the command prompt

In MATLAB on using the command prompt, when we type *edit* in the command window this will open the editor.

```
>> edit % will open the Editor window.
```

We should not get confused with the use of symbol '%' here as it is used to show that the text which appears after that symbol is not considered as instructions to MATLAB but they are statements used by us to make user code readable and user friendly. They are also called comments in the program. It is used very frequently in this book to include comments in the programs written.

Even when we directly type edit and then the filename (with '.m' extension) the editor screen of the stored file appears.

```
>> edit poly % by typing edit <filename> will open the saved file as Editor Window.
```

The above command creates the file in default MATLAB directory. This program files is saved in a specific folder of assigned directory path.

Following command creates a folder <name> by using specific command <mkdir> at the command prompt (>>):

```
>> mkdir progs      % create directory progs under default directory
>> chdir progs      % changing the current directory to progs
>> edit prog2.m     % edit the previously saved file named prog2.m
```

M-file functions are subprograms stored in text files with .m extensions. If a new m-file is to create for the first time MATLAB prompts confirm it by Clicking (New → Function) as shown in Figure 8.4.

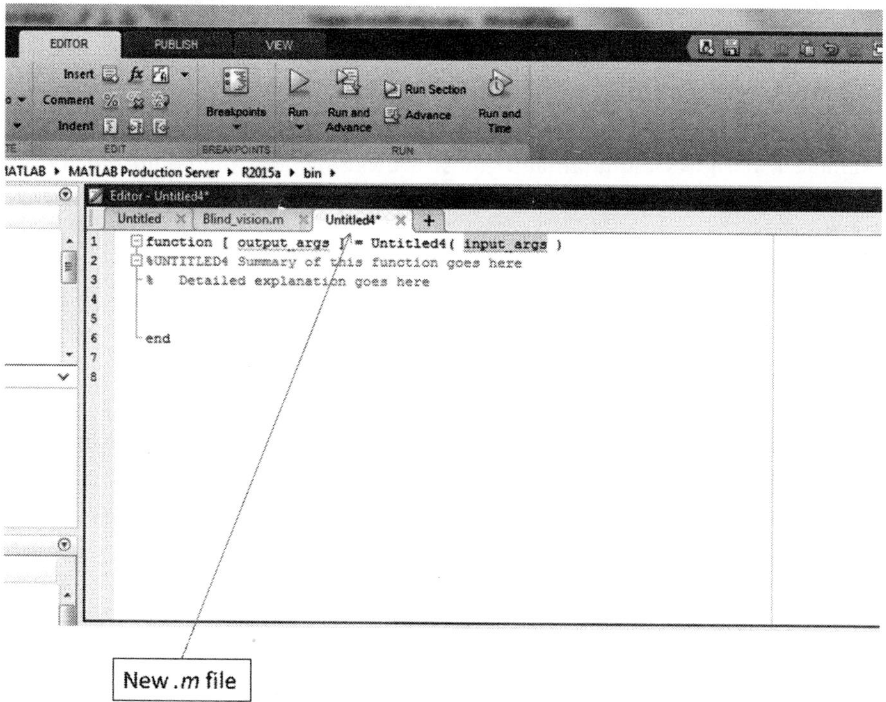

FIGURE 8.4   Illustration to open .m file.

Using the Independent Development Environment (IDE)

Using the IDE, we can choose NEW → Script, this will open the editor and creates a file named Untitled as shown in Figure 8.5. This can be saved in new file name after typing the code.

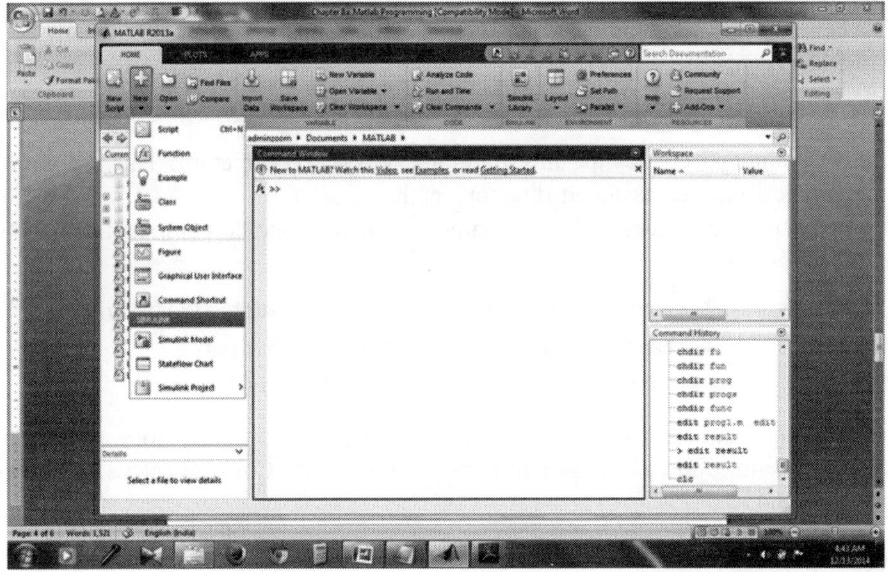

FIGURE 8.5   Editor window displayed by IDE.

Before, creating a script file and moving to the script editor, type the following program code in Example 8.1. shows the total strength of a department at the command prompt.

EXAMPLE 8.1

```
>> x = input('Number of Teaching Staff = ');
Number of Teaching Staff = 22
>> y = input('Number of Lab Staff = ');
Number of Lab Staff = 8
>> s = input('Number of ECE students = ');
Number of ECE students = 120
% when the above code is compiled and executed then MATLAB produces the following
result as:
>> z = x + y + s
z =
    150
```

Now, create a script file, of the above program code that shows the total strength of a department in the m-file. The m-file after creating and saving (say ECE) can be run it in two ways:

- Clicking the Run button on the editor window or
- Just typing the filename (without extension) in the command prompt: >> ECE

The command window prompt displays the result: 150. This is illustrated in Example 8.2. Complete procedure for creating and running the script file through Debug-run is as shown in Figure 8.6.

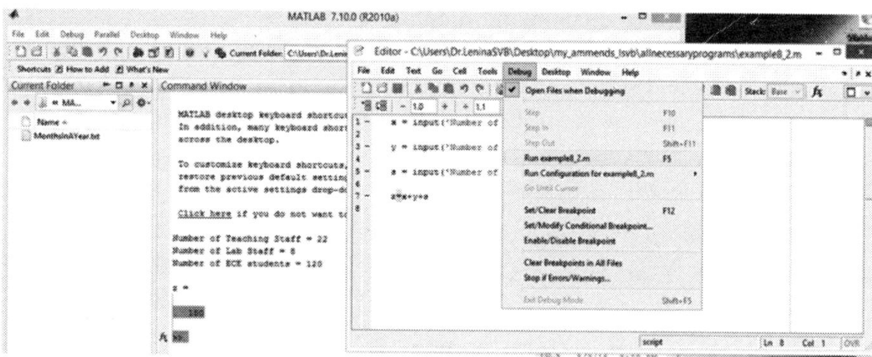

FIGURE 8.6   Complete procedure to run a script file.

EXAMPLE 8.2

```
Number of Teaching Staff = 22
Number of Lab Staff = 8
Number of ECE students = 120
z =
    150
```

Note: We need to provide the input through the keyboard as we have used input function in our code. Also whenever we are saving the script file, we need to save it at the desired location by changing the path or adding the path. The option to do so is displayed when we click on file in the editor window and choose save submenu available there.

Let us see another example, to create a script file, and type the following code:

EXAMPLE 8.3

```
>> a = 5; b = 7;c = a + b
>> d = c + sin(b);e = 5 * d
>> f = exp(-d)
```

When the above code is compiled and executed, MATLAB will produce the following results:

```
c =
    12
d =
    12.6570
```

```
e =

   63.2849

f =

   3.1852e-06
```

When the execution is completed the variable will remain in the workspace can be displayed by typing whos command at the command prompt.

The following example produces a plot of a random series using script file writing. The command lines of the whole script can be dragged-and-dropped in the Editor command window or alternately typed on the new script file by selecting File → New → Script.

EXAMPLE 8.4   % Random Plot: This script creates a random series of changes and display.

```
>> Level = cumprod (1+randn(600, 1)  or 100);
>> Dates = 1950 + 1 or24: 1 or12: 2000;
>> plot(Dates, Level, 'g')
>> title ('Levels during 1990 to 2000')
>> xlabel('Year'), ylabel ('Level of range')
>> grid
>> legend('First observation')
```

This script when typed into the Editor file will produce the result, when run button (green) is pressed or by typing the file name at the command window prompt after file name is saved. The above code when compiled and executed; produces the following display as shown in Figure 8.7.

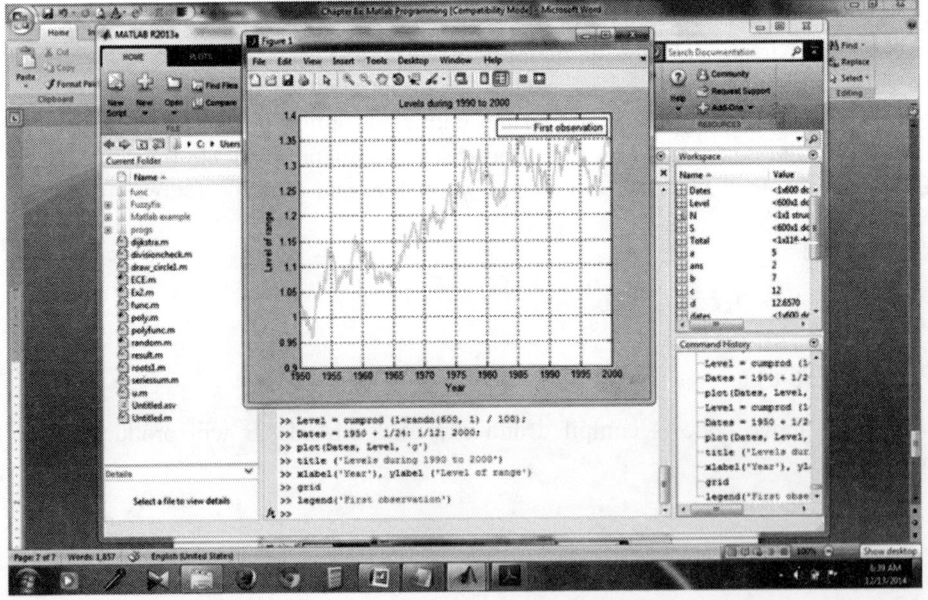

FIGURE 8.7   Results displayed after execution of Example 8.4.

The program written in the above example shows we cannot change the features of the script variables if written at command prompt. If we need to change the inputs to produce different graphs and different lengths or years then script needs to be written at the editor differently, so that it can be changed in an interactive manner. This will let us to enter the interactive information. In the forthcoming, Example 8.5, three lines at the beginning of the script are asked as input. When we run the program and enter the value the result will be displayed correspondingly.

EXAMPLE 8.5   The following example also produces a plot of a random series using script file writing.

```
% Random Plot: This script creates a random series of changes and display.
noOfLevel = input('Number of observation = ');
startDates = input('Starting year = ');
varTitle = input('Variation from the point = ');
Level = cumprod (1+randn(600, 1)  or 100);
endDates = startDates + 1 or24 + 1 or12*(noOfLevel-1);
Dates = startDates + 1 or24 : 1 or12 : endDates;
plot(Dates, Level, 'g')
title(varTitle)
xlabel('Year'), ylabel('Level')
grid
legend('First observation')
disp(['Start Date: ' num2str(startDates)])
disp(['End Date: ' num2str(round(endDates))])
disp(['Number of observation: ' num2str(noOfLevel)])
```

When the above code is compiled and executed, MATLAB will produce the following results:

```
Number of observation = 600
Starting year = 1960
Title of the graph = 10
Start Date: 1960
End Date: 2010
Number of observation: 600
```

This script when typed into the Editor file and run in MATLAB will produce the following display (Figure 8.8).

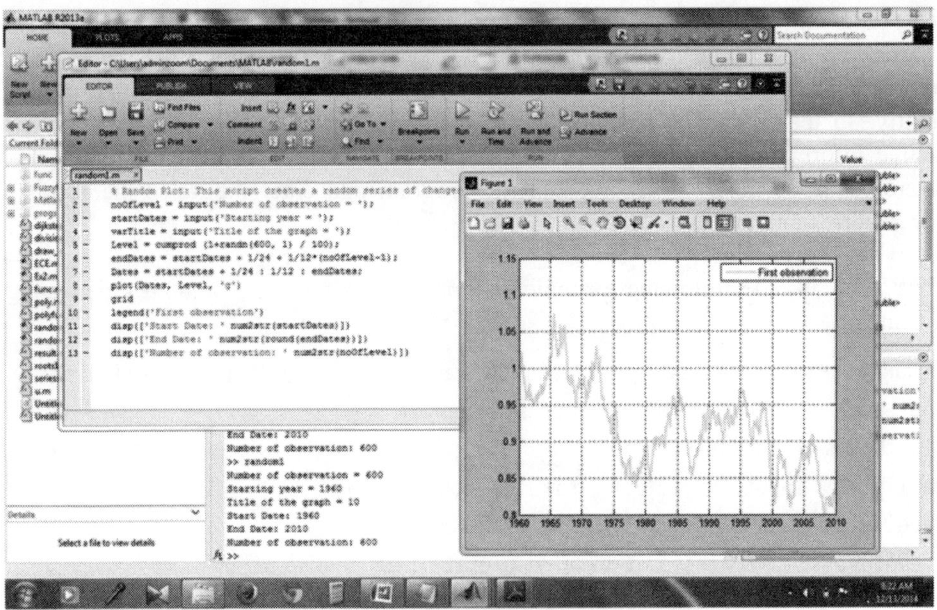

FIGURE 8.8 Results displayed after execution of Random Plot in file random1.m.

8.5 FUNCTIONS

The Function files are also known as program files with '.m' extension. Functions can accept input arguments and return output arguments. Internal variables are local to the function and have their own workspace.

8.5.1 Function M-files

In Function m-file, the input arguments process several times for different input values of a parameter and return output arguments. It provides different inputs to a built-in function to find an output that meets a given criterion. Figure 8.9 shows the function m-files.

Like a script M-file, a function M-file is a plain text file that resides in MATLAB working directory. The file name saved as a function name and that matches each other.

```
function [ output_args ] = Untitled11(input_args)
% UNTITLED11 Summary of this function goes here
% Detailed explanation goes here end
```

The first line Untitled11 specifies the name of the function, which identifies the file as a function M-file. The first line of the file contains a function statement, and describes both its input arguments (and parameters) and its output values.

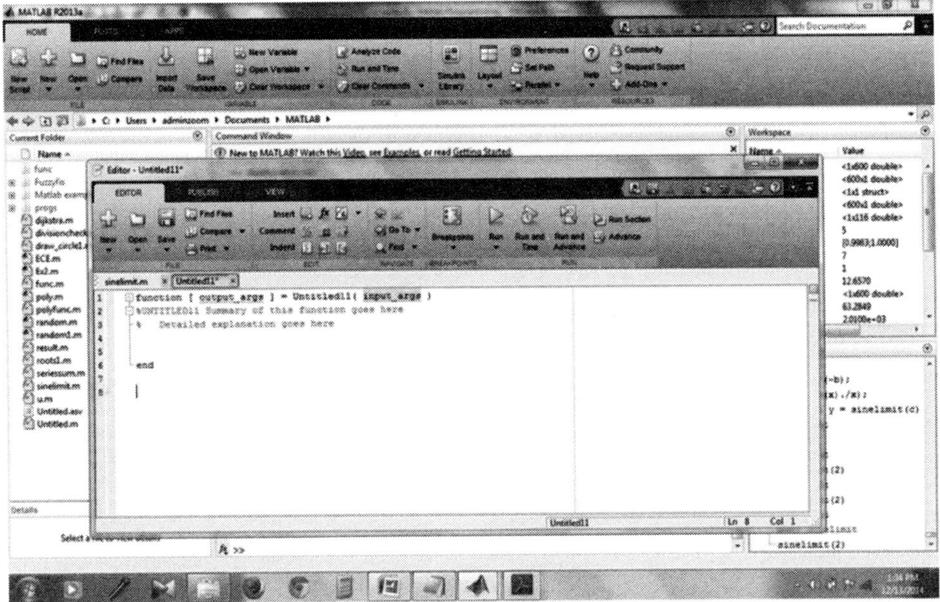

FIGURE 8.9 Illustration of function m-file.

The following example problem computes some values of $\dfrac{\sin(x)}{x}$ with $x = 10^{-b}$ for several values of b.

EXAMPLE 8.6   In the following example of function M-file is created, executed on function file [NEW $\rightarrow$ Function] and saved as *sinelimit.m file*.

```
function y = sinelimit(c);
% SINELIMIT computes sin(x) orx for x = 10^(-b),
% where b = 1, ..., c.
format long
b = 1:c;
x = 10.^(-b);
y = (sin(x)./x)';
end
```

The above code is compiled and executed as a saved file *sinelimit*. When the function with its value of $c = 4$ is called in MATLAB, will produce the following result:

```
>> sinelimit(4)
ans =
    0.998334166468282
    0.999983333416666
```

```
0.999999833333342
0.999999998333333
```

The answer of the values of *b* from 1 to 4 yields the desired results.

If only the function name is called then there will be an error display as shown below:

```
>> sinelimit
Error using sinelimit (line 5)
Not enough input arguments.
```

The function name structure is similar to other program except it should include with the input arguments. Complete procedure to create function file and execute it is demonstrated by Figure 8.10.

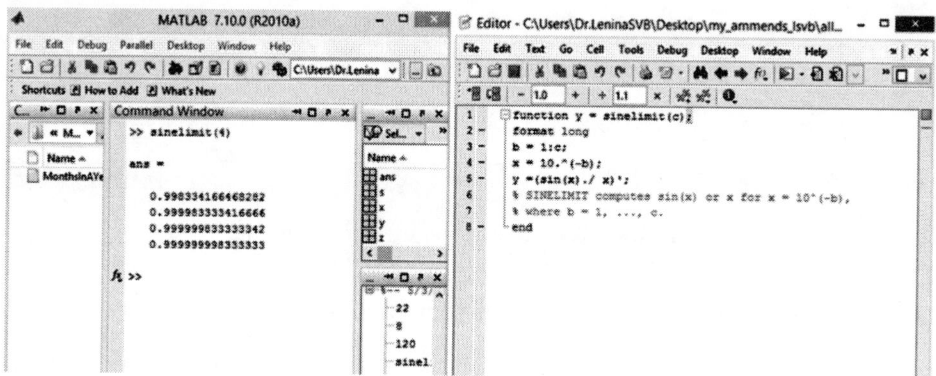

FIGURE 8.10   Illustration of function m-file for sinelimit.m file.

8.5.2 Parts of Function M-file

Files that contain MATLAB language code are called *M-files*. M-files can be *functions* that accept arguments and produce output, or they can be *scripts* that execute a series of MATLAB statements. For MATLAB to recognise a file as an M-file, its name must end in *.m*.

The function M-file consists of following parts as shown in Figure 8.11.

- Function definition line
- Function body
- Comments

We can create M-files using a text editor, and use them as MATLAB function or command. The process appears like this:

- Create an M-file using a text editor.
- Call the M-file from the command line, or from within another M-file.

From the toolbar when the function is pressed the M-file window to open. The following expression appears in the window of function file. The general default syntax of a MATLAB function is as follows:

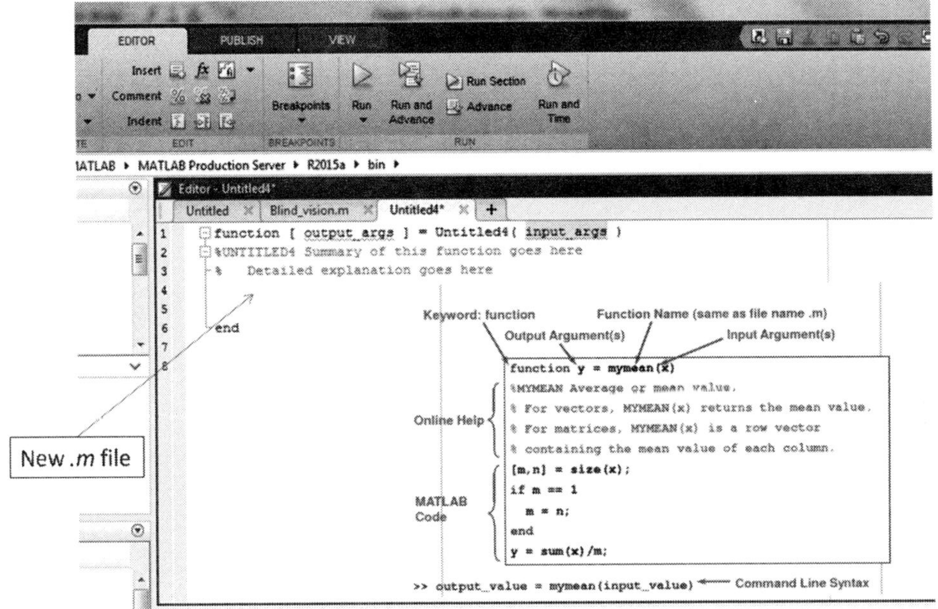

FIGURE 8.11   Parts of function m-file.

```
function [ output_args ] = Untitled4( input_args )
% UNTITLED4 Summary of this function goes here
% Detailed explanation goes here
  Code
Code
..
..
..
Code
code

end
```

The M-function is explained as mentioned below.

```
function [output_arg1, output_arg2, ..., output_argN ] = functionName(input_arg1, input_arg2, ..., input_argM )
```

```
        % Comment in the first line represent "lookfor"

        % these are additional lines is at first comment by "help"
```

```
        .
        .MATLAB commands is written here
        .
        output_arg1 = . . .
        .
        .
        .
        output_arg2 = . . .
        .
        .
        .
        .
        .
        .
        .
    output_argN = . . .
        .
        .
        .
        .
        .
        .
        .
```

The following explanation is referred to the above general default syntax of a MATLAB M-function:

- The M-file function is normally used with '.m' extension.
- The M-file function appears in lowercase letters at the start of the file.
- MATLAB M-functions have the input and output arguments listed in square brackets. The arguments in the parentheses are separated in by comma.
- When the MATLAB M-functions have a single input then square bracket is not needed.
- When there is no output argument then neither square bracket nor equal sign are used.
- In the first comment line, the 'lookfor' command is used for search and display when there is a matching.
- The 'help' or 'doc' is used in the first comment block.
- At the end of execution of the function, the last output argument is used.
- Finally the end of the functions is automatically returned.
- The M-file function name must match the name of the .m-file function.

Function name

The function definition line is M-file that defines a function subprogram. It is the first line of the file contains a function statement, and describes both its input arguments and its output values. The general form of the function definition line is:

```
function [ output_args ] = Untitled1( input_args )
```

In MATLAB, the function name begins with a letter, number and underscores. The name of the function file and the function name may not be identical and it is called by the function filename. Function M-file is either the MATLAB command line or from within other M-file. When the new function is opened its Editor Window is then its code is represented as:

```
function [ output_args ] = step( input_args )
```

When this function is saved then file name is assigned as *step.m* by itself.

EXAMPLE 8.7　MATLAB has a built-in function sign that performs this function for more general inputs as illustrated in this example.

```
function y = signum(x)
```

When this function is saved the file name is assigned as *signum.m* by itself.

Note:
(i) It is advisable to maintain the same name for the function name and the filename, as well.
(ii) It is necessary to include all arguments of the function while enclosing input arguments in parentheses and output arguments in square brackets.

EXAMPLE 8.8　In this example, here the two input step function is assigned to output variables that is defined in the function subprogram.

```
[X, Y] = step ([2 5], [1 2])
```

For the case of varying number of input and output arguments of the function can be passed by *varargin* and *varargout* functions.

Function body

The function of the body contain all the MATLAB statement that perform the required subtask computation. The subprogram statement contains the flow control, interactive input or output and statement assigned. Referring to Example 8.6 of the function body statement is given as follows:

```
b = 1:c;
x = 10.^(-b);
y = (sin(x). /x)';
```

Comments

The comment lines begin with a percentage sign (%). Comment lines appear anywhere in an m-file, that defines the response of the statement. Following are the comments added at the end of the statements: discussed in Example 8.6.

```
b = 1:c;      % Define the vector of values of the independent variable range from
1 to c
```

```
x = 10.^(-b); % the value of x computer from value b
y = (sin(x). /x)'; % Compute the desired values
```

8.5.3   Function Workspace

In MATLAB, the function occupies the separate memory space called MATLAB workspace. The function has its own variables that are separated from other functions and the base workspace. The variables that are passed to a function in the program workspace termed as program that return its output arguments to the function workspace of called program. If there are several functions then such variables are called as global. The following example is the command for the global variables.

EXAMPLE 8.9

```
global x y z;
```

8.5.4   Function Types

MATLAB function can be classified into different categories as follows:

- Subfunctions
- Nested functions
- Inline functions

Subfunctions

In MATLAB function, there are chances of more number of function codes. The first function is the file and is called primary function. The additional functions defined within the same file are called Subfunctions. Both the function and subfunction are the M-files.

EXAMPLE 8.10   In this example, we see a function to calculate percentage and division from score marks of student.

```
function[percent,division]=result(marks)
n=length(marks);
percent=pcent(marks,n)
division=divs(percent,n)
function percent=pcent(marks,n)
percent=sum(marks) orn;
function d=divs(p,n)
if p>60
    d='first'
else
    d='not_first'
end
```

When the above code is compiled and executed, MATLAB will produce the following results:

```
>> result(90)
percent = 90
d = first division
ans = 90
```

Here, the result is out of the primary function. It saved as *result.m file*. The subfunctions are pcent and divs. They are respectively stored as pcent.m and divs.m files.

Nested functions

In MATLAB, nested function is used to provide a way to pass information, without passing it through input or output arguments and without using global variables.

EXAMPLE 8.11 In this example, we see a function to calculate percentage and division from score marks of student.

```
function[percent,division]=result(marks)     % F1 = Primary function (...,)
n=length(marks);
percent=pcent(marks,n)
division=divs(percent,n)
function percent=pcent(marks,n)               % F2 = Nested function (...,)
percent=sum(marks) orn;
function d=divs(p,n)                           % F2 = Nested function (...,)
if p>60
    d='first'
else
    d='not_first'
end                                           % end of Nested function F1
end                                           % end of Primary function F1
```

A primary function contains several nested functions within itself. The primary and nested function is marked with an end statement.

Inline functions

In MATLAB, mathematical expression can be created as a function. This can above represented as an inline object from a string expression. The syntaxes of inline function are follows:

- inline(expr)   % constructs an inline function object from the MATLAB expression contained in the string expr.
- inline(expr,arg1,arg2,...)   % constructs an inline function whose input arguments are specified by the strings arg1, arg2,....
- inline(expr,n)   % constructs an inline function whose input arguments are x, P1, P2, ...

EXAMPLE 8.12 In this example, we create a simple inline function to square a number. The resulting inline function evaluated with the *char* function.

```
>> r = inline ('x^3 + 3*x^2 - 4')
f =
        Inline function:
fx(x) = x^3 + 3*x^2 - 4
```

The result can convert to a string using the *char* function as shown below:

```
>> char(f)
ans =
x^3 + 3*x^2 - 4
```

EXAMPLE 8.13 In this example, we create an inline function to represent the formula $f = 7 \cos 2x^2 + 5 \sin 2x^2$. The resulting inline function evaluated with the argnames (argument names) and formula functions.

```
f =
        Inline function:
f(x) = 7*cos(2*x.^2)+5*sin(2*x.^2)
```

The result can convert to a string using the *argnames* function as follows:

```
>> argnames(f)
ans =
    'x'
```

The result can be converted to a string using the *formula* function as follows:

```
>> formula(f)
ans =
7*cos(2*x.^2)+5*sin(2*x.^2)
```

EXAMPLE 8.14   In this example, we create an inline function to represent the formula $f = 7 \cos 2x^2 + 5 \sin 2x^2$.

```
function f = inline (7*cos(2*x.^2)+5*sin(2*x.^2), 'x', 'y')
end
```

Using the value of f at $x = 2$ and $y = 4$, the following result is displayed:

```
ans =
    3.9283
```

8.6   FEW INBUILT FUNCTIONS OF MATLAB RELATING TO STRINGS

MATLAB provides numerous inbuilt functions, few relating to strings are discussed in Table 8.1.

TABLE 8.1   Few inbuilt functions relating strings

MATLAB function	*Use*
General	
char	Create character array (string)
strings	Help for strings
cellstr	Create cell array of strings from character array
blanks	String of blanks
deblank	Remove trailing blanks
String tests	
iscellstr	TRUE for cell array of strings
ischar	TRUE for character array (string)
isspace	TRUE for white space characters
isstrprop	Check if string elements are of a specified category
String operations	
regexp	Match regular expression
regexpi	Match regular expression, ignoring case
regexprep	Replace string using regular expression
strcat	Concatenate strings
strcmp	Compare strings
strncmp	Compare first N characters of strings
strcmpi	Compare strings Ignoring case
strncmpi	Compare first N characters of strings ignoring case
strfind	Find one String with in another
strjust	Justify character array
strrep	Replace string with another
strtok	Find to ken in string
strtrim	Remove insignificant white space
upper	Convert string to uppercase
lower	Convert string to lowercase

8.7   MATLAB ERROR AND CORRECTION

MATLAB has error handling capabilities. There are different kinds of error checking and execution methods. There are basically two types of errors:

- Syntax errors
- Runtime errors

Syntax errors

They are caused by grammatical mistakes observed in the statements due to use or non-use of a comma, semicolon, bracket or parenthesis. It may be due to misspelled function name or wrong use of array indices and so on. The syntax error will appear during compilation describing the error in the program file. Syntax errors are easy to correct as they will notify by MATLAB compiler.

Runtime errors

They are caused due to use of wrong logic, wrong variable or incorrect variable for computation by the programmer. This will result in erroneous program output and runtime error become apparent. The runtime errors are more difficult to track as MATLAB does not report the type of error or its location. It is basically the programmers' capability to identify the error and resolve it.

Error identifier

In the MATLAB, there are different techniques that are useful in isolating the erroneous statement caused during runtime error. Following are some techniques used to isolate the errors:

Keyboard statement: Keyboard statement stops the execution of the program until the statement is given appropriate command.

Semicolon usage: Semicolon at the end of statement prevents the result of the statement to execute. So the programmer can choose semicolon at selected points in the program.

Script execution function: Script function is used with the function declaration for execution of statement. The script file input and output is fixed can be examined after execution.

8.8   MATLAB DEBUGGER

MATLAB has the facility to verify the programming errors in *.m files*. The debugger is used to identify the MATLAB programming error while executing the program in *.m files*. This will allow the user to view the contents of error and examine it for correction. The debugger executes the M-file statements line by line till the point without any routine errors. Debugger can also be used through its graphical user interface as well as commands.

8.8.1   MATLAB Setting Breakpoint

In the MATLAB, there is a method of executing the program by stopping the program for a while using breakpoints. This stops a program for a specific points and lines that allow the user to view or change the variables in the workspace functions. Thereafter, the execution can be resumed from the point of the program stops until the next breakpoint.

The breakpoint will not set if there are any syntax errors in the program. A breakpoint can be set at any executable statement if it is valid otherwise; it is set for next executable statement. Methods of breakpoint are as follows:

- Select the breakpoint (set or clear) icon form the toolbar.
- The cursor is moved the statement where the breakpoint is to be set. Click the icon of 'set or clear' breakpoint.
- A red circle sign ![breakpoint icon] will appear on left side of statement line where the breakpoint is desired.

The Figure 8.12 shows the Editor window showing the breakpoint set in the program.

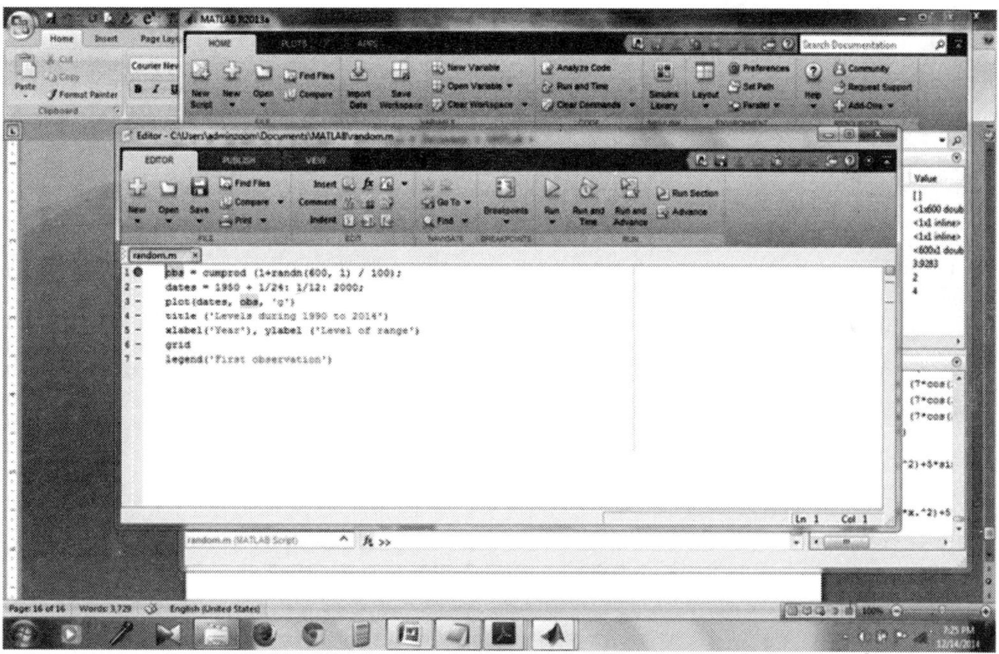

FIGURE 8.12   Illustration of breakpoints in m-file.

8.8.2   MATLAB Breakpoint Examine

The program written in editor workspace consists of different values of variables that need to be examined. The breakpoints are capable of verifying the execution of the program at the desired level. This will show the status of the variables at each point in the program. Methods of breakpoint examination are as follows:

- The breakpoint is a red circle point that is set for the statement, it shows green arrow appearing on left when the run button is clicked.
- The next statement can be verified when step icon is clicked line by line. This will show the result for each click.

- For each click the MATLAB function will examine the variable before returning to the calling function.

Figure 8.13 shows the Examination of breakpoint with green arrow set to the left of text.

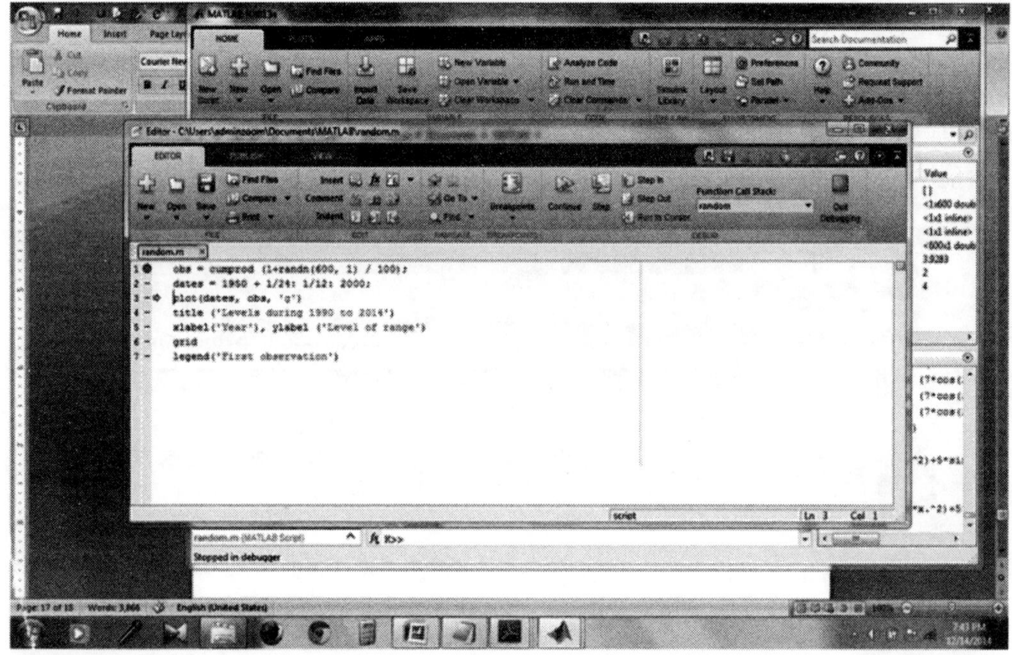

FIGURE 8.13   Examination of breakpoints in m-file.

MATLAB provides the facility to the user to examine the statement correctly up to the breakpoint. This will isolate the correct code and run time error in the m-file.

SUMMARY

In this chapter, we have discussed the MATLAB m-file. MATLAB editor has been discussed the illustration of menu bar and toolbar. Different types of function file discussed were the MATLAB script and editor. The types of function such as subfunction, nested function and inline function were also described in the chapters. The display of errors and also types of error such as syntax and runtime error were discussed. Method to isolate the error was described, i.e., using semicolon, keyboard and script function was explained. The MATLAB debugger and its features on breakpoints were also discussed.

REVIEW QUESTIONS

1. State various filters methods to open MATLAB Editor.
2. Write full form of IDE.
3. What do you understand by function files in MATLAB?
4. State various parts of function files.
5. Write syntax for function file and explain various parts of it with an example.
6. How do you insert comments in a function file?
7. What do you understand by subfunction, line function and nested function?
8. Mention types of error in MATLAB.
9. Identify the function of the symbol used to insert breakpoint in the editor window.
10. State the use of inline function.

PRACTICE EXERCISE

1. Write a MATLAB program to find sum, product, quotient and difference of two numbers.
2. Convert the word MATLAB to lowercase using MATLAB inbuilt function.
3. Print the following output using horzcat function "hello!!!Good luck to learn MATLAB".
4. Execute the following code using MATLAB editor and observe the output:

```
for k=1:4
name=['CHANDRAGUPTA' int2str(k) '.THE KING']
end
```

5. Write a function to find simple interest.

   [*Hint:* use Simple Interest=(Principle*Time*Rate)/100]
6. Write and save a programme with name firstsum.m in MATLAB editor to add two numbers and run it by typing firstsum at command prompt.
7. Write and save a programme with name firstmul.m in MATLAB editor to multiply two numbers and run it by using save and run icon in the script file.
8. State the command used to edit file named firstsum.
9. Use inline function to represent the formula $f = \sin x^2 + \cos x^2$.
10. Write code using nested functions to display your family tree of four generations.

CHAPTER **9**

MATLAB in Filter Application

LEARNING OBJECTIVES

This chapters focuses on the understanding of filter functions using MATLAB. By the end of this chapter, we will learn:

- The concept of different types of filters.
- IIR low pass, high pass, band pass and band stop filters.
- FIR low pass, high pass, band pass and band stop filters.
- Design of Butterworth, Chebyshev filters using MATLAB.
- To remove a high frequency signal from a desired signal using MATLAB.

INTRODUCTION

A filter is one which rejects unwanted frequencies from the input signal and allows the desired frequencies. The range of frequencies of the signal that are passed through the filter is called *passband* frequencies and those that are blocked are called *stopband* frequencies. The filters are of different types: Low pass filter, High pass filter, Band pass filter and Band reject filter.

Digital filtering is a widely used technique that is common in many fields of science and engineering. Digital filters also remove unwanted signals and noise from a received signal. There are many different kinds of digital filters, such as low pass, high pass, band pass and band stop filters.

Basically, a digital filter is a linear time-invariant discrete time system. Also, there are two different type. They are Finite Impulse Response (FIR) and Infinite Impulse Response (IIR). The FIR filters are of non-recursive type, whereby the present output sample depends on the present input samples and previous input samples, whereas IIR filters are of recursive type, whereby the present output sample depends on the present input, past input samples and output samples.

282

9.1 FIR FILTER DESIGN

The FIR filters are of non-recursive type, whereby the present output sample depends on the present input samples and previous or past input samples. We are discussing various subtypes of filter in the following subsections.

9.1.1 FIR Low Pass Filter MATLAB Code

Code for the FIR Low Pass Filter is as given in the following example.

EXAMPLE 9.1

```
fp=900;
fs=920;
rp=0.02;
rs=0.03;
f=5000;
num=-20*log10(sqrt(rp*rs))-13;
dem=14.6*(fs-fp)/f;
n=ceil(num/dem);
n=abs(n);
wp=2*fp/f;
ws=2*fs/f;
wn=(ws+wp)/2;

if (rem(n,2)==0)
    m=n+1;
else
    m=n;
    n=n+1;
end
  w=hann(m);
b=fir1(n,wn,'low',w);
freqz(b,1,n);
title('Magnitude and Phase response');
```

In the code above, following steps are taken to design the FIR low pass filter:

Step 1 Initialising the values of passband and stopband frequencies and ripple values.

Step 2 Initialising sampling frequency 'f'.

Step 3 Calculating filter order 'n' as a fraction 'num'(numerator) divided by 'dem' (denominator) .

Step 4 Normalisation and calculation of cutoff value 'wn'.

Step 5 Checking the order of filter, it will be an odd number and order of the filter is one less than that of window.

Step 6 Calculation of hanning window sequence using the function 'hann'.

Step 7 Finding fir filter coefficients using function 'fir1'.

Step 8 Frequency response is plotted using MATLAB function 'freqz'.

By executing the code, the signal is plotted as shown in Figure 9.1.

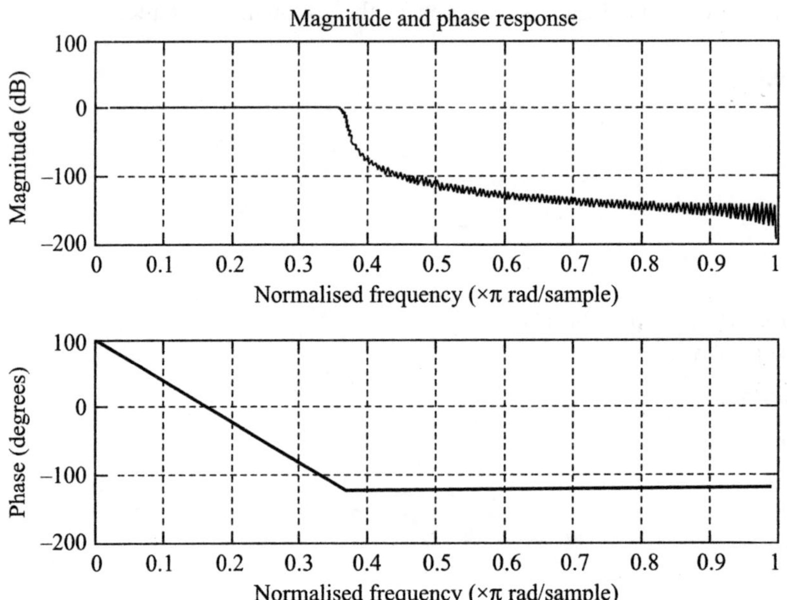

FIGURE 9.1 Magnitude and phase response: FIR low pass filter.

9.1.2 FIR High Pass Filter MATLAB Code

Code for the FIR High Pass Filter is as given in the following example.

EXAMPLE 9.2

```
fp=900;
fs=920;
rp=0.02;
rs=0.03;
f=5000;
num=-20*log10(sqrt(rp*rs))-13;
dem=14.6*(fs-fp)/f;
n=ceil(num/dem);
```

```
n=abs(n);
wp=2*fp/f;
ws=2*fs/f;
wn=(ws+wp)/2;

if (rem(n,2)==0)
     m=n+1;
else
     m=n;
     n=n+1;
end

w=hann(m);
b=fir1(n,wn,'high',w);
freqz(b,1,n);
title('Magnitude and Phase response');
```

We observe the following in the code above, use to design FIR high pass filter:

- Steps are similarly proceeded as for low pass filter in Example 9.1.
- We need to declare 'high' for a high pass filter with cutoff frequency 'wn' while using 'fir1' function in this case.

By executing the code, the signal is plotted as shown in Figure 9.2.

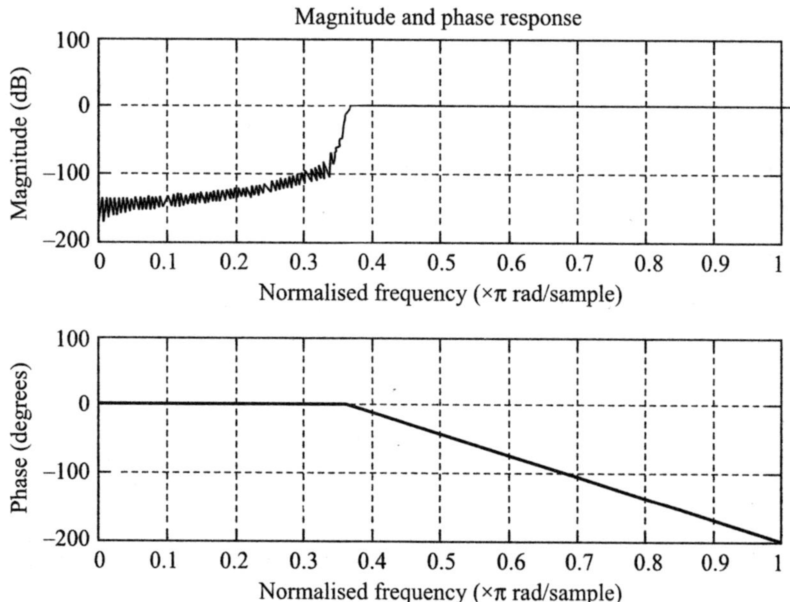

FIGURE 9.2   Magnitude and phase response: FIR high pass filter.

9.1.3   FIR Band Pass Filter MATLAB Code

Code for the FIR Band Pass Filter is as given in the following example:

EXAMPLE 9.3

```
fp=900;
fs=920;
rp=0.02;
rs=0.03;
f=5000;
num=-20*log10(sqrt(rp*rs))-13;
dem=14.6*(fs-fp)/f;
n=ceil(num/dem);
n=abs(n);
wp=2*fp/f;
ws=2*fs/f;
if (rem(n,2)==0)
    m=n+1;
else
    m=n;
    n=n+1;
end

w=hann(m);
wc=[wp,ws];
b=fir1(n,wc,w);
freqz(b,1,n);
title('Magnitude and Phase response');
```

We observe the following in the above code, use to design the FIR band pass filter:

- Band pass filter is designed with fp and fs as the passband frequencies.
- Cutoff frequencies are wp and ws (normalised values).

By executing the code, the signal is plotted as shown in Figure 9.3 and Figure 9.4 at two different frequencies.

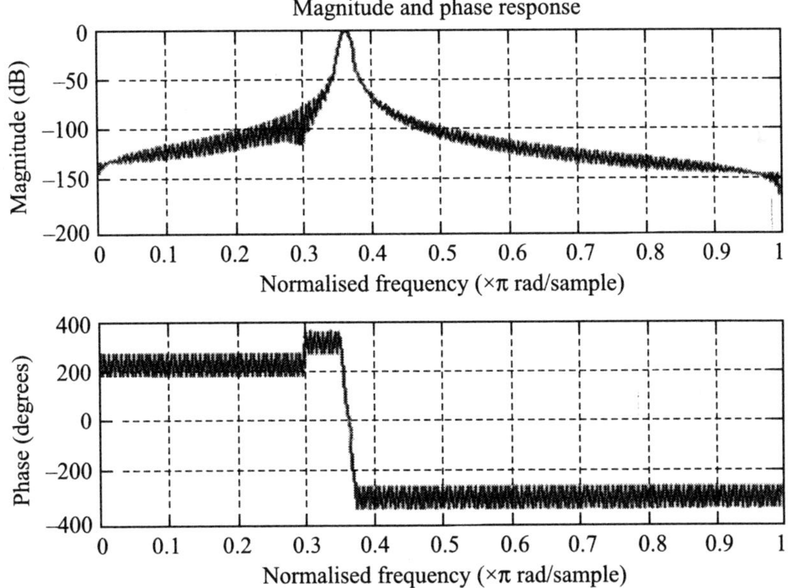

FIGURE 9.3   Magnitude and phase response: FIR band pass filter with fp=900, fs=920.

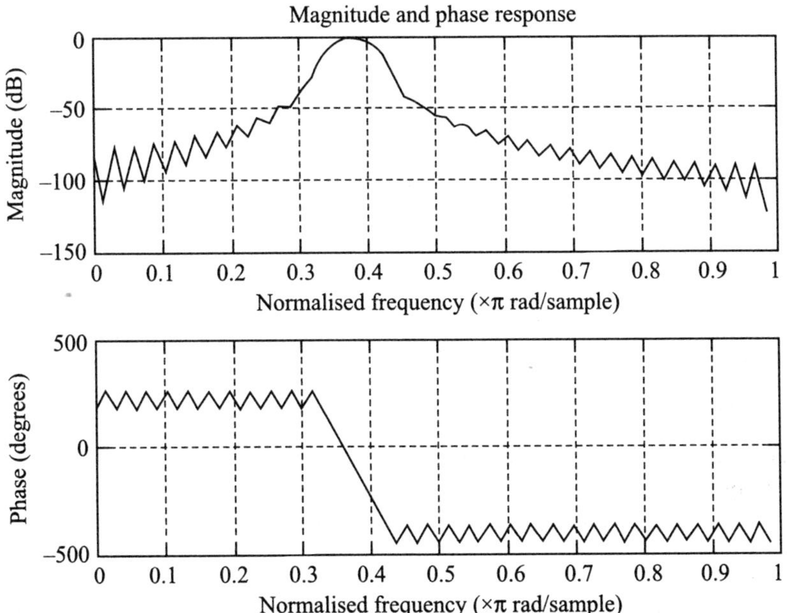

FIGURE 9.4   Magnitude and phase response: FIR band pass filter with fp=900, fs=1000.

9.1.4 FIR Band Stop Filter MATLAB Code

Code for the FIR Band Stop Filter is as given in the following example:

EXAMPLE 9.4

```
fp=900;
fs=920;
rp=0.02;
rs=0.03;
f=5000;
num=-20*log10(sqrt(rp*rs))-13;
dem=14.6*(fs-fp)/f;
n=ceil(num/dem);
n=abs(n);
wp=2*fp/f;
ws=2*fs/f;
if (rem(n,2)==0)
    m=n+1;
else
    m=n;
    n=n+1;
end

w=hann(m);
wc=[wp,ws];
b=fir1(n,wc,'stop');
freqz(b,1,n);
title('Magnitude and Phase response');
```

We observe the following in the above code, use to design the FIR Band Stop filter:

- Band stop filter is designed with fp and fs as the stopband frequencies.
- Cutoff frequencies are wp and ws (normalised values).
- Declare 'stop' for a band stop filter with cutoff frequencies [wpws] while using 'fir1' function.

By executing the code, the signal is plotted as shown in Figure 9.5 and Figure 9.6 at two different frequencies.

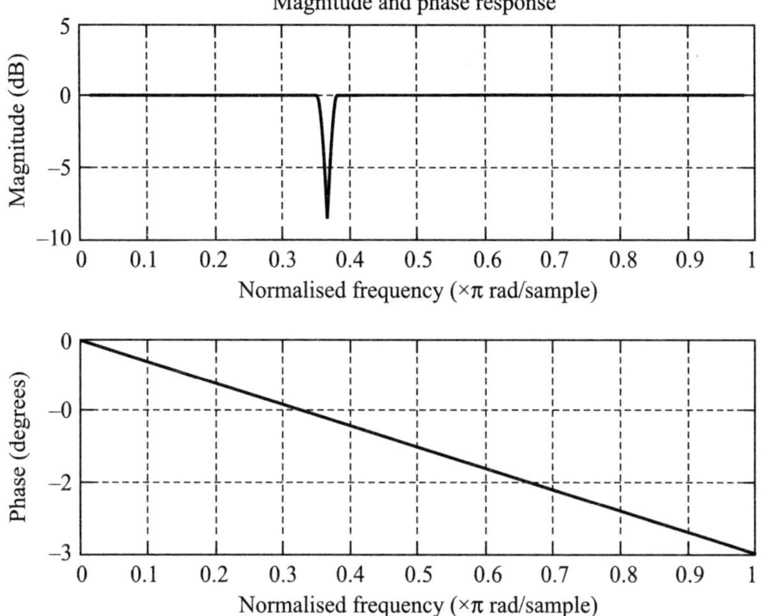

FIGURE 9.5   Magnitude and phase response: FIR band stop filter with fp=900, fs=920.

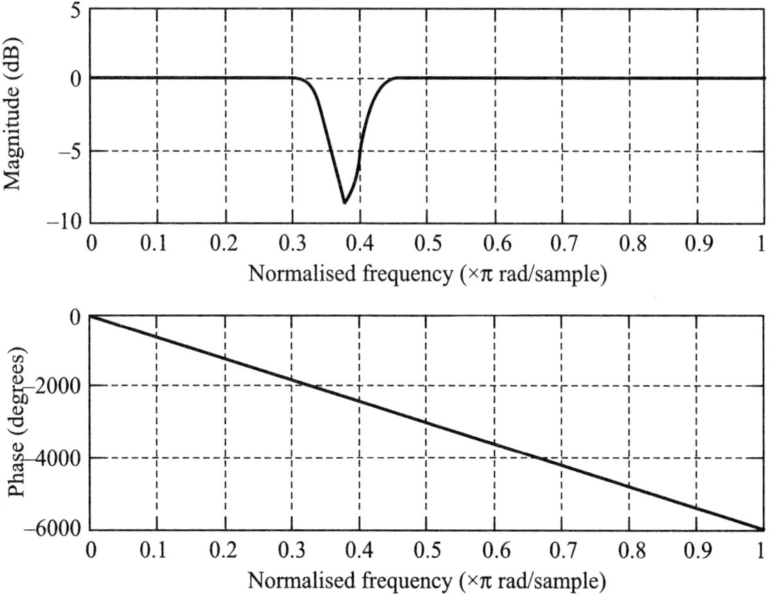

FIGURE 9.6   Magnitude and phase response: FIR band stop filter with fp=900, fs=1000.

Advantages of FIR filters are as follows:

- They can have linear phase exactly.
- They are always stable.
- Their design methods are generally linear.
- Their hardware realisation is efficient.
- Their startup transients have finite duration.

Only disadvantage of FIR filters is that, they often require a much higher filter order than IIR filters to achieve a given level of performance. Correspondingly, the delay of these filters is often much greater than for an equal performance IIR filter.

9.2   IIR FILTERS

IIR filters are digital filters with infinite impulse response. Unlike FIR filters, they have the feedback (a recursive part of a filter) are therefore known as *recursive digital filters*. The most commonly used design method to design IIR filter uses reference analog prototype filter. It is the best method to use when designing standard filters such as low pass, high pass, band pass and band stop filters. Butterworth, Chebyshev (Chebyshev I) and inverse Chebyshev filters (Chebyshev II) are commonly used for filter design.

Chebyshev filters are analog or digital filters having a steeper roll off and more passband ripple (type I) or stopband ripple (type II) than Butterworth filters. Chebyshev filters have the property that they minimise the error between the idealised and the actual filter characteristic over the range of the filter, but with ripples in the passband.

There are two basic methods used for IIR filter design which are as follows:

- Impulse invariance method
- Bilinear transformation method

In the impulse invariance method, the impulse response of analog filter is sampled. However, aliasing problem is predominant in the frequency domain.

In contrast, Bilinear Transformation (BLT) does overcome the aliasing limitations.

9.2.1   IIR Butterworth Filter

The Butterworth filter is a type of signal processing filter designed to have as flat a frequency response as possible in the passband. It is also referred to as a maximally flat magnitude filter.

Some special functions is used for the design of IIR Butterworth Type 1 filter are listed below:

Use of 'buttord' function

'buttord' is used to define Buttertworth filer order and cutoff frequency. 'buttord' calculates the minimum order of a digital or analog Butterworth filter also required to meet a set of filter design specifications.

[n,wn] = buttord(wp,ws,rp,rs) returns the lowest order, *n*, of the digital Butterworth filter with no more than rp dB of passband ripple and at least rs dB of attenuation in the stopband. The scalar (or vector) of corresponding cutoff frequency, wn, is also returned. Use the output arguments n and wn in butter.

Use of 'butter' function

'butter' function is used for Butterworth filter design. [b,a] = butter(n,Wn,ftype) designs is a low pass, high pass, band pass, or band stop Butterworth filter, depending on the value of f-type and the number of elements of wn.

Code for IIR Butterworth Low Pass Filter is as given in the following example:

EXAMPLE 9.5

```
fp=900;
fs=1500;
rp=4;
rs=50;
f=5000;

wp=2*fp/f;
ws=2*fs/f;

[n,wn] = buttord(wp,ws,rp,rs)
[b,a] = butter(n,wn,'low');

freqz(b,a,n);
title('Magnitude and Phase response');
```

We observe the following in the above code, use to design the IIR Butterworth low pass filter:

- Initialising the passband and stopband edge frequencies
- Initialising passband and stopband ripple
- Initialise the sampling frequency
- Normalisation of edge frequencies
- Calculating order and frequency scaling factor
- Finding filter coefficients using 'butter()'
- Plotting magnitude and phase responses

By executing the code, the signal is plotted as shown in Figure 9.7.

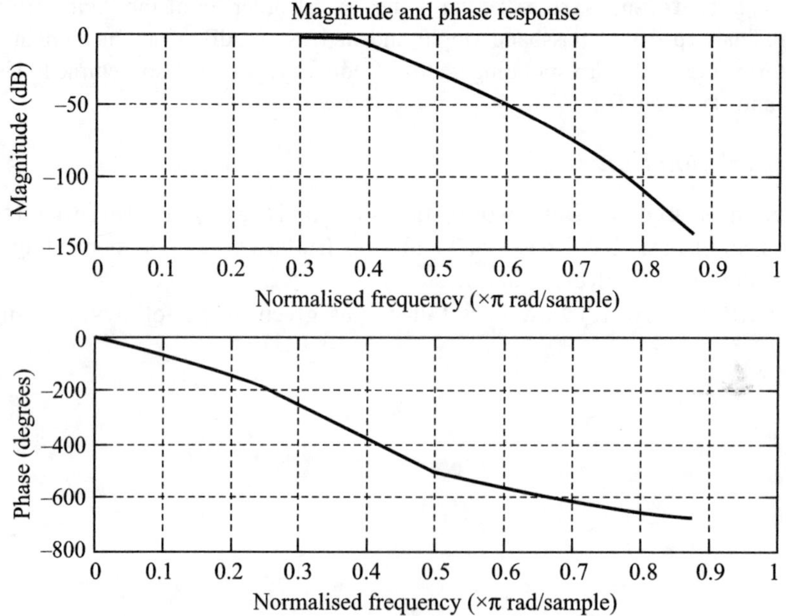

FIGURE 9.7   Magnitude and phase response: IIR Butterworth low pass filter.

9.2.2   IIR Butterworth High Pass Filter

Code for IIR Butterworth High Pass Filter is as given in the following example:

EXAMPLE 9.6

```
fp=900;
fs=1500;
rp=4;
rs=50;
f=5000;

wp=2*fp/f;
ws=2*fs/f;

[n,wn] = buttord(wp,ws,rp,rs)
[b,a] = butter(n,wn,'high');

freqz(b,a,n);
title('Magnitude and Phase response');
```

We observe the following in the above code, use to design the IIR Butterworth high pass filter:

- Initialisation steps are same as for low pass filter
- Filter coefficients are found using MATLAB function by declaring ftype as 'high'.

By executing the code, the signal is plotted as shown in Figure 9.8.

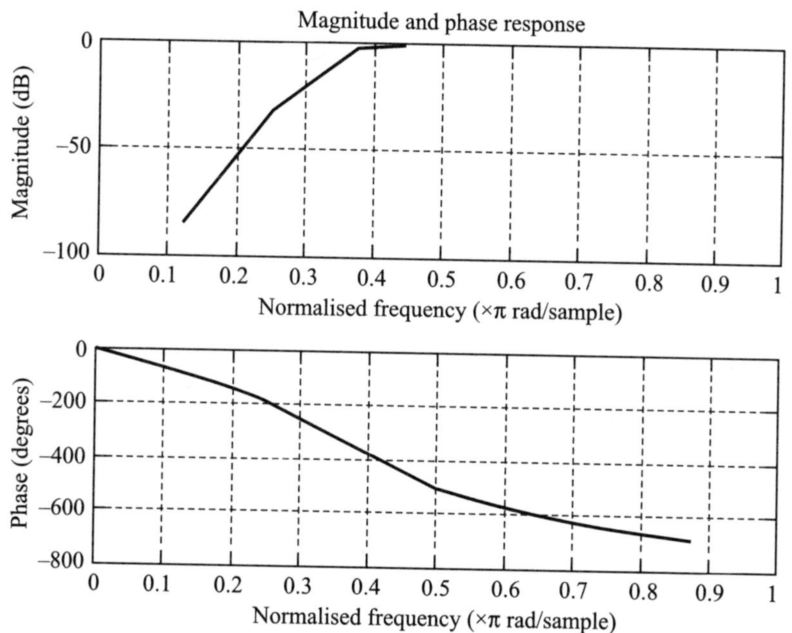

FIGURE 9.8 Magnitude and phase response: IIR Butterworth high pass filter.

9.2.3 IIR Butterworth Band Pass Filter

Code for IIR Butterworth Band Pass Filter is as given in the following example:

EXAMPLE 9.7

```
fp=[1000 1500];
fs=[800 1800]
rp=4;
rs=50;
f=5000;

wp=2*[fp]/f;
ws=2*[fs]/f;
```

```
[n,wn] = buttord(wp,ws,rp,rs)
[b,a] = butter(n,wn,'bandpass');


freqz(b,a,n);
title('Magnitude and Phase response');
```

We observe the following in the above code, use to design IIR Butterworth Band pass filter:

- Initialising a set of edge frequencies for the selected band
- Following steps for finding order and frequency scaling factor
- Finding filter coefficients by declaring ftype as 'bandpass'

By executing the code, the signal is plotted as shown in Figure 9.9.

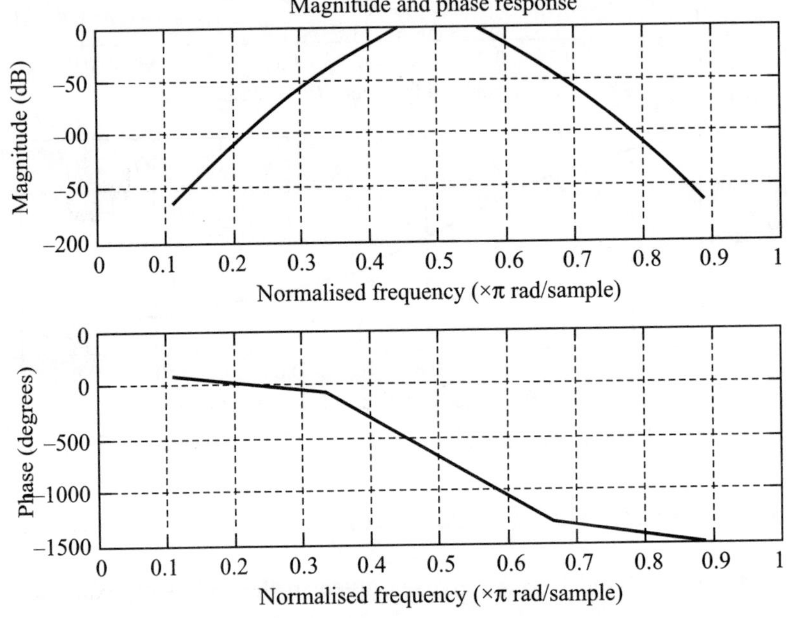

FIGURE 9.9   Magnitude and phase response: IIR Butterworth band pass filter.

9.2.4 IIR Butterworth Band Stop Filter

Code for IIR Butterworth Band Stop Filter is as given in the following example:

EXAMPLE 9.8

```
fp=[1000 1500];
fs=[800 1800];
rp=4;
```

```
rs=50;
f=5000;

wp=2*[fp]/f;
ws=2*[fs]/f;

[n,wn] = buttord(wp,ws,rp,rs)
[b,a] = butter(n,wn,'stop');

freqz(b,a,n);
title('Magnitude and Phase response');
```

We observe the following in the above code, use to design the IIR Butterworth Band stop filter:

- Initialisation steps are similar to band pass design
- Finding filter coefficients using MATLAB function by declaring ftype as 'stop'

By executing the code, the signal is plotted as shown in Figure 9.10.

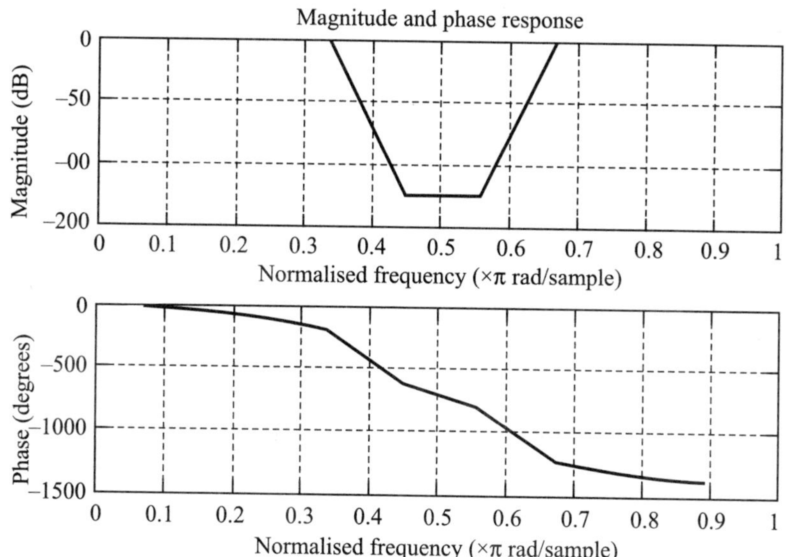

FIGURE 9.10   Magnitude and phase response: IIR Butterworth band stop filter.

9.2.5   IIR Chebyshev Type 1 Filter

In comparison to Butterworth filters, Chebyshev filters have a supplemental parameter: a ripple in amplitude. This ripple, which could be considered as non ideal, has the tremendous advantage to allow a steeper roll off between passband and stopband. Chebyshev Type I filters show a ripple in the passband.

Some special functions used for the design of IIR Chebyshev Type 1 Filter are listed below:

Use of 'cheb1ord' function

'cheb1ord' calculates the minimum order of a digital or analog Chebyshev Type I filter required to meet a set of filter design specifications. The syntax for it is:

```
[n,wp] = cheb1ord(wp,ws,rp,rs)
```

[n,wp] = cheb1ord(wp,ws,rp,rs) returns the lowest order *n* of the Chebyshev Type I filter that loses no more than rp dB in the passband and has at least rs dB of attenuation in the stopband. The scalar (or vector) of corresponding cutoff frequency wp, is also returned. Use the output arguments n and wp with the cheby1 function.

Use of 'cheby1' function

[b,a] = cheby1(n,rp,wp) returns the transfer function coefficients of an nth order lowpass digital Chebyshev Type I filter with normalised passband edge frequency wp and rp decibels of peak-to-peak passband ripple.

EXAMPLE 9.9   In this example, we will learn code for IIR Chebyshev Type 1 Low Pass Filter.

```
fp=900;
fs=920;
rp=4;
rs=50;
f=5000;

wp=2*[fp]/f;
ws=2*[fs]/f;

[n,wn] = cheb1ord(wp,ws,rp,rs)
[b,a] = cheby1(n,rp,wn,'low');

freqz(b,a,n);
title('Magnitude and Phase response');
```

By executing the code, the signal is plotted as shown in Figure 9.11.

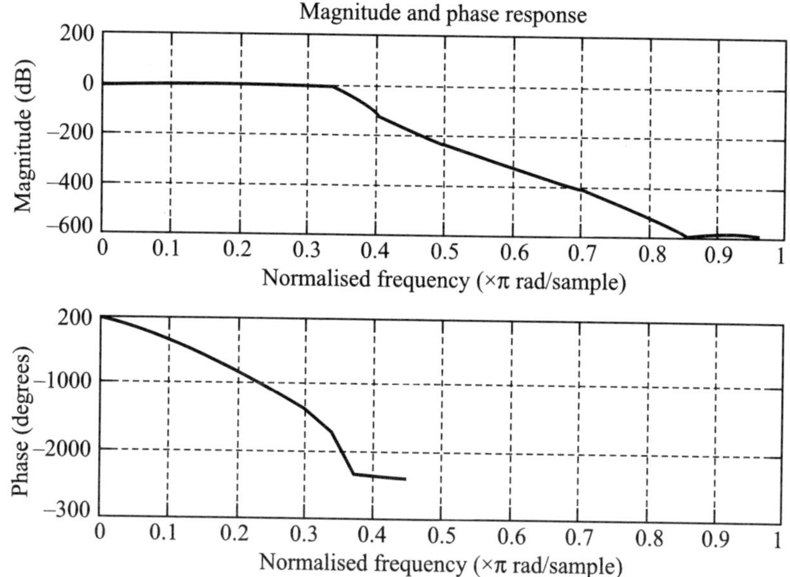

FIGURE 9.11   Magnitude and phase response: IIR low pass Chebyshev Type 1 filter.

9.2.6   IIR Chebyshev Type 1 High Pass Filter

Code for IIR Chebyshev Type 1 High Pass Filter is as given in the following example:

EXAMPLE 9.10

```
fp=1000;
fs=980;
rp=4;
rs=50;
f=5000;

wp=2*[fp]/f;
ws=2*[fs]/f;

[n,wn] = cheb1ord(wp,ws,rp,rs)
[b,a] = cheby1(n,rp,wn,'high');

freqz(b,a,n);
title('Magnitude and Phase response');
```

By executing the code, the signal is plotted as shown in Figure 9.12.

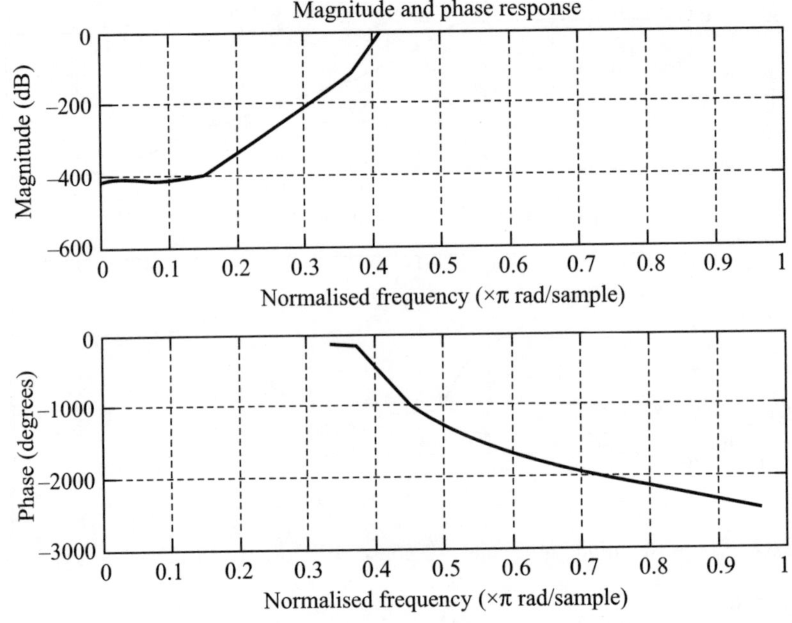

FIGURE 9.12   Magnitude and phase response: IIR high pass Chebyshev Type 1 filter.

9.2.7   IIR Chebyshev Type 1 Band Pass Filter

Code for IIR Chebyshev Type 1 Band Pass Filter is as given in the following example:

EXAMPLE 9.11

```
fp=[1000 1500];
fs=[800 1800]
rp=4;
rs=50;
f=5000;

wp=2*[fp]/f;
ws=2*[fs]/f;

[n,wn] = cheb1ord(wp,ws,rp,rs)
[b,a] = cheby1(n,rp,wn,'bandpass');

freqz(b,a,n);
title('Magnitude and Phase response');
```

By executing the code, the signal is plotted as shown in Figure 9.13.

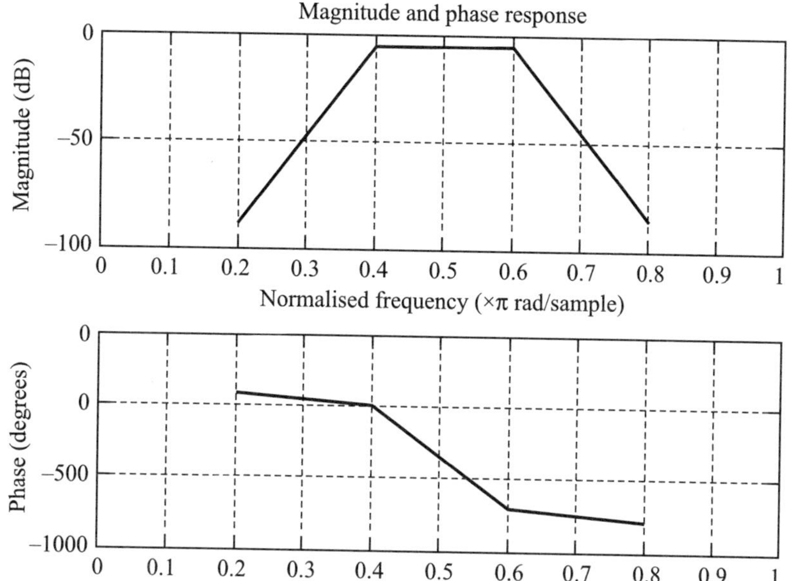

FIGURE 9.13　Magnitude and phase response: IIR band pass Chebyshev Type 1 filter.

9.2.8　IIR Chebyshev Type 1 Band Stop Filter

Code for IIR Chebyshev Type 1 Band Stop Filter is as given in the following example:

EXAMPLE 9.12

```
fp=[1000 1500];
fs=[900 1800]
rp=4;
rs=50;
f=5000;

wp=2*[fp]/f;
ws=2*[fs]/f;

[n,wn] = cheb1ord(wp,ws,rp,rs)
[b,a] = cheby1(n,rp,wn,'stop');

freqz(b,a,n);
title('Magnitude and Phase response');
```

By executing the code, the signal is plotted as shown in Figure 9.14.

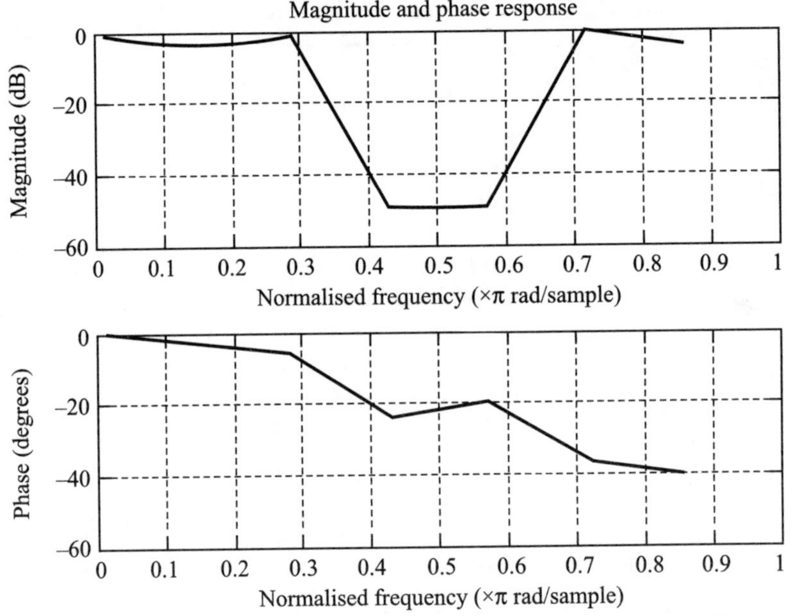

FIGURE 9.14 Magnitude and phase response: IIR band stop Chebyshev Type 1 filter.

9.2.9 IIR Chebyshev Type 2 Filter

Some special functions used for the design of IIR Chebyshev Type 1 filter are listed below:

Use of 'cheb2ord' function

'cheb2ord' is used to define Chebyshev Type II filter order. 'cheb2ord' calculates the minimum order of a digital or analog Chebyshev Type II filter required to meet a set of filter design specifications.

    `[n,ws]` = `cheb2ord(wp,ws,rp,rs)` returns the lowest order n of the Chebyshev Type II filter that loses no more than rp dB in the passband and has at least rs dB of attenuation in the stopband. The scalar (or vector) of corresponding cutoff frequency ws, is also returned. Use the output arguments n and ws in cheby2.

Use of 'cheby2' function

'cheby2' is used for Chebyshev Type II filter design. `[b,a]` = `cheby2(n,rs,ws,ftype)` designs a lowpass, highpass, bandpass, or bandstop Chebyshev Type II filter, depending on the value of *ftype* and the number of elements of ws. The resulting bandpass and bandstop designs are of order $2n$.

Code for IIR Chebyshev Type 2 Low Pass Filter is as given in the following example:

EXAMPLE 9.13

```
fp=800;
fs=1100;
rp=4;
rs=50;
f=5000;

wp=2*[fp]/f;
ws=2*[fs]/f;

[n,wn] = cheb2ord(wp,ws,rp,rs)
[b,a] = cheby2(n,rp,wn,'low');

freqz(b,a,n);
title('Magnitude and Phase response');
```

By executing the code, the signal is plotted as shown in Figure 9.15.

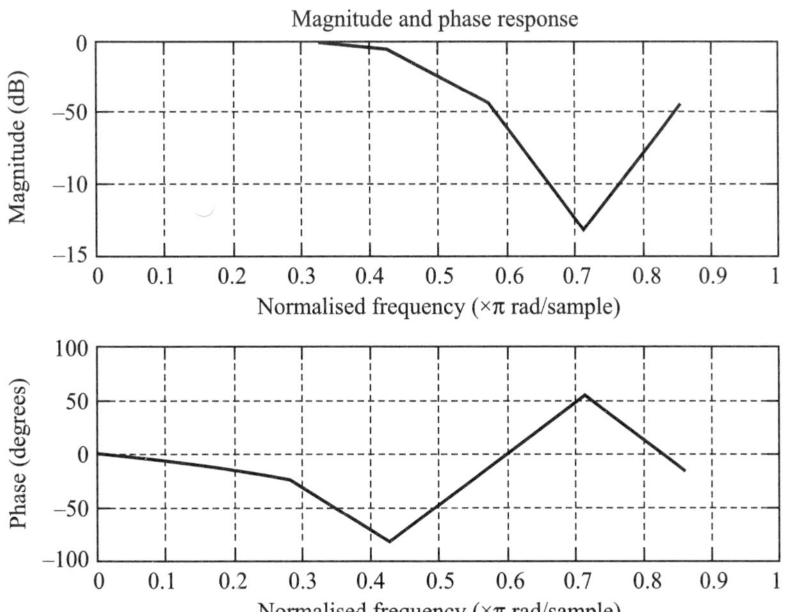

Figure 9.15 Magnitude and phase response: IIR Chebyshev Type 2 low pass filter.

9.2.10   IIR Chebyshev Type 2 High Pass Filter

Code for IIR Chebyshev Type 2 High Pass Filter is as given in the following example.

EXAMPLE 9.14

```
fp=800;
fs=1100;
rp=4;
rs=50;
f=5000;
wp=2*[fp]/f;
ws=2*[fs]/f;

[n,wn] = cheb2ord(wp,ws,rp,rs)
[b,a] = cheby2(n,rp,wn,'high');

freqz(b,a,n);
title('Magnitude and Phase response');
```

By executing the code, the signal is plotted as shown in Figure 9.16.

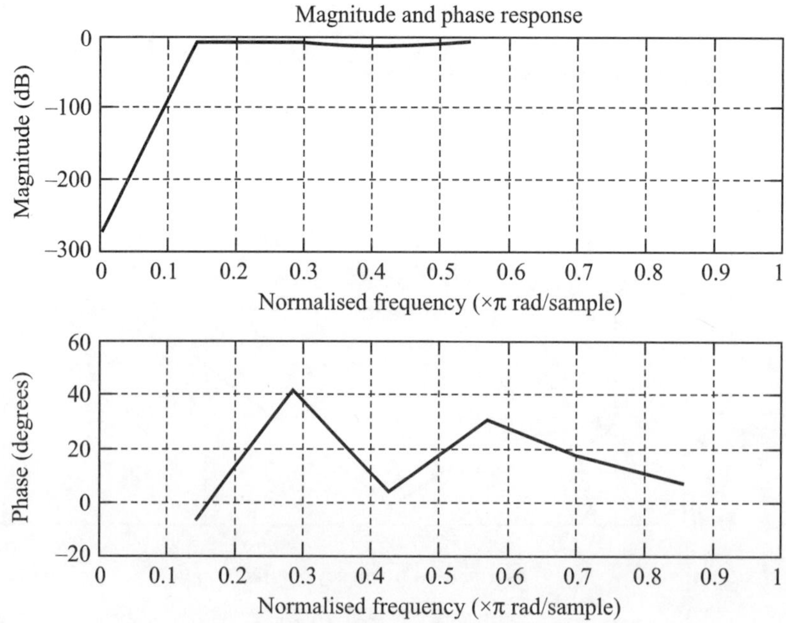

FIGURE 9.16   Magnitude and phase response: IIR Chebyshev Type 2 high pass filter.

9.2.11   IIR Chebyshev Type 2 Band Pass Filter

Code for IIR Chebyshev Type 2 Band Pass Filter is as given in the following example:

EXAMPLE 9.15

```
fp=[1000 1500];
fs=[500 1800]
rp=4;
rs=50;
f=5000;
wp=2*[fp]/f;
ws=2*[fs]/f;

[n,wn] = cheb2ord(wp,ws,rp,rs)
[b,a] = cheby2(n,rp,wn,'bandpass');

freqz(b,a,n);
title('Magnitude and Phase response');
```

By executing the code, the signal is plotted as shown in Figure 9.17.

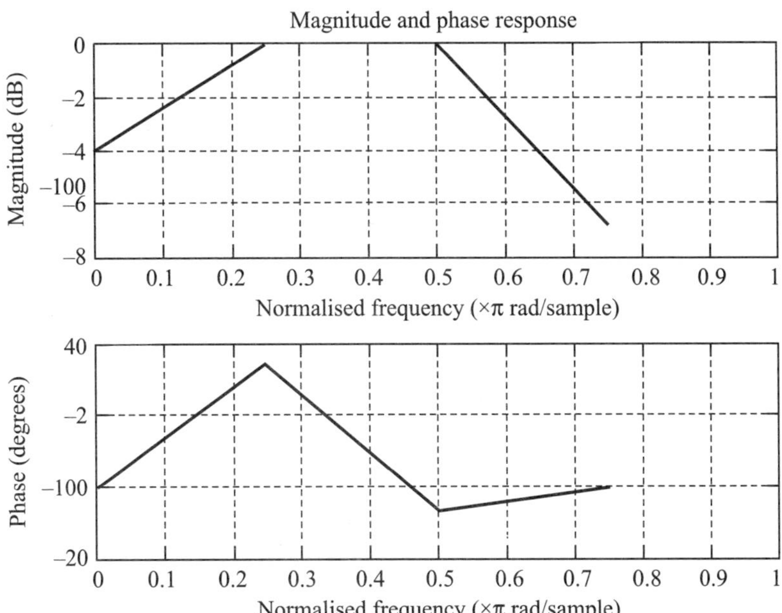

FIGURE 9.17   Magnitude and phase response: IIR Chebyshev Type 2 band pass filter.

9.2.12   IIR Chebyshev Type 2 Band Stop Filter

Code for IIR Chebyshev Type 2 Band Stop Filter is as given in the following example:

EXAMPLE 9.16

```
fp=[1000 1500];
fs=[800 1800]
rp=4;
rs=50;
f=5000;

wp=2*[fp]/f;
ws=2*[fs]/f;

[n,wn] = cheb2ord(wp,ws,rp,rs)
[b,a] = cheby2(n,rp,wn,'stop');

freqz(b,a,n);
title('Magnitude and Phase response');
```

By executing the code, the signal is plotted as shown in Figure 9.18.

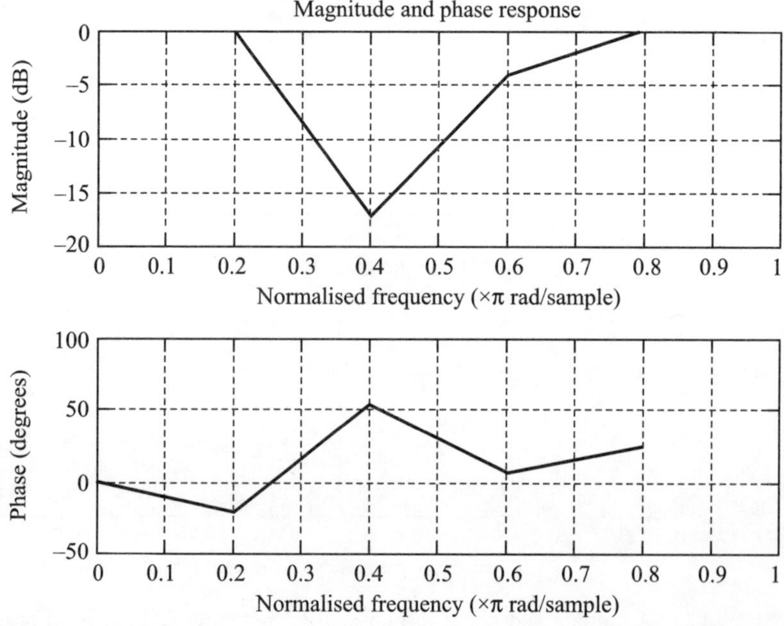

FIGURE 9.18   Magnitude and phase response: IIR Chebyshev Type 2 band stop filter.

9.3 SOME OTHER FILTER

Filtering is a broad subject. Following some related filters that you can understand from example.

9.3.1 The Moving Average Filter

The moving average is the most commonly used DSP filter as a digital filter. Inspite of its simplicity, the moving average filter reduce random noise while retaining a sharp step response. However, the moving average is the worst filter for frequency domain encoded signals, with little ability to separate one band of frequencies from another. Relatives of the moving average filter include the Gaussian, Blackman, and multiple pass moving average which have slightly better performance in the frequency domain, at the expense of increased computation time. The moving average formula is given as:

$$y[n] = \frac{1}{h} \sum_{p=0}^{h-1} x[n-p]$$

EXAMPLE 9.17

```
>> x=sin(2*pi*f*t);      % original signal
>> r=sqrt(v)*randn(1,length(t));       % noise
>> Xw=x+r;              % signal plus noise (filter input)
>> % I have chosen h=3
>> for n=3:length(Xw),
y(n)=sum(Xw(n-2:n))/3;      % y[n] is the filtered signal
end
>> plot(y);
>> hold;
Current plot held
>> plot(x,'r');      % plot the
original signal over top the filtered
signal to see the difference
```

By executing the code, the signal is plotted as shown in Figure 9.19.

The moving average filter is simple and effective. The only disadvantage of this filter is that it has a problem of lag associated with it.

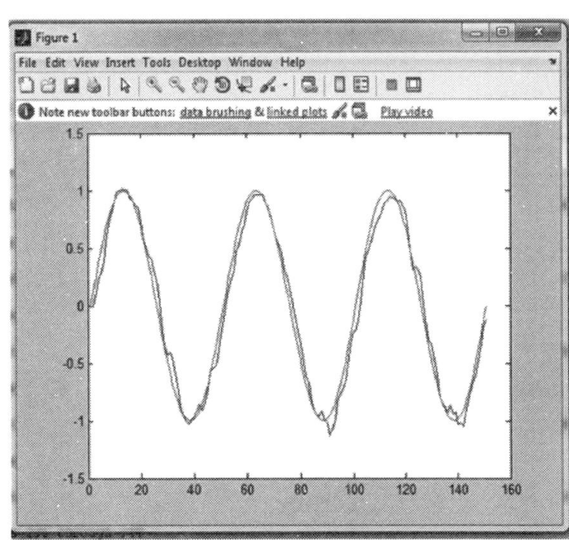

FIGURE 9.19 Response plot.

9.4   METHOD TO REMOVE HIGH FREQUENCY INTERFERENCE

In the communication system during the signal transmission in the noisy channel, the unwanted signal superimpose to the original signals. This signal changes the characteristics of the originality signals. So we need a device to incorporate, to identifiy and to remove it. The filters remove unwanted signals and noise from a received signal. In this discussion, we will learn to remove a high frequency signal from a received signal using MATLAB.

In the following example, the *filter* function is used to remove high frequency interference from a lower frequency signal using the given code.

EXAMPLE 9.18   In this example, initially the original signal is set with following code:

```
Fs = 200;
tmax = 10;
Nsamps = tmax*Fs;


% This is to create the initial signals
t = 1/Fs:1/Fs:tmax;
s1 = 5*cos(2*pi*t);
s2 = 5*cos(20*pi*t + pi/4);
s3 = s1 + s2;
```

The following code is to plot original signal in time domain.

```
figure
plot(t,s1)
xlabel('Time (s)')
ylabel('Amplitude (V)')
title('Original Signal')
ylim([-20 20])
```

By executing the code, the signal is plotted as shown in Figure 9.20.

In the following code, the original signal is combined with high frequency interference that is ten times higher. This combination of original with high frequency signal are shown in Figure 9.21.

```
figure
plot(t,s3)
xlabel('Time (s)')
ylabel('Amplitude (V)')
```

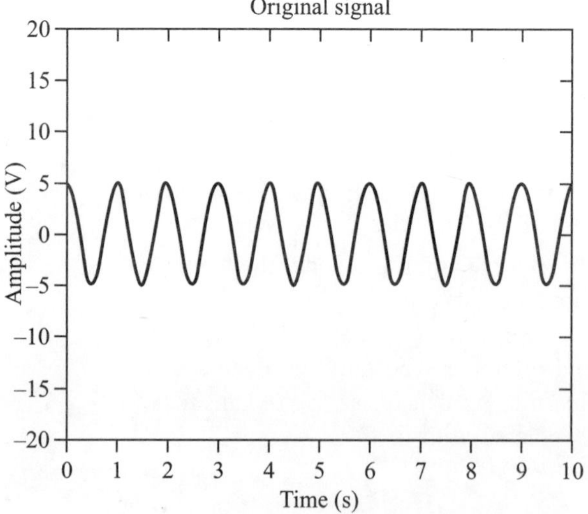

FIGURE 9.20   Original signal plot.

```
title('Original Signal Combined With High Frequency Signal')
ylim([-20 20])
```

By executing the code, the signal is plotted as shown in Figure 9.21.

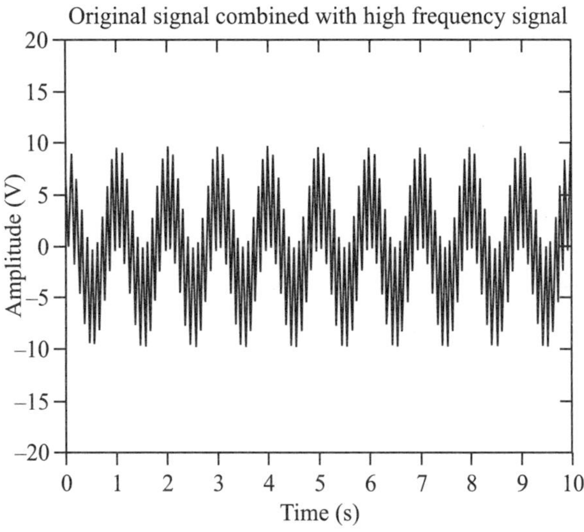

FIGURE 9.21   Original signal combination plot.

The combined signal is filtered through low pass filter. This will distort the original signal by removing the high frequency interference signal but this will keep the information in the desired signal intact.

```
% the simple Low-Pass Filter
b = 2;
a = [2 -2];
% y = filter(b,a,x) filters the input data, x, using a rational transfer function
defined by the numerator and denominator coefficients b and a, respectively.
% by applying filter
s3_f = filter(b,a,s3);

% by scale output
s3_f = s3_f/15;

% the plot of filtered signal
figure
plot(t,s3_f)
xlabel('Time (s)')
ylabel('Amplitude (V)')
```

```
title('Filtered Signal')
ylim([-20 20])
```

By executing the code the signal is plotted as shown in Figure 9.22.

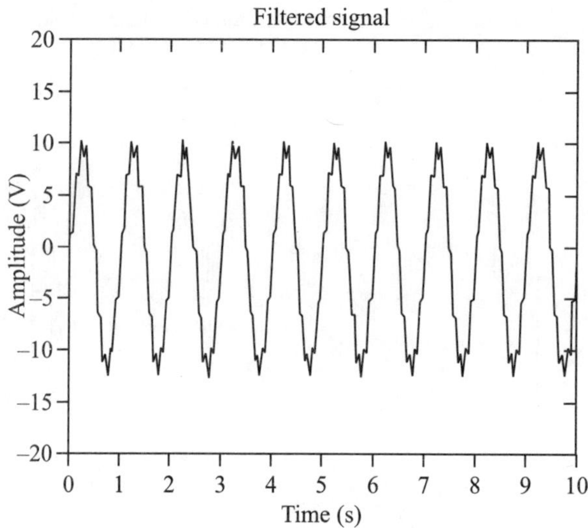

FIGURE 9.22   Filtered signal plot.

```
% the frequency domain. The frequency responses of the signals from the combined
signal derived before filtering.
f = Fs*(0:Nsamps/2-1)/Nsamps;      % Prepare freq data for plot

% the combination of original with high frequency signal.
s3_fft = abs(fft(s3));
s3_fft = s3_fft(1:Nsamps/2);         % Discard Half of Points

% Plotting of combined signal before filtering
figure
plot(f, s3_fft)
xlabel('Frequency (Hz)')
ylabel('Amplitude')
title('Frequency Response of Combined Signal Before Filtering')
ylim([0 5000])
```

By executing the code, the signal is plotted as shown in Figure 9.23.

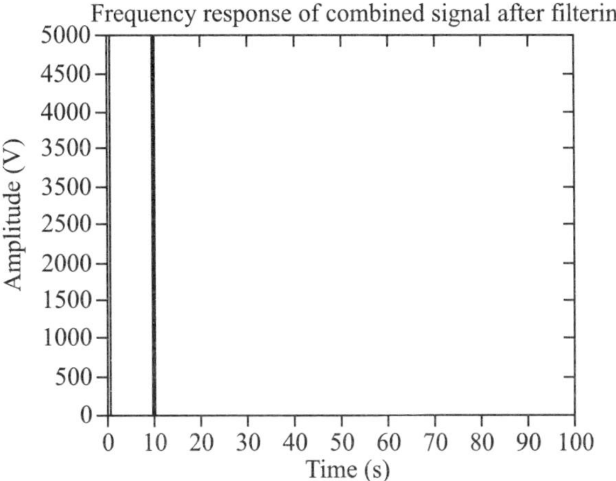

FIGURE 9.23 Combined signal before filtering plot.

% the Filter signals. The frequency responses of the signals from the combined signal derived after filtering.

```
s3_f_fft = abs(fft(s3_f));
s3_f_fft = s3_f_fft(1:Nsamps/2);        % Discard Half of Points

% Plotting of combined signal after filtering
figure
plot(f, s3_f_fft)
xlabel('Frequency (Hz)')
ylabel('Amplitude')
title('Frequency Response of Combined Signal After Filtering')
ylim([0 5000])
```

By executing the code, the signal is plotted as shown in Figure 9.24.

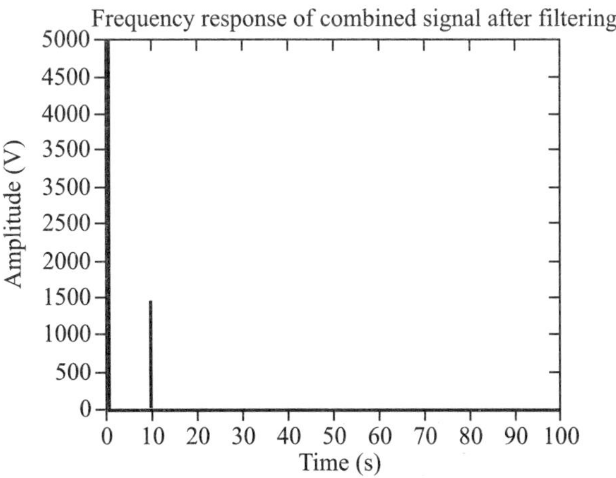

FIGURE 9.24 Combined signal after filtering plot.

Finally, the signal at 10 Hz is greatly attenuated after filtering, while the signal at 1 Hz is almost the same as before filtering.

SUMMARY

In this chapter we have learnt about the different types of filters. We have also learnt the MATLAB code for filters like FIR filter variants like low pass, high pass, band pass and band stop. IIR filters like Butterworth, Chebyshev Type 1 and Type 2. All variants of IIR filters were also studied in detail. This chapter was just to give us the glimpse of filter design. However, it is the up to the user to make efficient use of MATLAB for analysis, design, visualise the filters and their response. Also, we have learnt to remove a high frequency signal from a received signal using MATLAB.

REVIEW QUESTIONS

1. What do you understand by filter?

2. State different types of filters.

3. Elaborate the given code and state function of each variable involved in it.

   ```
   [n,wn] = cheb2ord(wp,ws,rp,rs)
   ```

4. What do you understand by order of a filter?

5. Explain the characteristics of IIR filter.

6. What is the difference between order of ideal filters and practical filters?

7. Explain the characteristics of FIR filter.

8. Explain the Butterworth filter frequency response.

9. What do you understand by magnitude response of a filter?

10. What do you understand by frequency response of a filter?

11. Explain the Chebyshev filter frequency response.

PRACTICE EXERCISE

1. Design a low pass FIR filter for data sampled at 35 kHz. The passband edge frequency is 5 kHz. The passband ripple is 0.02 dB and the stopband attenuation is 70 dB. Constrain the filter order to 100.

2. Using MATLAB code to design a linear system filter and observe the output. Consider a aperiodic pulse as shown below which has Fourier transform $X(s) = 4 * \mathrm{sinc}(4 * f)$.

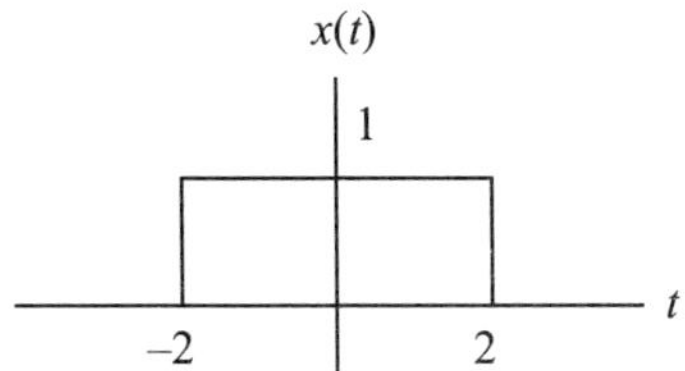

Hints: Type and observe the result.

```
>> f= -4:.001:4;
>> X=4*sinc(4*f);
>> subplot(1,2,1)
>> plot(f,abs(X))
>> subplot(1,2,2)
>> plot(f,angle(X))
```

3. Design a low pass FIR filter for data sampled at 60 kHz. The passband edge frequency is 10 kHz. The passband ripple is 0.01 dB and the stopband attenuation is 90 dB. Constrain the filter order to 110.

4. Using MATLAB code to design a low pass filter of linear system as shown below.

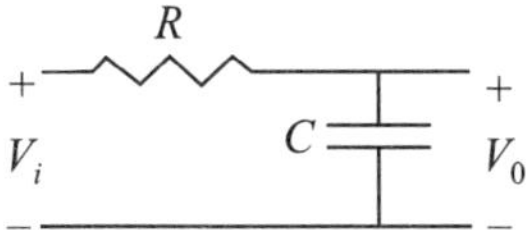

Consider the filter frequency response function as $H(ij) = 1/1 + 2j2\pi fRC$

Hints: Type and observe the result.

```
>> R=1.5E6;
>> C=1E-6;
>> H=1./(1+j*2*pi*f*R*C);
>> subplot(1,2,1)
>> plot(f,abs(H))
>> subplot(1,2,2)
>> plot(f,angle(H))
```

5. Design an elliptic filter with the same sampling frequency, cutoff frequency, passband-ripple constraint, and stopband attenuation as the 100th order FIR filter. Reduce the filter order for the elliptic filter to 15.

6. Considering the Butterworth filters, design a low pass filter to pass 150 Hz and block the 250 Hz portion of the signal using MATLAB.

   Hints: Type and observe the result.

   In this method, use two frequency signal $x(t) = \cos(c\pi100t) + \cos(2\pi400t)$

```
>> t=0:2E-4:.05;
>> x=cos(2*pi*100*t)+cos(2*pi*400*t);
>> plot(t,x)
```

CHAPTER 10

Digital Signal and Image Processing with MATLAB

INTRODUCTION

Today's era is an era of communication through images or pictures. It is rightly said that image speaks thousand words. The chapter intends to provide basic understanding of signal and image. It also focuses on how MATLAB can be used to process digital signals and images.

10.1 SIGNAL

Signal is a physical parameter which is function of physical variable. Examples of physical parameters are temperature, air pressure, voltage etc. They are also called dependent variable and are functions of independent variable called time. The term signal described the physical state of an object and helps to register or transform information about it. Sometimes, we say temperature on so and so day was recorded to be 50°C. Here the physical parameter is the temperature (dependent variable) quantified by 50°C measured on a particular day (time) which forms an independent variable. 'Signal' is a word derived from Latin word *Signum* meaning sign. Mathematically, signals are represented as $v(t)$, $f(t)$, $x(t)$, etc. That is a dependent variable as a function of an independent variable. They are measured using instruments or devices like thermometer, oscilloscope, voltmeter, ammeter, seismograph drums, etc. However, these signals are called as analog signals. Word analog derived from word *analogous* as these signals give complete analogy of physical parameters or physical state of an object. However these analog signals are not ready in format to be readable by computer. They needs to be digitised and made ready for a computer to read. Digitisation again is not direct process as the analog signal first needs discretisation. Signals recorded by a sensor or transducer or any recording device are converted in to digital signal by transformation given by Figure 10.1. A signal can be represented as analog, discrete and digital signal. Values of signals are tabulated in Table 10.1 which are obtained from the function defined as:

$$f(t) = 1.25^t$$

TABLE 10.1   Values of $f(t)$

Time instants (t) in seconds	Samples of $f(t)$ at discrete time instants	Digitised values of $f(t)$	Binary equivalent of digitised $f(t)$
0	1.0000	1	001
1	1.2500	1	001
2	1.5625	2	010
3	1.9531	2	010
4	2.4414	2	010
5	3.0518	3	011
6	3.8147	4	100
7	4.7684	5	101
8	5.9605	6	110
9	7.4506	7	111

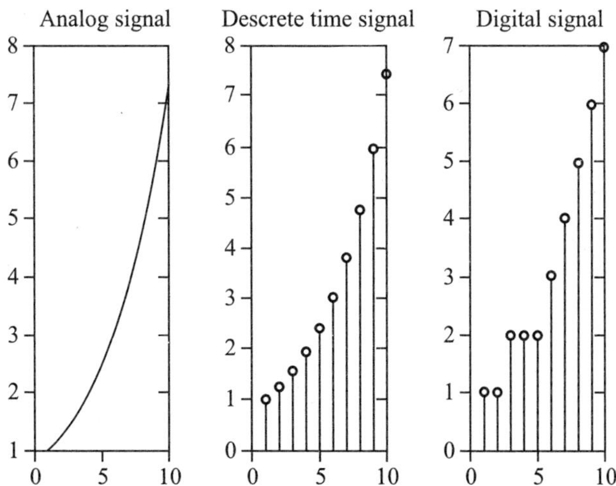

FIGURE 10.1   Illustration of analog, discrete and digital signals.

10.1.1   Signal Processing Toolbox of MATLAB

Toolbox called Signal Processing Toolbox is available in MATLAB. It is a software collection of tools supported by MATLAB environment. This toolbox supports variety of signal processing operations. Operations like waveform generation to filter design and implementation, parametric modelling, and spectral analysis are supported by MATLAB. We can find two categories of tools in this toolbox of Signal processing. They are command line functions/objects and graphical user interfaces.

Command line functions and objects are available in the following categories:

- Discrete time filter design, analysis, and implementation
- Analog filter design, analysis, and implementation
- Linear system transformations
- Window functions
- Spectral analysis and cepstral analysis
- Transforms
- Statistical signal processing
- Parametric modelling
- Linear prediction
- Multirate signal processing
- Waveform generation

Let us see the functions of one such category signal processing. Few examples based on these functions are as follows. Example 10.1 illustrates various signals used in signal processing. Output of Example 10.1 is shown in Figure 10.2.

EXAMPLE 10.1

```
t = (0:0.001:1)';

imp= [1; zeros(99,1)]; subplot(5,1,1); plot(imp);title('Impulse','FontSize', 11);
% Impulse

unit_step = ones(100,1); subplot(5,1,2); plot(unit_step);title('Step','FontSize',
11); % Step (with 0 initial cond.)

ramp_sig= t; subplot(5,1,3); plot(ramp_sig);title('Ramp','FontSize', 11); % Ramp

quad_sig=t.^2; subplot(5,1,4); plot(quad_sig);title('Quadratic','FontSize', 11);
% Quadratic

sq_wave = square(4*pi*t); subplot(5,1,5); plot(sq_wave);title('Square
Wave','FontSize', 11); % Square wave with period 0.5
```

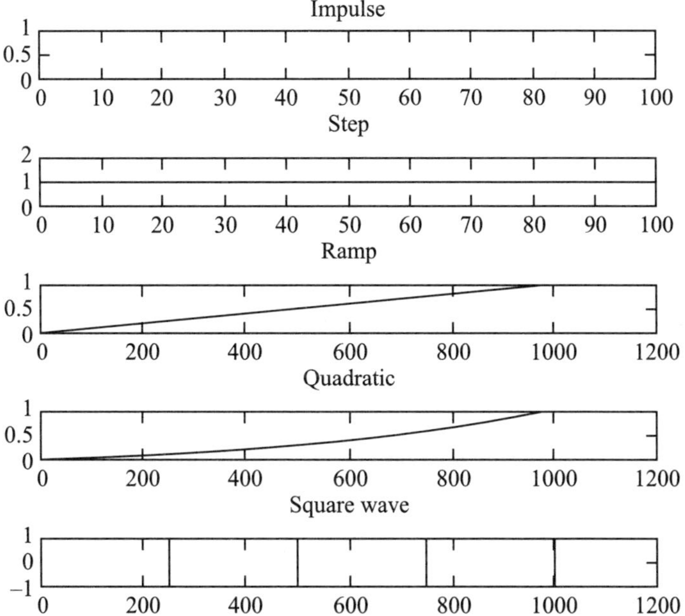

FIGURE 10.2   Various signals used in signal processing plotted in MATLAB.

Sinc function is most commonly known function in signal processing. MATLAB code of Example 10.2 can generate *Sinc* function. Its output is as shown in Figure 10.3.

EXAMPLE 10.2

```
x = linspace(-10,10);
y = sinc(x);
plot(x,y);subplot(1,1,1); plot(y);title('Sinc Function','FontSize', 11);
```

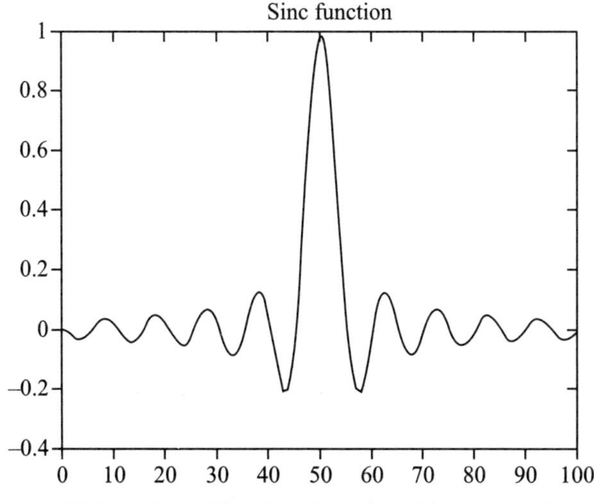

FIGURE 10.3   Sinc function plotted in MATLAB.

10.1.2   Statistical Signal Processing

Signal Processing Toolbox provides functions that we use to measure common distinctive features of a signal such as denoise, smooth, and detrend signals for further analysis. Each of signal functions are further divided as per the application. For example, under statistical signal processing various operations can be carried out on the given signal.

Signal Processing Toolbox functions can be used for the following applications:

- Remove noise, outliers, and spurious content from data.
- Enhance signals, visualise signals, and discover patterns.
- Change the sample rate of a signal or make constant for irregularly sampled .signals or signals with missing data.
- Extract key signal characteristics and reduce data sets without losing information.
- Locate signal peaks and determine their height, width, and distance to neighbours.
- Measure time-domain features such as peak-to-peak amplitudes and signal envelopes.
- Measure pulse metrics such as overshoot, locate signal peaks and duty cycle.

Some of the operations are as listed below:

- *corrmtx:* Data matrix for autocorrelation matrix estimation
- *cpsd:* Cross power spectral density
- *dspdata:* DSP data parameter information
- *dspdata.psd:* Power spectral density
- *mscohere:* Magnitude squared coherence
- *pburg:* PSD using Burg method
- *pcov:* PSD using covariance method
- *peig:* Pseudospectrum using eigenvector method
- *periodogram:* PSD using periodogrampm
- *cov:* PSD using modified covariance method
- *pmtm:* PSD using multitaper method (MTM)
- *pmusic:* Pseudospectrum using MUSIC algorithm
- *pwelch:* PSD using Welch's method
- *pyulear:* PSD using Yule-Walker AR method
- *rooteig:* Frequency and power content using eigenvector method
- *rootmusic:* Root music algorithm
- *spectrogram:* Spectrogram using short-time Fourier transform
- *spectrum:* Spectral estimation
- *tfestimate:* Transfer function estimate
- *xcorr:* Cross-correlation
- *xcorr2:* 2D cross-correlation
- *xcov:* Cross-covariance

10.1.3   Signal Processing Functions in MATLAB

Signal Processing Toolbox™ provides a family of correlation and convolution functions that let us to detect signal similarities. It determines periodicity; find a interest hidden signal in a long data record. It computes the response of a linear time-invariant (LTI) system to an input signal, perform polynomial multiplication, and carry out circular convolution.

- *conv:* Convolution and polynomial multiplication
- *conv2:* 2D convolution
- *corrcoef:* Correlation coefficients
- *cov:* Covariance matrix
- *cplxpair:* Sort complex numbers into complex conjugate pairs
- *deconv:* Deconvolution and polynomial division
- *fft:* Discrete Fourier transform
- *fft2:* 2D discrete Fourier transform
- *fftshift:* Shift zero-frequency component to center of spectrum
- *filter2:* 2D digital filter
- *freqspace:* Frequency spacing for frequency response
- *ifft:* Inverse discrete Fourier transform
- *ifft2:* 2D inverse discrete Fourier transform
- *unwrap:* Correct phase angles to produce smoother phase plots

Convolution

The convolution of two functions $f(t)$ and $g(t)$ on the interval $(0, T)$, is defined as

$$(f * g)(\tau) = \sum_{i=0}^{N} f(t_i)g(t_i - \tau)$$

where,

* denote the convolution, T is defined from $(0, T)$, $f(t)$ and $g(t)$.

Correlation

The cross-correlation of two functions is similar to their convolution of the difference in the reversal of the time variable.

$$R_{fg}(\tau) = \int_0^T f(t)g(t + \tau)\, dt = \int_0^T g(t)f(t + \tau)\, dt = [f(t) * g(-t)](\tau)$$

10.2 IMAGE

An image is defined as a two-dimensional function $f(x, y)$, where x and y are spatial co-ordinates (or pixel co-ordinates), and the amplitude of f is called the intensity of the image at the selected point as shown in Figure 10.4. Physical image captured with the help of a camera is divided into tiny regions called *pixels* or *picture elements* or *pels*. Image is a 2D (two-dimensional) signal. Digital is a two-dimensional rectangular array of quantised values which are sampled. Integer value of a pixel represents the brightness or darkness of the image at that point. The term gray level in an image is used often to refer to the intensity of monochrome images. Colour images are formed by a combination of individual monochrome images. In an RGB colour system, a colour image consists of three individual monochrome images, referred to as the red (R), green (G), and blue (B) component of images. Digitising the co-ordinate values is called *sampling* and digitising the amplitude values is called *quantisation*. If x, y and the amplitude values of f are all finite and discrete quantities, then the image is called as a *digital image*.

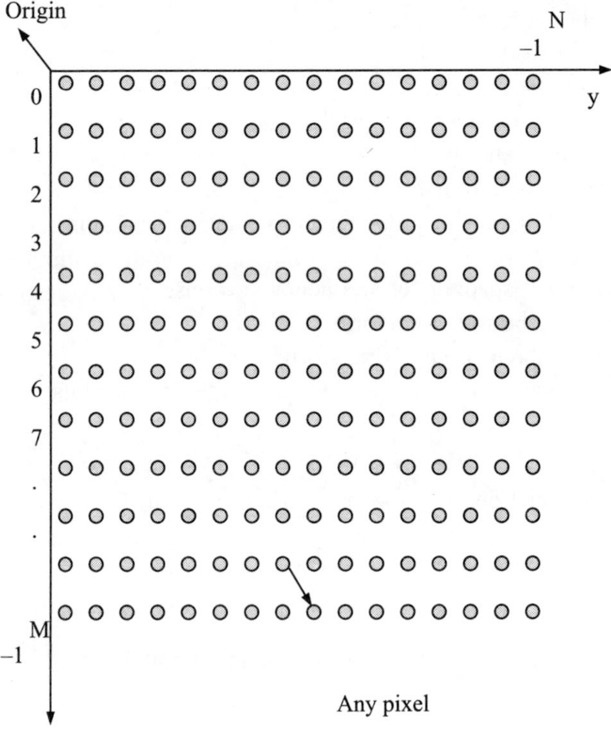

FIGURE 10.4   Conventional co-ordinates of an image.

Image representation as a matrix

- Image f as a function of x and y (2-dimensional).
- Image is of size $M \times N$.
- Image origin is defined to be at $(0, 0)$.
- In an image processing toolbox (in MATLAB documentation, etc.), image origin is defined to be at $(1, 1)$.
- Image as a Matrix (in general) is given as:

$$f(x, y) = \begin{bmatrix} f(0,0) & f(0,1) & \cdots & f(0,N-1) \\ f(1,0) & f(1,1) & \cdots & f(1,N-1) \\ \vdots & \vdots & \cdots & \vdots \\ f(M-1,0) & f(M-1,1) & \cdots & f(M-1,N-1) \end{bmatrix}$$

- Each element of this matrix is called an image element, picture element, pixel, or pel in short deriving p from *p*icture and *el* from *el*ement.

- Image is a collection of pixels.
- A digital image representation as a MATLAB matrix is given as:

$$f(x, y) = \begin{bmatrix} f(1,1) & f(1,2) & \cdots & f(1,N) \\ f(2,1) & f(2,2) & \cdots & f(2,N) \\ \vdots & \vdots & \cdots & \vdots \\ f(M,1) & f(M,2) & \cdots & f(M,N) \end{bmatrix}$$

10.2.1   Image Processing

Processing an image means modifying the image pixels at programmers will. The processed image is once again made user interpretable by displaying it on the computer screen. Resolution of an image is measured in terms of gray-scale resolution. Gray-scale resolution is the number of gray levels per unit measure of image amplitude. For example, if an image is said to be stored in eight bit bytes, such image yields a 256 ($2^8 = 2*2*2*2*2*2*2*2$) level gray scale. Image processing in MATLAB allows us to read and write images and also to analyse them. MATLAB supports following categories of functions to compute images.

Format-specific information in MATLAB

This section provide information about the support for specific formats, listed in alphabetical order by format name. There are format-specific syntaxes in MATLAB. They need to be considered while processing them in MATLAB. Each of the formats in turn support various level scales for storage (for example, 8 bit byte means 256 gray levels). Various formats supported by MATLAB are as follows:

- *BMP* — Windows Bitmap
- *JPEG* — Joint Photographic Experts Group
- *PNG* — Portable Network Graphics
- *CUR* — Cursor File
- *JPEG 2000* — Joint Photographic Experts Group 2000
- *PPM* — Portable Pixmap
- *GIF* — Graphics Interchange Format
- *PBM* — Portable Bitmap
- *RAS* — Sun Raster
- *HDF4* — Hierarchical Data Format
- *PCX* — Windows Paintbrush
- *TIFF* — Tagged Image File Format
- *ICO* — Icon File
- *PGM* — Portable Graymap
- *XWD* — X Window Dump

Reading an image in MATLAB

Basic requirement to read an image into MATLAB, the destined image we wish to read should be present in some form of memory. The `imread` function reads an image from any supported graphics bit depths. Most of the images that we read into memory are stored as class uint8. The main exception to this rule is MATLAB support for 16-bit data for PNG and TIFF images.

Images are read into the MATLAB environment using function *imread*, whose basic syntax is

```
imread ('filename.format')
```

where, filename is a string containing the complete name of the image file (including any applicable extension).

Following Example 10.3 illustrates the *imread* function use to read an image in MATLAB.

EXAMPLE 10.3

```
clc;
close all;
clear all;
a= imread ('cameraman.tif');
b= imread ('D:\myimages\rose.jpg');
```

We observe the following in the above code:

- 4th line reads the image from the TIF file cameraman into image array *a*.
- 5th line reads the image 'rose.jpg' stored in a user folder into an image array *b* (image should be present in users' folder otherwise there would be an error!!).
- The use of single quotes (') to delimit the string filename.
- The semicolon at the end of a statement is used by MATLAB for suppressing output.
- If a semicolon is not included, MATLAB displays on the screen the results of the operation specified in that line.
- Image 'cameraman.tif' is saved as an image matrix named *a*, where matrix contents will be intensity levels of each pixel.
- The values are available in the variable editor by double clicking 'variable name' stored in the workspace. They are displayed as in Figure 10.5.

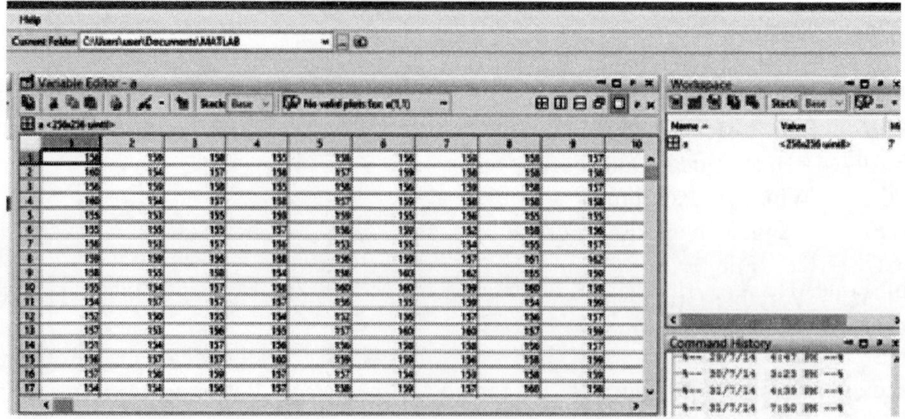

FIGURE 10.5 Workspace values for cameraman image MATLAB.

EXAMPLE 10.4   In this example, we will learn how to read the image ngc6543a.jpg into the workspace variable RGB and then displays the image using the image function:

```
RGB = imread('ngc6543a.jpg');
image(RGB)
```

By running the code, Figure 10.6 image is appeared on the screen.

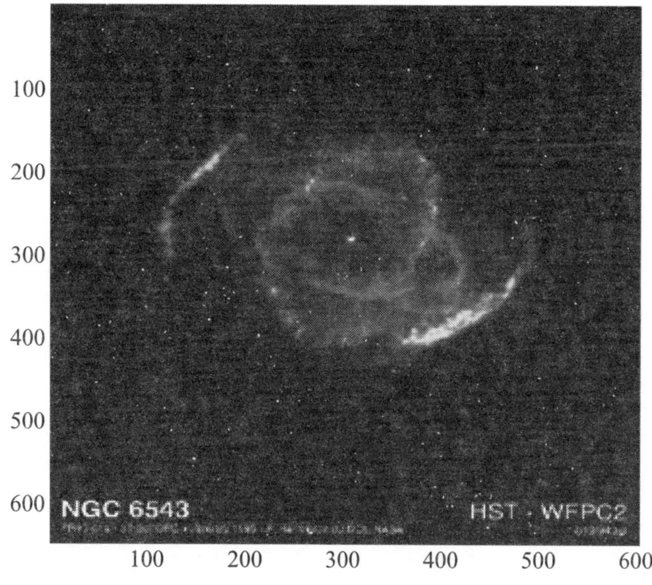

FIGURE 10.6   Image 'ngc6543a.jpg'.

Writing images in MATLAB

Images are written to the current directory using function *imwrite*, which has the following basic syntax:

```
imwrite(a, 'filename with format')
```

With this syntax, the string contained in filename must include a recognised file format extension which is valid for *imread* function. For example, the following command writes 'a' to a file called *bwcameraman.tif*

```
imwrite(f, 'bwcameraman.tif')
```

Function *imwrite* writes the image as a TIFF file because it recognises the *.tif* extension in the filename. Newly written image contents can be checked by using function *iminfo* can also be displayed by using *imshow* command.

When you save an image in MATLAB using *imwrite*, the default behaviour is automatically reduce the bit depth to uint8. The rule for saving the image data PNG and TIFF images format is that uint8 can be saved as uint16. Because these two formats the 8-bit data, can override the MATLAB default behaviour by specifying `uint16` using *imwrite* command. The following example shows writing a 16-bit PNG file using *imwrite*.

EXAMPLE 10.5   In this example we will learn to write (save) image data using the `imwrite` function using the following statements:

```
>> load clown
>> imwrite(X,map,'clown.bmp')
```

Size of an image

Any image read in MATLAB has finite size that is number of rows and columns used to store the intensity values of that image. There are different commands in MATLAB to extract the size of an image and store for reference or processing purpose. Type the command 'doc size' at command prompt for more details. Also, typing 'size' at the prompt (>>) gives the row and column dimensions of an image as described in Example 10.6.

EXAMPLE 10.6

```
clc;close all;clear all;
a=imread ('cameraman.tif');
size(a)
[M,N] = size(a)
Z1=size(a,1)
Z2=size(a,2)
Z3=size(a,3)
whos a
```

We observe the following in the above code:

- 3rd statement gives the number of rows and columns of image matrix *a*.
- 4th statement gives rows in *M* and columns in *N*.
- 5th statement gives number of rows, which is the first selected dimension.
- 6th statement gives number of columns, which is the second selected dimension.
- 7th statement gives the third dimension entry.
- 8th statement displays additional information about the image array such as size, number of bytes and class.
- Result displayed in the command window is as follows:

```
ans =
256 256
M =
256
N =
256
```

```
Z1 =
256
Z2 =
256
Z3 =
1
Name    Size        Bytes     Class Attributes
a       256x256     65536     uint8
```

Class of image

Although we work with integer co-ordinates, the values (intensities) of pixels are not restricted to be integers in MATLAB. There are different classes as shown in Table 10.2.

TABLE 10.2 Different classes of images in MATLAB

Name	*Description*
double	Double-precision, floating-point numbers in the approximate range $\pm\ 10^{308}$ (8 bytes per clement).
single	Single-precision floating-point numbers with values in the approximate range $\pm\ 10^{38}$ (4 bytes per element).
ulnts	Unsigned 8-bit integers in the range [0, 255] (1 byte per element).
umt16	Unsigned 16-bit integers in the range [0, 65535] (2 bytes per element).
uint32	Unsigned 32-bit integers in the range [0, 4294967295] (4 bytes per element).
into	Signed 8-bit integers in the range [–128, 127] (1 byte per element).
lnti6	Signed 16-bit integers in the range [–32768, 32767] (2 bytes per clement).
int32	Signed 32-bit integers in the range |–2147483648, 2147483647] (4 bytes per element).
char	Characters (2 bytes per element).
logical	Values are 0 or 1 (1 byte per clement).

Displaying an image

Images are displayed on the MATLAB desktop using function *imshow*, which has the basic syntax:

```
imshow(a)
```

Image show

We should make sure that for displaying an image it should be first read or loaded into MATLAB environment and only then it can be displayed. If another image, *b*, is to be displayed using *imshow*, MATLAB replaces the image in the figure window with the new image and only the latest image will be displayed. To keep the first image and output a second image, use *figure*, function with syntax in Example 10.7, so that the output as shown in Figure 10.7. will be displayed.

```
figure, imshow(b)
```

EXAMPLE 10.7

```
clc; close all; clear all;
a=imread ('cameraman.tif');
b= imread('trees.tif')
imshow(a),title('cameraman.tif');
figure,imshow(b),title('Trees.tif');
```

We observe the following in the above code:

- 4th line displays the image cameraman.tif.
- More than one command can be written on a line, provided that different commands are delimited by commas or semicolons.
- Title displays the given title on the top of the figure.

FIGURE 10.7   Use of imshow and figure functions in MATLAB.

Image tool

The Image tool in the image processing toolbox provides a more interactive environment for viewing and navigating within images, displaying detailed information about pixel values, measuring distances, and other useful operations. To start the Image Tool, use the *imtool* function. Use of this function and output of Example 10.8 is shown in Figure 10.8.

EXAMPLE 10.8

```
clc; close all; clear all;
a=imread ('cameraman.tif');
imshow(a),title('cameraman.tif');
```

```
imtool(a);
imtool('trees.tif');
```

We observe the following in the above code:

- Toolbar has the tools in the respective order, navigate image using overview, inspect pixel values, display image information, adjust contrast, help, crop image, measure distance, zoom in, zoom out, drag image to pan, adjust contrast/brightness via mouse motion.
- 5th statement also displays the image tool for the image mentioned in quotes.

FIGURE 10.8   Output of imtool in MATLAB.

Description of various tools in MATLAB is in Table 10.3.

TABLE 10.3   Description of various tools in MATLAB

Tool	Description
Pixel Information	Displays information about the pixel under the mouse pointer
Pixel Region	Superimposes pixel values on a zoomed-in pixel view
Distance	Measures the distance between two pixels
Image Information	Displays information about images and image files
Adjust Contrast	Adjusts the contrast of the displayed image
Crop Image	Defines a crop region and crops the image
Display Range	Shows the display range of the image data
Overview	Shows the currently visible image

Binary transformation of an image

MATLAB also allows image conversions from one type to another. In following case, the image is converted to black and white levels.

```
BW = im2bw(I, level)
```

It converts the gray scale image I to a binary image as shown in Figure 10.9. The output image BW replaces all pixels in the input image with luminance greater than level with the value 1 (white) and replaces all other pixels with the value 0 (black). Specify level in the range [0,1]. This range is relative to the signal levels possible for the image class. Therefore, a level value of 0.5 is midway between black and white, regardless of class.

EXAMPLE 10.9

```
clc;close all;clear all;
a=imread ('cameraman.tif');
imshow(a),title('cameraman.tif');
b=im2bw(a);
imwrite(b,'BWcameraman.tif');
figure,imshow(b);
```

Output of the code is shown in Figure 10.9.

FIGURE 10.9   Gray scale Cameraman image converted to binary image.

Some of the image formats supported by '*imread*' and '*imwrite*':   There are some selected image formats which are compatible with '*imread*' and '*imwrite*' MATLAB functions and are shown in Table 10.4.

TABLE 10.4   Image formats supported by MATLAB

Format name	Description	Recognised extensions
BMP[†]	Windows Bitmap	.bmp
CUR	Windows Cursor Resources	.cur
FITS[†]	Flexible Image Transport System	.fts, .fits
GIF	Graphics Interchange Format	.gif
HDF	Hierarchical Data Format	.hdf
ICO[†]	Windows Icon Resources	.ico
JPEG	Joint Photographic Experts Group	.JP9, .jpeg
JPEG 2000[†]	Joint Photographic Experts Group	.jp2, .jpf, .jpf, .jpx, j2c, j2k
PBM	Portable Bitmap	.pbm
PGM	Portable Graymap	.pgm
PNG	Portable Network Graphics	.png
PNM	Portable Any Map	.pnm
RAS	Sun Raster	.ras
TIFF	Tagged Image File Format	.tif, .tiff
XWD	X Window Dump	. xwd

[†]Supported by imread, but not by imwrite.

RGB to Gray transformation

Digital images are classified in four broad types according to its pixel format: binary images, gray scale images, indexed images, and true colour images. Transformations can be done among these. MATLAB syntax for *rgb* to gray transformations is:

```
I = rgb2gray(RGB)
```

It converts the true colour image RGB to the gray scale intensity image I. '*rgb2gray*' converts RGB images to gray scale by eliminating the hue and saturation information while retaining the luminance.

EXAMPLE 10.10

```
clc;close all;clear all;
a=imread ('onion.png');
imshow(a);
b=rgb2gray(a);
figure,imshow(b);
c=im2bw(b);
figure,imshow(c);
```

Output of the code is shown in Figure 10.10.

Original image   Gray scale image   Black and white image

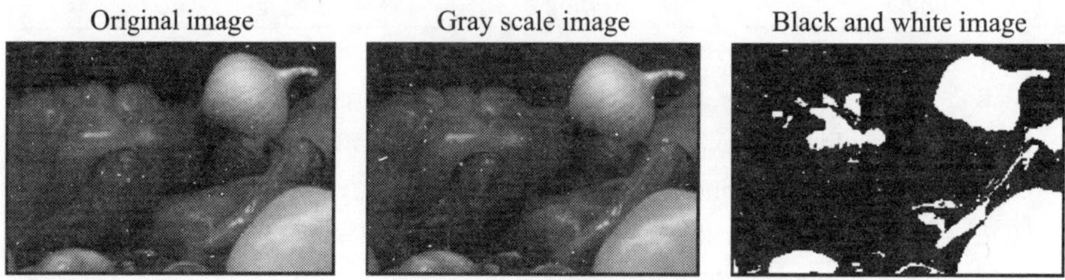

FIGURE 10.10   Image transformations RGB to Gray and Black and white image.

The above discussed sections are the very basic levels of implementing Digital Image Processing using MATLAB software. The image is assumed to be a matrix with its elements as pixel/intensity levels. Processing is done on these pixels. All manipulations are easily implementable mathematically using MATLAB. MATLAB allows different kinds of operations to be performed on images. They as listed below:

- *Image display and exploration:*   Display, import, and export images
- *GUI tools:*   Modular interactive tools and associated utility functions.
- *Spatial transformation and image registration:*   Resizing, rotating, copping and registration
- *Image analysis and statistics:*   Image analysis, texture analysis, view pixel values, and calculate image statistics
- *Image arithmetic:*   Add, subtract, multiply, and divide images
- *Image enhancement and restoration:*   Enhance and restore images
- *Linear filtering and transforms:*   Linear filters, filter design, and image transforms
- *Morphological operations:*   Morphological image processing
- *ROI-based, neighbourhood, and block processing:*   ROI-based, neighbourhood, and block operations
- *Colour maps and colour space:*   Manipulate image colour
- *Utilities:*   Array operations, demos, preferences and other toolbox utility functions

The user needs to judge the type of application he/she intends to use from the image processing toolbox as per his/her applications.

SUMMARY

This chapter has discussed signals as an array of integers. They are ready for processing as vectors and various mathematical operations can be performed on them for proper interpretations. Also, image is represented as a matrix in MATLAB. Each element of this matrix is called an image element or pixel. Image is a combination of pixels. It also discussed retrieving an image from a disk using the function *imread.* Some basic processing can be done on an image matrix by transforming it into Black and White or to gray level. This chapter has also equipped reader with saving of an image to the current directory. It is left to the reader to decide the application and make use of the tool as per requirements.

REVIEW QUESTIONS

1. Define signal.
2. List various statistical signal processing commands in MATLAB.
3. List signal processing commands in MATLAB.
4. Define image.
5. State the command to read an image in MATLAB.
6. State the command to write an image in MATLAB.
7. What are the three basic steps required in digitizing a signal?
8. Define pixel.
9. Write an expression for digital image representation in MATLAB.
10. Name the function used for reading an image.
11. What is M and N in size M×N of an image?
12. List out different classes of images in MATLAB.
13. Differentiate between *imshow* and *imtool* functions.
14. Write syntax for *imwrite* and mention its uses.
15. Name the function which transforms a gray image into a binary image.
16. Name the function which transforms coloured RGB image into a gray image.
17. List image formats supported by *imwrite* and *imread* in MATLAB.

PRACTICE EXERCISE

1. Create a sample signal y consisting of two sinusoids, one at 100 Hz and one at 150 Hz with twice the amplitude. (***Hint:*** $y = \sin(2*pi*25*t) + 2*\sin(2*pi*20*t)$)

2. With the help of sequence below which generates 1.5 s of a 50 Hz sawtooth wave with a sample rate of 10 kHz and plot 0.2 s

```
fs = 10000;
t = 0:1/fs:1.5;
x = sawtooth(2*pi*50*t);
plot(t,x), axis([0 0.2 -1 1])
```

   Generate square and sine waveforms with appropriate assumptions and modifications.

3. Execute the given code and display the output.

```
clc;
clear all;
```

```
close all;
yc=[];
xc=[];
q=[];l_v=[];
I=zeros(30,30);
Column=15;
      Row=15;
      p= zeros(36,180);
for r= 1:1:14;
      N=359;
      t=(0:1:N)*2*pi/N;
      x=r*cos(t)+Column;
      y=r*sin(t)+Row;
      X=round(x);
      Y=round(y);
yc=[yc; Y];
xc=[xc; X];
  IMG1= roipoly(I,X,Y);
hold on
imshow(IMG1,[])
end
```

4. Execute the following commands and see the output:
   (i) `imshow(imread('westconcordaerial.png'))`
   (ii) `imshow(imread('rice.png'))`
   (iii) `imshow(imread('moon.tif'))`
   (iv) `imread('ngc6543a.jpg')`

5. Transform the imgaes in 10.2. into rgb.

6. Display the following image using imtool function (***Hint:*** use *imtool((imread(('board. tif')))))*.

7. Execute the following code and appreciate contrast stretching of an image.

```
[X, map] = imread('forest.tif');
S = decorrstretch(ind2rgb(X, map),'tol',0.01);
figure, imshow(X,map)
figure, imshow(S)
```

8. Explore the following command to change shape of the patch shown below.

```
patch([0 .5 .5], [0 1 0], [1 0 0])
```

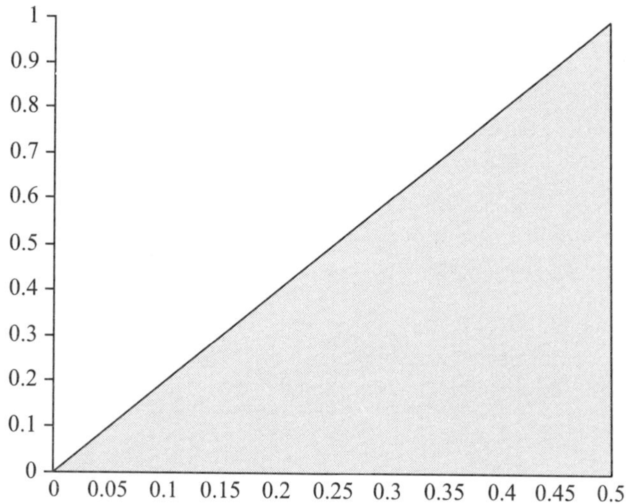

9. Read *rice.png* and display as following image is displayed using the given code:

```
I = imread('pout.tif'); imshow(I)
i1=imadjust(I);figure,imshow(i1)
i2=cat(2,I,i1);figure,imshow(i2)
```

10. Read *rice.png* and remove background of the image using appropriate code.

11. Read *rice.png, pout.tif* adjust their size and concatenate them horizontally.

CHAPTER 11

MATLAB and Simulink

LEARNING OBJECTIVES

This chapter aims to provide the basic ideas on Simulink and its tools using MATLAB. At the end of this chapter, one should be able to understand:

- How to start Simulink and the effectiveness to use Simulink tools using MATLAB.
- Methods to build models in the Model editor using Simulink.
- How to design and evaluate the performance of Simulink facility as a tool.
- Methods to use Simulink resources.
- How to model Simulink with graphical user interface.
- How to use Simulink resources to deal with different systems and observe various inputs.
- What is a range of design problems using Simulink.

INTRODUCTION

Simulink (Simulation and Link) is an extension of MATLAB. *Simulink* is a software package that is graphical extension to MATLAB modelling, simulating and analysing under a Graphical User Interface (GUI) environment. The software package is widely used in academic and industry. The *Simulink* is a part of MATLAB used to simulate dynamic system models drawn on the screen as block diagrams using analysis tools in MATLAB.

In this window, the components of the system models are created and edited primarily by mouse driven commands. The construction of a model is simplified with click-and-drag mouse operations. *Simulink* is integrated with MATLAB and data can be easily transferred between the programs. This includes a comprehensive block library for creating standard components such as sinks, sources, connectors, linear and nonlinear components. *Simulink* provides a GUI for building models as block diagram using click-and-drag mouse operations.

Data and information from various blocks in *Simulink* can be forward to another block by line connecting relevant block library of sinks, sources, linear and nonlinear components, and connector. Signal can be fed into static and dynamic blocks and can be observed in scopes, displays or can also be saved in a file. As *Simulink* is an integral part of MATLAB, it is easy to switch back and forth during the analysis process take full advantage of features offered in both the environments.

In this chapter, we will get to know the basic introduction of *Simulink* and get experience of its simulation by simulating dynamic systems. The chapter includes different types of *Simulink* examples and lets us customise and create our own blocks. *Simulink* works on UNIX, Macintosh, and Windows environments and simulation results can be put in the MATLAB workspace for postprocessing and visualisation.

11.1 TRADITIONAL WINDOW

In the traditional method to evaluate the physical documents, we need several iterations as shown in Figure 11.1. There are several problems with traditional development method. In the traditional methods to design the process, we need to develop physical structure based on the input parameters. Finally the design blocks are implemented for testing using various tools and then verified. The traditional development process is not rapid and takes several sets of iterations. The design of physical prototype is expensive because it passes through several stages for reconstruction. The design of traditional prototype implementation consumes lots of time and cause human errors. The final verification may lead to error in the later stage of process.

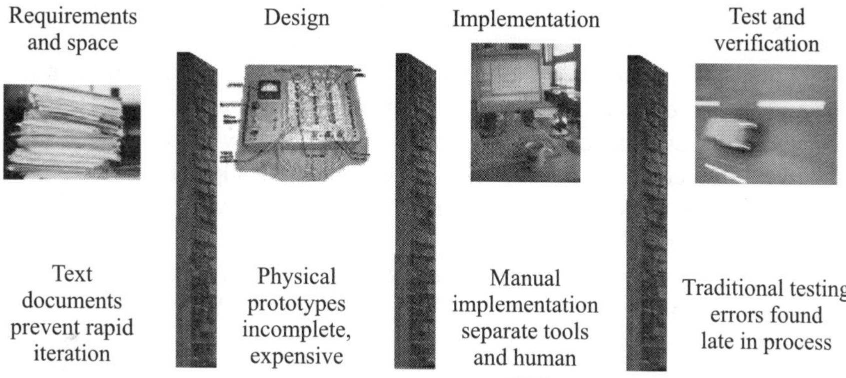

FIGURE 11.1   Problem with traditional development Model-based Design.

11.1.1 Adopting Model-based Design

The traditional method always have certain limitations. By adopting the model-based design, it becomes imperative to design and successfully test the modular model which is suitable for practical applications. Figure 11.2 shows the Adopting Model-based Design.

In Figure 11.2, stage 1 represents executable specifications. Using the software simulation like MATLAB, Simulink which supports the adopting model. This section shows unambiguous specifications which are supplemented by text is replaced by a set of models for all teams including in the simulate environment. It represents the block diagram description with early validation and test development.

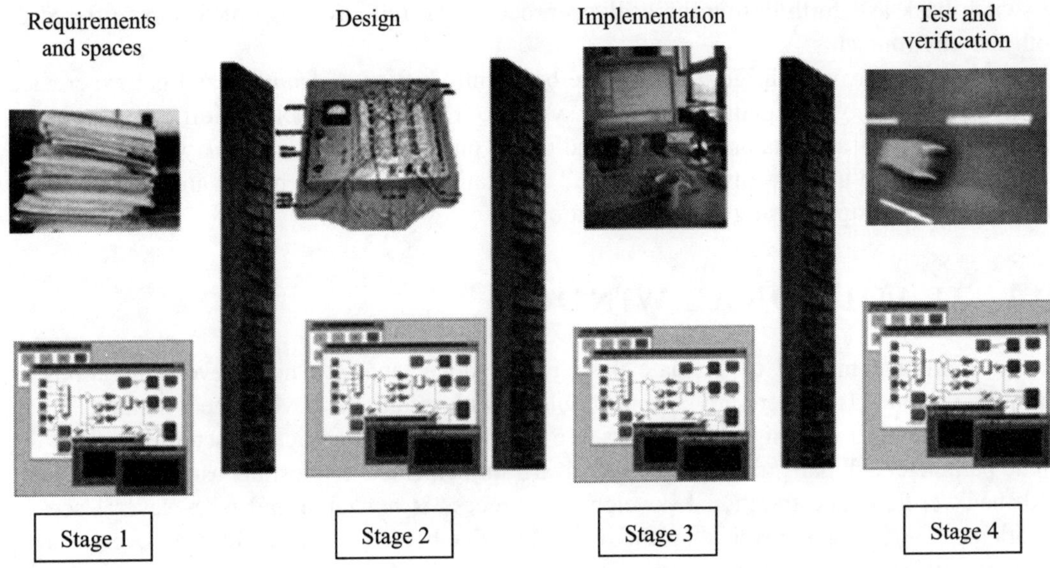

FIGURE 11.2   Model-based design stages.

Stage 2 represents design with simulation. The systematic design exploration and optimisation shows the fast design that is easy to analyse. The design model can be corrected number of times for troubleshooting before implementation. The hardware part can be specifically simulated stage by stage in an incremental way from system level implementation.

Stage 3 represents automatic code generation. Based on systematic design, the code is generated for the hardware implementation. This design is mostly error free for repeated test on improvement of design. Such code generation bridges the knowledge between software and hardware domain.

Stage 4 represents continuous test and verification to detect errors in the early stage of development so as to reduce dependency on physical prototypes. Such implementations appear successfully, when repeatedly tested across development stages.

11.2   SIMULINK WINDOW

Simulink is a platform for multi-domain simulation and model-based design for dynamic systems. It provides an interactive graphical environment and a customisable set of block libraries, and can be extended for specialised applications. Simulink model-based design is shown in Figure 11.3.

Foundation for model-based design represents automatic code generation, verification and validation. The Simulink open architecture also consists of integrating models from other tools to support applications in controls, signal processing, communications and other system engineering areas.

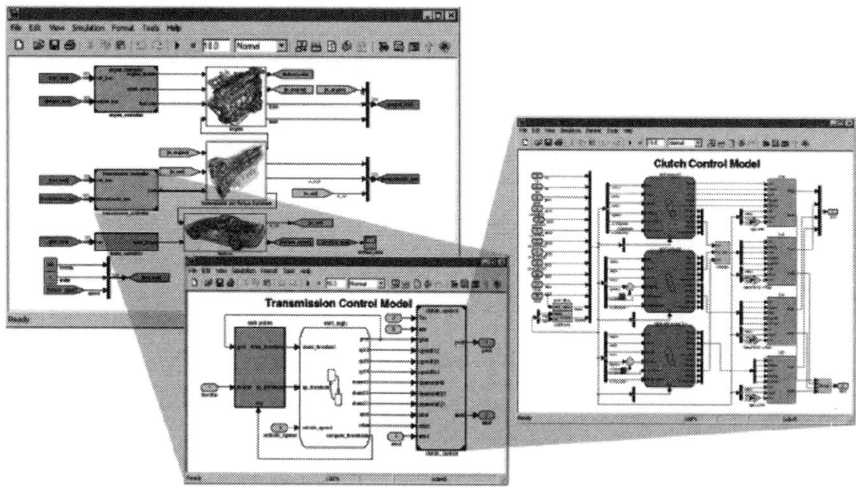

FIGURE 11.3 Simulink foundation model based.

11.2.1 Simulink Startup

The Simulink Library Browser contains basic and add-on blocks. It consists of editor window. We can start the computer and log into it. Click on the Microsoft 'Start' button in the bottom corner of screen and click MATLAB or directly on MATLAB icon. Simulink can be started by using one of the following methods:

To invoke Simulink, in MATLAB type `Simulink` at command prompt '>>'. Simulink is started from the MATLAB command prompt using the command form:

```
>> Simulink
```

This will open a window as shown in Figure 11.4.

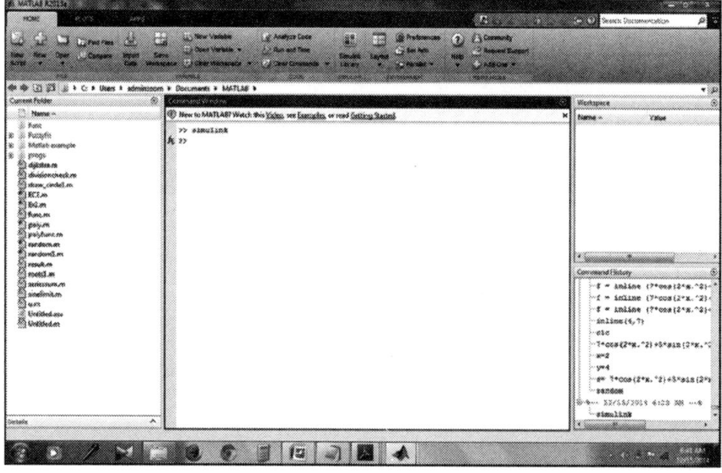

FIGURE 11.4 Simulink from MATLAB window.

Alternatively, the New *Simulink* Model button at the top of the MATLAB command window can be started by clicking on the icon of '*Simulink Library*' toolbar of the MATLAB Command Window as shown in Figure 11.5.

Simulink block diagram editor facilitates the buildup of a model or subsystem block diagram to represent the problems. The Simulink Library Browser contains basic and add-on blocks.

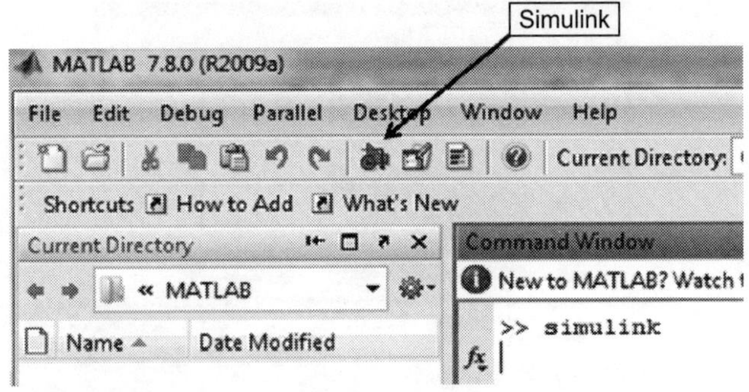

FIGURE 11.5   Simulink toolbar from MATLAB screen.

11.2.2   Simulink Dependency on MATLAB

Simulink depends on the MATLAB workspace to define and evaluate model and block parameters. The platform of Simulink is defined to model inputs and to store model outputs for analysis. Simulink can integrate calls to MATLAB operators and functions in models.

11.3   SIMULINK LIBRARY

The *Simulink* Library Browser view different displays of a tree-structured from *Simulink* library. We can build models by copying blocks from the library browser into a model window. The Simulink library consists of block set group represented in 'grey' blocks and every block in the blocks set is represented by 'white' block.

Simulink library browser window block set contains a number of blocks of different categories as listed in Table 11.1.

TABLE 11.1   Commonly used Block of Simulink Library Browser window

Block names	*Block names*
• Commonly Used Blocks	• Model-wide Utilities
• Continuous	• Port and Subsystems
• Discontinuities	• Signal Attributes
• Discrete	• Signal Routing
• Logic and Bit operations	• Sinks
• Lookup Tables	• Sources
• Math Operations	• User-defined Functions
• Model Verification	• Additional Math and Discrete

11.3.1   Browse for Blocks

When we click start button, *Simulink* Library Browser will pop-up presenting the block set for model construction in Figure 11.6. Simulink brings up the main Simulink window and a blank, untitled, model window drawn into a new model.

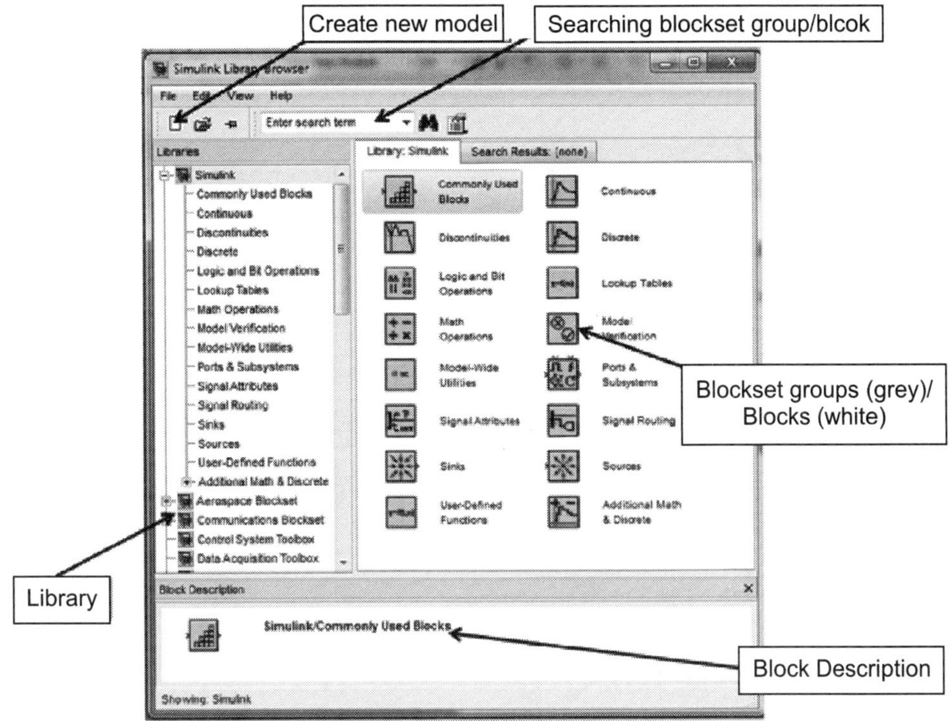

FIGURE 11.6   Simulink block.

To browse through the block libraries, select a functional area in the left pane of Library display, the blocks for the design. To get detailed information about a block right-click on a block, and then select Help forthe <block name>. The Help browser opens with the reference page for the block.

Further, to view block parameters right-click on a block, and then select the block parameters to open the dialog box.

11.3.2   Simulink Sub-block Sets

The Simulink option has several sub-options which are required to design the models. The block set extends Simulink with a comprehensive library of sub-blocks to design and simulate the physical layer of the systems and components.

When we select a block (left mouse click) in the library browser, we can read a short description and view its appearance in our worksheet, at the bottom of the library browser window. The most frequently used boxes like Bus Creators, Constant, Gain, Ground, etc., are the part of the sub-blocks.

11.3.3   Commonly Used Blocks

Commonly Used Blocks are used to list a lot of blocks which are usually used. Double-click on the commonly used blocks icon in the main Simulink windows to bring up the commonly used window. The commonly used blocks set appearance consist of several blocks as shown in Figure 11.7.

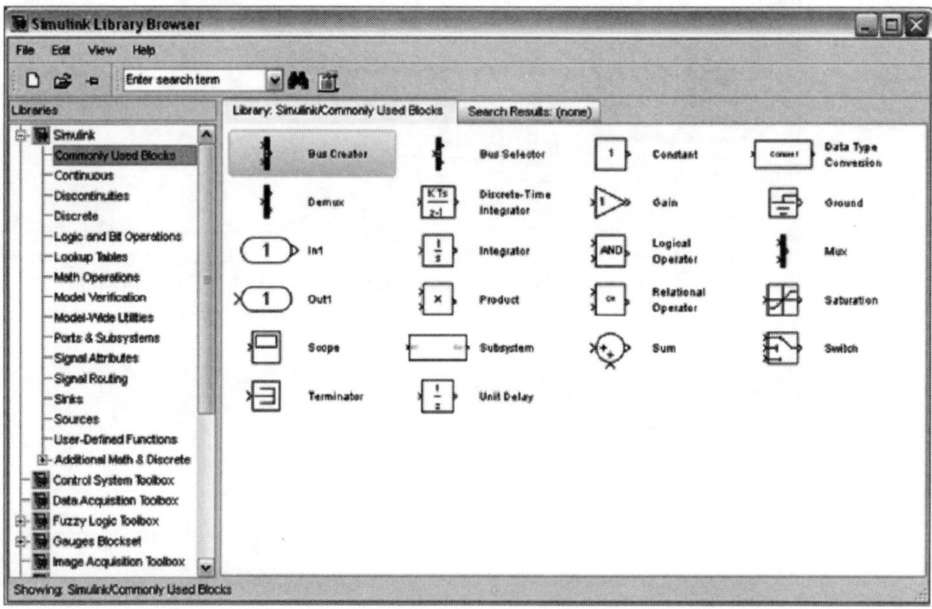

Figure 11.7   Commonly used blocks set appearance.

Bus creator

The Bus Creator block combines a set of signals into a bus.

Bus selector

The Bus Selector block outputs a specified subset of the elements of the bus at its input. The block can output the specified elements as separate signals or as a new bus.

Constant

The Constant block generates a real or complex constant value. The constant output value is displayed in the middle of the block, with a default value of 1.

The Continuous block sets in the given group appear as shown in Figure 11.8. It includes Derivative, Integrator, Transfer Function, Pole-zero, etc. in the sub-blocks.

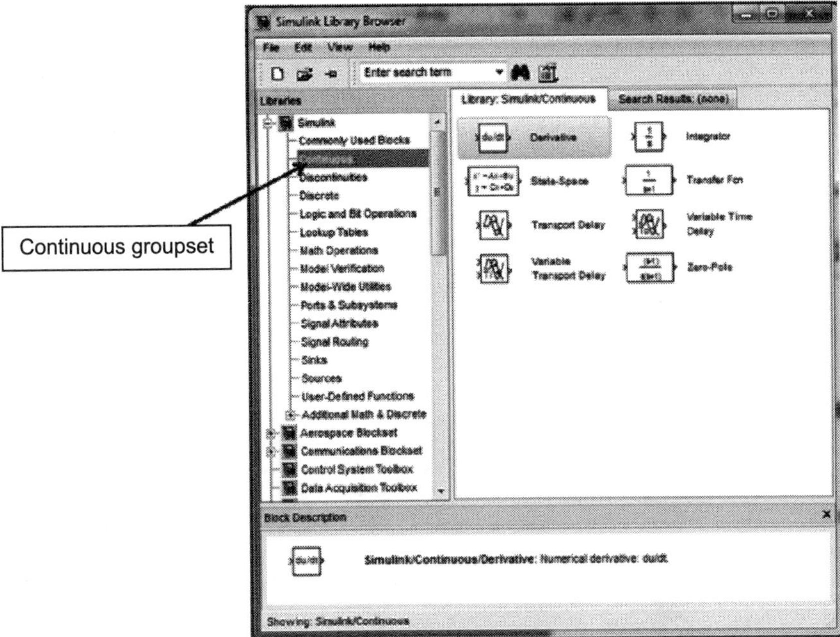

FIGURE 11.8 Simulink Library Browser.

Similarly, block sets for the other sections are also able to form and available while designing system with Simulink. We can design any system using more than one individual blocks to get a desired results. By varying the different parameters of the individual blocks, we can analyse the change in the output of the optimise system for the end-user applications.

In order to examine there blocks, create a new model window (by selection get *New* from the *File* menu in the Simulink window or hit *ctrl+N*) as shown in Figure 11.9.

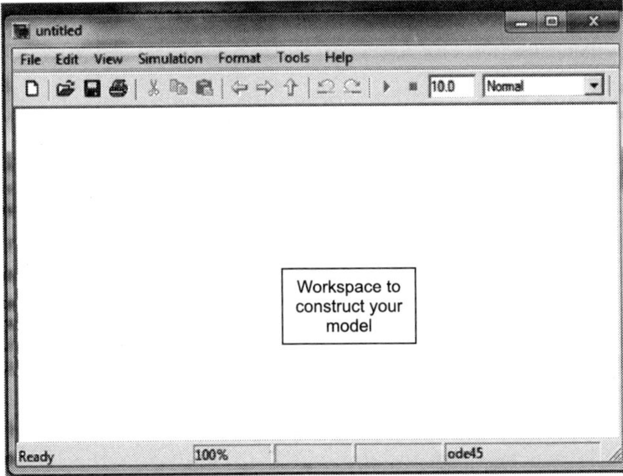

FIGURE 11.9 New window appearance.

11.4   SIMULINK BASIC ELEMENTS

There are two major classes of items in Simulink. They are *blocks* and *lines*.
   Blocks are used to generate, modify, combine, output, and display signals.
   Lines are used to transfer signals from one block to another. *Lines* can never inject a signal into another line; it is combined through the use of a block such as a summing junction.

11.4.1   Resources of Simulink

The following model of window as shown in Figure 11.10 represents the simulation screen display and its different tools and labels.

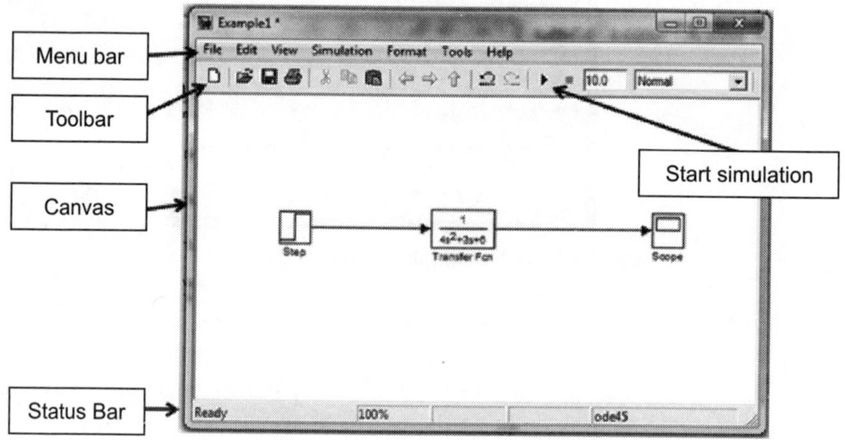

FIGURE 11.10   The simulation model block.

The components of the simulation display are briefly explained here are as follows:

Menu bar: It contains commands for creating, editing, viewing, printing and simulating models.

Toolbar: It holds the most frequently used commands and allowing execution of the commands with a click of a mouse button.

Status bar: This bar provides the information regarding the status of the model.

Context menus: This menu is displayed when the right button of the mouse is clicked over the canvas.

Canvas: It displays model's block diagram to edit the blocks for modification.

11.4.2   Opening an Existing File

The Simulink saved file can be open by any of the following methods:

* Opening can be done by click on the open [open model] icon on the toolbar of the Simulink library browser.

- By selecting open [Open] toolbar from the file menu in the Simulink library browser.
- By pressing the [Ctrl + O] from the keyboard.

11.4.3 Creating a New File

We can create a new file in Simulink by any of the following methods:

- Click on the new [new model] file icon on the toolbar of the Simulink library browser.
- By select New → Model bar from the file menu in the Simulink library browser.
- By press [Ctrl + N] keyboard.

Blocks

There are several general classes of blocks:

- *Sources:* These are to generate various input signals.
- *Sinks:* These are used to output or display signals.
- *Discrete:* Linear, discrete-time system elements (transfer functions, state-space models, etc.)
- *Linear:* Linear, continuous-time system elements and connections (summing junctions, gains, etc.)
- *Nonlinear:* Nonlinear operators (arbitrary functions, saturation, delay, etc.)
- *Connections:* Multiplex, Demultiplex, System Macros, etc.

Lines

The blocks are connected using lines. Lines transmit signals in the direction indicated by the arrow. It must always transmit signals from the output terminal of one block to the input terminal of another block. We can observe the exception, a line can tap off from another line, splitting the signal to each of two destination blocks, as shown in Figure 11.11.

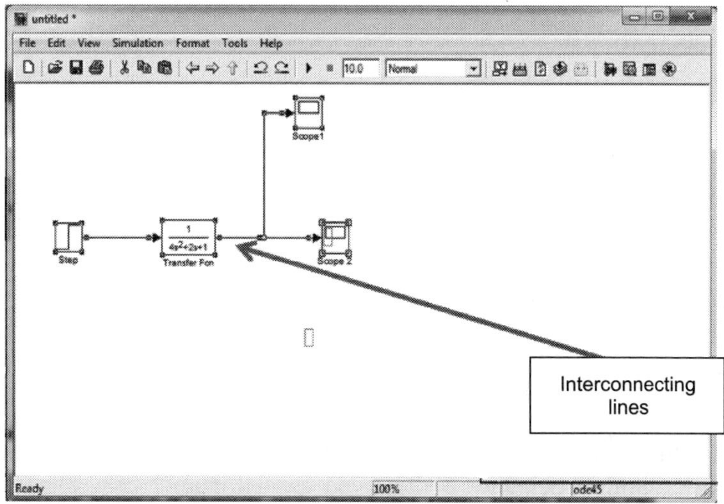

FIGURE 11.11 Destination blocks.

Lines can never inject a signal into another line; lines must be combined through the use of a block such as a summing junction. A signal can be either a scalar signal or a vector signal.

11.4.4 Simulation of Blocks

In Simulink, a model is a collection of blocks which, in general, use to draw a model in a blank model window, or saved model files can be loaded either from the File menu or from the MATLAB command prompt as shown in Figure 11.12.

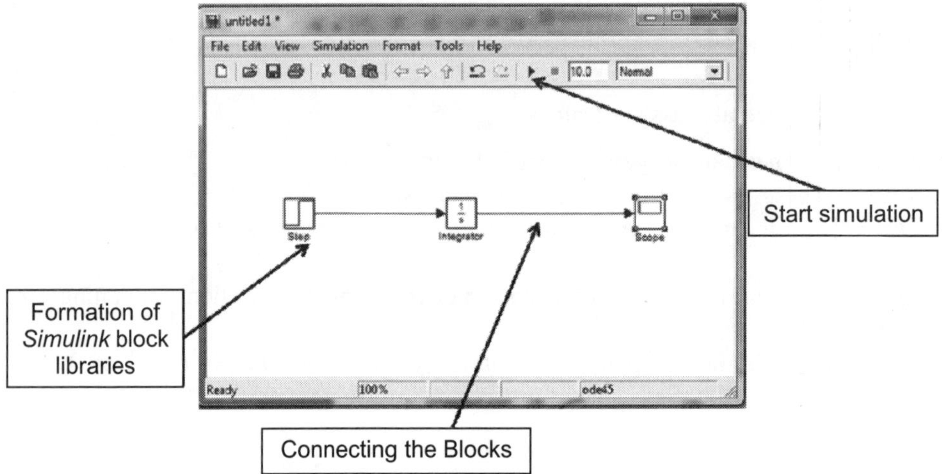

FIGURE 11.12   The model window of defined blocks.

The simple model consists of three blocks: *Step*, *Transfer Function* and *Scope*.

- The *Step* is a source block from which a step input signal originates.
- The *Transfer function* is a linear block that modifies its input signal and produces a new output signal.
- The *Scope* is a sink block used to display a signal. It is similar to an oscilloscope.

From the Simulink library, blocks are dragged and dropped on the newly opened window. Connections between step, transfer function and scope blocks are made by just pressing the left button of the mouse over the source and dragging to the destination port.

After the connections are made, the system is ready and it is saved as filename.mdl.

To run the model, click at the 'Start Simulation' option button it will start the simulation. More detail discussion of the concept will be done in the following sections.

11.5 MODEL CREATION IN SIMULINK

Type *Simulink* in the MATLAB command window and then open the new model window. The *Simulink* new 'untitled' window is displayed as in Figure 11.13. The *Simulink* window incorporates the required model from the library browser window.

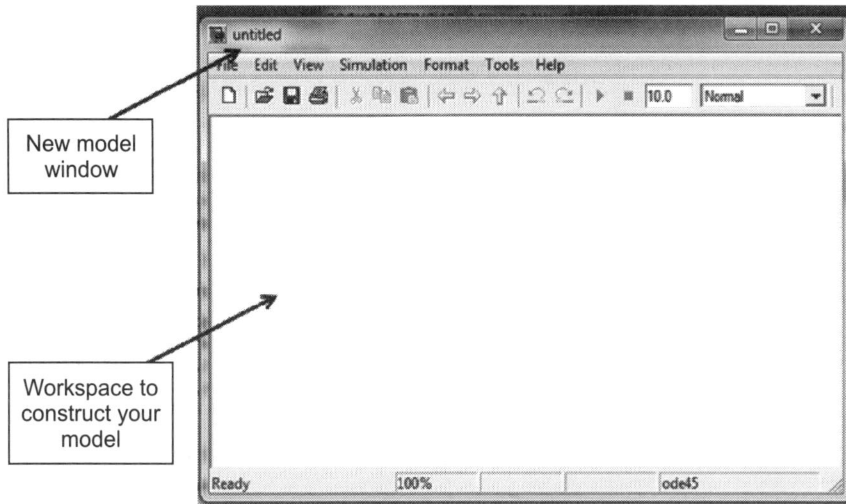

FIGURE 11.13   New untitled simulink window.

To become familiarised with the structure and the environment of Simulink, we are encouraged to explore the toolboxes and scan their contents. Even through we may not know what they are all about but these toolboxes will guide us for a design.

The desired block can be selected by clicking on the block library. The tool is user friendly and helps to move and add this block the model window. This is done by clicking on it and also dragging it to the desired location. The desired block is selected from particular category by dragging and dropping into the model window. These models are joined by connecting lines from the output terminal of one block to input terminal of other block.

A complete model in *Simulink* can be made with the help of following steps:

1. Creation of model using blocks
2. Labelling of blocks
3. Modifying block parameters
4. Interconnecting blocks design
5. Labelling the signal lines
6. Simulation of block
7. Saving the model

11.5.1 Creation of Model Using Blocks

We can create the model as shown in Figure 11.14 to represent the model window of dragged and dropped blocks.

Following steps are used for creating a new model from the *Simulink* Library Browser.

*   *Selection of desired block from library:*   The design model can be created my altering the model until desired blocks that fits, is found.
*   *Drag and drop blocks in window:*   For the design of new model window, the drag and drop of model using mouse or keyboard creates the model.

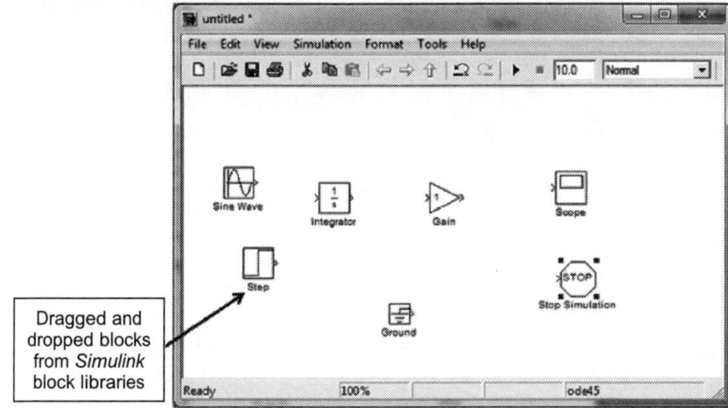

FIGURE 11.14   The model window of dragged and dropped blocks.

- *Expansion of the block library:*   The blocks available in the Simulink Library Browser can be expanded by clicking on it. On clicking on the commonly used block library the parameters can be modified.

11.5.2   Labelling of Blocks

The labelling is to change the standard name of the block. This is changed by click on the standard label of the block and deletes the existing label to edit with new label. Labelling is used to provide different identification labels anywhere in the model. This is done by double click at the desired location as shown in Figure 11.15. We can refer to the model that is selected for changing label.

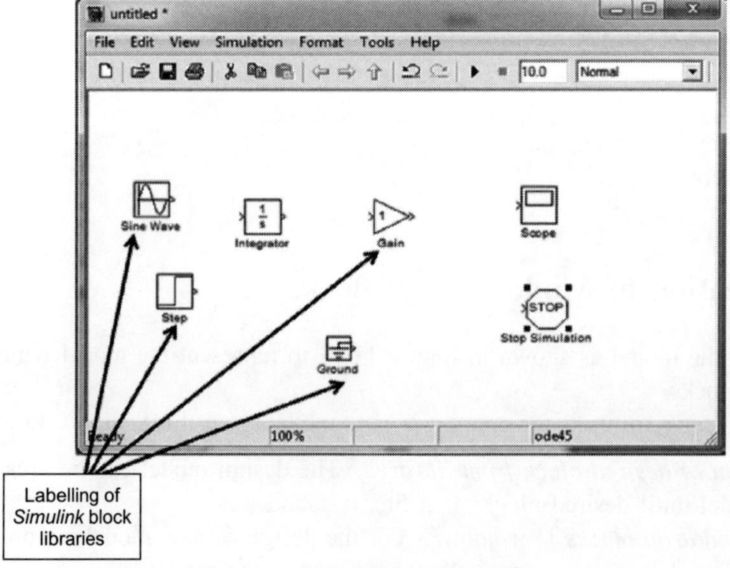

FIGURE 11.15   Label of standard block changed.

11.5.3   Modifying Block Parameters

In the *Simulink* Library Browser, the blocks are in default mode having standard forms. At times, it becomes necessary to modify the contents of the Simulink model formed. For that the Simulink editor can be used. The parameters can be modified to make them suitable as per the requirement to solve the problem. A block can be modified by double-clicking on it. Double click on block will pop-up the dialog box. Figure 11.16 shows the pop-up dialogue box of 'Source Block Parameters step'.

The default parameters in this dialog box generate a step function occurring at time =1 s, from an initial level of zero to a level of 1.

The arrow shows the transformation from Simulink library to formation of block using step 1 and for modification of setup parameter the arrow step 2 is marked in Figure 11.16.

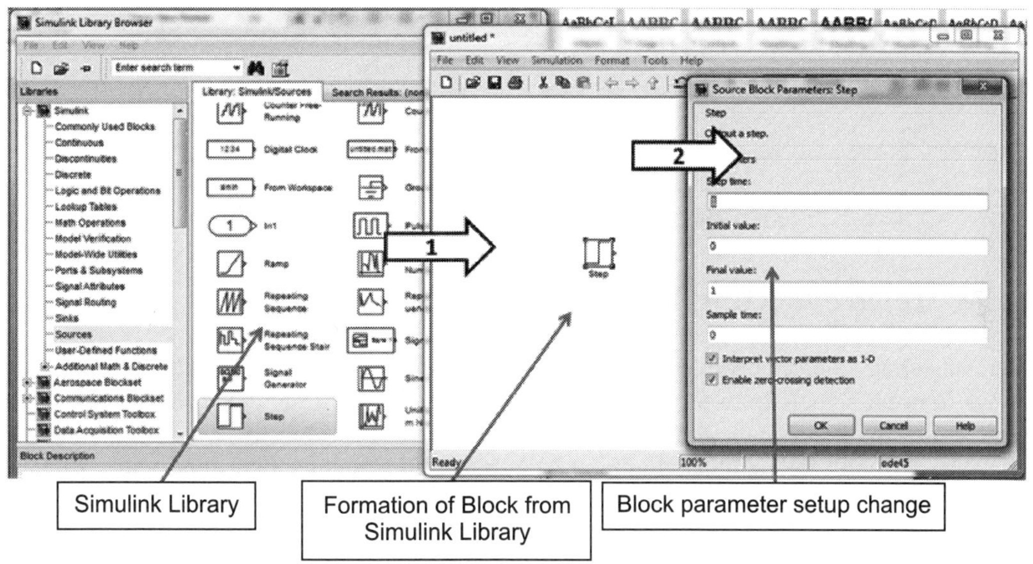

FIGURE 11.16   Pop-up dialogue box of 'Step function'.

EXAMPLE 11.1   In this example, we learn to modify the transfer function block parameters.

Open a transfer block dialog box by double-click on it, to observe the transfer function parameters. This dialog box contains fields for the numerator and the denominator of the block transfer function. By entering a vector containing the coefficients of the desired numerator or denominator polynomial, the desired function can be formed.

Let us see how to implement transfer function $[1/(4s^2 + 2s + 1)]$. We can change the vector variable coefficient of transfer function block by modifying the values of the parameters as displayed in the Figure 11.17. By changing the numerator and denominator the result will be appear in the block. For easy way of understanding, we have entered the following into the denominator field: [4 2 1] to form the denominator value as $4s^2 + 2s + 1$ and 1 in the numerator field.

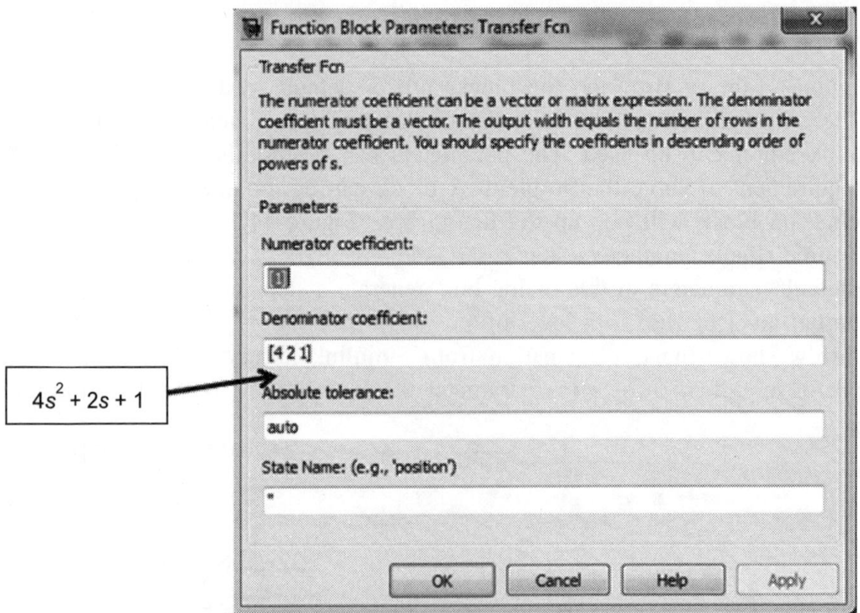

FIGURE 11.17   Transfer function block parameters.

11.5.4   Interconnecting Blocks

Interconnecting lines transmit signals in the direction indicated by the arrow. Lines must always transmit signals from the output terminal of one block to the input terminal of another block. After the blocks are selected based on desired design and labelled (if needed), these are connected with one another. Figure 11.18 shows the resulting line filled with arrowhead for interconnecting blocks.

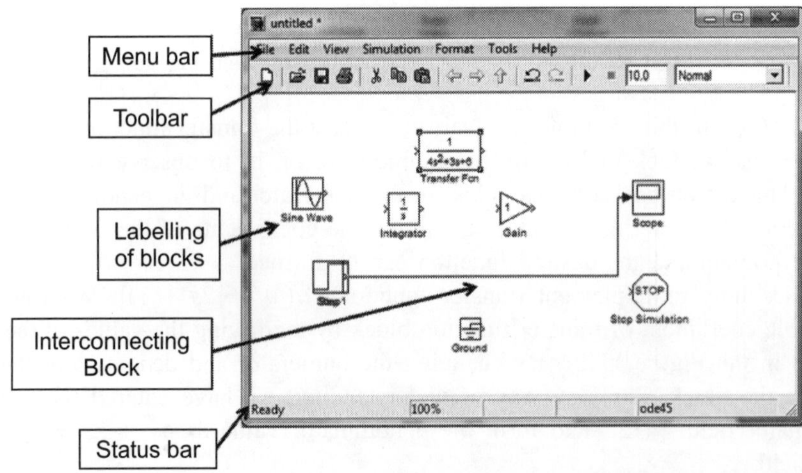

FIGURE 11.18   Interconnecting blocks with arrowhead line.

To interconnect the blocks, the mouse pointer is draged to input and/or output ports indicated by angle brackets on the side that connects by solid line with an arrowhead that indicates the direction of signal flow.

Further, if the signal blocks need to provide a feedback then it can be connected by connecting line. Figure 11.19 shows the connecting tapped feedback signal line from output side block to input side.

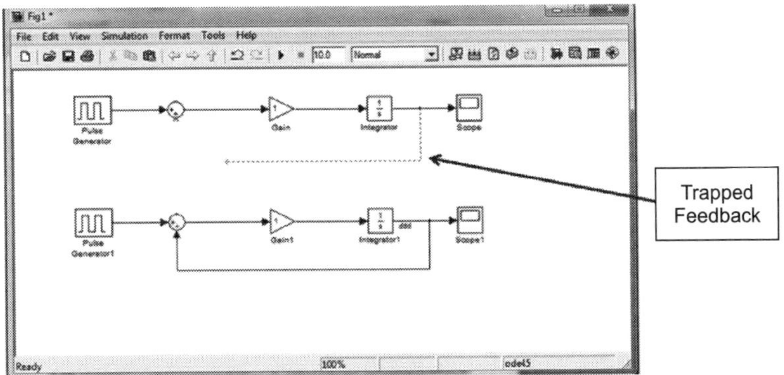

FIGURE 11.19　Connecting tapped feedback signal line.

The feedback signal line can be drawn by pointing the mouse on the output line at desired point. Click the mouse at the point, press and hold the 'Ctrl' key then again click and drag the mouse pointer till the destination block is reached. Initially, a dashed line with an open arrow head will appear. This is the incomplete line from output terminal. The line when drawn to the input terminal, the branching line will be complete. Finally, the blocks are realigned to appear in order by connecting correct lines.

11.5.5　Labelling the Signal Lines

Labelling is used to provide different identification labels anywhere in the model. This is done by doubleiclick at the desired location as shown in Figure 11.20.

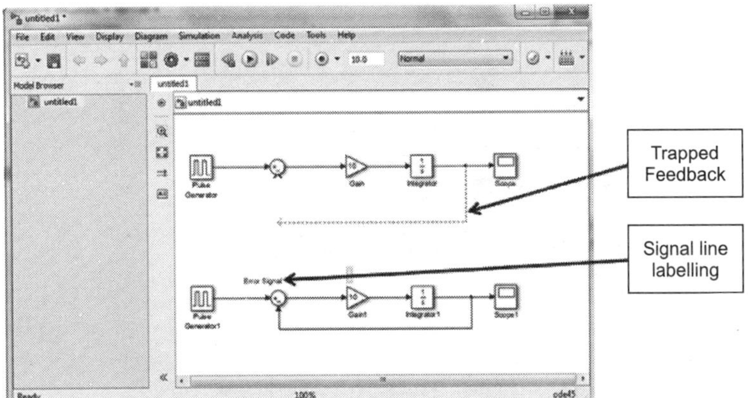

FIGURE 11.20　Labelling of signal lines.

11.5.6   Simulation of the Model

The procedure to run a simulation of the design model is shown in Figure 11.21.

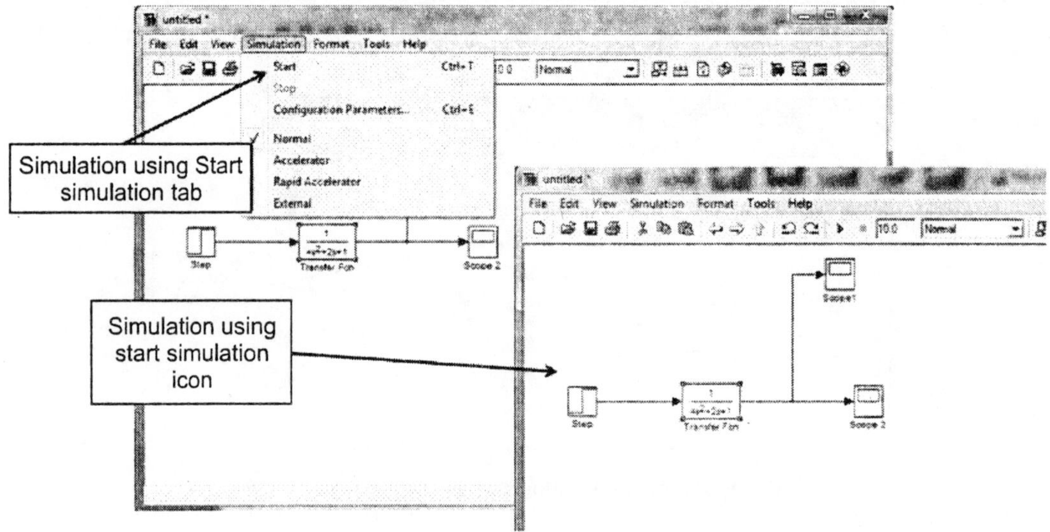

FIGURE 11.21   Simulation of model.

Before running a simulation of this system, first open the scope window by double-clicking on the scope block. Then, to start the simulation, either select **Start** from the **Simulation** menu or directly click on the icon.

The simulation should run very quickly and we can see that the scope window will appear as shown in Figure 11.22.

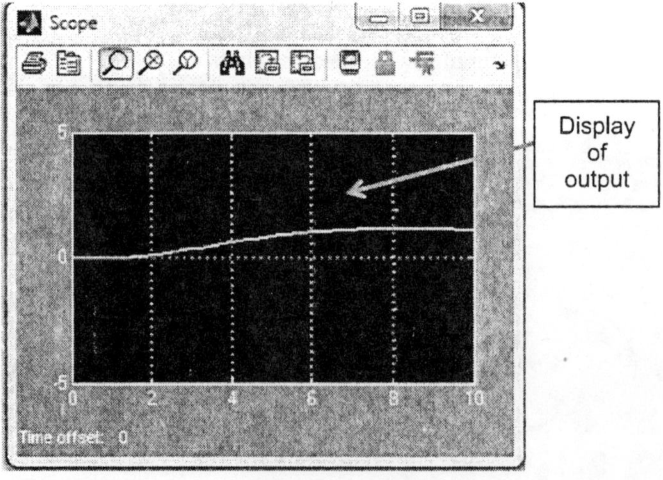

Figure 11.22   Scope window.

Simulink Performs Simulation

The Simulink performs simulation as per flowchart shown in Figure 11.23. Once the model is designed then the simulation is started to observe the output results. After the simulation is complete, it is terminated by cleaning up memory.

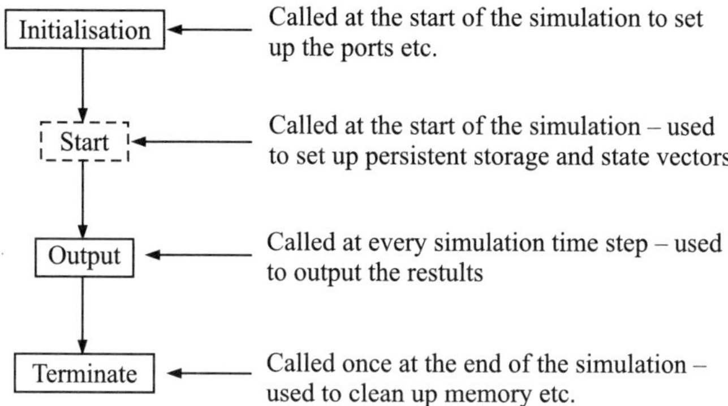

FIGURE 11.23   Simulation flowchart.

11.5.7   Saving the Model

The design model can be saved like Window desktop by clicking 'save as' from *File* menu in the model window. The click on [save] icon in the toolbox saves the model.

Save or *CTRL+S* command save all *Simulink* model file and it will have an extension '.mdl'.

11.6   SIMULINK EXAMPLES

The *Simulink* model after being created and completed, the model can be simulated to visualise for analysing the result. The signal appears in the scope and it will be displayed by double-click in the window. Following examples give better insight of the *Simulink* model.

11.6.1   Step Response Modelling and Simulation

The simple model consists of three blocks: Step, Transfer function, and Scope. The Step is a **source block** which originates a step input signal. The Transfer function is a **linear block**. The Transfer function can be modified by its input signal and it outputs a new signal. The Scope is a **sink block** used to display a signal much like an oscilloscope. We can understand the above blocks in the following examples.

EXAMPLE 11.2   In this example, we learn to find the step response of the transfer functions $\dfrac{1}{(4s^2 + 2s + 1)}$ for Figure 11.24 using Simulink.

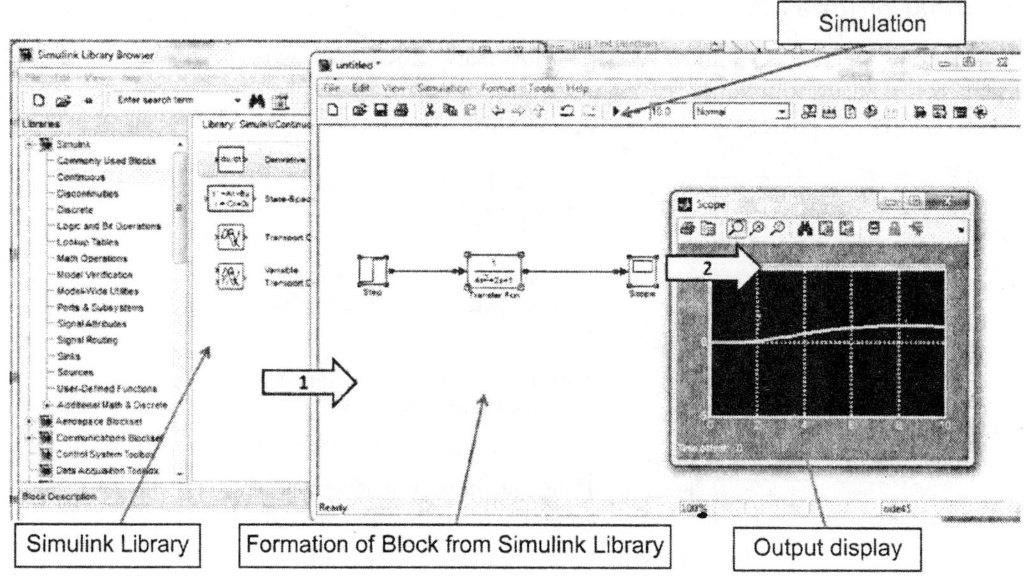

FIGURE 11.24   Step response example.

In Simulink, a model for the given example is created from collection of library blocks to create a model window as shown by the arrow 1. Then the simulation is done by clicking the run icon or by clicking on the toolbar Simulation → Start.

Before running a simulation of this system, first open the 'Configuration parameter' option of Simulation menu and select 'Data Import/Export'. On completion 'Run' the simulation and verify the result on scope block window by double-clicking on it. Once the simulation run it out put will appear in the scope window. The time response of the system of the example is shown in Figure 11.25.

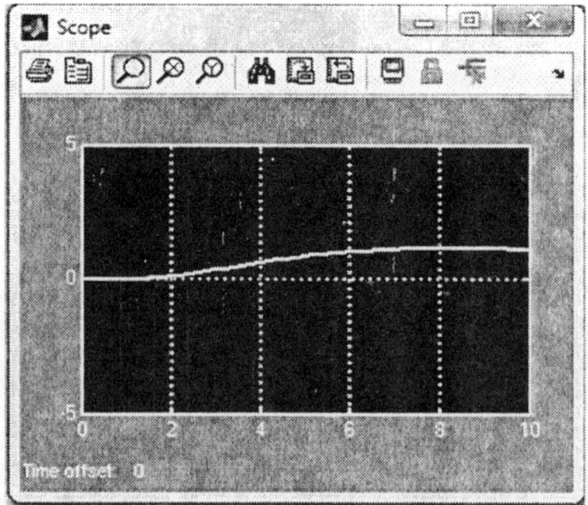

FIGURE 11.25   Simulation response for Example 11.2.

If we change start time from 0.0 to 5, the parameters of the simulation model window, will show the new result. The simulation parameter options produce new result as shown in Figure 11.26.

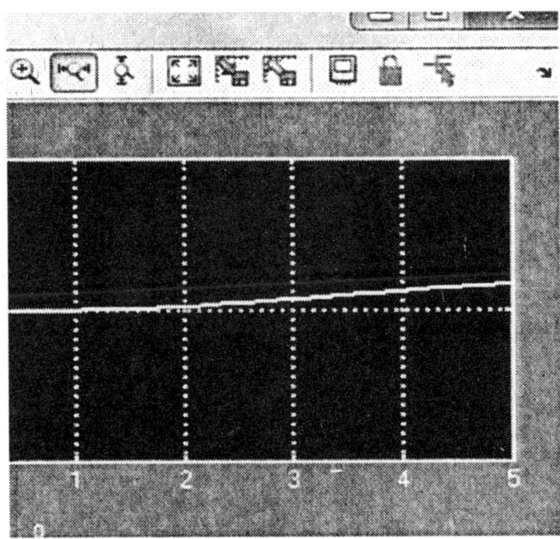

FIGURE 11.26　Simulation response for Example 11.2.

Note that the simulation output as shown in yellow colour is at a very low level relative to the axes of the scope. To fix this, we can hit the autoscale button icon (binoculars) to see the better appearance of display. Figure 11.27 shows the autoscale window.

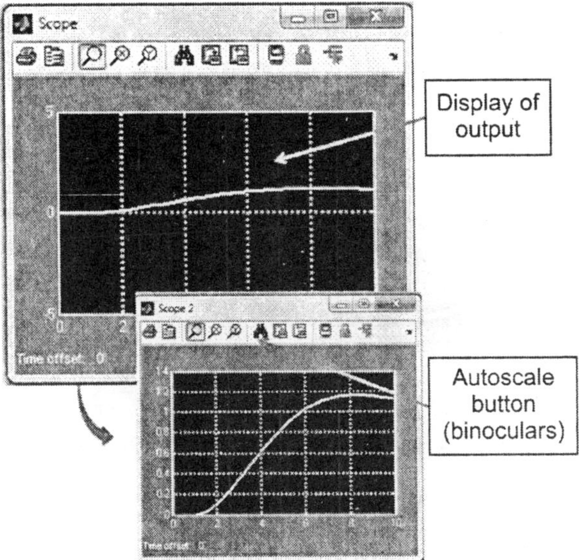

FIGURE 11.27　Autoscale window.

We can also change the parameters of the simulation. In the model window, select **Configuration Parameters** from the **Simulation** menu. We will see the following dialog box as shown in Figure 11.28.

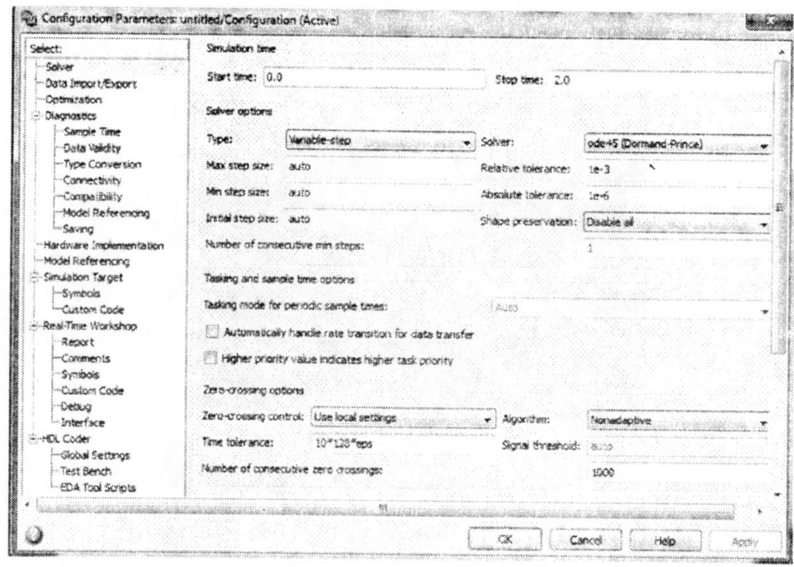

FIGURE 11.28   Configuration parameter window.

In the confirmation parameter window, we can select the start and stop times, which tell Simulink about time period to perform the simulation. We can try by changing **Start time** from 0.0 to 1 and change **Stop time** from 10.0 to 2.0, to observe the display shown in Figure 11.29.

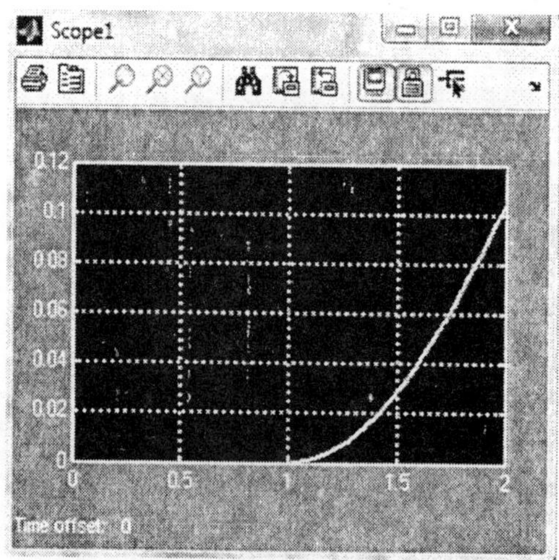

FIGURE 11.29   Configuration parameter scope window.

EXAMPLE 11.3 In this example, we see a sine wave block (a source) which generates a sine wave signal displayed by the scope. The integrated sine signal is sent to scope for display. These two signals are multiplex via Mux to display the output as shown in Figure 11.30.

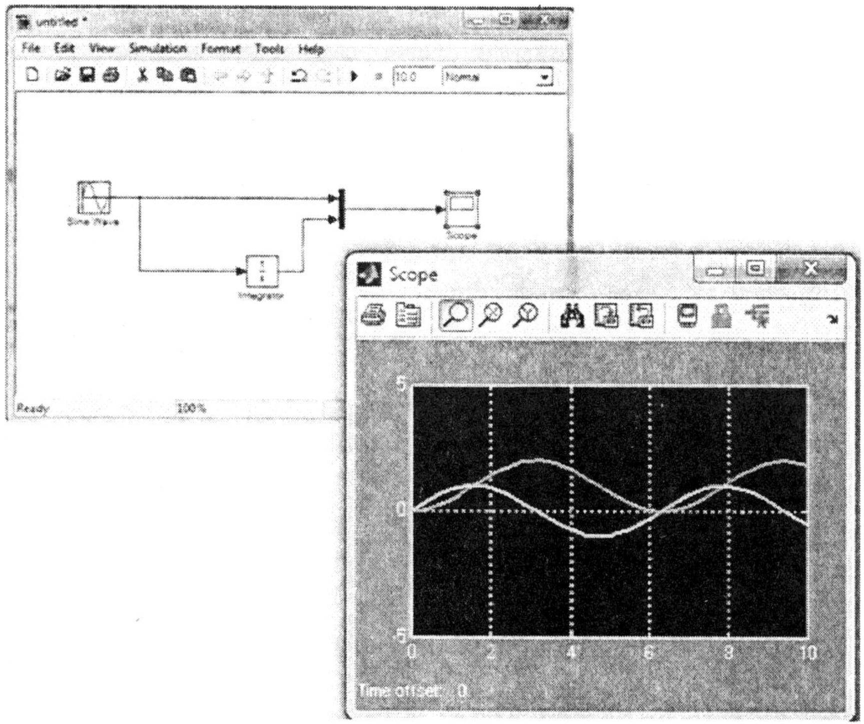

FIGURE 11.30 Simulink simulation of Example 11.3.

The output signal on scope can be viewed/edited with the parameters by done simply double-clicking on the block of interest.

EXAMPLE 11.4 In this example, we learn to find the response of the controller transfer functions $10\left(\dfrac{s+2}{s}\right)$ using *Simulink* for Figure 11.31.

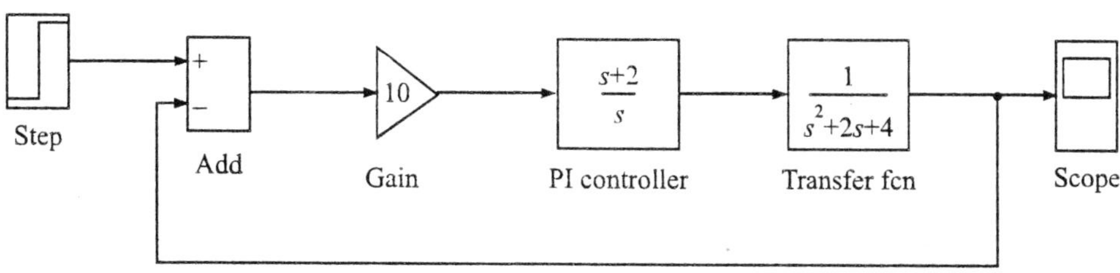

FIGURE 11.31 Controller transfer functions $10\left(\dfrac{s+2}{s}\right)$

In this case, the complete controller transfer function is entered into *Simulink* manually by entering the numbers in the block dialog boxes.

The block in the Simulation menu is selected and by 'Configuration parameter' toolbar the 'Data Import/Export' parameter is set. Selected block is simulated by clicking on Run tool icon. The simulation output is viewed by double-click on the Scope block, shown in Figure 11.32.

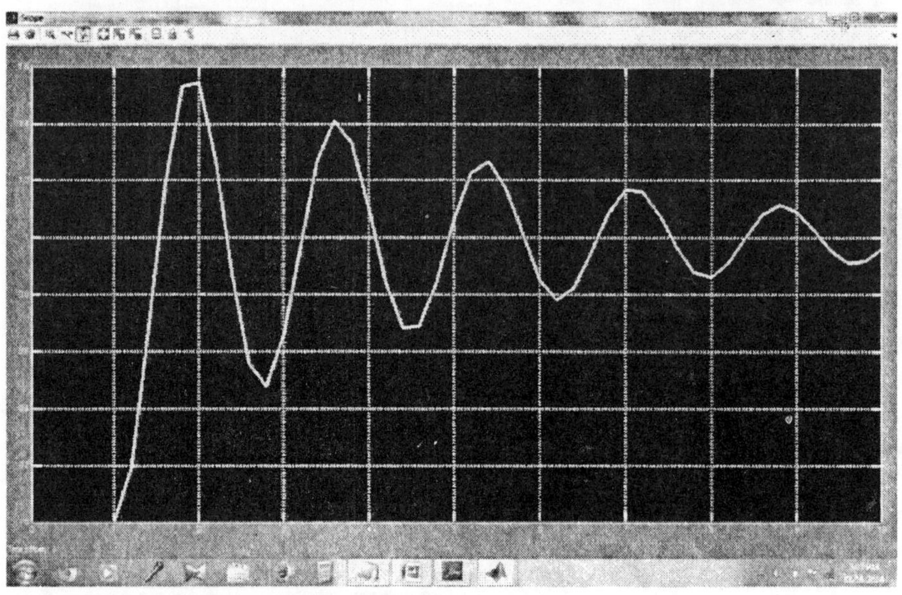

FIGURE 11.32   Simulation response for Example 11.4.

EXAMPLE 11.5   In this example, we learn to find the response of the controller transfer function using *Simulink* for Figure 11.33.

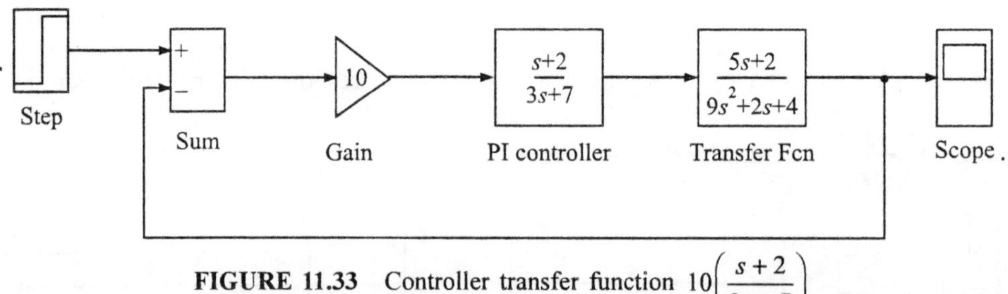

FIGURE 11.33   Controller transfer function $10\left(\dfrac{s+2}{3s+7}\right)$

Based on controller transfer function for given example, blocks are created from collection of Library blocks model window in Simulink.

Selected block in the Simulation menu 'Configuration parameter' toolbar the 'Data Import/Export' parameter is set. Selected block is simulated by clicking on Run tool icon. The simulation output is viewed by double-click on the Scope block, shown in Figure 11.34.

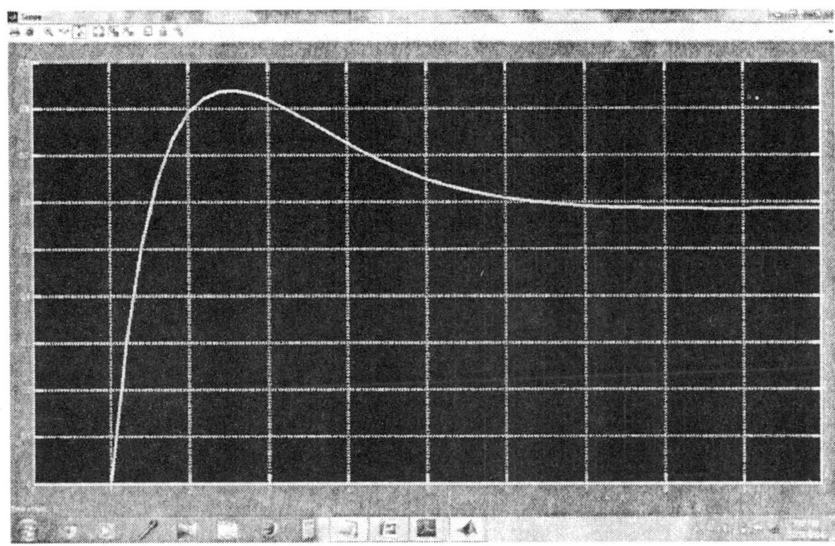

FIGURE 11.34   Simulation response for Example 11.5.

In the Simulink sometimes, we would like to use the results of a simulation in the MATLAB command window for further calculations and plotting. In such case, both the output signal and the control signal for calculations in MATLAB need to observe. These two signals are considered as two variables. The two variablesare saved as a time signal from our Simulink model. Following example shows the simulation results of these variables.

EXAMPLE 11.6   Consider the response of the controller transfer function $10\left(\dfrac{s+2}{3s+7}\right)$ using *Simulink* for Figure 11.35.

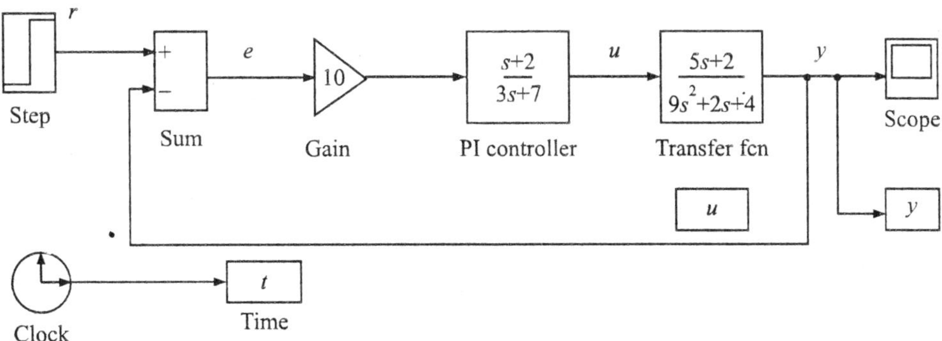

FIGURE 11.35   Controller transfer function $10\left(\dfrac{s+2}{3s+7}\right)$ for time function.

Based on controller transfer function for given example selected block in the simulation menu 'Configuration parameter' toolbar the 'Data Import/Export' parameter is set. Selected block is simulated by clicking on Run tool icon. The simulation output is viewed by double-click on the Scope block shown in Figure 11.36.

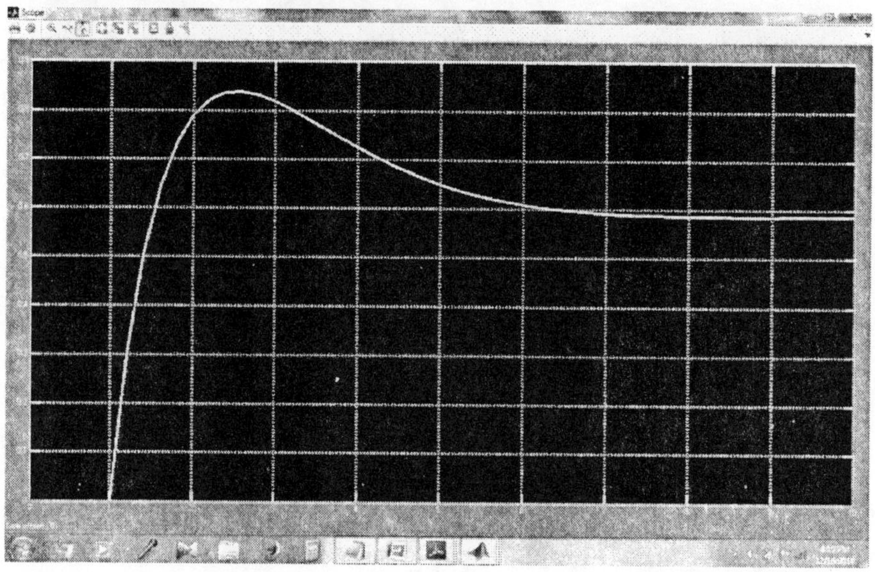

FIGURE 11.36   Simulation response of output.

MATLAB variable u and the output signal to the MATLAB variable y is as shown in Figure 11.37.

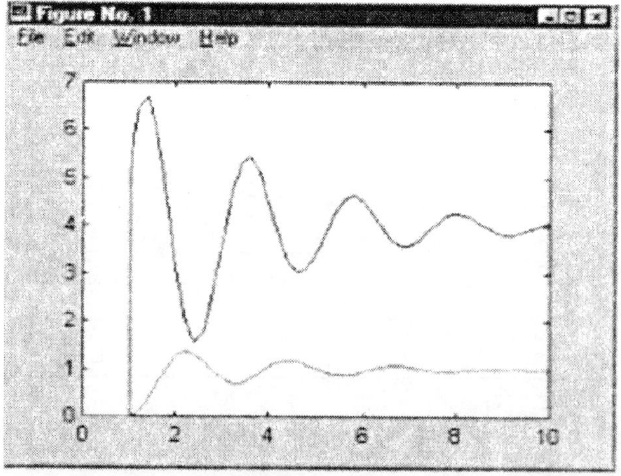

FIGURE 11.37   Simulation response of variable.

EXAMPLE 11.7   In this example, we learn to find the response of the controller transfer functions $\left(\dfrac{1}{2s+1}\right)$ using *Simulink* for Figure 11.38.

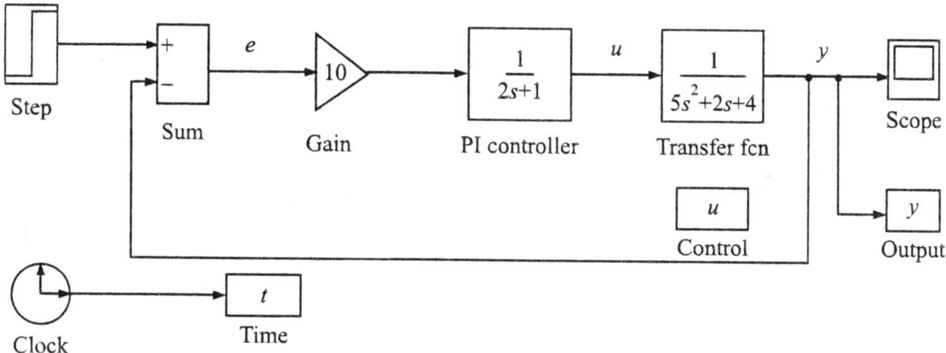

FIGURE 11.38   Block diagram of Example 11.6.

Here, both the output signal and the control signal are used for the calculations in MATLAB. We can save the two variables as well as a time signal from *Simulink* model.

The Workspace block near the Plant block will output the control signal to the MATLAB variable *u* and the output signal to the MATLAB variable *y* is as shown in Figure 11.39.

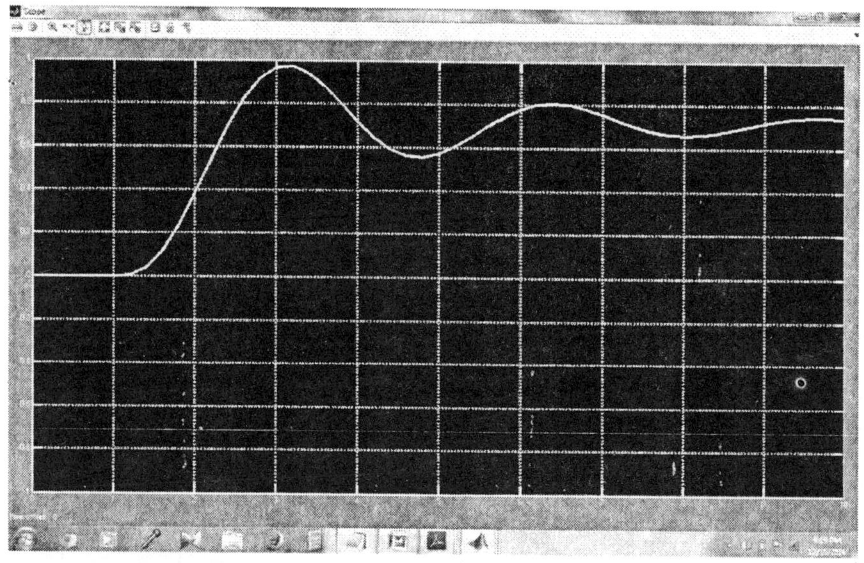

FIGURE 11.39   Simulation response for Example 11.7.

11.6.2   Multiplying Two Sinusoidal Using *Simulink* Diagram

A state of art using the Simulink library browser, drawn two sinusoid signal blocks are selected from the Sources block-set. Signals are dragged on to the canvas. Two sinusoidal signals are operated in different frequencys. These two signals are multiplied by the product block, selected from the commonly used blocks and dragged to canvas from the library. Finally, running the simulation will results the following output in Figure 11.40.

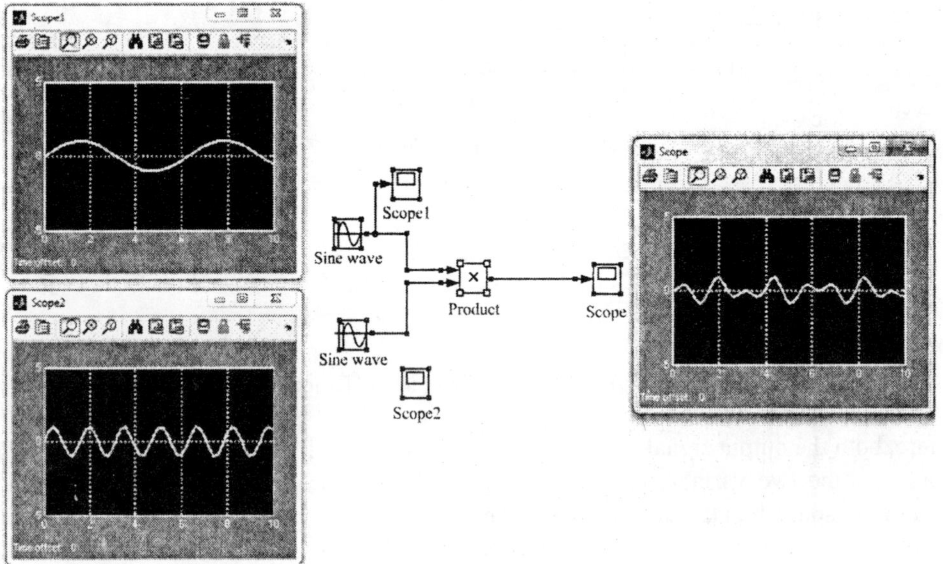

FIGURE 11.40   Model to multiply two sinusoidal signals.

11.6.3   Generating an AM Signal from *Simulink* Diagram

Using a state of art Simulink library browser, two sinusoid signal blocks are selected from the Sources block-set. Signals blocks are dragged on to the canvas, connections are made and the scope is added. The frequency values of the source are modified to suit the AM generation requirement as shown in Figure 11.41.

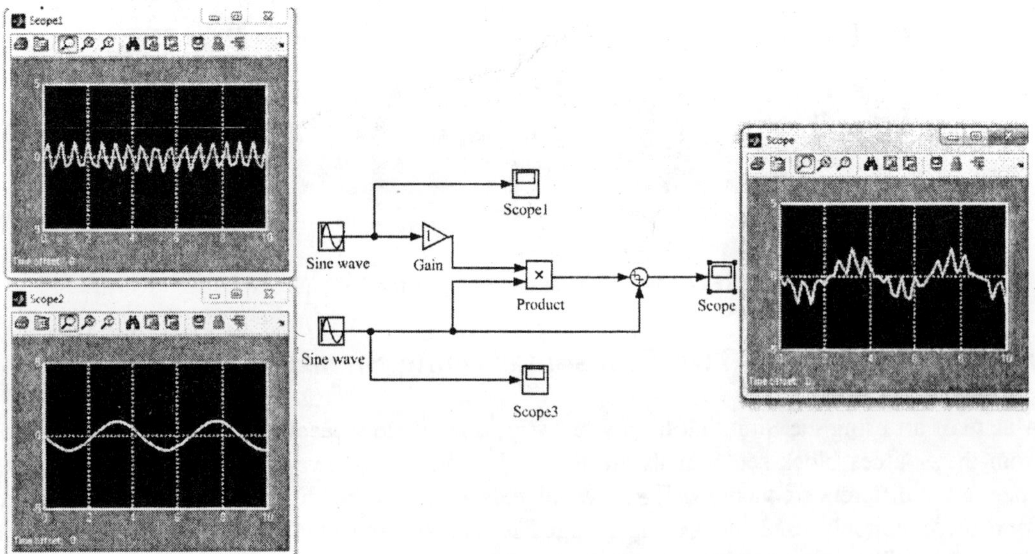

FIGURE 11.41   AM signal generation.

11.6.4   Adding Derivative of Two Sinusoidal Using *Simulink* Diagram

Using a state of art Simulink Library Browser, two sinusoid signal blocks are selected from the Sources block-set. Signals are dragged on to the canvas. Two sinusoidal signals passed to derivative block and the resultant waveforms are combined together. These two signals are multiplied from the Commonly Used Blocks from the library. Finally, running the simulation will results the following Figure 11.42.

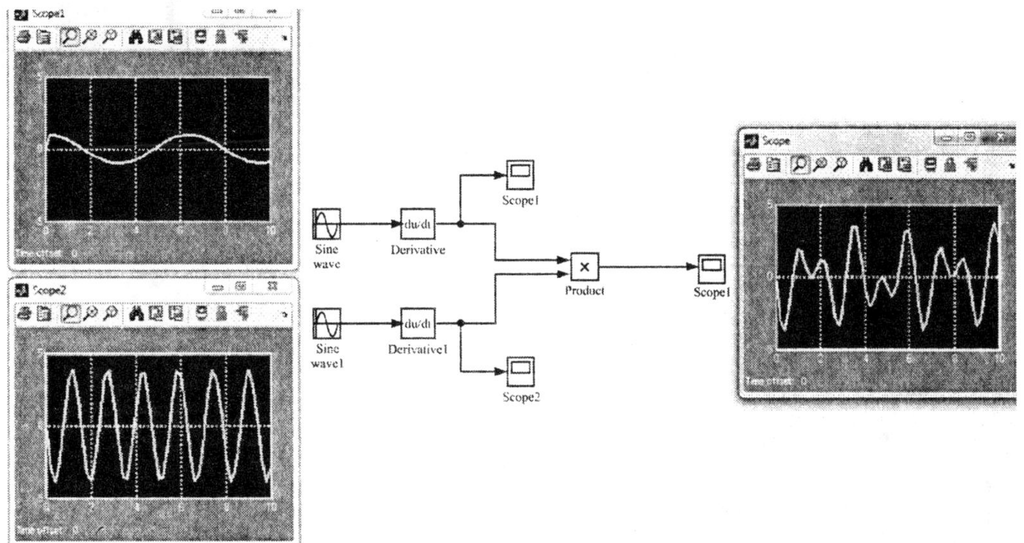

FIGURE 11.42   Derivative of two signals.

11.6.5   Design of Second Order Closed Loop System

Using a state of art Simulink library browser, to design a second order closed loop system blocks are selected from the Sources block-set. Step response of a closed loop second order system is shown in Figure 11.43.

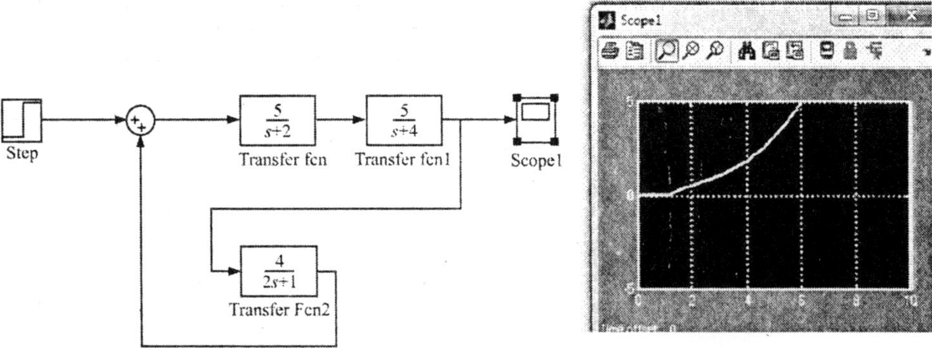

FIGURE 11.43   Step response of second order closed loop.

Similarly, for sinusoidal response of a closed loop second order system is shown in Figure 11.44.

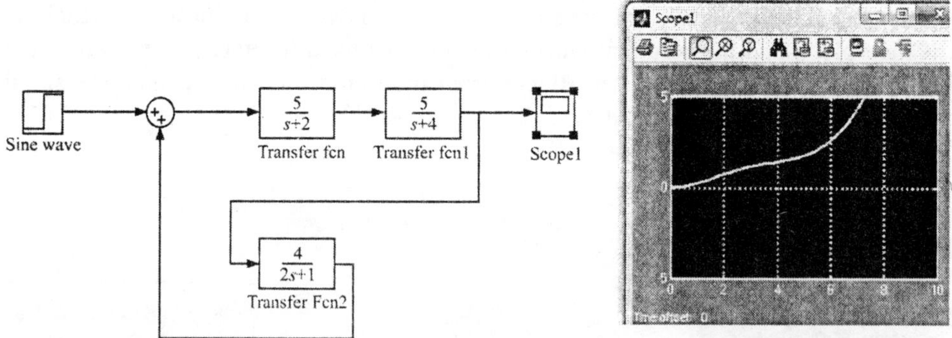

FIGURE 11.44   Sinusoidal input response of second order closed loop.

11.6.6   Step Response Modelling and Simulation

The Workspace block of state-space model of dynamic system response described by matrix of differential equations is represented in the following example by using Simulink.

In this *Simulink* model window, the state-space model is created from 'continuous block library' using the *Simulink* Library Browser as shown in Figure 11.45.

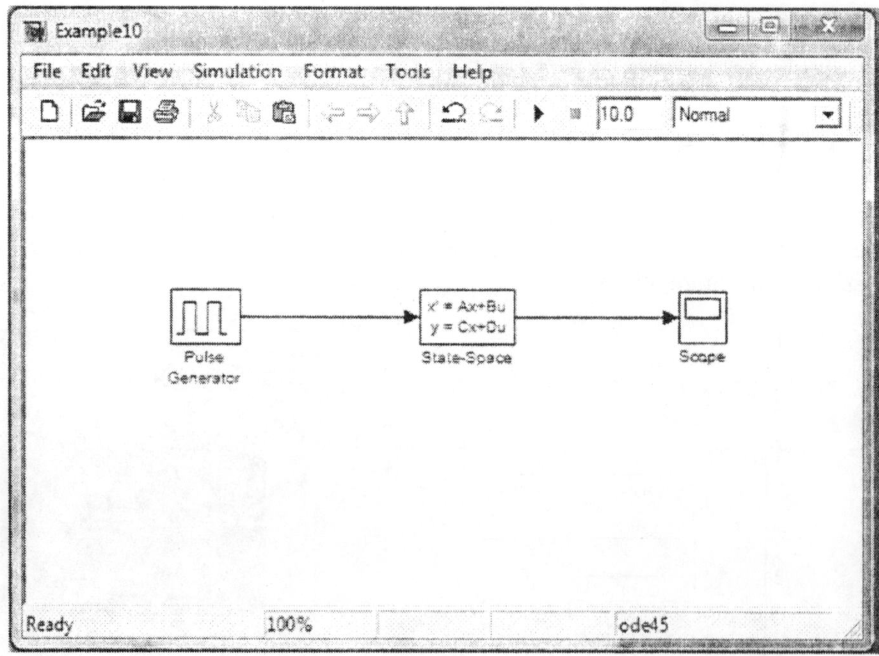

FIGURE 11.45   State-space model.

State-space block model parameters consist of A, B, C and D matrix vectors. The system is simulated as described in the earlier example procedure.

EXAMPLE 11.8   Using *Simulink* find the unit step response of a following control system described by the following state variable.

$$x = \begin{bmatrix} 2 & 5 & -5 \\ -7 & 3 & 9 \\ 6 & -1 & -7 \end{bmatrix} \begin{bmatrix} x_1 \\ x_2 \\ x_3 \end{bmatrix} + \begin{bmatrix} 4 \\ 2 \\ 7 \end{bmatrix} u \text{ and } y = [2 \ 5 \ 1] x$$

Solution: The *Simulink* model is constructed for the above equation by drag and drop of blocks of state-space model from 'Sources, Continuous and Sink block library'. We will get the state-space model as shown in Figure 11.45.

By double-click on state-space dialogue box enter the value of the matrices and vectors of *A*, *B*, *C* and *D* from the example in the respective dialog box.

Start the simulation by selecting 'start simulation' or by click on 'run' icon and view the scope block by double-clicking. The response is shown in Figure 11.46.

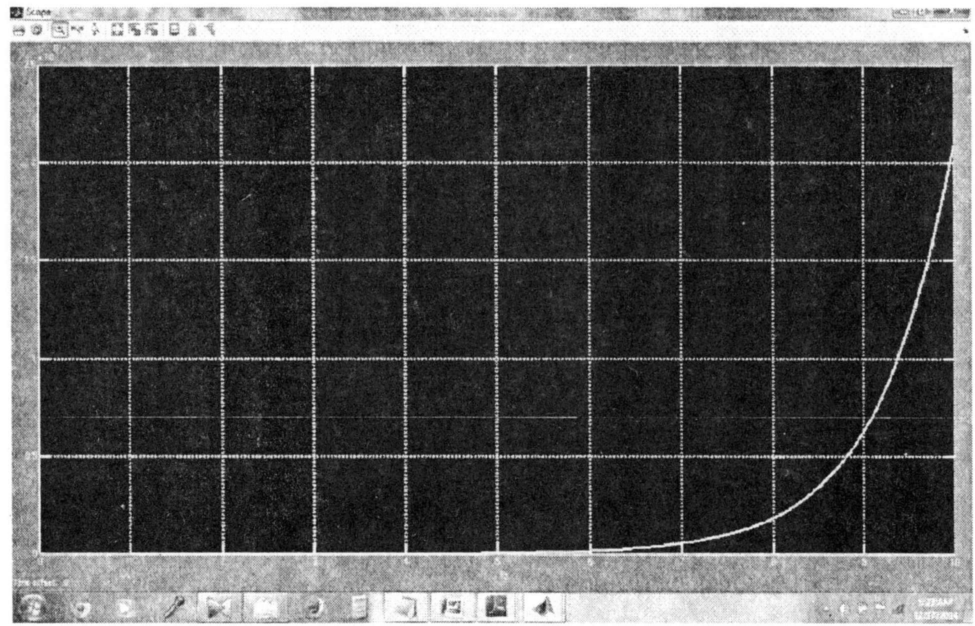

FIGURE 11.46   Simulation response for Example 11.8.

11.6.7   State-space Model from *Simulink* Diagram

A state-space linear model consists of ordinary differential equations. These differential equations can be extracted from a given *Simulink* model using *linmod* function. Following are the syntax:

```
[a,b,c,d] = linmod('sys')
[a,b,c,d] = linmod('sys',x,u)
```

where,

sys name is to obtain state-space model of the Simulink.

x, u are state vector and input vector as specified.

ss2tf converts a state-space representation of a given system to an equivalent transfer function representation. Its syntax is as follows:

```
[b,a] = ss2tf(A,B,C,D,iu)
```

tf2ss convert transfer function filter parameters to state-space form representation. Its syntax is as follows:

```
[A,B,C,D] = tf2ss(b,a)
```

EXAMPLE 11.9   In this example, we use MATLAB to convert the transfer function filter parameters to state-space form using tf2ss.

```
>> [A,B,C,D]=tf2ss(1,[2,0.7,1])
A =
    -0.3500    -0.5000
     1.0000          0
B =
     1
     0
C =
     0     0.5000
D =
     0
```

EXAMPLE 11.10   Following example illustrates to obtain state-space model from *Simulink* diagram. In this example, find the state-space model and transfer function for the system shown in Figure 11.47.

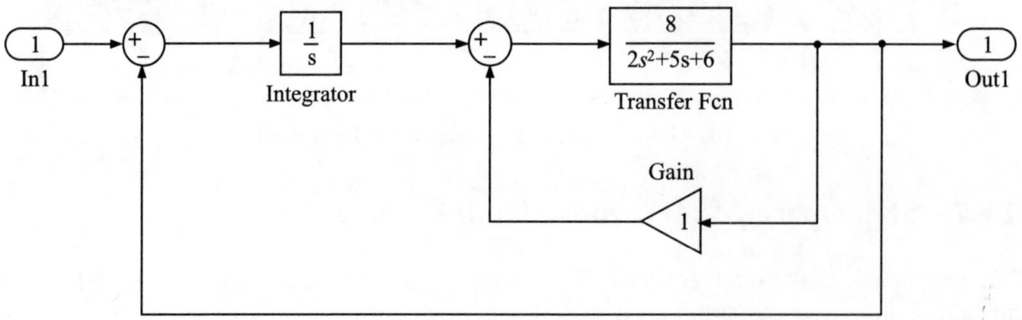

FIGURE 11.47   State-space model of Example 11.10.

Solution: The *Simulink* block diagram shown in simulation Window is saved as '.mdl'.

'Example5.mdl'

```
>> [a,b,c,d]=linmod('Example5')
```

The desired state-space model will be extracted from the *Simulink* diagram, and we will get the following results:

```
a =

       -8        -22         1
        1          0         0
        0        -10         0

b =

        0
        0
        1

c =

        0         10         0

d =

        0
```

State-space model can be converted into transfer function form by the following command in the Command Window:

```
>> [n,d]=ss2tf(a,b,c,d)
```

The numerator and denominator polynomial of the transfer function obtained are as follows:

```
n =

        0     0.0000    -0.0000    10.0000

d =

   1.0000     8.0000    22.0000    10.00


  -2.5000    -7.0000     1.0000
   1.0000          0          0
        0    -4.0000          0
```

The transfer function of state-space model is represented as:

$$G(s) = \frac{8}{s^3 + 2.5s^2 + 7s + 4}$$

SUMMARY

Introduction and methods to start *Simulink* are discussed in this chapter. By this time, we could have understood the method to start Simulink. The *Simulink* modelling, editing and simulation were discussed in different forms with its example. A *Simulink* Library Browser block is illustrated with creating workspace by examples. Further, state-space model with examples using *Simulink* was also discussed.

REVIEW QUESTIONS

1. List out various types of toolboxes available in Simulink Library Browser.
2. Explain the concept of Simulation Configuration Parameters.
3. Design a circuit of OR, AND and NOT gate using *Simulink*.
4. Design a Sine wave using *Simulink*.
5. Combine two waves and show the display using *Simulink*.
6. Using *Simulink* show the AWGN channel using PN sequence Generator.

PRACTICE EXERCISE

1. Create a Simulink model to simulate the function $y = 3x^2 + 5x + 6$, for $x = 3$.
2. Draw the Simulink block diagram and show the result for the step response of the system whose transfer function $y = \dfrac{10}{3x^2 + 5x + 2}$.

CHAPTER 12

MATLAB in Fuzzy Logic

<table>
<tr><td align="center">LEARNING OBJECTIVES</td></tr>
</table>

The chapter on Fuzzy Logic is discussed using MATLAB useful graphical interface. At the end of the chapter, the reader will learn the following:

- The use of Fuzzy function and graphical interface of Fuzzy Logic toolbox using MATLAB.
- Fuzzy Logic design for viewing and analysing using Fuzzy interface system.
- Standard Mamdani and Sugeno-type Fuzzy interference systems.
- Methods to evaluate AND, OR and NOT logic using user-defined rules.
- GUI of Fuzzy logic examples using MATLAB.

INTRODUCTION

Fuzzy Logic (FL) means imprecise judgment. The fuzzy logic concept was developed by *Dr. Lotfi Zadeh*, a Professor at the University of California, Berkely. Professor Zadeh introduced the term fuzzy logic in his seminal work 'Fuzzy sets', in 1965 that describes the concept of mathematics of fuzzy set theory.

FL is not based on accurate quantitative model to control a system or determine appropriate action. FL provides the opportunity for modelling conditions that are inherently imprecisely defined. Its advantage is its ability to deal with vague systems and its use of linguistic variables. Fuzzy techniques in the form of approximate reasoning provide decision support and expert systems with powerful reasoning capabilities.

In this chapter, we will learn how MATLAB is used to implement FL and its basic methods to control any systems. Here, we introduce FL concepts such as fuzzy sets and their properties, FL operators, hedges, fuzzy proposition and rule-based systems, fuzzy maps and inference engine, defuzzification methods, and the design of a FL decision system.

12.1 FUZZY LOGIC

'Fuzzy logic' concept represents the variation or imprecision in logic by using natural language in logic for solving the problems. It is based on approximate reasoning that take into account multi-valued logic that allows intermediate value to be defined between linguistic variables such as true/false, yes/no etc. FL poses the ability to mimic the human mind to effective reasoning that is approximate rather than exact. With FL, we specify mapping rules in terms of words rather than numbers. Computing with the words to explore imprecision and tolerance.

Fuzzy logic analyse the relative measure of precision using a rough answer. Henri Matisse stated that 'Precision is not truth'. FL can model nonlinear functions of arbitrary complexity to a desired degree of accuracy. It maps a multi-input space to a multi-output space system using FL tools that provide vague, ambiguous, imprecise, noisy, or missing input information. In this context, FL can be implemented in hardware, software, or a combination of both ranging from small, embedded microcontrollers to large, networked, and control systems.

12.1.1   Fuzzy Logic Evolution

The Fuzzy Logic (FL) concept was envisaged by *Lotfi Zadeh*. He reasoned that people do not require precise or numerical input information, to control the output. By imprecise inputs, the system can be capable of controlling highly adaptive systems. The controller can be designed based on noisy or imprecise input for effective and easier outputs. Unfortunately, *Lotfi Zadeh* concept was not accepted by the U.S. manufacturers while the Europeans and Japanese valued his work and aggressively put into building real products globally.

The Fuzzy Logic Toolbox with MATLAB is a tool for solving problems with fuzzy logic. There is several fascinating area of FL research that trading off between significance and precision, for various applications and domains. For example, Figure 12.1 shows that depending on the fabric the iron tool is used to remove the wrinkles by keeping the precision temperature of 180–220°C. But if someone unknowingly try to touch its hot iron plate then significant word (Hot, Very hot) is sufficient to keep one away from it.

Precision   Significance

FIGURE 12.1   Precision and significance in the heating box.

Imprecision in measurement is associated with a lack of precise knowledge. That are inaccurate, inexact, or of low confidence. Fuzzy logic is a suitable way to map an input parameter to an output parameter. This is the mapping of inputs to the appropriate outputs via a black box that significantly works. Lotfi Zadeh, is considered to be the father of fuzzy logic, has remarked that "in almost every case you can build the same product without fuzzy logic, but fuzzy is faster and cheaper".

12.1.2 Fuzzy Logic Use

FL provides several unique features for many control problems. Following are the list of general observations about fuzzy logic:

Fuzzy logic concept is easy

Nonlinear systems are generally difficult or not viable to model mathematically. However, FL solves mathematical concepts with fuzzy reasoning that is very simple and easy to understand. It is based on natural significant language for solving complex problems.

Fuzzy logic is flexible

FL system, has the flexibility to solve the problems in an easy way. This opens ways for control systems automation that is normally unfeasible for conventional methods. Using the rule-based operation, for any reasonable number of inputs produces numerous outputs by implementation.

Fuzzy logic is imprecise data, set with approximate range

In the FL system, most things are imprecise and its values need to set with its range appropriately. The logic is intrinsically robust which does not require precise inputs. It produces the smooth controlled output despite wide range of input variations. Hence, FL designs are based on understanding the process and its range setting.

Fuzzy logic can model complex problems

FL match the input and output data based on nonlinear functions of arbitrary complexity. The procedure is made by adaptive techniques using ANFIS (Adaptive Neuro-fuzzy Inference Systems), in the Fuzzy Logic Toolbox to solve the complex problems.

Fuzzy logic supports other soft tools

FL system, modelled with other soft tools like neural networks that train data and generate interdependent variable for fuzzy logic system. The soft computing includes fuzzy logic, neural networks, probabilistic reasoning, and genetic algorithms are used to design an intelligence system.

Fuzzy logic can hybrid with conventional control techniques

FL systems can be modelled with conventional control by hybrid with fuzzy rules for implementation. FL controller method is a user-defined rules leading the control system on system performance. It uses the governing rules to control the system using FL techniques.

Fuzzy logic is based on Lingusitic language

FL used the linguistic variable to solve the problems. Linguistic language is a natural language that is used for human communication. Based on this language statements, fuzzy logic is implemented.

12.1.3   Restriction on Use of Fuzzy Logic

Fuzzy logic is not the end solution for every system. FL is a suitable way to map an input space to an output space, as mapping is the starting point for everything. A graphical representation of an input-output map is shown in Figure 12.2.

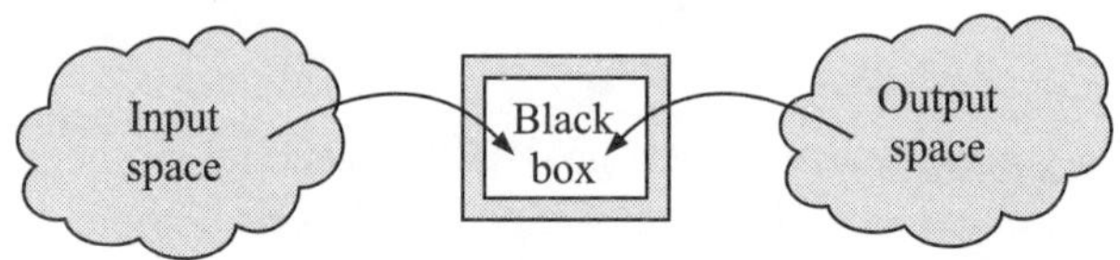

FIGURE 12.2   Fuzzy logic input-output map.

This is a very powerful tool for dealing quickly and efficiently with imprecision, uncertainty, robustness, nonlinearityand partial truth to achieve tractability. The relation between input and output can be significantly improved when the norms are the part of appropriate relations. If it is not convenient, then it is better to switch over. Fuzzy logic is the codification of common sense to analyse the relation of input and output to make the right decision. In many applications, the hybrid or the independent FL is used to design a controller.

12.1.4   Fuzzy Logic Toolbox

The Fuzzy Logic Toolbox has significant functions such as to create and edit fuzzy inference systems. Figure 12.3 shows the Fuzzy Logic Toolbox. FL systems make use of graphical tools or command-line functions, or adaptive neuro-fuzzy techniques.

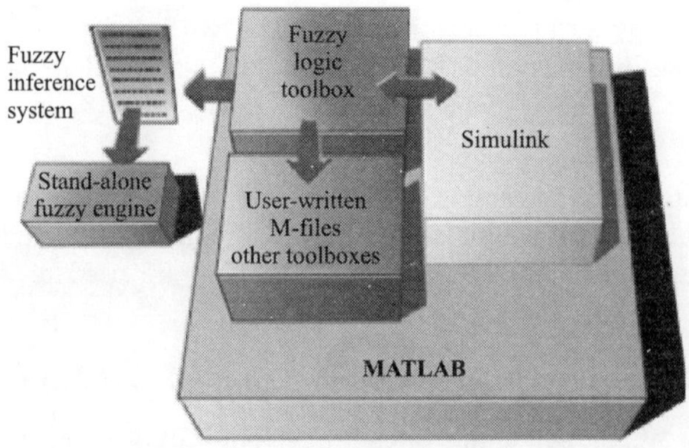

FIGURE 12.3   Fuzzy logic toolbox.

In the Fuzzy Logic, the toolbox provides MATLAB functions, apps, and a Simulink block for analysing, designing, and simulating. The product guides provided many methods for learning. Using the toolbox, we can model complex system behaviours and implement rules of a stand-alone fuzzy inference engine. Alternatively, a fuzzy inference block supports the Simulink and simulates the fuzzy systems model of the system.

FL systems also support the Simulink to test fuzzy system block diagram for simulation environment. The toolbox runs by a stand-alone Fuzzy Inference Engine for a MATLAB session. Even user can create their own tools to customise the FL toolbox for the control system, neural network, or optimisation toolbox, etc.

12.1.5   Steps to Use Fuzzy Logic Toolbox

Following steps explain about how we should use the Fuzzy Logic Toolbox.

(i)   In this step we define the control objectives and criteria of a system using FL Toolbox. This is to identify the design parameters that need to control the system and to identify the response etc.

(ii)   Determine the input and output relationships with a minimum number of variables that applies to FL engine.

(iii)   Using the rule-based structure of FL. This defined the system desired output response for given system input conditions using 'IF X AND Y THEN Z'. The number and complexity of rules depends on the number of inputs as well as the number of fuzzy variables of each parameter.

(iv)   FL membership functions define the relation of Input/ Output terms based on the rules.

(v)   Finally, the FL system is verified to evaluates the result. This is based on the rules and membership functions, to retest until satisfactory results are obtained.

In nutshell FL is inherently robust, to process any reasonable number of inputs and outputs. 'IF X AND Y THEN Z' rules are used to describe the desired system response in terms of linguistic variables rather than mathematical formulas to produce the desired results.

12.2   FUZZY SETS

Fuzzy Sets is a part of Fuzzy logic. Fuzzy logic deals with approximate reasoningrather on fixed value. It deals with uncertainty in slope designs that are nonrandom in nature. Figure 12.4 shows the classical Fuzzy set that contain two elements, i.e., includes and excludes elements. In this figure includes are set of 'Star' symbol vs. excludes are set of 'Plus' and 'Cross' so on.

Such sets which says 'Plus' or 'Cross'may be either a set in cluster of 'Star' or not in 'Star'.

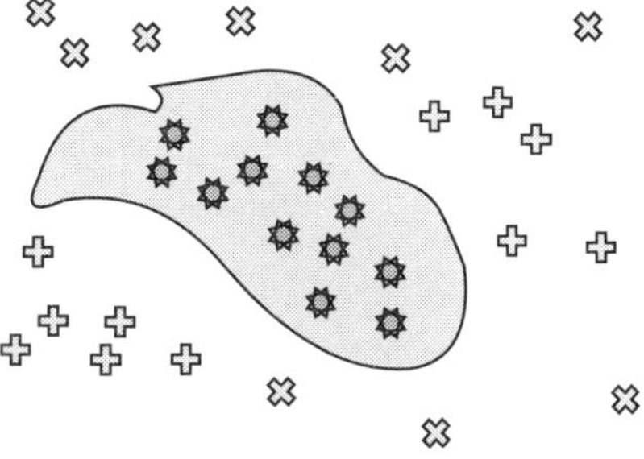

FIGURE 12.4   Show the classical Fuzzy set.

The membership function of a fuzzy set is an indicator function of the sets elements. FL represents the degree of truth as an extension of valuation of fuzzy membership functions.

12.2.1   Crisp and Fuzzy Membership Functions

The crisp set A has a binary behaviour instead of fuzzy set $\tilde{A}$, with a bell-shaped (Gaussian) curve. The fuzzy set is dynamic in behaviour. The support is the limit which a membership function has in x-axis.

The crisp $(0, 1)$ is an element of membership function. The crisp set 'A' of real objects are described by a unique membership function such as $\mu_A(x)$ shown in Figure 12.5.

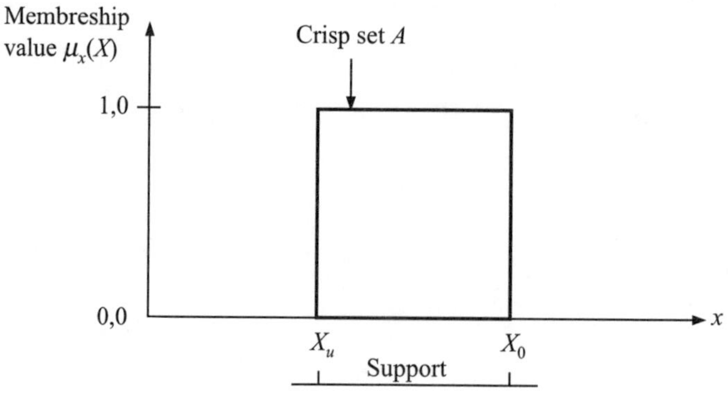

FIGURE 12.5   Crisp membership function.

A membership function for fuzzy sets defines how many element of 'A' is inside all possible sets. This mean in fuzzy, the element a can be part of n sets described by $\mu_A(x)$.

A FL set is an extension of a crisp set. In crisp sets, condition may be either full or no membership. Hence fuzzy sets will have the intermediate range of partial membership. A fuzzy set membership function $\mu_A(x)$ is shown in Figure 12.6.

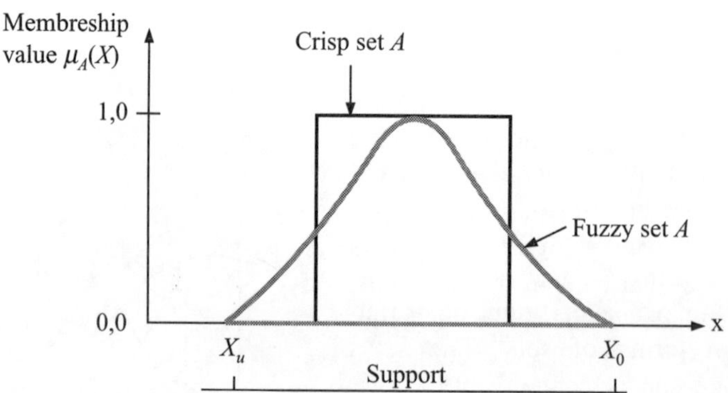

FIGURE 12.6   Fuzzy membership function.

Fuzzy set contains members of a given element at a time. Consider a fuzzy set A in U that represents ordered pairs of a generic element x with its membership function $\mu_A(x)$ is given by,

$$A = \{(x, \mu_A(x)) | x \in U\}$$

A linguistic variables x is the universe of discourse U is characteristic of set of terms $T(x) = \{T_A^1, T_A^2, T_A^3, \ldots, T_A^m\}$ and membership function $\mu_A(x) = \{\mu_A^1, \mu_A^2, \mu_A^3, \ldots, \mu_A^m\}$.

The fuzziness is the human thought process with fuzzy logic conditions and fuzzy rules of inference. Figure 12.7 shows the example on plot of Crisp and Fuzzy membership function.

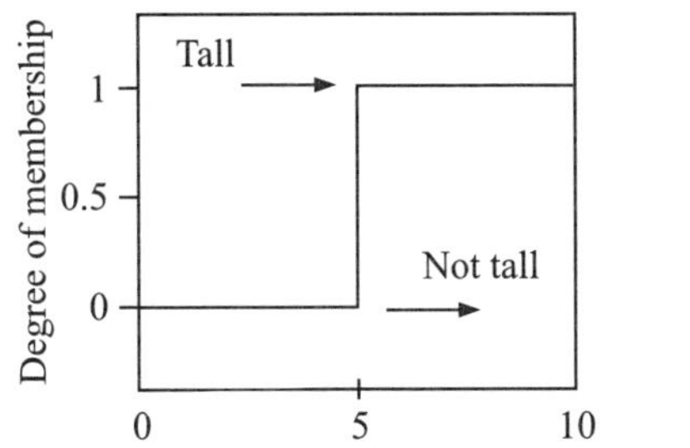
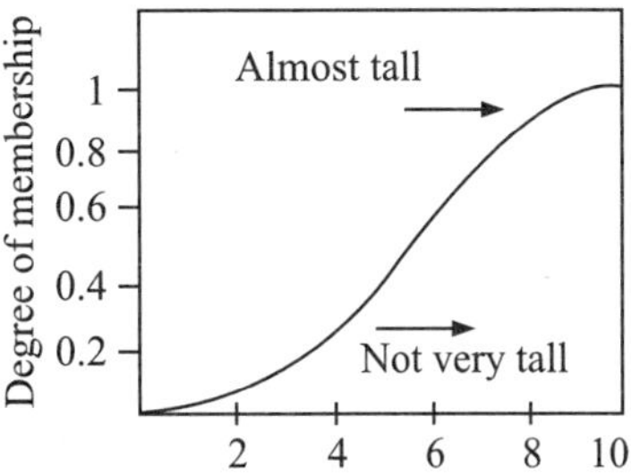

FIGURE 12.7   Crisp and Fuzzy membership heights example.

This example is related to human heights. The crisp set shows the condition of two level heights only, whereas fuzzy represents different level of heights using a natural language.

12.2.2 Linguistic Variables

A linguistic variable values are names of fuzzy sets. Fuzzy sets represent in linguistic variables language interms of slow, fast, small, large, heavy, low, medium, high, tall, etc. These values are described by fuzzy sets and membership functions. Some of the linguistic variables scales are listed below:

- Attitude: {poor, good, excellent}
- Speed: {slow, medium, fast}
- Temp: {freezing, cool, warm, hot}
- Cloud Cover: {cloudy, partly cloudy, sunny}

Consider the example of linguistic variable scale of 'academic performance', with values poor, good and excellent, with its membership functions is shown in Figure 12.8.

The membership value of linguistic variable is represented in terms of sets. The set of memebership grade shows contant upto 2.5 and then set decreases as the response increases. The membership grade of 5 is good set. Beyond 5, an answer of 5 in either side is considered with

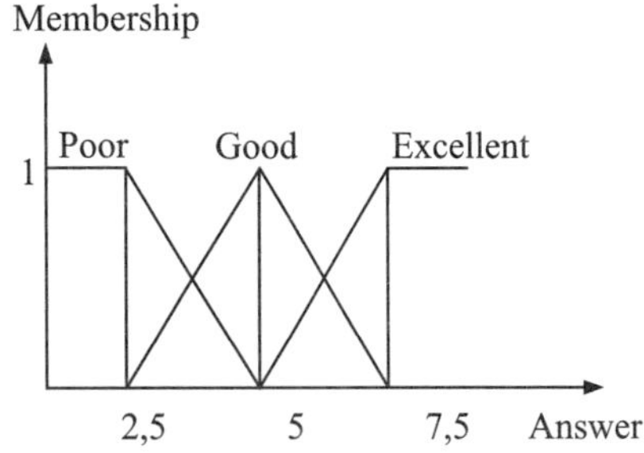

FIGURE 12.8   Example of Linguistic variable.

the poor or excellent set. Membership functions may have different shapes, depending on the context of poor, good and excellent which are extremely subjective.

12.2.3   Fuzzy vs. Probability

Fuzzy theory discuss about the uncertainty whereas the probability discuss about the amount of occurrence of the events. Fuzzy theory and Probability treat different kinds of uncertainty. Fuzzy theory is analysed based on varying boundary level conditions. FL theory calculates the proximity of elements with some set.

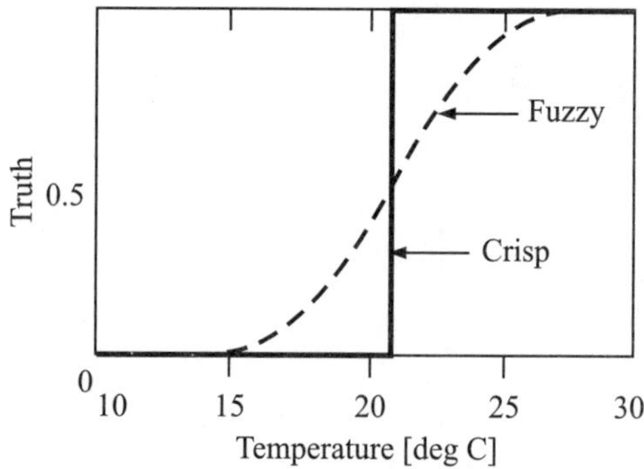

FIGURE 12.9   Fuzzy vs. Probability example.

Fuzzy vs. Probability as shown in Figure 12.9 express the example of temperature in furnace. Imagine temperature of furnace at different time is needed to identify.

Let the temperature set between minimum to maximum is 10 to 30°C. Considering that a highest temperature reached within time frame in the space S is 27°C. If we consider between 0 to 1 membership periods, three times temperature reached above 17°C. The probability of the temperature in given time is P(*a*) = 3/20 = 0.15, or a probability of 15%. Whereas, the fuzzy value calculation is based on center of gravity of the number of membership function.

12.3   TYPES AND FEATURES OF MEMBERSHIP FUNCTION

A fuzzy set is completely characterised by its membership function (MF) which expressed it as a mathematical formula.

12.3.1   Types of Membership Functions

There are different types of membership functions as shown in Figure 12.10 like Triangular MFs, Trapezoidal MFs, Gaussian MFs, and Generalised bell MFs which are represented with three parameters *a*, *b* and *c*.

Triangular MF:

$$f(x; a, b, c) = \max(\min((x\text{-}a)/(b\text{-}a), (c, x)/(c\text{-}b)), 0)$$

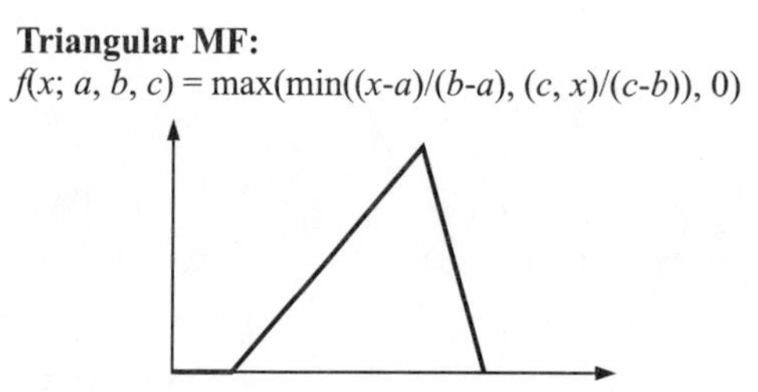

Gaussian MF:

$$f(x; a, b, c) = e^{-\frac{1}{2}\left(\frac{x-a}{\sigma}\right)}$$

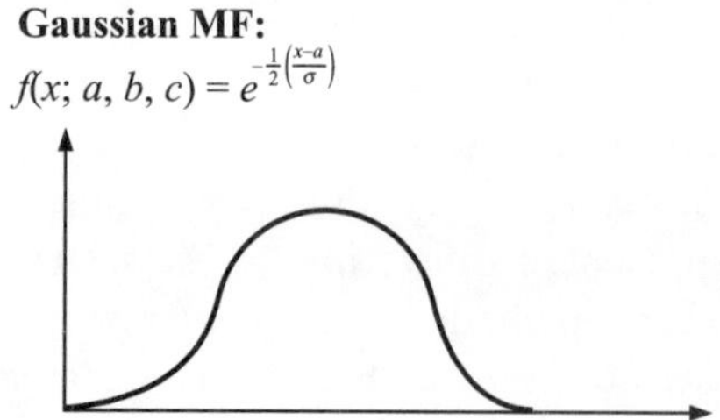

FIGURE 12.10   (*Contd.*)

Trapezoidal MF:
$f(x; a, b, c, d) = \max(\min((x\text{-}a)/(b\text{-}a), (c, x)/(c\text{-}b)), 0)$

Generalised bell MF:
$f(x; a, b, c) = 1/(1 + |(x\text{-}c)/b|^{2b})$

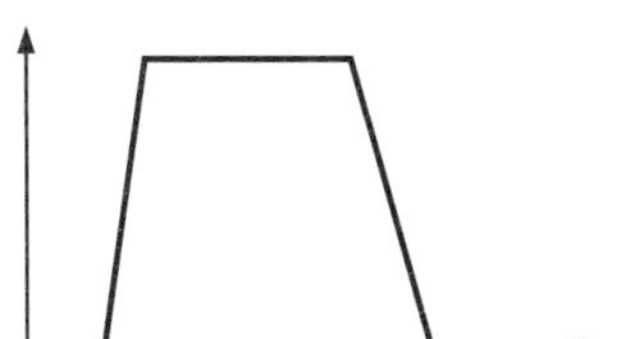
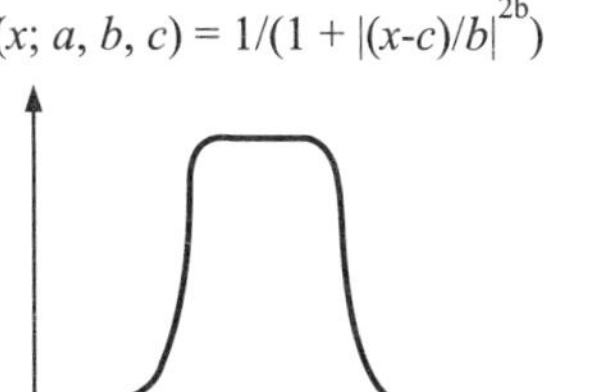

FIGURE 12.10   Types of membership functions.

Triangular MFs

A triangular MF is specified by three parameters $\{a, b, c\}$ as follows:

$$\text{triangular}(x; a, b, c) \begin{cases} 0 & x \leq a \\ \dfrac{x-a}{b-a} & a \leq x \leq b \\ \dfrac{c-x}{c-b} & b \leq x \leq c \\ 0 & c \leq x \end{cases}$$

The parameters $\{a, b, c\}$ (with $a < b < c$) determine the x-co-ordinates of the three corners of the underlying triangular MF.

Trapezoidal MFs

A trapezoidal MF is specified by four parameters $\{a, b, c, d\}$ as follows:

$$\text{trapezoidal}(x; a, b, c, d) \begin{cases} 0 & x \leq a \\ \dfrac{x-a}{b-a} & a \leq x \leq b \\ 1 & b \leq x \leq c \\ \dfrac{d-x}{d-b} & c \leq x \leq d \\ 0 & d \leq x \end{cases}$$

Gaussian MFs

A Gaussian MF is specified by two parameters:

$$\text{gaussian}(x; c, s) = e^{-\frac{1}{2}\left(\frac{x-c}{\sigma}\right)^2}$$

A Gaussian MF is determined complete by c and σ; c represents the MFs centre and σ determines the MFs width.

Generalised bell MFs

A generalised bell MF (or Bell-shaped Function) is specified by three parameters $\{a,\ b,\ c\}$:

$$\text{bell}(x;\, a, b, c) = \cfrac{1}{1 + \left| \cfrac{x - c}{a} \right|^{2b}}$$

where, the parameter b is usually positive that shows the shape of this MF is upside-down bell.

Sigmoid MFs

A sigmoid MF is defined by

$$\text{sig}(x;\, a, c) = \frac{1}{1 + \exp\left[-a(x - c)\right]}$$

where, a controls the slope at the crossover point $x = c$.

12.3.2   Features of Membership Function

The membership function is a graphical representation of each input magnitude. It associates a weighting overlap functional between inputs to determines the response of output. The rules are used with the input membership weighting factors value to determine the fuzzy output values. The membership functions for input and output response can be represented as triangular, trapezoidal, generalised bell shaped, Gaussian curves, polynomial curves, and sigmoid functions where, the triangular is common.

Once the functions are inferred, it is scaled, and combined. They are defuzzified into a crisp output for the system. This illustrates in Figure 12.11, where we discuss about the features of the triangular membership function for mathematical simplicity.

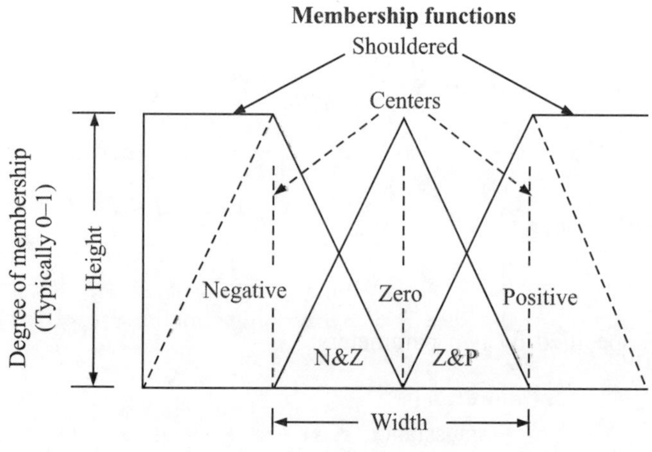

FIGURE 12.11   The features of a membership function.

12.4 FUZZY SET OPERATIONS

Fuzzy logic reasoning is a superset of standard Boolean logic. Following are the binary operations defined by standard fuzzy operations as shown in Figure 12.12.

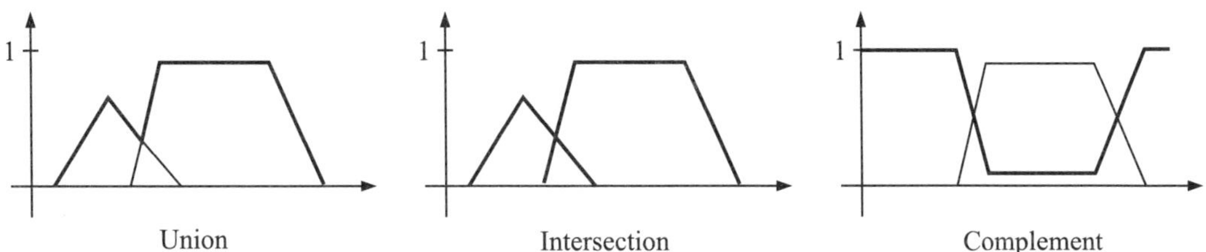

FIGURE 12.12 Standard fuzzy operations.

12.4.1 Union

The membership function of union of two fuzzy sets A and B with membership functions μ_A and μ_B respectively is defined as the maximum of the two individual membership functions (μ_{AB} = max μ_A, μ_B). This is called the maximum criterion.

$$\text{Union: } \mu_{AB}(x) = \max\ \{\mu_A(x),\ \mu_B(x)\},\ x \in X$$

The Union operation in fuzzy set theory is similar to Boolean algebra OR operation.

12.4.2 Intersection

The membership function is the Intersection of two fuzzy sets A and B. Their membership functions μ_A and μ_B respectively is defined as the minimum of two individual membership functions (μ_{AB} = min μ_A, μ_B). This is called the minimum criterion.

$$\text{Union: } \mu_{AB}(x) = \min\ \{\mu_A(x),\ \mu_B(x)\},\ x \in X$$

The Intersection operation in fuzzy set theory is the equivalent of the AND operation in Boolean algebra.

12.4.3 Complement

The membership function of the Complement of a fuzzy set A with membership function μ_A is defined as the negation of the specified membership function ($\mu_A = 1 - \mu_A$). This is called the negation criterion.

$$\text{Complement: } \mu_A(x) = 1 - \mu_A(x),\ x \in X$$

The complement operation in fuzzy set theory is the equivalent of the NOT operation in Boolean algebra.

The bivalent logic uses the Boolean operators AND, OR, and NOT to perform the intersection, union and complement operations defined using the following truth table is listed in Table 12.1.

TABLE 12.1   Boolean operators AND, OR, and NOT.

x	y	x AND y	x OR y	NOT x	NOT y
0	0	0	0	1	1
0	1	0	1	1	0
1	0	0	1	0	1
1	1	1	1	0	0

The generalised form for these three operators is listed in Table 12.2 as follows:

TABLE 12.2   Generalised form of three operators AND, OR, and NOT.

x OR y	max (x, y)
NOT x	$1 - x$

These generalised definitions of the operators work well for fuzzy numbers as well as bivalent sets.

12.5 FUZZY INFERENCE SYSTEM

The Fuzzy Logic Toolbox in MATLAB provides tools for building Fuzzy Inference System (FIS). This is shown in Figure 12.13. Fuzzy inference and rule formulate the mapping process from a given input to the output using fuzzy logic.

FIS maps crisp inputs data to a crisp output of application. These inputs are fuzzified (mapped to fuzzy sets), based on linguistic variables with rules in a given situation. The linguistic rules are IF-THEN statements constitute a key aspect in the performance of a fuzzy inference system. The next steps is the aggregation process, of fuzzy set for each output variable that needs defuzzification. This means once the output fuzzy set is computed through the process of inference, a defuzzification is used to generate crisp outputs as per application. The process of fuzzy inference involves the membership functions, fuzzy logic operators and if-then rules.

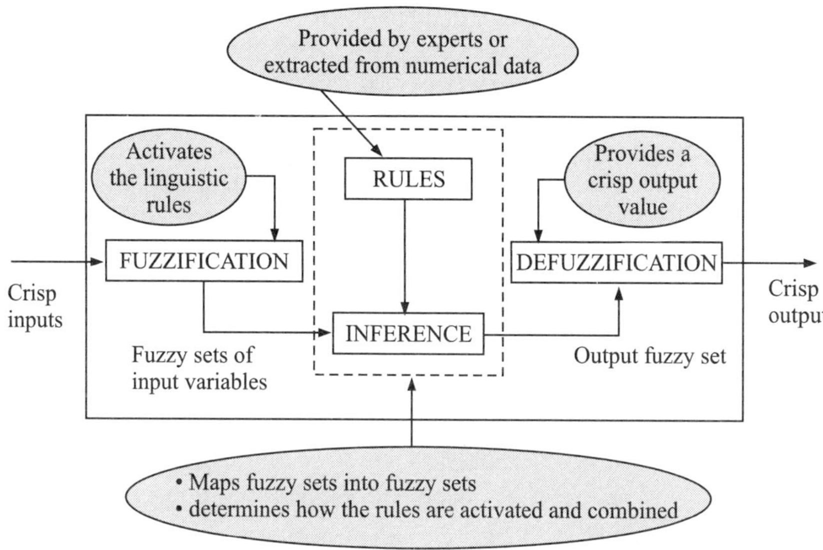

FIGURE 12.13   Block structure of Fuzzy system.

Fuzzy inference process consists of five parts such as fuzzification of the input variables, choosing membership functions, constructing rules, making decision and defuzzification. Figure 12.14 shows the fuzzy inference viewer available in the MATLAB Fuzzy Logic Toolbox, where we can change the input values by click and drag the input vertical lines and see the consequent MFs and overall output MF.

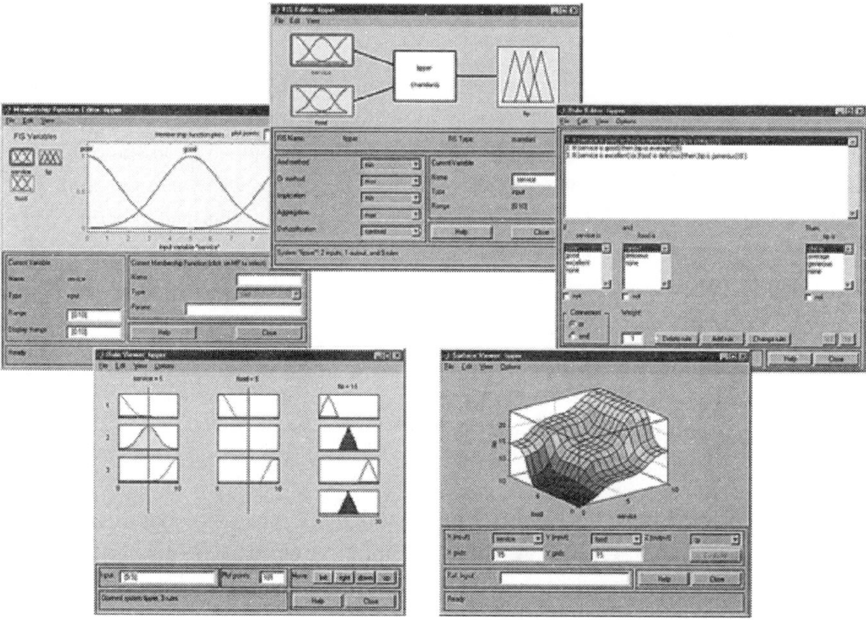

FIGURE 12.14   Fuzzy inference viewer.

12.5.1   Mamdani-type FIS vs. Sugeno-type FIS

There are two types of fuzzy inference systems that can be implemented in the Fuzzy Logic Toolbox: *Mamdani-type* and *Sugeno-type*. Mamdani's fuzzy inference methods are most commonly used and seen fuzzy methodology and it is widely accepted for capturing expert knowledge. It describes the expertise in more intuitive, more human-like manner. However, Mamdani-type FIS entails a substantial computational burden.

On the other hand, Sugeno method is computationally efficient, better optimisation and use adaptive techniques to solve problems for dynamic nonlinear systems. These adaptive techniques customise the membership functions so that fuzzy system models the data.

The most fundamental difference between Mamdani-type FIS and Sugeno-type FIS is the way the crisp output generated from the fuzzy inputs. Mamdani-type FIS uses the technique of defuzzification of a fuzzy output, while Sugeno-type FIS uses weighted average to compute the crisp output. For example:

- Mamdani: If A is X_1, and B is X_2, then C is X_3. (X_1, X_2, X_3 are fuzzy sets).
- Sugeno: If A is X_1 and B is X_2 then $C = aX_1 + bX_2 + c$ (linear expression) (a, b, and c are constants)

The Sugeno has better processing time but consume time for the defuzzification process. Due to such limitation Mamdani-type FIS is widely used for decision support application. Other differences are that Mamdani FIS has output membership functions whereas Sugeno FIS has no output membership functions. Also, Mamdani FIS is less flexible in system design in comparison to Sugeno FIS as latter can be integrated with ANFIS tool to optimise the outputs.

12.6   GUI OF FL EXAMPLES USING MATLAB

To demonstrate the fuzzy logic control capabilities of MATLAB, we consider a very simple example on control of motor speed for given variation of inputs. Based on motor set point speed, if the motor runs faster, we can slow down by reducing the input voltage and vice versa.

Linguistic variables of the input speed words are: *Too slow*, A*bout right* and *Too fast*.

Linguistic variables of the output stroke words are: *Slow down* and *Speed up. Less voltage slow down, no change* and *more voltage speed up the motor.*

The rule-base is defined as:

1. If the speed of the motor *Too slow*, then raise more voltage.
2. If speed of the motor is A*bout right*, then no change in voltage.
3. If motor speed is *Too fast*, then reduce voltage.

Figure 12.15 shows the condition of the membership functions for input and output variables.

As we have seen the initial mapping of input and output variable based on certain rules. Also, the membership function defined for this example. Now, we will discuss its fuzzification with the help of Fuzzy Inference System viewers in the following section.

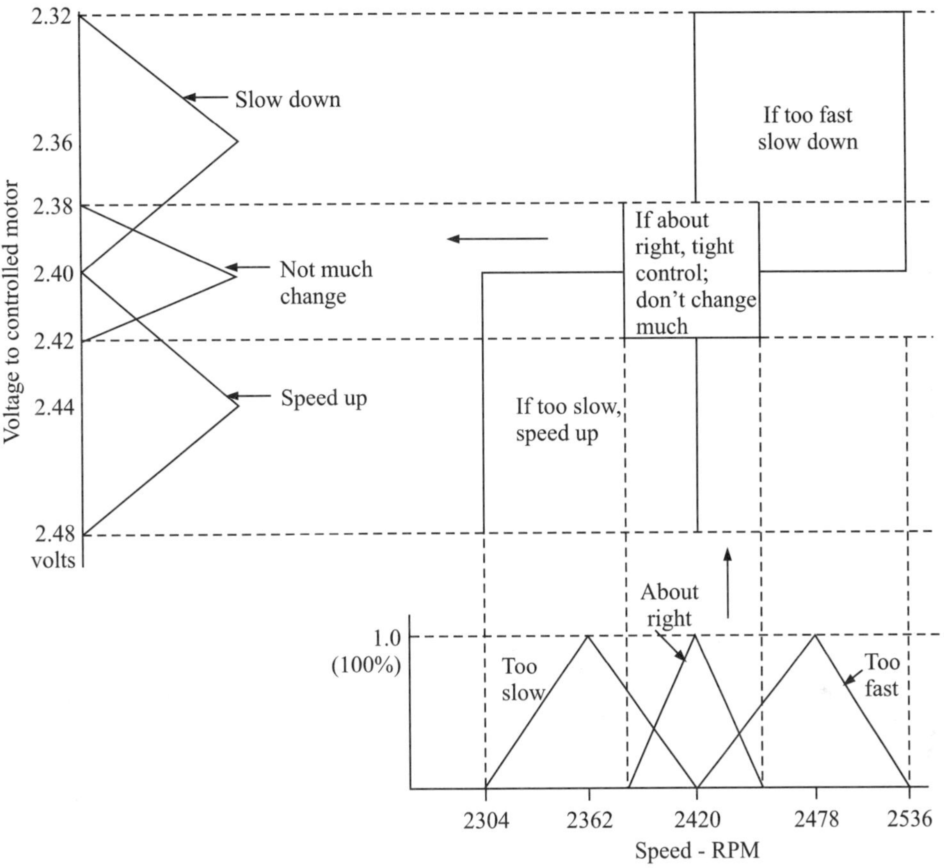

FIGURE 12.15   Membership function.

12.6.1   Fuzzy Logic Designer

Fuzzy Inference System (FIS) toolbox is the powerful Graphical User Interface (GUI) to design a fuzzy systemin MATLAB. The FIS displays information about a fuzzy inference viewer. To open the Fuzzy Logic Designer, following command prompt is to type:

```
>> fuzzyLogicDesigner
```

The FIS editor is the main GUI that is used to represent results graphically. We can start a new FIS file with the FIS editor, by typing the following command into MATLAB Command Window.

```
>> fuzzy
```

The window will open the Fuzzy Inference System editor window. With the FIS editor the input and output membership functions, the rule base and the fuzzy operators are defined. In the default system, the FIS has one input and one output with membership function editor as shown in Figure 12.16.

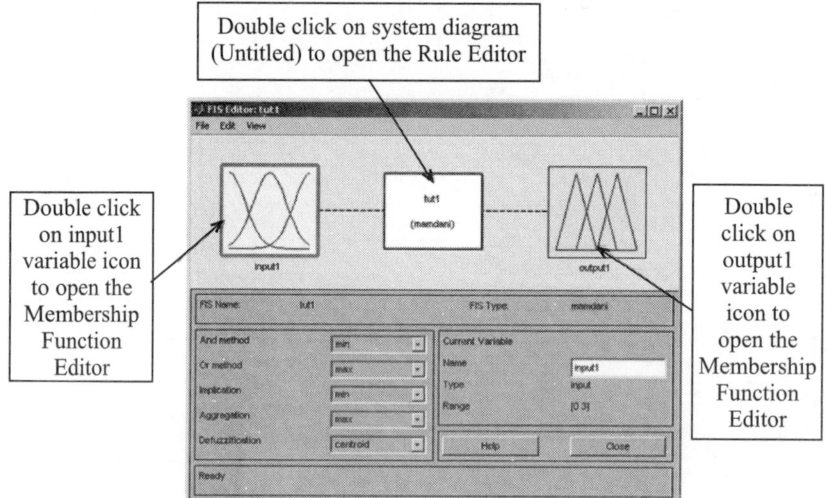

FIGURE 12.16   Fuzzy inference system editor window.

The Fuzzy Logic Designer opens and displays a Fuzzy Inference System editor windowdiagram with the names of each input variable on the left, and output variable on the right. The untitled membership functions boxes icons shown in the centre portion of FIS. Figure 12.17 shows the diagram with the name of the system and the type of inference used.

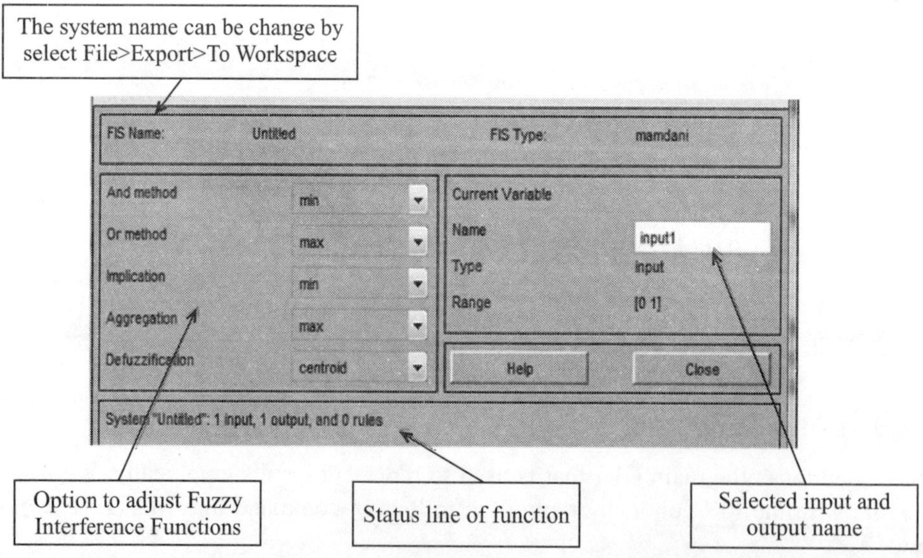

FIGURE 12.17   Fuzzy inference system name modification.

We can start the FIS type design in MATLAB using MamdaniFuzzy inference engine as shown in Figure 12.18. The input and output uses the MamdaniFIS and aggregation method. This editor illustrates the fuzzy controller, fuzzification, inference, and defuzzification functions.

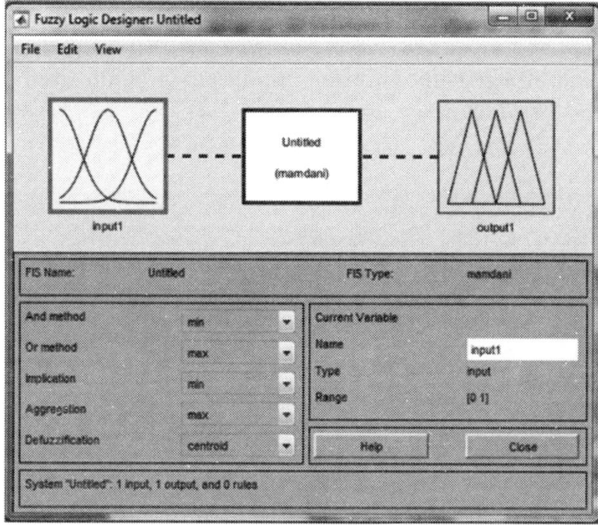

FIGURE 12.18　Mamdani Fuzzy inference system name.

Initially by double-click the linguistic variable which is defined for the input box (input1). This will display membership function editor to enter the value.

Now, redefine the linguistic variables of the input grade words *Too slow*, *About right* and *Too fast* into three membership functions, mf1, mf2, and mf3. The range period for input can be set from 2200 to 2600. You can redefine the parameters for *Too slow* are [2304 2362 2420]; *About right* are [2385 2420 2455] and *Too fast* are [2420 2478 2536]. If we increase the speed from 2430 to 2450 rpm set point, this will correspondingly change the membership function. Figure 12.19 shows the *updated input membership functions* with the different set parameters.

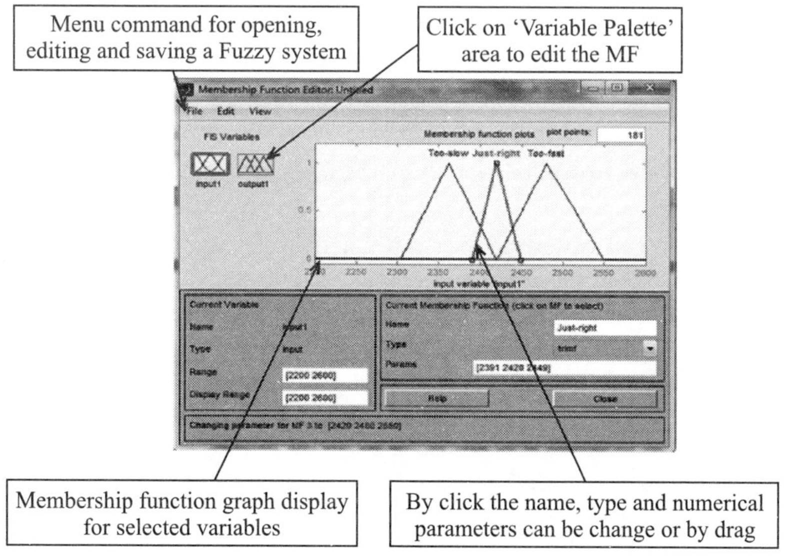

FIGURE 12.19　Input membership function.

Similarly, the output membership functions defined by linguistic variables *Less voltage* (*Slow down*), *No change* and *More voltage* (*Speed up*) are also created. The three membership functions, mf1, mf2, and mf3 redefined for the output range width from 2.28 to 2.52. We can redefine the parameters for *Slow down* are [2.3 2.34 2.4]; *No change* are [2.35 2.4 2.45] and *Speed up* are [2.4 2.46 2.5] that will appear as shown in Figure 12.20.

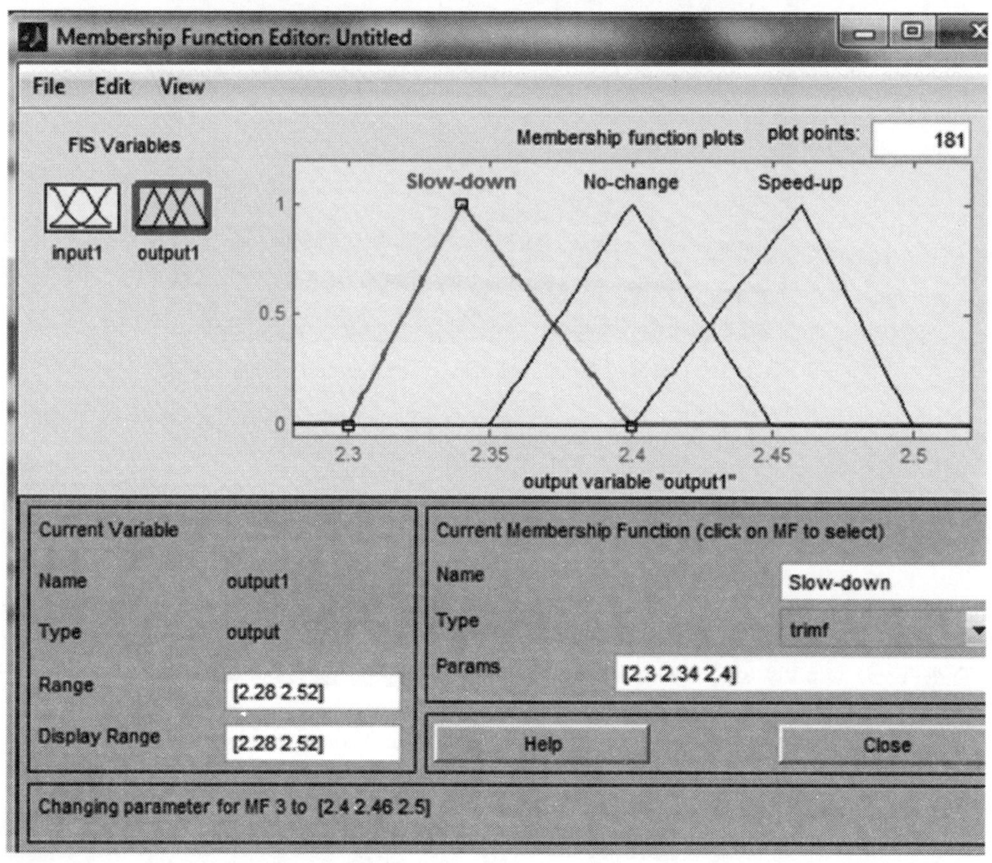

FIGURE 12.20   Output membership function.

In the next step, the FIS editor membership functionrules are defined. By double-click on the tut1 Mamdani in between the input and output membership functions to pop-up the Rule Editor. The linguistic inference rules are defined using the fuzzy membership functions labels input and output. We can select the rule based on application by selecting the 'if' option and 'then' option and click 'add rule' at the bottom. Finally, the Rule editor will appear like in Figure 12.21.

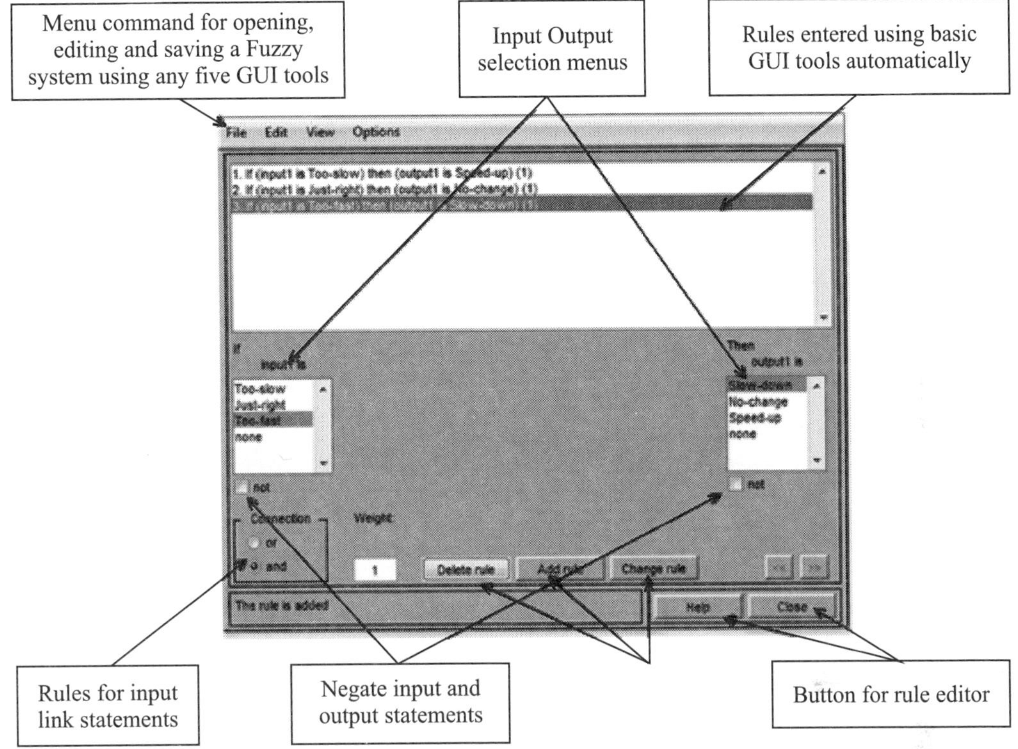

FIGURE 12.21   Rules editor.

The Fuzzy window can be exported to the Matlab Simulink model. To do this we can select the FIS editor tab followed by file, export, workspace and finally enter the name of the Simulink model saved as 'tut1'. Further in Simulink, change the refresh rate to 0.01by double-click on the Fuzzy logic controller and set the FIS matrix to tut1. The simulation run for three seconds and then the Rule Viewer window will pop-up as shown in Figure 12.22.

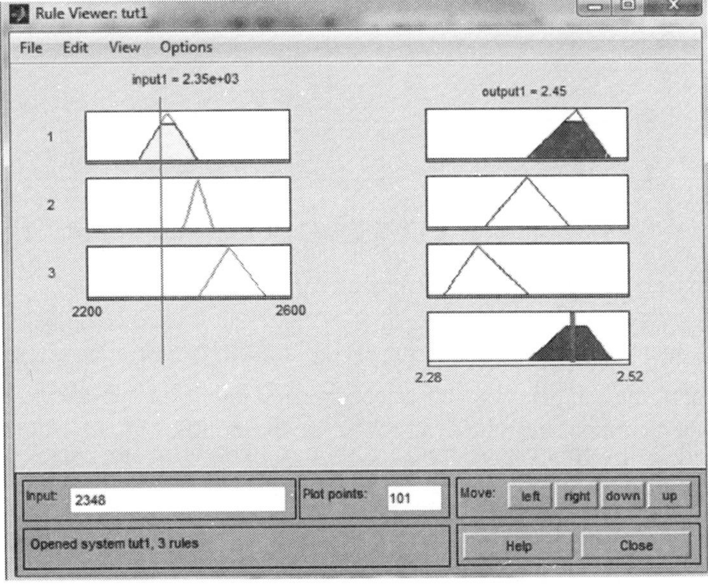

FIGURE 12.22   Rules viewer.

The Rule Viewer window will display the relevant input and output membership functions for the required condition as desired based on each rule. We can observe fuzzified result is input membership function 2.35e+03 and output membership function 2.45 based on firing and the aggregate value. Even the default defuzzification process display as the red line indicates the centroid and output.

The surface view can be seen on clicking the view tab, the surface will then pop-up as shown in Figure 12.23.

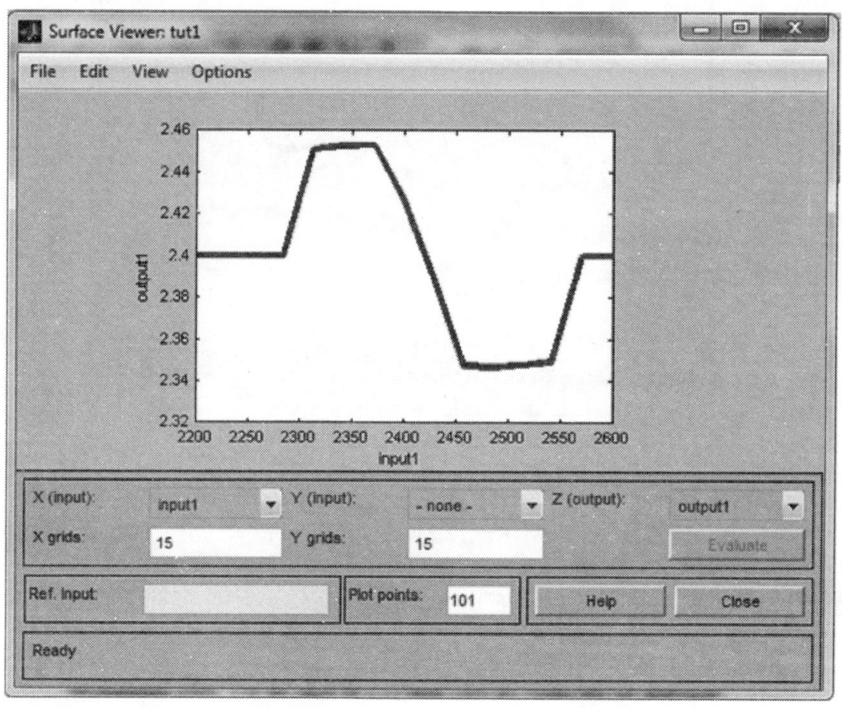

FIGURE 12.23   Surface viewer.

Even video link view will display the input variation corresponding to the result of each rule of aggregate output. When inputs exceeds more than one, the User Interface Layout view appears to be three-dimensions as shown in Figure 12.24.

Takagi-Sugeno-Kang method of fuzzy inference is almost similar to the Mamdani method. In many aspects for input fuzzifying and fuzzy operator, are same. As compared to Mamdani the Sugeno output membership functions appears to be linear or nearly constant.

This can be obtained by clicking on **File → New FIS → Surgeon**. Then the Sugeno-type FIS will pop-up and similar activities like earlier to create plots after simulating for same application.

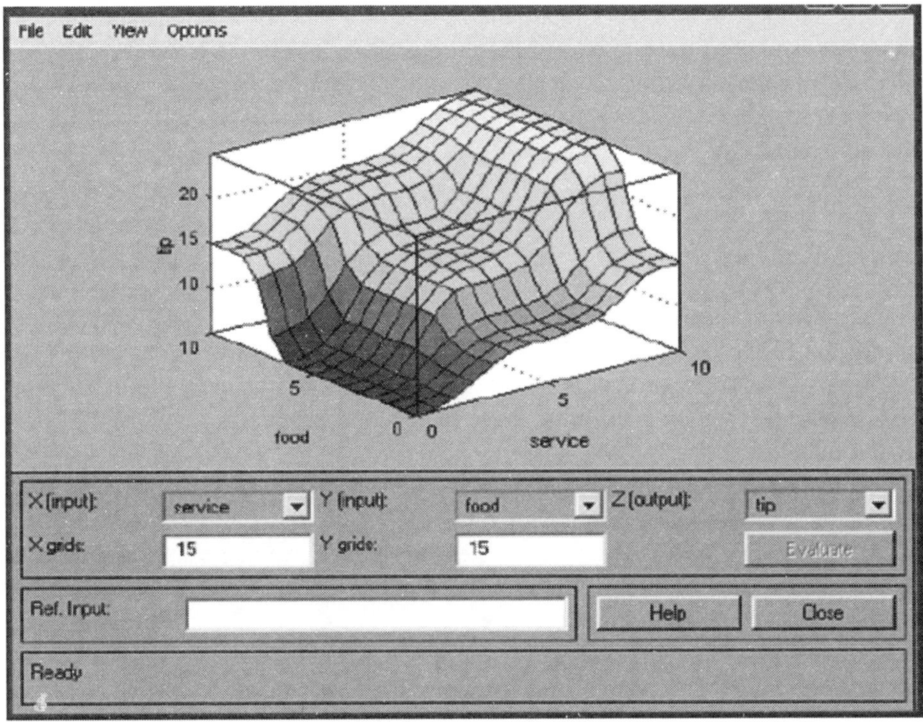

FIGURE 12.24   UIL: Surface viewer.

12.7 FIS COMMON COMMAND LINE

Some of the common command-line functions associated with FIS construction are as follows:

- *fuzzy:* command used to invoke the fuzzy GUI tool
- *mfedit:* command used to invoke the MF GUI tool
- *newfis:* command used to define the name of the new variable that identifies the FIS being created
- *ruleview:* command used to display the Rule Viewer
- *surfview:* command used to display the Surface Viewer
- *addvar:* command used to add the variables, input or output to the FIS
- *addmf:* command used to add the MF to the variable. Input or output to the FIS
- *addrule:* command used to add an If-Then rule to the FIS
- *readfis:* command used to read the FIS into the MATLAB workspace
- *setfis:* command allows user to change any property of an FIS
- *getfis:* command used to get the FIS information
- *plotfis:* command used to display the whole FIS system as a block diagram
- *plotmf:* command used to plot all the MFs associated with given variables

- *evalfis:* command used to evaluate the output of a FIS for a given plot
- *writefis:* command used to save the FIS to disk
- *showrule:* command used to display all rules in verbose format for the FIS associated with the matrix
- *gensurf:* command used to generate a plot of two inputs to one output of a given system

SUMMARY

In this chapter we have learnt about the Fuzzy Logic Toolbox of MATLAB with its command. The introduction of the chapter starts with Fuzzy Logic concept and purpose. The explanation of Fuzzy logic provides us an insight of how to represent linguistic and subjective attributes of the real world in computing. We may have understood the basics of fuzzy logic, linguistic variable and membership function concept as described.

Further, in this chapter we have discussed Fuzzy Interference System consists of input variables, output variables, aggregation of outputs and defuzzification. Also, the concept of fuzzy rules If-then is explained with examples. Moreover, we you have experienced about the different features of FIS editor, Membership function editor, Rule editor, Rule viewer and Surface viewer.

Fuzzy control systems with example of the process was explained and simulated. Finally, the commands of Fuzzy Toolbox were discussed.

REVIEW QUESTIONS

1. How to prepare the fuzzy GUI tool from the Fuzzy Logic Toolbox?

2. Design a Fuzzy controller for the common water level in the tank.

3. Shows how to use Fuzzy Logic Toolbox software for image processing. Shows how to detect edges in an image.

PRACTICE EXERCISE

1. Design the controller using Fuzzy Logic to implement in real-time process to control the room temperature. Select the parameters appropriately.

2. Design the controller using Fuzzy Logic to implement in real-time process of Rice cookers by automatically controlling the heat and timing, and at the same time release up a heating element on the range.

3. Design the traffic light controller using Fuzzy Logic in real-time process for optimum selection of relationship between traffic and timing of traffic lights to activate.

MATLAB in Neural Network

INTRODUCTION

Artificial neural network (ANN) is a field within artificial intelligence and have been in research study for several years. They have found applications in data aggregation, video games, image processing, security, and optimisation techniques.

ANN is a technique that mimics the behaviour of human brain. In traditional ways, it is used to model linear and nonlinear systems. This technique has been applied in various engineering applications and other fields. A neural network can be compared to a parallel distributed processor for computing based applications.

Neural Network is the mimic of the brain emulating some of its strength for computation. These are mainly divided into various pattern association and pattern classification. Neural Network has supervised and unsupervised learning methods. The supervised learning supports with feed-forward, radial basis, and dynamic networks. Also, it supports unsupervised learning with self-organising and layers.

MATLAB has a Neural Network Toolbox™ that also comes with a GUI. This toolbox provides functions and apps for modelling complex nonlinear systems. This is difficult to model with a closed-form equation.

In this chapter, we are focusing on the use of MATLAB in neural network as lot of research on soft computing technique takes place in various applications of ANNs. Further, we will discuss how to solve the neural network problems using MATLAB.

13.1 ABOUT NEURAL NETWORK

Neural Network is very commonly referred to as an 'artificial neural network or in short ANN. This was found by Dr. Robert Hecht–Nielsen. According to him neural network define as "a computing system made up of a number of simple, highly interconnected processing elements, which process information by their dynamic state response to external inputs".

ANNs are software processing devices (algorithms) and hardware that consist of hundreds or thousands of processor units. Such processor is like a billions of neurons in brain to perform as human thoughts. The neural network performs based on mathematical model which gives at least an operational understanding of their structure and function.

13.1.1 Benefits of Neural Networks

A Neural network has some remarkable ability to solve the complicated or imprecise data. Some of the advantages of ANN are as follows:

(i) *Adaptive learning:* An ANN has the ability to perform task based on input data using the training mode and learning experience.

(ii) *Self-organisation:* An ANN can generate the organisation structure based on learning time.

(iii) *Real time operation:* An ANN computation supports real time operation of process devices. This operates the controller in precise and in speed.

(iv) *Fault tolerance:* An ANN can protect the variation and partial degradation performance of a network. Even ANN recover the network from major damage.

13.2 HUMAN AND ARTIFICIAL NEURONS

Like in human brain, Neural network is a networks in which nodes correspond to neurons and edges represent chemical or electrical trigger (synaptic) connections between neurons. A simple biological neuron diagram of the human brain, consisting of basic component of neuron is depicted in Figure 13.1. A neuron consists of number of cell body, having various extensions from the cell. These are branches that are called dendrites which transmit the signal from one neuron to other neuron.

A biological neuron is represented with the dendrites and axon terminals in the shown figure.

Neurons receive electrical signals from other neurons (or sensory inputs) via their dendrites. The Figure 13.2 shows the connection of two neurons with a unidirectional synaptic connection where the left neuron is sending the signal and the right

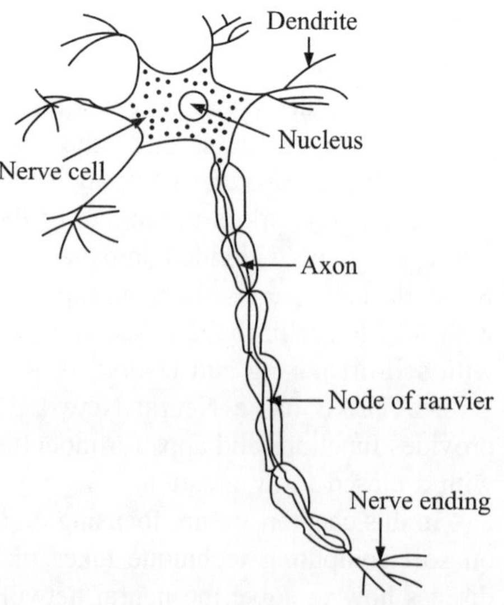

FIGURE 13.1 Components of a neuron.

neuron receiving it. The electrical wave propagates down the cell body of the sending neuron and finally terminate at the synapse to release neurotransmitter into the synaptic cleft.

Depending upon the strength and timings of electrical wave inputs, signal transmit along neuron axon send out to other neurons.

The average human brain contains around 100 billion neurons each with approximately 7000 connections which

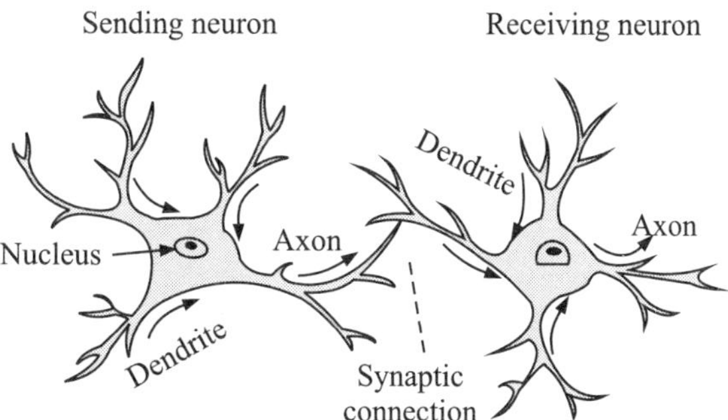

FIGURE 13.2   Connection of a neuron.

make about 700 trillion connections. Each neuron size is as small as 0.004 mm and the average power consumption of a human brain is around 20 W. When neurons die the global operation is unaffected; so such neural networks are very fault tolerant.

If we consider the Core i7 processor, it contains 1.4 billion transistors. Each transistor in this processor is 0.00000022 mm in size and each with two inputs and one output. The power consumption of this Core i7 is approximately 200 W. But in the CPU (central processing unit) of a Core i7 if a single transistor fails then the whole computer collapse; so it is not at all fault tolerant.

From this, discussion we can imagine that human brains are far more powerful than computers. It has many advantages including fault tolerance, low power consumption, multiple parallel processing and large data storage. For these reasons, Neurophysiologist Warren McCulloch and a mathematician Walter Pitts study of neurons as computational devises has been ongoing research since 1940s.

13.3   THE ARTIFICIAL NEURON

The artificial neuron is the model of the real neuron or in other word it is the mimic of the human brain. The idea behind this simple model is to develop the architecture of the neurons that is easier to understand and can be simulated. This makes them computationally viable; even for the complex models. The artificial neuron is represented by the diagram in Figure 13.3.

The neuron transmits the electrical spikes signal through a thin and long stand known

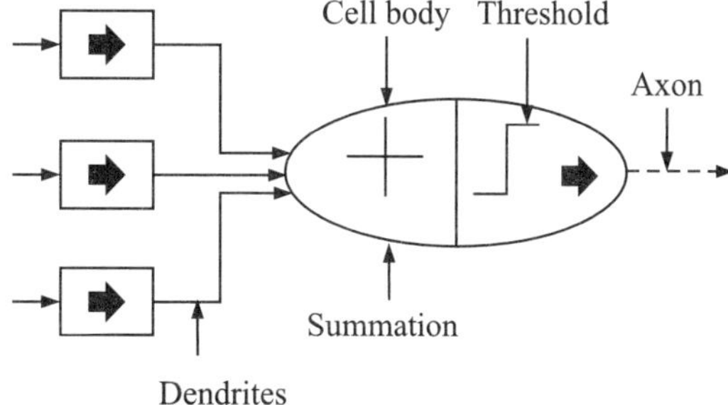

FIGURE 13.3   The artificial neuron model.

as an *axon*. This signal is further splits into thousands of branches. At the end of axon for each branch, a structure called a *synapse* converts the activity from the axon into electrical signal. The dashed line in the figure is the axon hillock, where transmission of signals starts up. Finally, this electrical signal inhibits or excites activity in the next connected neurons.

Figure 13.4 shows the artificial neural networks model functions that deduce the essential features of neurons and their interconnection. Here, each input neurons is multiplied by designated weight values and then summed these weighted inputs before being passed into an activation function.

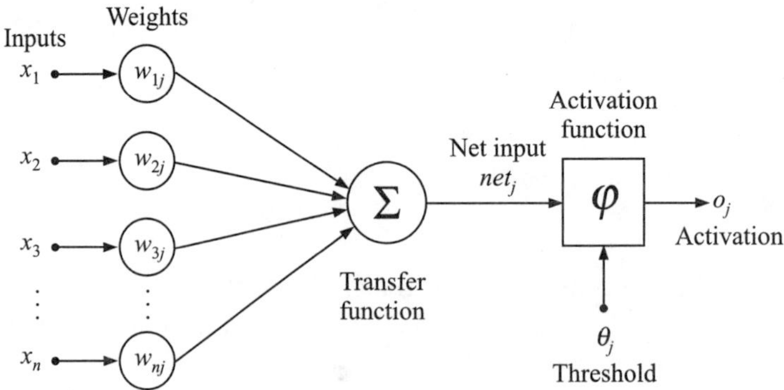

FIGURE 13.4   The artificial neuron model functions.

An artificial neuron is a device with number of inputs and one output. Here each neuron input is multiplied by a weight associated with the connection and these are summed before being passed into an activation function. By writing a code, the ANN can simulate these models like a real networks of neurons with the activation function changing from model to model.

In the artificial neural network, there are two modes of operation in the neuron; the training mode and the learning mode. The training mode, constitute of firing the neuron based on input patterns. Whereas, in the learning mode, the learned input pattern is processed for the current output.

The neuron compares the received signal from excitatory input with its inhibitory input, and correspondingly sends a spike of electrical activity via axon [chemical interaction of the neurotransmitter and the postsynaptic receptor initiates events that lead to either depolarisation (excitation) or hyperpolarisation (inhibition) of the postsynaptic cell]. This develops the mode of learning process and influence the effectiveness of the synapses that exhibit changes of one neuron on another. If the input pattern does not belong to the trained then the firing rule is applied to determine the output based on desire condition.

13.4 ARCHITECTURE OF NEURAL NETWORKS

The architecture of neural network consists of following networks.

13.4.1 Feed-forward Networks

Feed-forward ANNs consideredbeing straight forward networks that associate inputs with outputs. This allows signals to travel from input network to output network in one way. There is no feedback loop, i.e., the layer does not affect by the produced output. This type of network structure is also referred as bottom-up or top-down. Feed-forward ANNs are extensively used in pattern recognition application.

13.4.2 Feedback Networks

Feedback ANNs is a loop network where signals travel in either direction of the network. Feedback networks are dynamic, powerful and extremely complicated. The network 'state' changes continuously until the desired equilibrium point is attained.

13.4.3 Network Layers

The artificial neural network consists of three groups, or layers, of units. The first layer is a layer of 'input' units. The third layer is a layer of 'output' units. The second layer is a 'hidden' unit, connected to a 'input' and 'output' layer units as shown in Figure 13.5.

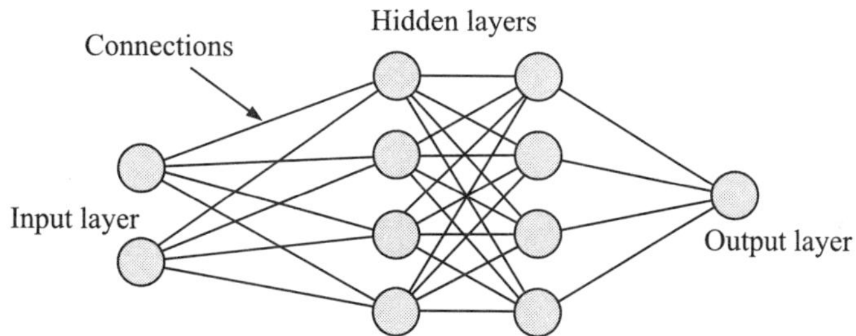

FIGURE 13.5 Neural network layer.

This simple type of network is the representations of weights between the input and hidden units and outputs. Each hidden unit is weights is modified to determine the required outputs. So, layers in Figure 13.5 are defined as follows:

The *input unit* represents the raw data that is fed into the first layer of the network.

The *hidden unit* determines the activities of the input units and the weights bias. This layer connects the input and the hidden units.

The *output unit* depends on the activities of the hidden units and the weights between them.

13.5 THE MCCULLOCH-PITTS MODEL OF NEURON

In 1943, Warren McCulloch and Walter Pitts introduced the early model of artificial neuron. A more complicated neuron as shown in Figure 13.6 is the McCulloch-Pitts model (MCP) of neuron. This model has the 'weighted' inputs; that change each input parameter depending on the particular input weight. The weight is multiplied with the input.

The McCulloch-Pitts neural model is also known as *linear threshold gate*. The inputs $(x_1, x_2, x_3, ..., x_n)$ and weights $(w_1, w_2, w_3, ..., w_n)$ connections are typically real values. It has both positive (+) and negative (−) values.

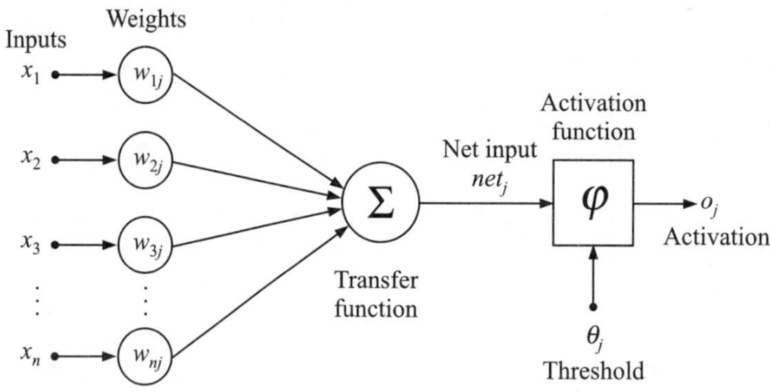

FIGURE 13.6   An MCP neuron.

In the McCulloch-Pitts neural network, the linear threshold gate simply classifies the set of inputs to sum the binary output *y*. Such a function can be expressed mathematically in equations as:

$$\text{Sum} = \sum_{i=1}^{N} x_i w_i$$

$$\text{Output } (y) = f(\text{Sum})$$

The inputs $(x_1, x_2, x_3, ..., x_n)$ with $(w_1, w_2, w_3, ..., w_n)$ weight values are normalised to the range of either (0, 1). This is compared to the threshold constant θ_j as:

$$x_1 w_1 + x_2 w_2 + x_3 w_3 + \cdots > \theta_j$$

The McCulloch-Pitts model of neuron is a simple mathematical definition and has considerable computing potential. However, this model only generates a binary output based on fixed weighted and threshold values as shown in Figure 13.7. Moreover, the neural computing algorithm is needed to obtain the neural model for diverse applications with more flexible computational features.

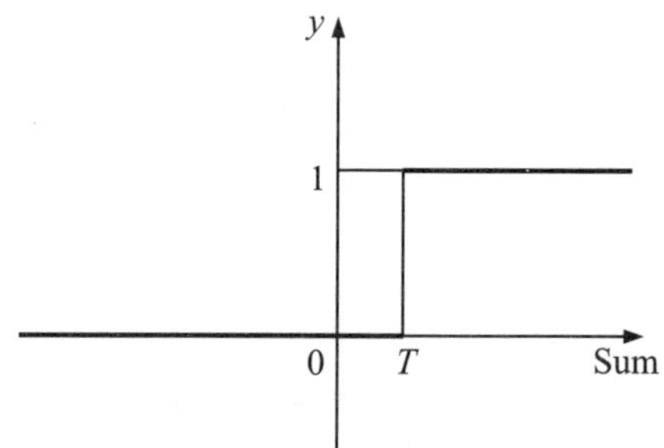

FIGURE 13.7   Linear threshold function.

13.6   THE PERCEPTRON

In late 1950s, Frank Rosenblatt introduced a network composed of the units based on the enhanced version of McCulloch-Pitts Threshold Logic Unit (TLU) model. As per Rosenblatt's model of neuron, a *perceptron* was the hybrid result of two concepts of McCulloch-Pitts model of an artificial neuron and Hebbian learning rule of adjusting weights. Additionally, Frank Rosenblatt's model has variable weight values so, the perceptron model added with extra input known as *bias*.

The perceptron learning algorithm is an adaptive network. This method self-organises a network to compute the desired behaviour. The closed loop learning algorithms present the input-output mapping to the network. This is executed until the network learns to produce the desired response by iteration.

Figure 13.8 shows the learning algorithm modelled in a closed loop of system for corrections of the network parameters.

Network layers are constructed from a number of interconnected nodes which contain an activation function. This can be single or multiple layer perceptron. A pattern of the network communicates to one or more hidden layers, is done via a system of weighted connections. The hidden layers then link to an output layer as shown in Figure 13.9.

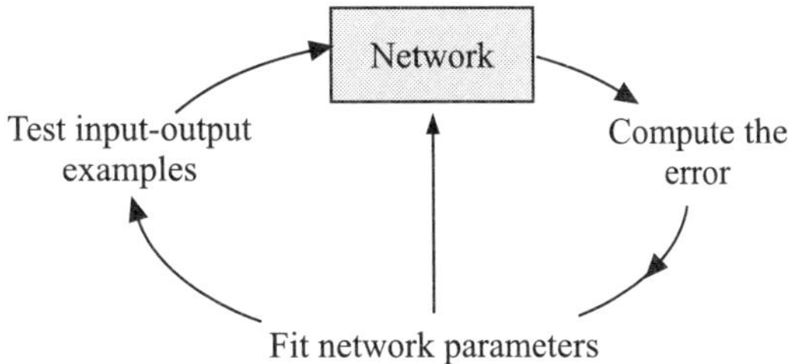

FIGURE 13.8   Learning process in a parametric system.

The weight w_i will be positive when x_i tends to cause the perceptron to fire. And the weight w_i will be negative when x_i inhibits the perceptron. These weighted inputs are summed together and compared with the preset threshold value. If the threshold value exceeds then the neuron fires otherwise the neuron cease the fire. In mathematical terms, the neuron fires if it exceeds threshold value;

$$x_1w_1 + x_2w_2 + x_3w_3 + \cdots > \theta_j$$

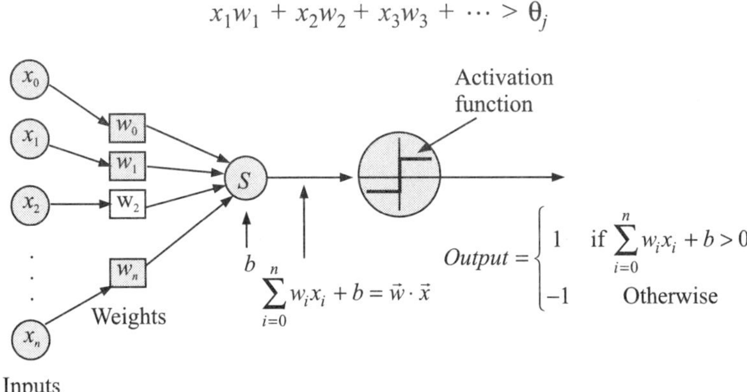

FIGURE 13.9   Weighted perceptron.

In machine learning, the perceptron is an algorithm for supervised learning of input binary classifiers functions. Thus, the modified equation is represented as:

$$\sum_{i=1}^{N} x_i w_i + b$$

where, b consider as bias input value.

When such network is a simple open loop system then it is called feed-forward networks. However, when the neuron network likes to change its weights and/or threshold then such network is termed as feedback networks.

In the modern computation, the perceptron is an algorithm for learning a binary classifier. It is a function that maps real value input x to binary output value y and represented as:

$$f(x) = \begin{cases} 1 & \text{if } w * x + b > 0 \\ 0 & \text{otherwise} \end{cases}$$

Where, w is real-valued weights vector, $w * x$ is the dot product in $\sum_{i=1}^{N} x_i w_i$, where N is the number of inputs and b is the *bias* to the perceptron. The bias is the decision boundary and it is not depend on input value. The value of $f(x)$ used to classify whether x is positive or negative in problems classification.

If b is negative, then the weighted combination of inputs produce a positive value greater than $|b|$. This shift the classifier neuron over the zero threshold.

In 1960s Frank Rosenblatt did the most influential work on ANN under the heading of 'Perceptrons'. This is distinguished as single-layer and multilayer perceptron architectures. In the single-layer perceptron, all units are connected to output node. Whereas in a multilayer perceptron (MLP) network consists of a set of input source layer, one or more hidden layers and an output layer of nodes. The input signal propagates through the network layer and the hidden layer does the computation to generate output.

13.6.1   Linearly Separable Regions

Perceptron computable functions are those points whose function value is separated in 0 and 1 value points using a line. Based on this concept, we can now plot the decision boundaries of logic gates. Figure 13.10 shows two possible separations to compute the OR, AND and NOT functions.

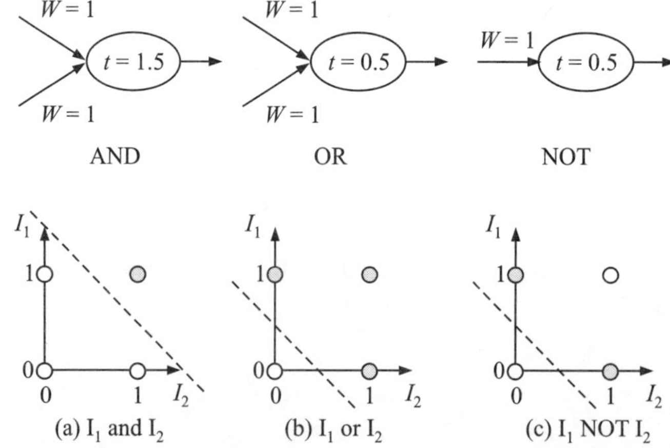

FIGURE 13.10   Separations of input space corresponding to OR, AND and NOT.

Since the perceptron outputs are a non-zero value, based on the weighted sum and threshold C, we can write down the output of this perceptron as follows:

$$\text{output of } P = \begin{cases} 1 & \text{if } Kx + Ly > C \\ 0 & \text{if } Kx + Ly \le C \end{cases}$$

Recall that $Kx + Ly > C$ and $Kx + Ly < C$ are the two regions on the xy plane separated by the line $Kx + Ly + C = 0$. If we consider the input (x, y) as a point on a plane, then the perceptron is separated by a single line, are called **linearly separable regions**.

We can apply linearly separable regions concept to observe logic functions such as the boolean AND, OR and NOT operators, i.e., they can be performed by using a single perceptron. This is illustrated by 2D plot on each graph as shown in Figure 13.11.

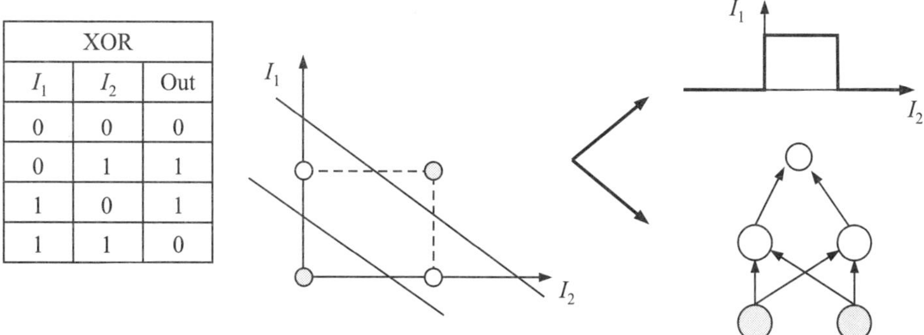

FIGURE 13.11   Linearly separable regions.

In the Boolean expression, the logic operators are not linearly separable. For instance, the XOR operator is not linearly separable by a single perceptron. As it is difficult to draw a line that divide the regions containing either 1 or 0. Hence, the XOR function is not linearly separable. Such situation in dealing with XOR is rather obvious. So there is need of two straight lines to separate the different outputs/decisions as shown in Figure 13.12.

XOR		
I_1	I_2	Out
0	0	0
0	1	1
1	0	1
1	1	0

FIGURE 13.12   Dual decision boundary for XOR.

The difficulty in dealing with XOR can be resolved by using an appropriate weight vector for each case, a single perceptron functions. This can be done by changing the transfer function to form more than one decision boundary. Even for the complex network more complex decision boundaries need to be generated. This is done by arranging more than one perceptron in feed-forward networks.

Note: To deal with the linear inseparability problem of single layer network XOR, the two-layer perceptron should be applied to compute XOR shown in Figure 13.13.

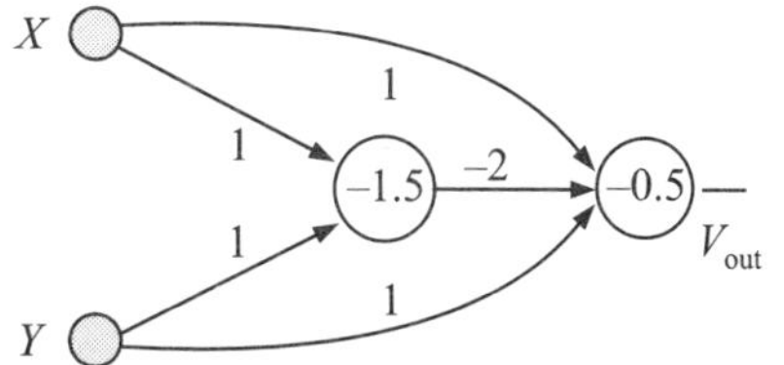

FIGURE 13.13   Two-layer perceptron.

The output is +1 if and only if $x + y - 2 \Theta (x + y - 1.5) - 0.5 > 0$

EXAMPLE 13.1   In this example we learn to design a two-input perceptron.
A two input hard limit neuron is trained to classify five input vectors.

```
>> X = [ -0.5 -0.5 +0.3 -0.1;  ...
-0.5 +0.5 -0.5 +1.0];
>> T = [1 1 0 0];
>> plotpv(X,T);
```

The output of the MATLAB code is shown in Figure 13.14.

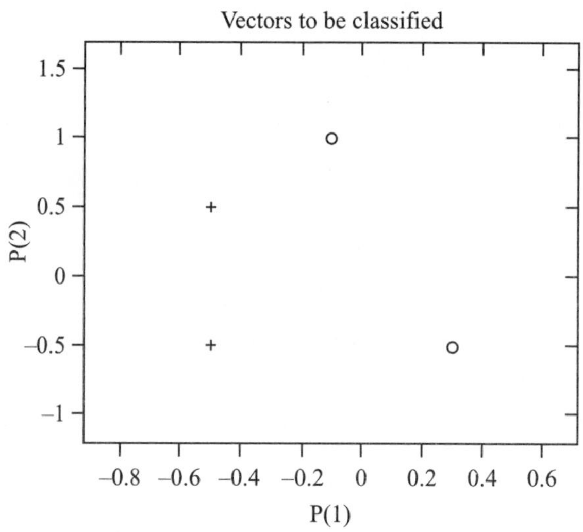

FIGURE 13.14   Two input perceptron.

The network is then configured to the data, so we can examine its initial weight and bias values, use the given commands form,

```
>> net = perceptron;
net = configure(net,X,T);
```

The input vectors are replotted with the neuron's initial classification, use the given commands form

```
>> plotpv(X,T);
plotpc(net.IW{1},net.b{1});
```

ADAPT updates the network for each time step in the series to perform as a better classifier. Following example illustrates the use of above commands and adapt function.

EXAMPLE 13.2

```
>> XX = repmat(con2seq(X),1,3);
TT = repmat(con2seq(T),1,3);
net = adapt(net,XX,TT);
plotpc(net.IW{1},net.b{1});
```

The output of the MATLAB code is shown in Figure 13.15.

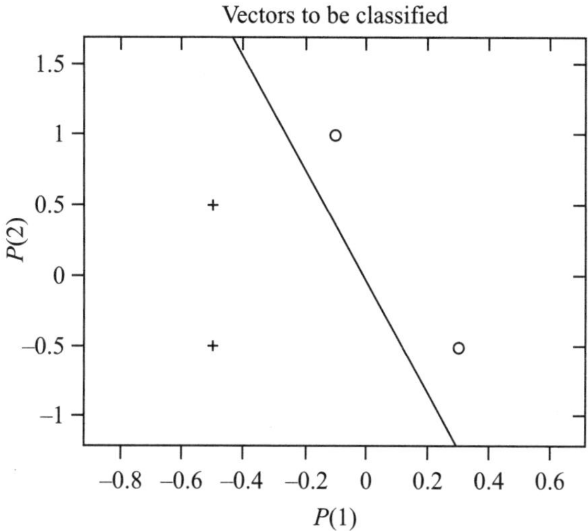

FIGURE 13.15   Vector classified.

13.7 TRANSFER FUNCTION

The behaviour of an ANN (Artificial Neural Network) depends on both the weights and the input–output function based on transfer function for a specified units. This function is divided into following three categories:

1. Linear (or ramp)
2. Threshold
3. Sigmoid

In the **linear units**, the output activity is proportional to the total weighted output.

In the **threshold units**, the output is set at one of the two levels. It depends on whether the total input is greater than or less than some threshold value.

In the **sigmoid units**, the output varies continuously but not linearly as the input changes.

Out of all three, the sigmoid units bear a greater resemblance to real neurons than linear or threshold units. However, all three are considered for rough approximations.

$$f(x) = \frac{1}{1 + e^{-\beta x}}$$

The sigmoid function as shown in Figure 13.16 is also very useful in multilayer networks, as the sigmoid curve allows differentiation.

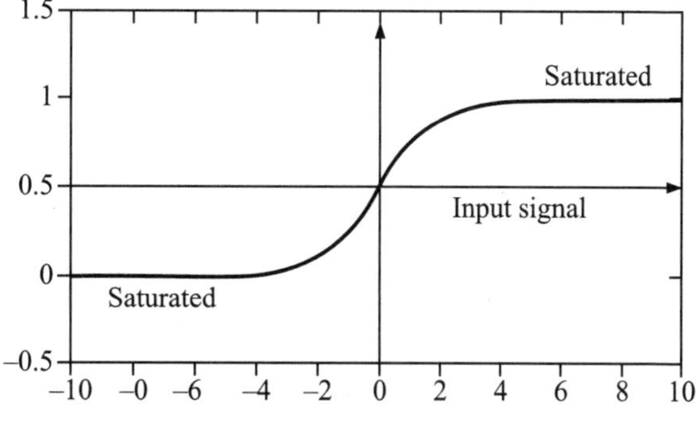

FIGURE 13.16   Sigmoid function.

EXAMPLE 13.3   In this example, we write a program to generate a few activation functions in neural networks whose output is shown in Figure 13.17.

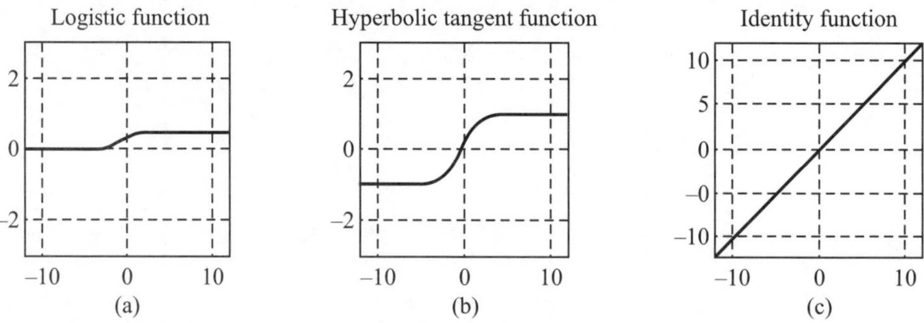

FIGURE 13.17   Plot of neuron of Example 13.3.

```
x = -12:0.15:12;
tmp = exp(-x); % variable
y1 = 1./(2+tmp); % y1 plot condition
y2 = (2-tmp)./(2+tmp); % y2 plot condition
y3 = x; % y3 plot condition
subplot(321); plot(x, y1); grid on;
axis([min(x) max(x) -3 3]);
title('Logistic Function');
xlabel('(Fig a)');
axis('square');

subplot(322); plot(x, y2); grid on; % second plot
axis([min(x) max(x) -3 3]);
title('Hyperbolic Tangent Function');
xlabel('(Fig b)');
axis('square');

subplot(323); plot(x, y3); grid on; % third plot
axis([min(x) max(x) min(x) max(x)]);
title('Identity Function');
xlabel('(Fig c)');
axis('square');
```

EXAMPLE 13.4   Let us see, how to define the Neuron weights and by running the given code observe, the following output will appear.

```
>> w = [6 -4]
w =
     6     -4
```

```
% Neuron bias
>> b = -1
b =

    -1
% Activation function
>> func = 'tansig'
func =
tansig
```

Similarly, following functions can also be tested:

```
% func = 'purelin'
% func = 'hardlim'
% func = 'logsig'
```

EXAMPLE 13.5   In this example, we learn to calculate Neuron outputs, by using the following codes:

```
>> r = [9 5];
>> s = [6 -2];
>> b = -4;
% by running the code the following command the output's appears.
>> activation_potential = r*s'+b

activation_potential =

    40
>> neuron_output = feval(func, activation_potential)
neuron_output =
    1
```

EXAMPLE 13.6   In this example, we learn to plot neuron output over the range of inputs.

```
[s1,s2] = meshgrid(-15:.2:15);
z = feval(func, [s1(:) s2(:)]*w'+b );
% [y1, y2, ...] = feval(fhandle, x1, ..., xn) evaluates the function
z = reshape(z,length(s1),length(s2));
plot3(s1,s2,z)
grid on
xlabel('Input 1')
ylabel('Input 2')
zlabel('Neuron output')
```

By running the above code, the following output appears as shown in Figure 13.18.

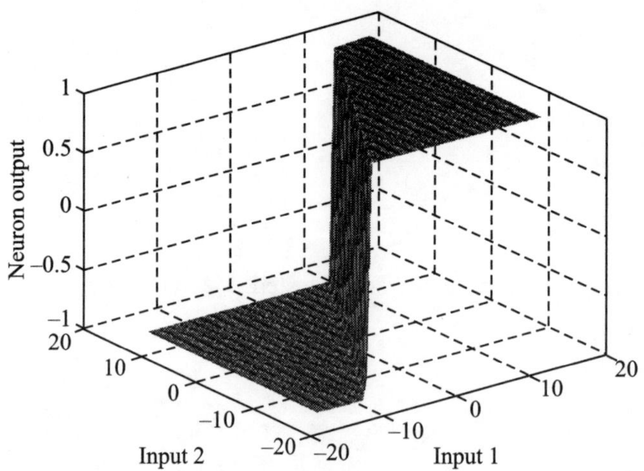

FIGURE 13.18   Plot of neuron Example of 13.6.

13.8   NEURAL NETWORK TOOLBOX

Neural Network Toolbox™ provides functions and apps for modelling complex nonlinear systems. Such toolbox supports modelling of a closed-form equation. So, Neural Network Toolbox is used to model a closed-form equation using supervised learning with feed-forward, basis, and networks. Neural Network Toolbox also supports unsupervised learning with self-organising and layers. We can design, train and simulate neural networks for applications.

Further, Neural Network Toolbox is used for following functions:

- *Nonlinear:*   A neural network can creates relationships between inputs and outputs applications.
- *Pattern recognition:*   A neural network is trained for class identification.
- *Clustering:*   A neural network is used to identify the natural distributions and category relationships.
- *Dynamic systems:*   A neural network can be used model nonlinear dynamic system for predicting sequential data.
- *Control systems:*   Neural Network can control nonlinear systems using model-predictive and model-reference.
- *Architectures:*   A neural network is used to define architectures and algorithms for sophisticated applications.

EXAMPLE 13.7   In this example, we will learn to design a single input and output variables using the following codes:

```
>> inputs = [1 : 5]' % input vector (5-dimensional pattern)
```

```
inputs =
     1
     2
     3
     4
     5
>> outputs = [2   3]' % corresponding target output vector
outputs =
     2
     3
```

EXAMPLE 13.8   In this example, we will learn to design a single input and two output network using the following codes:

```
% network to create
net = network( ...
1, ... % number of inputs,
2, ... % number of layers
[1; 0], ... % biasConnect,
[1; 0], ... % inputConnect,
[0 0; 1 0], ... % layerConnect,
[0 1] ... % outputConnect,
);
% View network structure
view(net);
```

By running the code, the following output appears as shown in Figure 13.19.

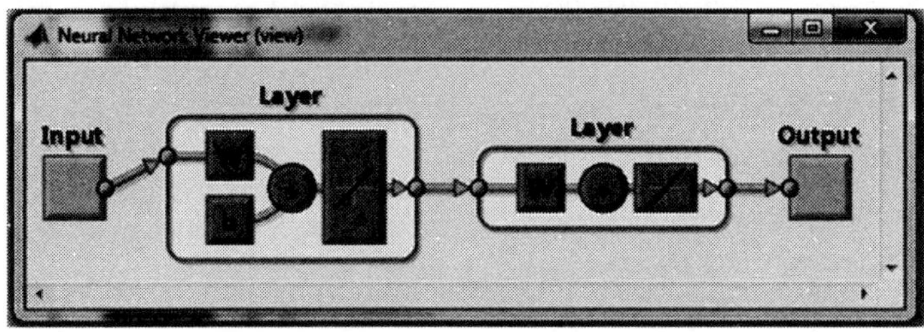

FIGURE 13.19   Perceptron layer.

EXAMPLE 13.9   Use the following codes to construct a classification of clusters of data in a two-dimensional input space:

```
N=30; % number of samples
% to define inputs and outputs
```

```
offset = 6; % offset class
x = [randn(2,N) randn(2,N)+offset]; % inputs
y = [zeros(1,N) ones(1,N)]; % outputs
% Plot input samples with PLOTPV (Plot perceptron input/target vectors)
figure(1)
plotpv(x,y);
```

By running the code, the following outputs appears as shown in Figure 13.20.

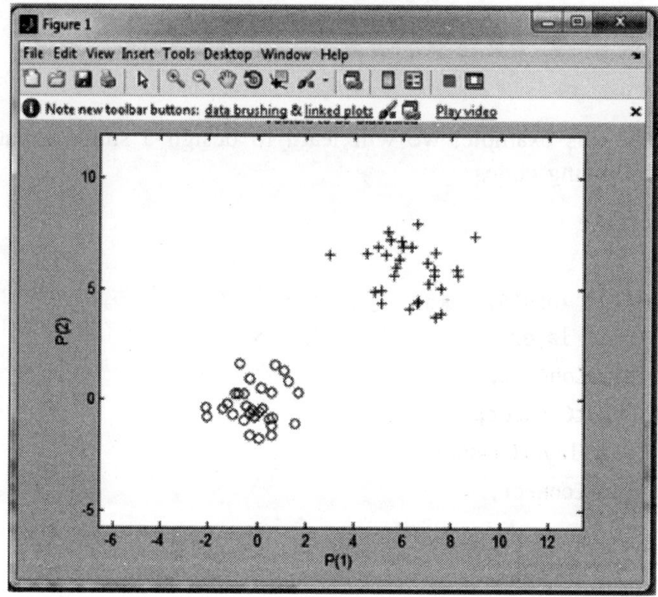

FIGURE 13.20   Cluster of perceptron in two-dimensional.

EXAMPLE 13.10   Use the following codes to construct a Perceptron for the classification of clusters of data in a three-dimensional input space:

```
N=10; % number of samples
% to define inputs and outputs
offset = 8; % offset class
x = [randn(3,N) randn(3,N)+offset]; % inputs
y = [zeros(1,N) ones(1,N)]; % outputs

% Plot input samples with PLOTPV (Plot perceptron input/target vectors)
figure(1)
plotpv(x,y);
```

By running the code, following output appears as shown in Figure 13.21.

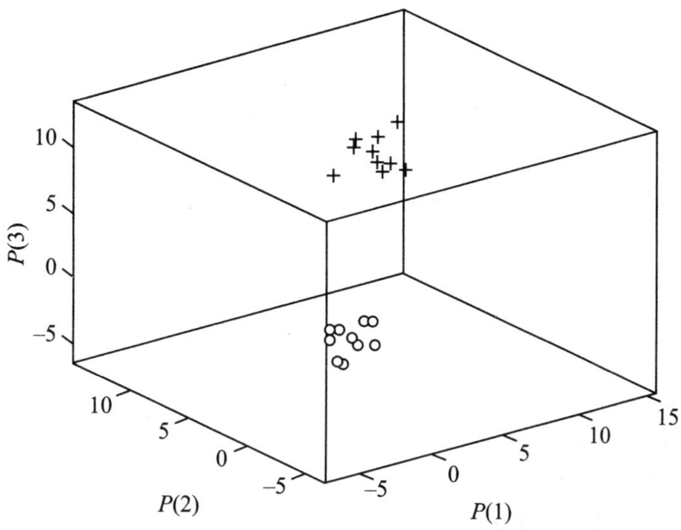

FIGURE 13.21   Cluster of perceptron in three-dimensional space.

EXAMPLE 13.11   In the example, we find the weight of simple perceptron to a two-input OR using the following codes:

```
input = [0 0; 0 1; 1 0; 1 1];
numIn = 4;
desired_out = [0;1;1;0];
bias = -1;
coeff = 0.5;
rand('state',sum(30*clock));
weights = -1*4.*rand(2,1)
```

By running the code, the following weight appears:
```
weights =
    -0.1318
    -3.1172
```

EXAMPLE 13.12   In this example, we use trained perceptron to classify an input vector of [0.7; 1.2], using the following codes:

```
>> p = [0.7; 1.2]
>> y = net(p)
% compare response with output coding (a,b,c,d)
p =
0.7000
1.2000
```

```
y =
1
1
```

EXAMPLE 13.13   In the example, we learn to design the NAND gate perceptron in MATLAB and find the performance using the following codes:

```
S = [0 1 1 1 ; 0 1 0 1];    % number of input vector dimension
R = [1 1 1 0];    % no. of layers
net = newp([0 1; 0 1], 1)
weight_int = net.IW{1, 1}
bias_int = net.b{1}
net.trainParam.epochs = 15
net = train(net,S,R);
weight_final = net.IW{1, 1};
bias_final = net.b(1);
simulation = sim(net, S)
```

By running the code, the display will be as follows:

```
net =
      Neural Network object:
      architecture:
            numInputs: 1
            numLayers: 1
         biasConnect: [1]
        inputConnect: [1]
        layerConnect: [0]
       outputConnect: [1]


weight_int =
      0       0
bias_int =
      0
simulation =
      1     0     0     0
```

By running the code, the following neural network training appears as shown in Figure 13.22.

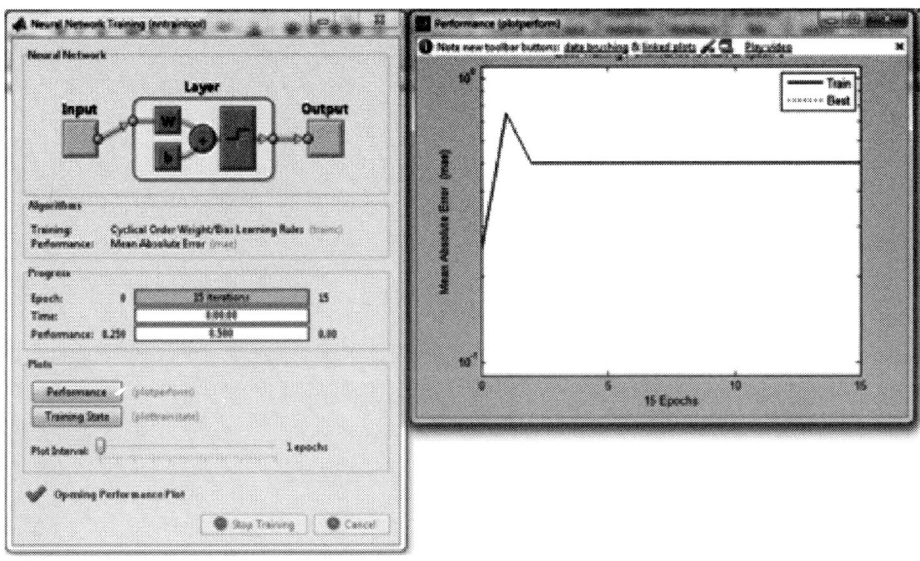

FIGURE 13.22   Neural network block and performance plot for Example 13.13.

EXAMPLE 13.14   In this example, we learn to design the NOR gate Perceptron in MATLAB and find the performance using the following codes:

```
S = [0 0 1 1 ; 0 1 0 1];    % number of input vector dimension
R = [1 0 0 0];    % no. of layers
net = newp([0 1; 0 1], 1)
weight_int = net.IW{1, 1}
bias_int = net.b{1}
net.trainParam.epochs = 15
net = train(net,S,R);
weight_final = net.IW{1, 1};
bias_final = net.b(1);
simulation = sim(net, S)
```

By running the code, the display will be as follows:

```
weight_int =
       0       0
bias_int =
       0
net =
     Neural Network object:
     architecture:
           numInputs: 1
```

```
           numLayers: 1
        biasConnect: [1]
       inputConnect: [1]
       layerConnect: [0]
      outputConnect: [1]
simulation =
        1     0     0     0
```

By running the code, the following neural network training appears as shown in Figure 13.23.

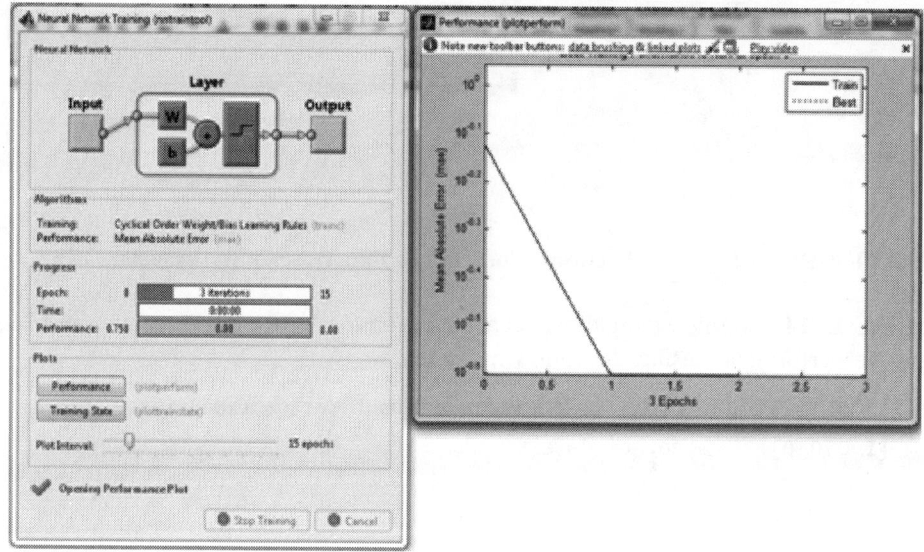

FIGURE 13.23   Neural network block and performance plot for Example 13.14.

13.9   ACTUAL MODEL

The neural networks can model any input to output relations. We can try on some simple MATLAB modelling using neural network.

Let us consider, a model for data generation that has three inputs a, b and c to generate an output y as

$$y = 3a + bc + 8c$$

We can write a MATLAB script to generate the data by using the codes given in the following example.

EXAMPLE 13.15

```
>> net=train(net,I,0);
>> a= rand(1,750);
```

```
>> b= rand(1,750);
>> c= rand(1,750);
>> n= rand(1,750)*0.02;
>> y=a*3+b.*c+8*c+n;
>> I=[a; b; c];
>> O=y;
>> R=[0 2; 0 2 ; 0 2];
>> S=[6 1];    % Size matrix has the v-size of all the layers
>> net=train(net,I,O);  % train neural network with the data
```

In actual cases, we do not have the mathematical model to generate the data by running the real system.

By running the code, the following neural network training appears as shown in Figure 13.24.

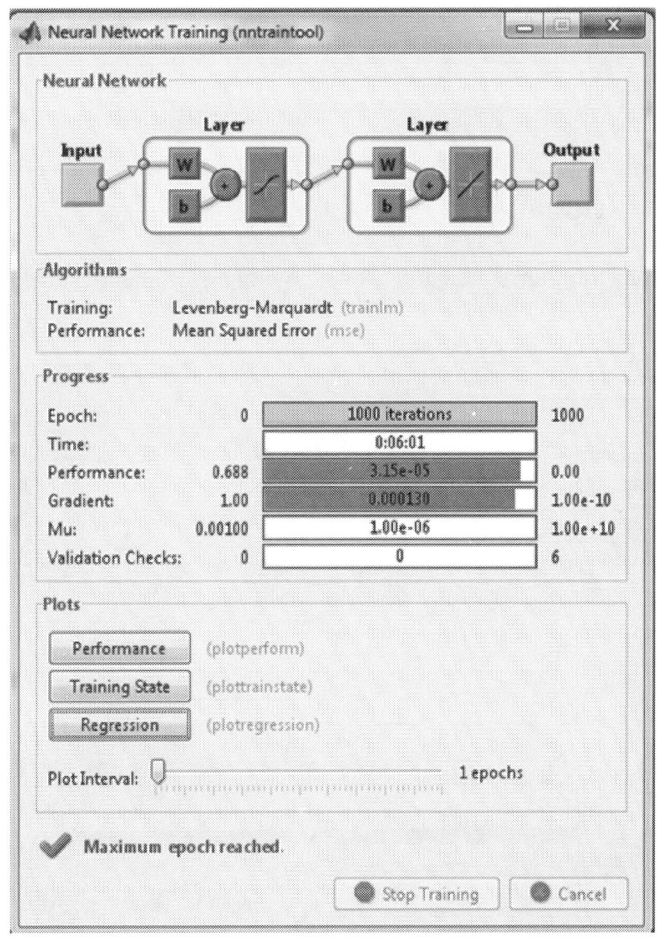

FIGURE 13.24   Neural network training for Example 13.15.

We can see the performance curve shown in Figure 13.22, by clicking the push button (performance) as it gets trained (Figure 13.24).

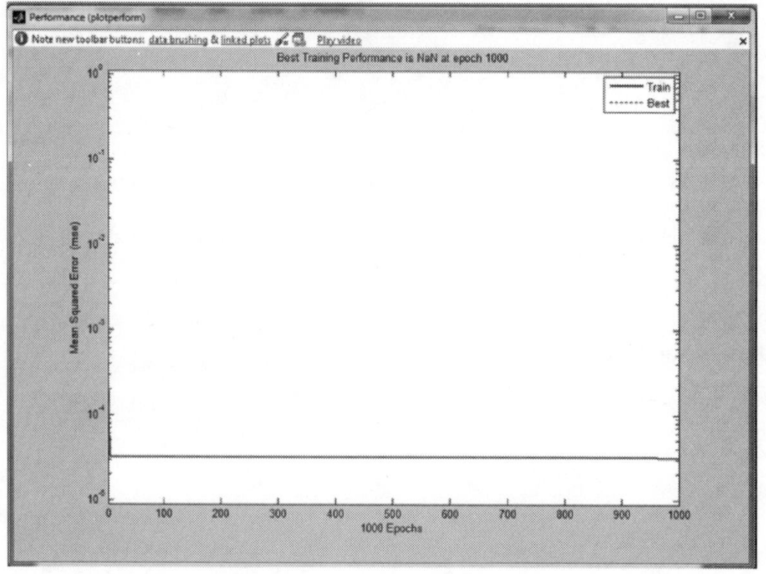

FIGURE 13.25   Performance curve for Example 13.15.

We can see the training state plot shown in Figure 13.26, by clicking the push button (training state).

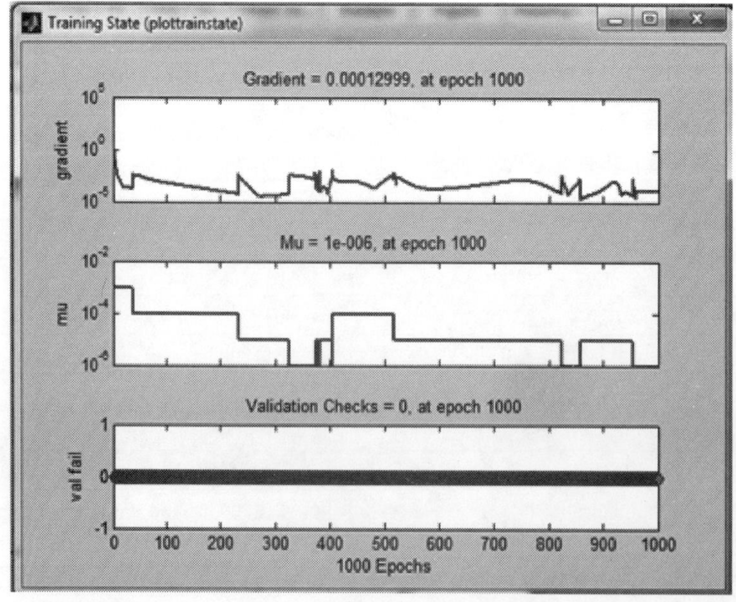

FIGURE 13.26   Training state for Example 13.15.

We can see the regression curve as shown in Figure 13.27, by clicking the push button (regression).

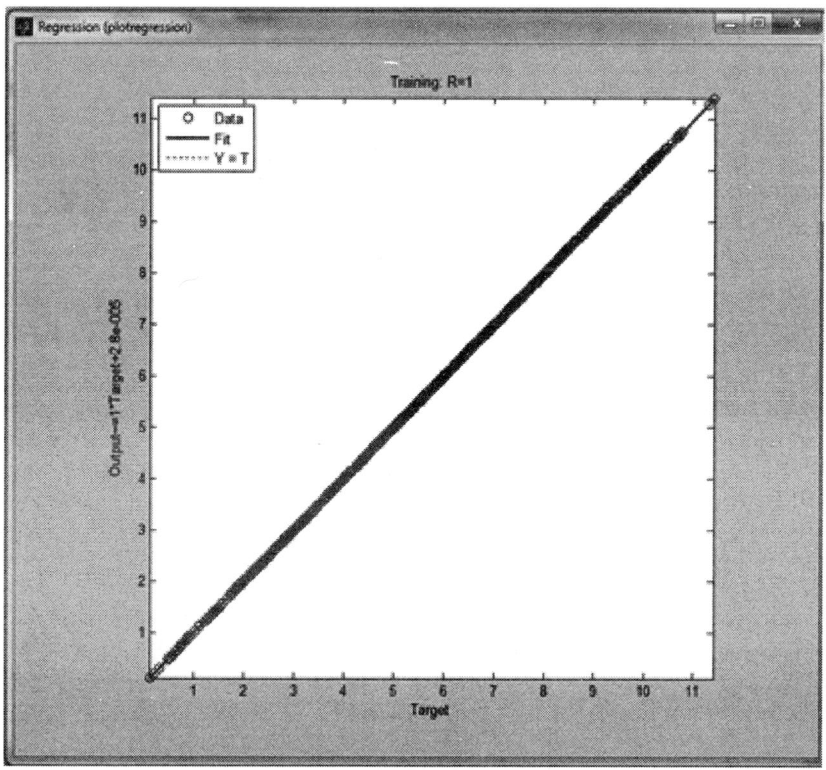

FIGURE 13.27   Regression for Example 13.15.

13.10   APPLICATIONS OF NEURAL NETWORK

Here, we are listed some of the applications of neural network that is useful in the field of artificial intelligence as follows:

- *Pattern recognition:*   Pattern Recognition is probably the most often used application. Some of the examples are facial recognition, optical character recognition, etc.
- *Time series prediction:*   Neural networks can be used to make predictions of events such as is it going to be rainy or be sunny.
- *Signal processing:*   Neural networks can be trained to process an audio signal by filter out unnecessary noise and amplify the sound level.
- *Soft sensors:*   Neural networks can be employed to process the input data from many individual sensors and evaluate them as a whole. A soft sensor refers to the process of analysing and a collection of many measurements.

- *Control:* Neural networks are often used to manage steering decisions of physical vehicles.
- *Image compression:* Neural networks can receive and process vast amounts of information in image compression.
- *Stock market prediction:* The day-to-day business of the stock market is examined by neural networks for predicting the information quickly. Many factors related to stock market can be analysed.
- *Medicine, electronic nose, security, and loan applications:* Neural networks support some applications that are in their proof-of-concept stage or not to grant a loan, information security and medical electronics fields.

These are some very interesting applications of neural networks. This is by no means a comprehensive and complete list of applications of neural networks. But hopefully, it gives an overall sense of the features and possibilities.

SUMMARY

In this chapter, we have discussed the essential features of ANNs to understand the Neural Network toolbox. The Neural Network and its different biological forms are described. The examples were used to cover the Neural Network toolbox using command line segments. We have learnt how model are used to generate logic functions. The learning rules were explained in this chapter for clear understanding. An overview of multi-layer perceptron was also described in this chapter.

REVIEW QUESTIONS

1. Define artificial neural network.
2. What are the three layers in the preceptron?
3. Explain the working of perceptron.
4. Define activation functions.
5. Explain the algorithm for training the perceptron net.
6. What are different types of learning in the contest of ANN?
7. Give a brief note on multi-layer perceptron.
8. Define bias and threshold.
9. Describe the application of neural networks.
10. What are the main requirements of the McCulloh-Pitts neuron?
11. Generate the XOR function by MATLAB code using McCulloh-Pitts neuron.
12. Generate a AND, NOT function using McCulloh-Pitts neuron using M-file.

PRACTICE EXERCISE

1. Write a MATLAB program to generate activation function for neural networks for `x=-12:0.1:12`.

2. Write a MATLAB program to generate output for a activation function when it is (a) binary and (b) bipolar sinusoidal for the net input to output neuron is 0.35.

3. Generate a MATLAB block model of preceptron for the function `y=a*4+b*2+c*3`.

4. Realise the XOR function using McCulloh-Pitts neuron.

5. Design a single neuron having an input vector with just two elements. Using net = newp([-2 2;-2 +2],1); the bias equal to 0 and the weights to 1 and –0.8, net.b{1} = [0]; w = [1 –0.8]; net.IW{1,1} = w.

   [*Hint:* The input target pair is given by p = [1; 2]; t = [1].]

CHAPTER 14

MATLAB Graphical User Interfaces

<table>
<tr><td align="center">**LEARNING OBJECTIVES**</td></tr>
</table>

This chapter aims to teach students about building of a new GUI by following ways:

- A different pop-up windows are explained about GUI template, GUIDE quick start layout editor, preference window and component name in Palette.
- All the examples related to GUI and its interface with GUI code are discussed.
- The snap shot of GUI is explained in simple way.
- Different GUIDE tools summary are tabulated.

INTRODUCTION

MATLAB GUIDE, is the 'MATLAB graphical user interfaces development environment' that provides a tool set to create Graphical User Interfaces (GUIs). GUI consists of a figure window that contains menus, buttons, text, graphics, etc. A user can interactively use the GUI figure window with the mouse and keyboard. These tools are user friendly to build GUIs for a process.

Creating a GUI involves two main steps. One is designing its layout, and the other is writing callback functions that perform the desired operations when the user selects different features. In this chapter, we shall discuss how to build a GUI and its interfaces. The methods to generate an M-file framework and its components are also elaborated.

14.1 GUIDE: GRAPHICAL USER INTERFACES DEVELOPMENT ENVIRONMENT

GUIDE, provides a set of tools for creating a process of designing and building GUIs. GUIDE tools have the following features:

Laying out the GUI

The GUI components are placed into the layout by simply clicking and dragging them into the layout area. It allows the user to create menus, GUI size, components alignment, set tab order and view a hierarchical list of component objects.

GUIDE Layout Editor, can also layout a GUI easily by clicking and dragging GUI components like menu, panels, buttons, text fields, sliders, list boxes, and so on into the layout area. GUIDE stores the GUI layout in a FIG-file.

Programing GUI

When the GUI layout is saved, GUIDE automatically generates an M-file that controls the GUI operations. This kind of programming is called *event-driven programming*. The M-file initialises the GUI and each component in the GUI is associated with one or more user written routines known as *callbacks*. Using the M-file editor, we can add code to the callbacks to perform the functions.

14.2 LAYING OUT A GUI

MATLAB provides an interactive tool called GUIDE that greatly simplifies the task of building a GUI. Here, we discuss GUIs with the MATLAB 2013a version of GUIDE that has significantly enhanced features over previous versions.

14.2.1 Starting GUIDE

To Start GUIDE, type 'guide' at the MATLAB command prompt. This displays the GUIDE Quick Start dialog window, as shown in Figure 14.1.

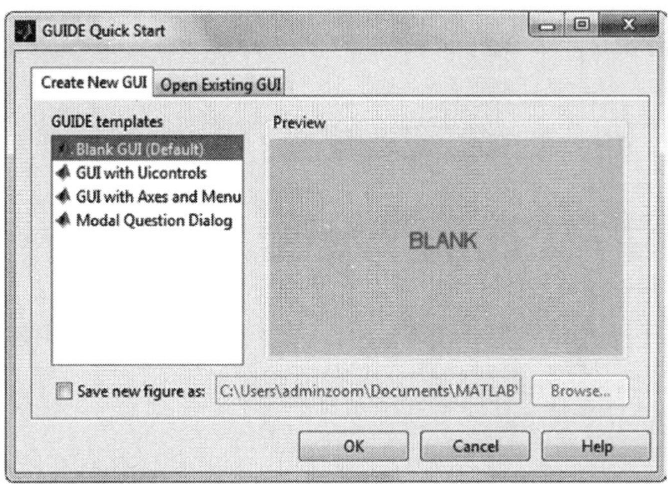

FIGURE 14.1   The guide quick start window.

From the GUIDE Quick Start dialog box, create a new GUI from one of the GUIDE templates. This is prebuilt GUIs that can be modified for our own purposes. To start with new GUI select the 'Blank GUI' template and click on the OK button at the bottom. This will pop-up the Layout Editor window as shown in Figure 14.2. Also, there is a possibility of opening the saved GUIs.

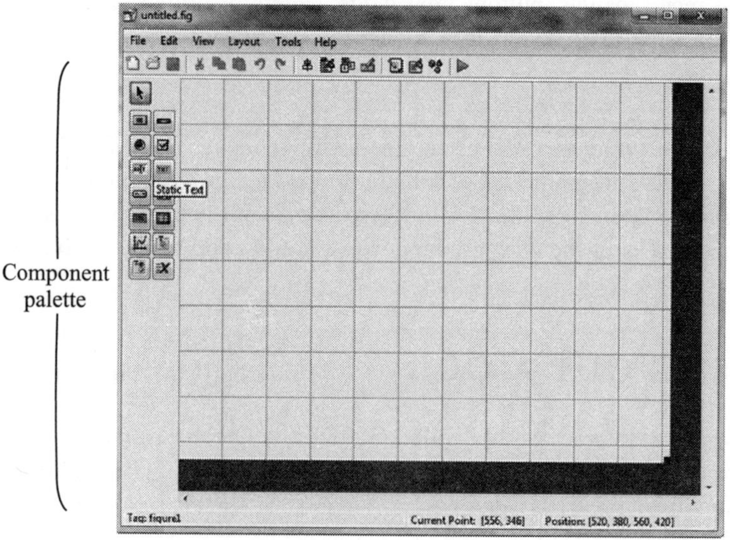

Component palette

FIGURE 14.2   The blank GUI template.

The component palette on the left side of the Layout Editor is difficult to comprehend. To display the name of the GUI components in the component palette, preference is selected from the MATLAB desktop window 'File' menu. The GUIDE preferences Window is shown in Figure 14.3. From the left part of the window, GUIDE option is to select and from the right part of the window 'Show the name in component palette' is to select followed by OK button.

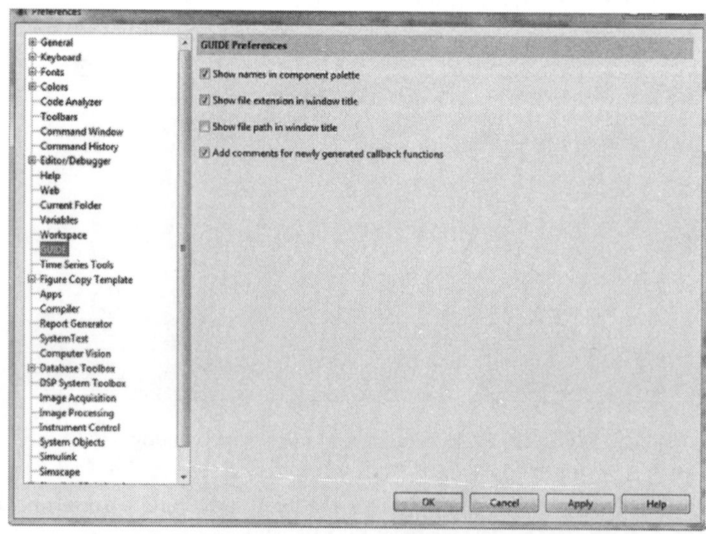

FIGURE 14.3   Guide preference window.

The new pop-up of GUIDE Quick start layout Editor with component name palette will be displayed as shown in Figure 14.4.

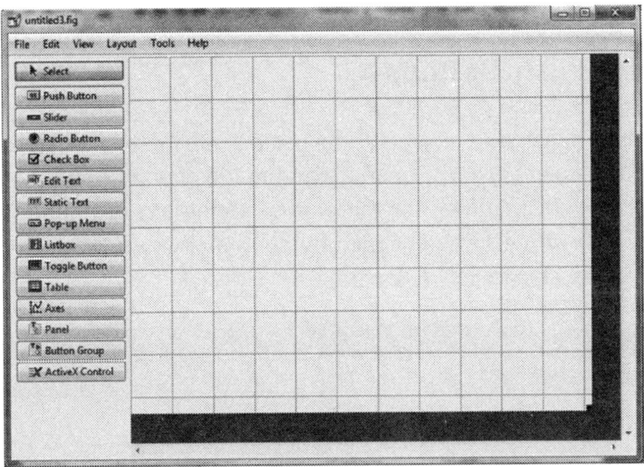

FIGURE 14.4   Palette component name in Layout editor.

14.2.2   The Layout Editor

When GUI is open, the Layout Editor enables us to select GUI components from the *palette* and arrange them in the blank GUI templatelayout area. In the Layout Editor, the GUI components such as axes, push buttons, pop-up menus, etc., are some component palette. These component palette is at the left side of the Layout Editor, can be created by dragging into the layout area.

To start the Layout Editor, first open the GUIDE Quick Start dialog box by entering *guide* command in the command prompt. Then click **OK** in the dialog box to open a blank GUI template in the Layout Editor. If we drag a push button, radio button, axes, select text and check box into the layout area, they will appear as shown in Figure 14.5.

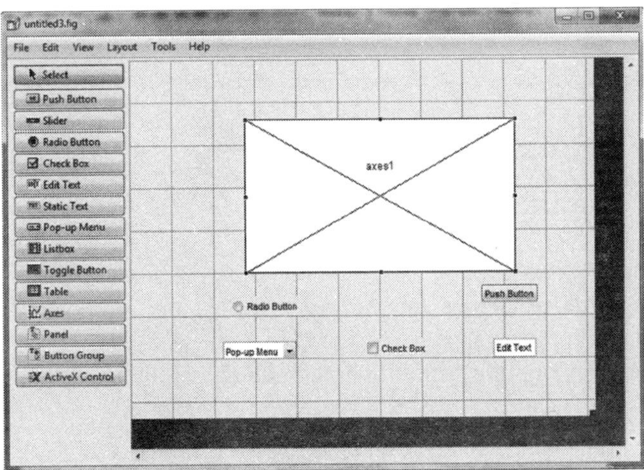

FIGURE 14.5   Component dragged into Layout area.

Further, we can also use the Layout Editor to create menus and set basic properties of the GUI components. For more information about Layout Editor and setting of property values, see 'Creating a GUI' in the MATLAB documentation.

14.2.3   Label the Push Buttons

From the 'View' menu select the 'Property Inspector' tab or by double-clicking on selected button from the Layout area. This will open a window displaying options that can be changed.

Forexample in this GUI, the label for the pop-up menu text in Figure 14.5 can be changed to read *Choose* Data. This can also be changed by double-click on 'Pop-up Menu' button. Then it will display window as shown in Figure 14.6.

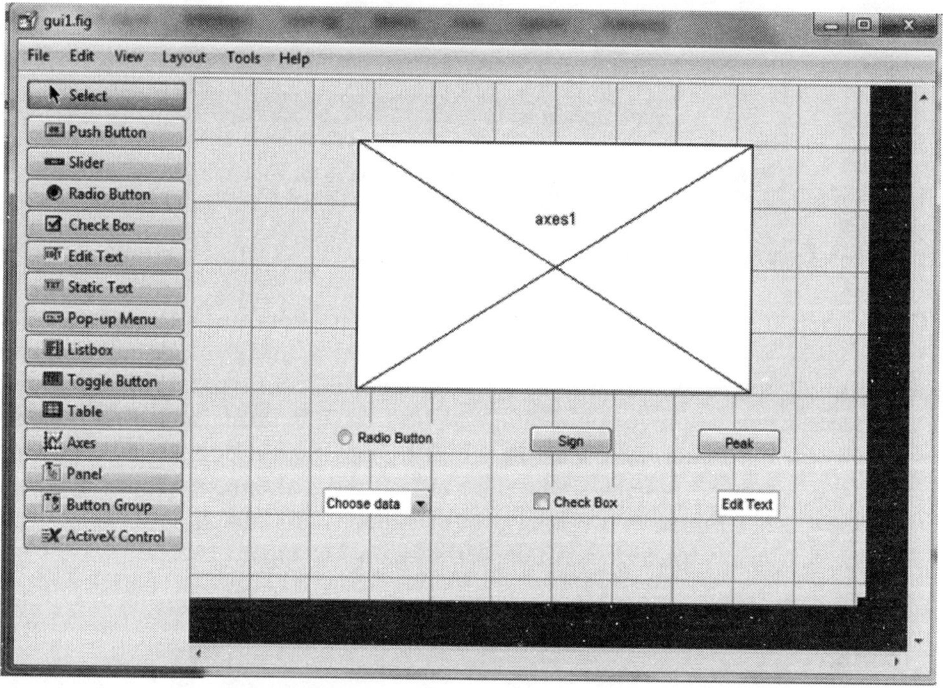

FIGURE 14.6   Label push button.

14.2.4   Modify the Static Text

In order to modify the text of 'Static Text' double-click on the text field. This will bring up a new window filled with properties for the text is called the *inspector*. We can change the 'Static Text' to 'Image Fun!' as shown in Figure 14.7.

Scroll down to observe option 'title of choice' which can be used to change 'Image Fun!' to a title of our choice.

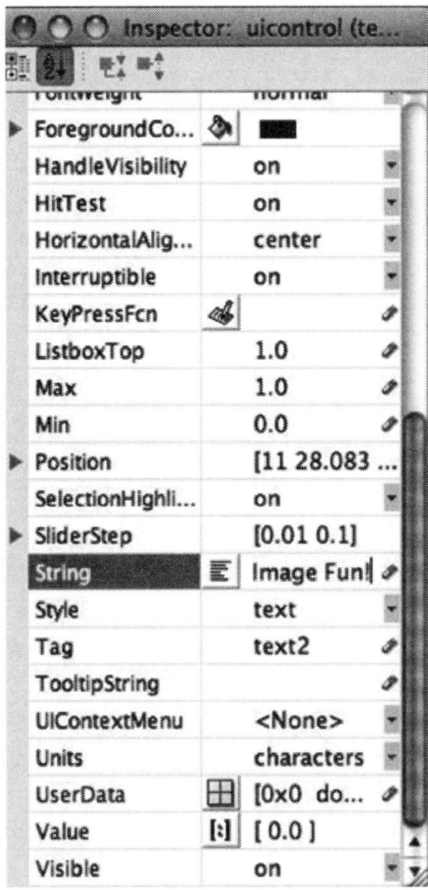

FIGURE 14.7　Modify push button.

14.2.5　GUI Layout Saving

To save a GUI, select **Save As** from the **File** menu and type file name without an extension. When we save the GUI, the GUIDE creates two files, a FIG-file and a code file. The extension .fig, is a binary file of FIG-file, that contains a description of the layout. The MATLAB code file functions, save with extension .m, to control the GUI behaviour. Once saved, run the GUI from the Command Window by typing itsname, whether or not GUIDE is running. When we save a GUI for the first time, the M-file appears ina separate Editor/ Debugger window. The copy of the GUI will appear in a separate window, without menus and buttons of the Layout Editor.

GUIDE then displays a dialog box with the text as shown in Figure 14.8.

"Activating will save changes to your figure file and M-file. Do you wish to continue?"

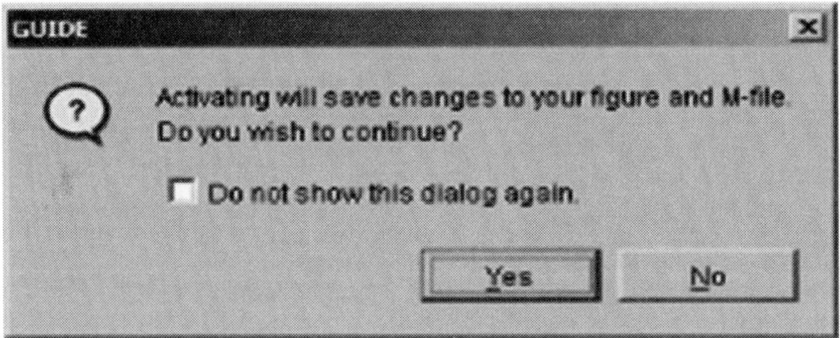

FIGURE 14.8   GUIDE dialog box.

Click **Yes.**

GUIDE opens a **Save As** dialog box in current directory shown in Figure 14.9 and prompts for a FIG-file name to save it.

FIGURE 14.9   Save As dialog box.

14.2.6 Open Saved File

MATLAB open the saved GUI file by using the following commands.

To open the saved MATLAB code type the following command:

```
>> open gui1.m
```

The MATLAB Editor Window with GUI M-filewill be opened as shown in Figure 14.10.

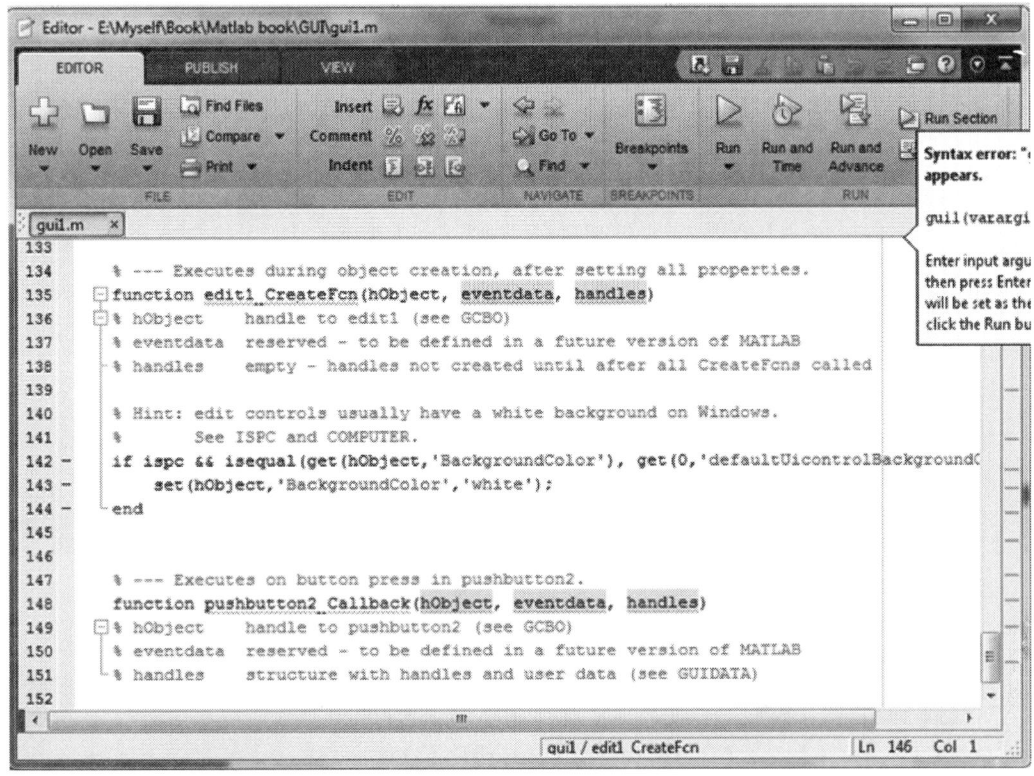

FIGURE 14.10   MATLAB editor window with GUI m-file.

A box opens in our current folder as GUIDE and **Save As** for a FIG-file name.

• The simulation of save file of the GUI can be activated by selecting Tools → Run.

To run a GUI created with saved GUIDE, execute its code file by typing its name as shown in the following command form:

```
>> open gui1.fig
```

We can also use the run command with the code file, for example,

```
>> run gui1.fig
```

This will display GUI Window as shown in Figure 14.11.

Remember and do not attempt to run a GUIDE GUI by opening its GUI Figure Window file outside of GUIDE. If done so, the figure opens and appears ready to use, but the GUI does not initialise.

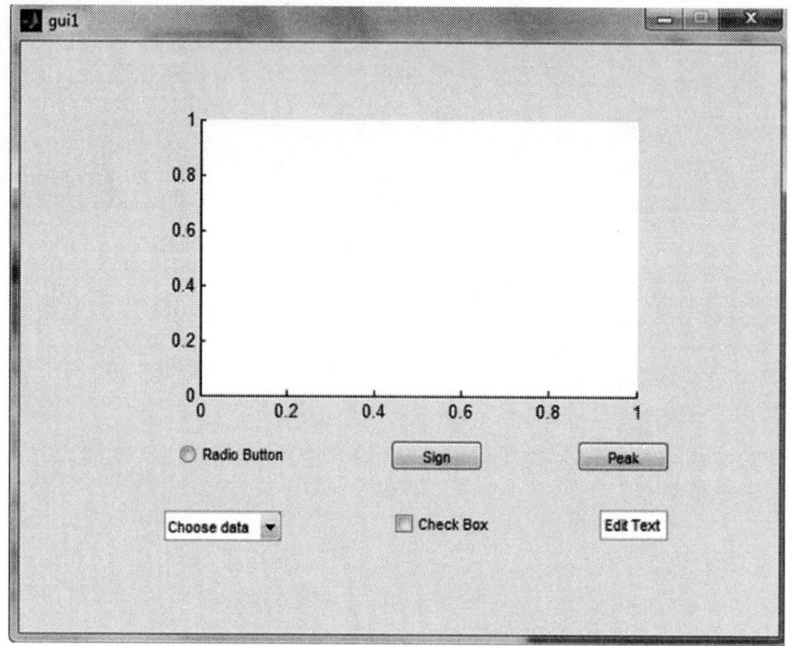

FIGURE 14.11   GUI figure window.

14.2.7   Interlink of Code with GUIDE GUI

GUIDE created two files: a FIG-file *filename.fig* that contains the GUI layout and a code file, *filename.m*, that contains the code of the GUI. The code consists of set of MATLAB functions that are not responding as per GUI because the functions contain no statements that perform actions yet. Following example of GUI Figure Window use MATLAB code to show how to add code to the file to make the GUI work as per the instructions.

EXAMPLE 14.1   Develop a GUI that will plot the generated data by the clicks button.

Solution: In this example, *opening function* generates data by calling MATLAB functions. The opening function, initialises a GUI, by GUIDE generated GUI code file.

To run a GUI created with saved GUIDE, type its name first then its code file can be executed by typing its name.

```
>> open gui4.fig
```

The *gui4.m* is the code for the Figure 14.12 GUI of Layout window.

Also in this example, add code that creates three data sets to the opening function. The code uses the MATLAB functions *peaks*, *membrane* and *sinc*. Following steps are taken to create data sets for the opening function:

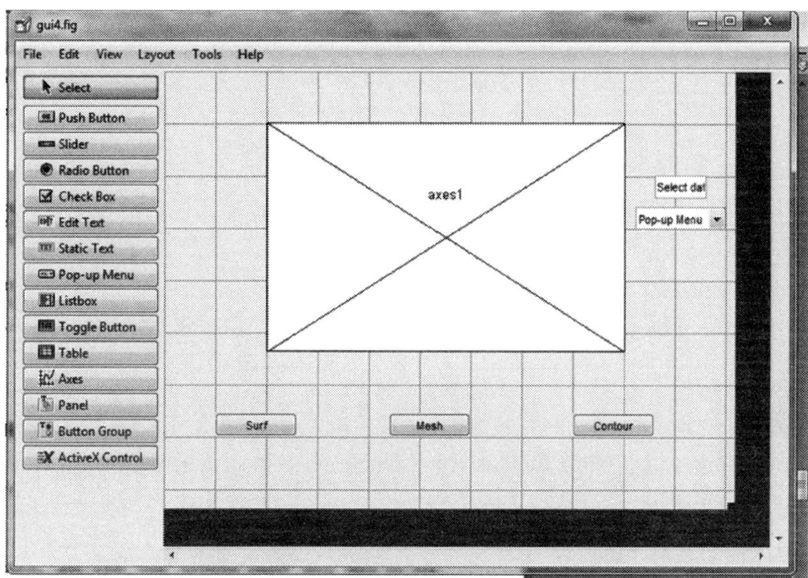

FIGURE 14.12   GUI layout window.

1. Open the filename.m file in the MATLAB Editor. This is done by opening the Layout Editor by selecting View → Editor.
2. In the NAVIGATE section of EDITOR tab, click Go To and then select filename.

The opening function code is as follows:

```
% --- Executes gui4 layout.
function gui4_OpeningFcn(hObject, eventdata, handles, varargin)
% The function has no output args.
% hObject     handle to figure
% eventdata   reserved
% handles     structure with handles and user data
% varargin    command line arguments to gui4
% Update handles structure
guidata(hObject, handles);

% UIWAIT makes gui4 wait for user response
% uiwait(handles.figure1);

% Create the data to plot.
handles.peaks=peaks(35);
handles.membrane=membrane;
[x,y] = meshgrid(-10:.2:10);
```

```
r = sqrt(x.^3+y.^3) + eps;
sinc = sin(r)./r;
handles.sinc = sinc;
% Set the current data value.
handles.current_data = handles.peaks;
surf(handles.current_data)
% Choose default command line output for gui4
handles.output = hObject;
```

Here, the first six executable lines create the data using the MATLAB functions *peaks*, *membrane* and *sinc*. The data in the handles structure is an argument that is stored to provide callbacks.

The callbacks for the push buttons can retrieve the data from the handles structure. The current data value is created from the last two lines. This will then display the *surf* plot for peaks. The GUI displays is shown in Figure 14.13.

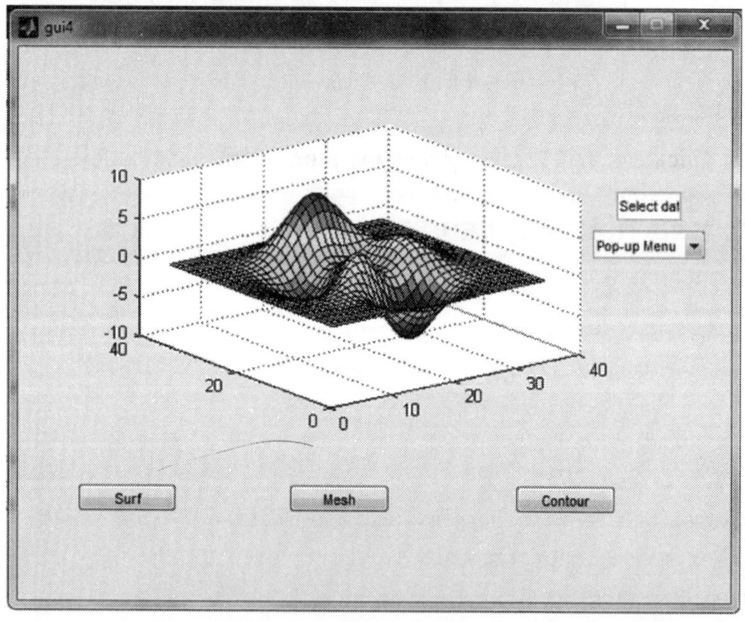

FIGURE 14.13   GUI figure window.

14.3   BUILDING SIMPLE GRAPHICAL USER INTERFACE IN MATLAB

MATLAB is a powerful mathematical tool for matrix calculations and almost any other mathematical function. MATLAB also has the ability to form windows like applications with its programming language to solve the issues. Following are the simple way to understand the GUI creation:

Open the MATLAB program and wait for it to finish loading

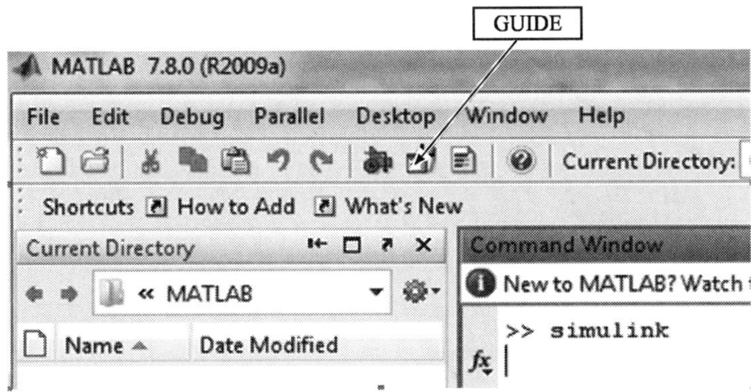

FIGIRE 14.14   GUIDE icon.

On MATLAB launch pad the GUIDE icon as shown in Figure 14.14 is clicked to start GUI creation.

The GUI builder will appear

In the launch pad Click on 'MATLAB' to expand the list and then double-click on 'GUIDE (GUI builder)'. If we cannot see the launch pad, click on view followed by launch pad. The GUI builder will appear as shown in Figure 14.15.

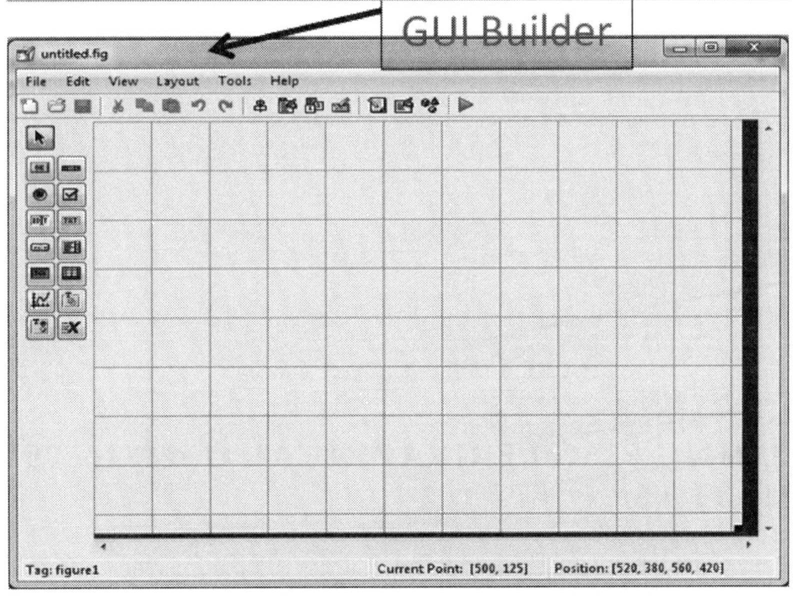

FIGURE 14.15   GUI builder.

Creation of push button

Click on the 'required' button in the left hand side of the window. We can drag and drop a push button from window as shown in Figure 14.16. Move the mouse to somewhere on the grey area in the center of the window and drop the icon.

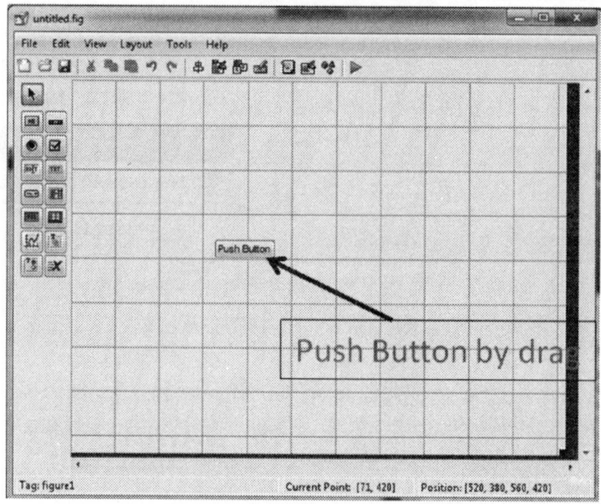

FIGURE 14.16　Push button icon on window.

Reshaping the push button

Click once and hold down the button and drag the mouse until the square that this formed is of the desire size as shown in Figure 14.17.

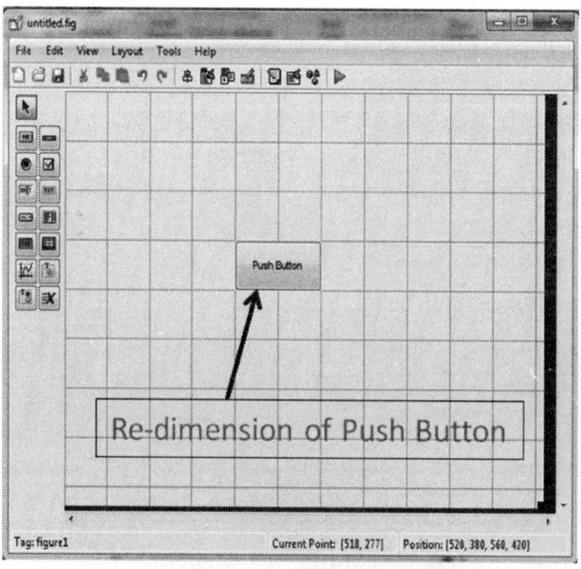

FIGURE 14.17　Reshape of push button.

Release the mouse button and we will see our push button appear on the same window.

Property manager

Double-click on the push button, we have just created. A property manager will pop-up as shown in Figure 14.18.

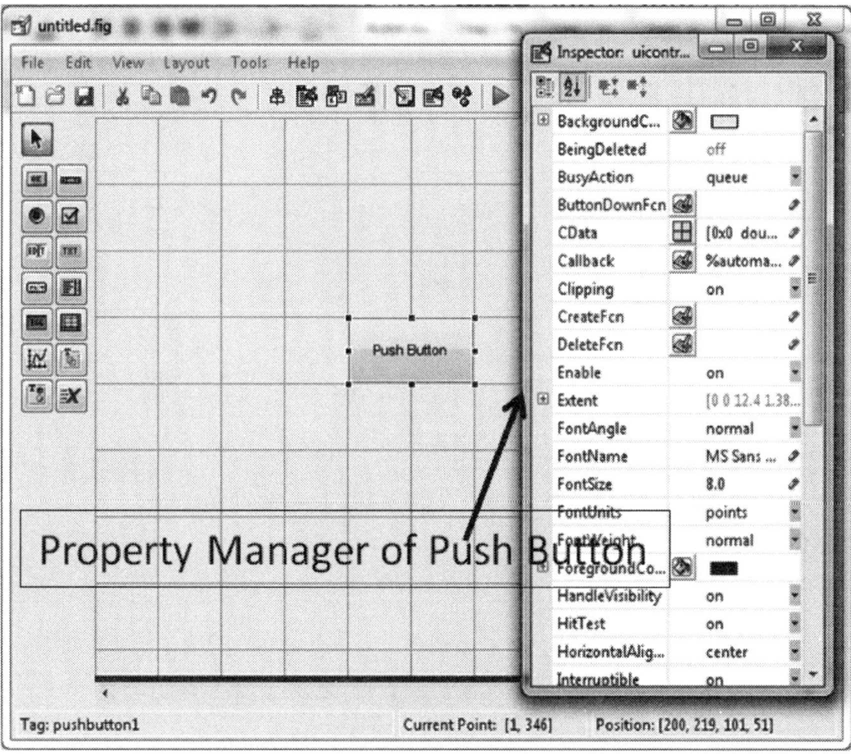

FIGURE 14.18   Property manager.

Changing the string content

Locate the 'string field' and click the area to the right of it and type 'START'. Then press OK. A window as shown in the Figure 14.19 will appear.

Save

Now, we click first on file then on save to save our work in required directory. This will also pop-up the code for our program as shown in Figure 14.20.

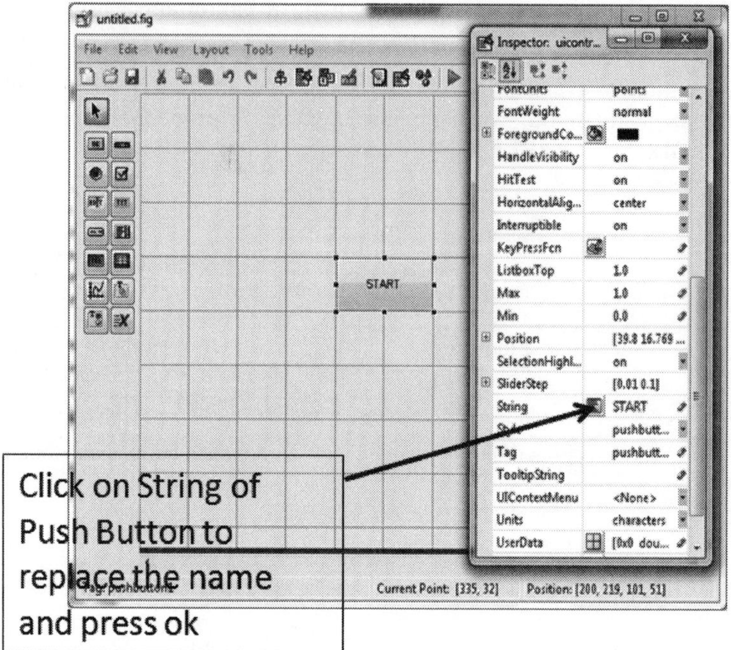

FIGURE 14.19   String button for content change.

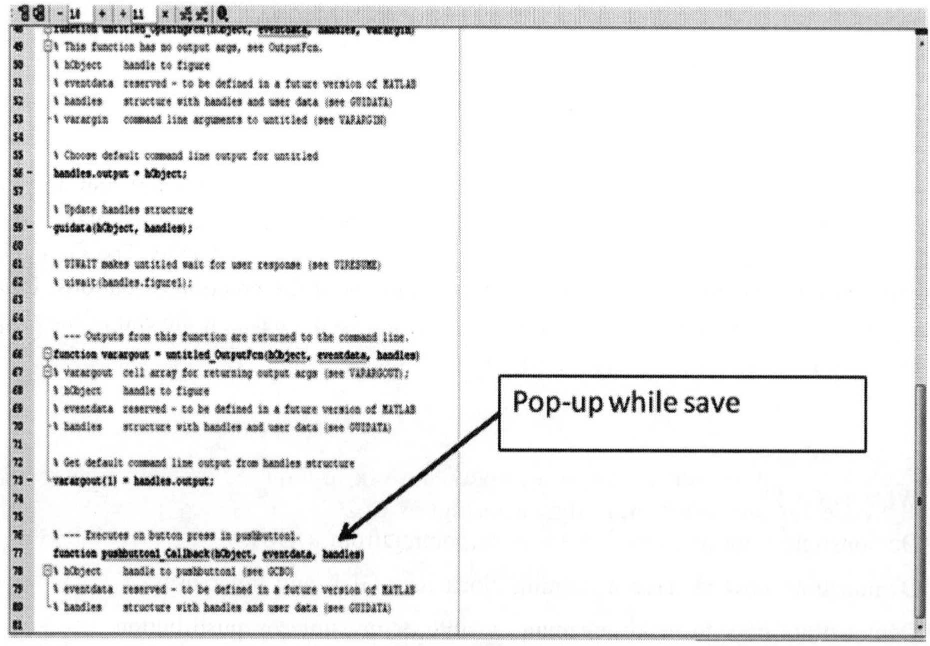

FIGURE 14.20   Save pop-up program code.

14.4 GUIDE TOOLS SUMMARY

The GUIDE tools summary available in the Layout Editor are described in Table 14.1.

TABLE 14.1   The Guide Summary

Layout editor	Components are selected from the component palette, at the left side of the Layout Editor, and arrange them in the layout area.
Figure resize tab	The GUI size is set displayed initially when we run it.
Menu editor	Create menus and context, i.e., pop-up, menus.
Align objects	Align and distribute groups of components. Grids and rulers also enable us to align components on a grid with an optional snap-to-grid capability.
Tab order editor	Set the tab and stacking order of the components in your layout.
Toolbar editor	Toolbars containing predefined and custom push buttons and toggle buttons is created.
Icon editor	Create and modify icons for tools in a toolbar.
Property inspector	It provides a list of all the properties that can set and displays their current values.
Object browser	Display a hierarchical list of the objects in the GUI.
Run	Save and run the current GUI.
Editor	Display, the default editor, the code file associated with the GUI.
Position readouts	Continuously display the mouse cursor position and the positions of selected objects

SUMMARY

In this chapter, we have learnt about the concept of GUI. Also, we have learnt how to build a new GUI. The discussion on different pop-up window is carried out on GUI template, GUIDE quick start layout editor, preference window and component name in Palette. The GUI related example and its pictorial display made us to understand about the creation of buttons. Finally, we have understood about different GUIDE tools summary as tabulated at the end of the chapter.

REVIEW QUESTIONS

1. What is GUI?
2. Demonstrate how to control the mouse pointer from a GUI.
3. Demonstrate how to have a running clock in a GUI, and timer use.
4. Demonstrate how to make an image visible or invisible by push button.
5. Demonstrate how to use an image as a background of a GUI.

Appendix

LANGUAGE FUNDAMENTALS

Entering Commands

`ans`	Most recent answer
`clc`	Clear Command Window
`diary`	Save Command Window text to file
`format`	Set Command Window output display format
`home`	Send cursor home
`iskeyword`	Determine whether input is MATLAB keyword
`more`	Control paged output for Command Window

MATRICES AND ARRAYS

Array Creation and Concatenation

`accumarray`	Construct array with accumulation
`blkdiag`	Construct block diagonal matrix from input arguments
`diag`	Create diagonal matrix or get diagonal elements of matrix
`eye`	Identity matrix
`false`	Logical 0 (false)
`freqspace`	Frequency spacing for frequency response
`linspace`	Generate linearly spaced vector
`logspace`	Generate logarithmically spaced vector
`meshgrid`	Rectangular grid in 2D and 3D space
`ndgrid`	Rectangular grid in N-D space
`ones`	Create array of all ones

`rand`	Uniformly distributed random numbers
`true`	Logical 1 (true)
`zeros`	Create array of all zeros
`cat`	Concatenate arrays along specified dimension
`horzcat`	Concatenate arrays horizontally
`vertcat`	Concatenate arrays vertically

Indexing

`colon`	Create vectors, array subscripting, and for-loop iterators
`end`	Terminate block of code, or indicate last array index
`ind2sub`	Subscripts from linear index
`sub2ind`	Convert subscripts to linear indices

Array Dimensions

`length`	Length of largest array dimension
`ndims`	Number of array dimensions
`numel`	Number of array elements
`size`	Array dimensions
`height`	Number of table rows
`width`	Number of table variables
`iscolumn`	Determine whether input is column vector
`isempty`	Determine whether array is empty
`ismatrix`	Determine whether input is matrix
`isrow`	Determine whether input is row vector
`isscalar`	Determine whether input is scalar
`isvector`	Determine whether input is vector

OPERATORS AND ELEMENTARY OPERATIONS

Arithmetic

`plus`	Addition
`uplus`	Unary plus
`minus`	Subtraction
`uminus`	Unary minus
`times`	Element-wise multiplication

`rdivide`	Right array division
`ldivide`	Left array division
`power`	Element-wise power
`mtimes`	Matrix multiplication
`mrdivide`	Solve systems of linear equations xA = B for x
`mldivide`	Solve systems of linear equations Ax = B for x
`mpower`	Matrix power
`cumprod`	Cumulative product
`cumsum`	Cumulative sum
`diff`	Differences and approximate derivatives
`prod`	Product of array elements
`sum`	Sum of array elements
`ceil`	Round toward positive infinity
`fix`	Round toward zero
`floor`	Round toward negative infinity
`idivide`	Integer division with rounding option
`mod`	Remainder after division (modulo operation)
`rem`	Remainder after division
`round`	Round to nearest decimal or integer

Relational Operations

Relational Operators	Relational operations
`eq`	Determine equality
`ge`	Determine greater than or equal to
`gt`	Determine greater than
`le`	Determine less than or equal to
`lt`	Determine less than
`ne`	Determine inequality
`isequal`	Determine array equality
`isequaln`	Determine array equality, treating NaN values as equal

Logical Operations

Logical Operators: Short-circuit	Logical operations with short-circuiting
`and`	Find logical AND
`not`	Find logical NOT
`or`	Find logical OR

xor	Logical exclusive-OR
all	Determine if all array elements are nonzero or true
any	Determine if any array elements are nonzero
false	Logical 0 (false)
find	Find indices and values of nonzero elements
islogical	Determine if input is logical array
logical	Convert numeric values to logicals
true	Logical 1 (true)

Numeric Types

double	Convert to double precision
single	Convert to single precision
int8	Convert to 8-bit signed integer
int16	Convert to 16-bit signed integer
int32	Convert to 32-bit signed integer
int64	Convert to 64-bit signed integer
uint8	Convert to 8-bit unsigned integer
uint16	Convert to 16-bit unsigned integer
uint32	Convert to 32-bit unsigned integer
uint64	Convert to 64-bit unsigned integer
cast	Cast variable to different data type
typecast	Convert data types without changing underlying data
isinteger	Determine if input is integer array
isfloat	Determine if input is floating-point array
isnumeric	Determine if input is numeric array
isreal	Determine whether array is real
isfinite	Array elements that are finite
isinf	Array elements that are infinite
isnan	Array elements that are NaN
eps	Floating-point relative accuracy
flintmax	Largest consecutive integer in floating-point format
Inf	Infinity
intmax	Largest value of specified integer type
intmin	Smallest value of specified integer type
NaN	Not-a-Number
realmax	Largest positive floating-point number
realmin	Smallest positive normalized floating-point number

PROGRAMMING SCRIPTS AND FUNCTIONS

Control Flow

`if, elseif, else`	Execute statements if condition is true
`for`	Execute statements specified number of times
`parfor`	Parallel for loop
`switch, case, otherwise`	Execute one of several groups of statements
`try, catch`	Execute statements and catch resulting errors
`while`	Repeat execution of statements while condition is true
`break`	Terminate execution of for or while loop
`continue`	Pass control to next iteration of for or while loop
`end`	Terminate block of code, or indicate last array index
`pause`	Stop MATLAB execution temporarily
`return`	Return control to invoking function

DESKTOP ENVIRONMENT

Start-up and Shutdown

`matlab (Windows)`	Start MATLAB program from Windows system prompt
`matlab (Mac)`	Start MATLAB program from Mac Terminal
`matlab (Linux)`	Start MATLAB program from Linux system prompt
`exit`	Terminate MATLAB program (same as quit)
`quit`	Terminate MATLAB program
`matlabrc`	Start up file for MATLAB program
`startup`	Start up file for user-defined options
`finish`	Termination file for MATLAB program

Basic Settings

`prefdir`	Folder containing preferences, history, and layout files
`preferences`	Open Preferences dialog box

Platform and License

`version`	Version number for MATLAB and libraries
`ver`	Version information for MathWorks products

```
verLessThan          Compare toolbox release or version to specified string
license              Get license number or perform licensing task
ispc                 Determine if version is for Windows (PC) platform
ismac                Determine if version is for Mac OS X platform
isunix               Determine if version is for Linux or Mac platforms
isstudent            Determine if version is Student Version
javachk              Error message based on Java feature support
usejava              Determine if Java feature is available
```

Help and Support

```
doc                  Reference page in Help browser Search for term in documentation
help                 Help for functions in Command Window
docsearch            Help browser search
lookfor              Search for keyword in all help entries
demo                 Access product examples in Help browser
echodemo             Run example script step-by-step in Command Window
```

Reference

For more details visit
http://in.mathworks.com/help/matlab/functionlist.html, dated 9/10/2015

Suggested Reading

Abrahim, Ahmad M., *Introduction to Applied Fuzzy Electronics*, Prentice-Hall of India, Delhi, 2004.

Ahlersten, K., *An Introduction to MATLAB*, bookboon.com, 2012.

Attaway, S., *MATLAB: A Practical Introduction to Programming and Problem Solving*, 3rd ed., Butterworth-Heinemann imprint of Elsevier, Oxford (UK), 2009.

Bansal, R.K., Goel, A.K., and Sharma, M.K., *MATLAB and its Application in Engineering*, Pearson Education, Delhi, 2009.

Chapman, S.J., *Essential of MATLAB Programming*, 2nd ed., Cengage Learning, Delhi, 2009.

Driscoll, T.A., *Learning MATLAB*, SIAM, Philadelphia, 2009.

Gilat, A., *MATLAB an Introduction with Application*, 4th ed., Wiley India, New Delhi, 2013.

Gonzalez, R. and Woods, R., *Digital Image Processing*, 3rd ed., Pearson Education Inc., New Delhi, 2014.

Gonzalez, Rafael C., Woods, Richard E., and Eddins, Steven L., *Digital Image Processing Using MATLAB*, Prentice-Hall, New Jersey, 2003.

Gray, Michael A., *Introduction to Simulation of Dynamics Using Simulink*, CRC Press, Florida, 2011.

Hahn, Brain H. and Valentine, Daniel T., *Essential MATLAB*, Academic Press (Elsevier), India, 2013.

Hanselman, D. and Littlefield, B., *Mastering MATLAB 7*, Prentice Hall, New Delhi, 2011.

Higham, Desmond J. and Higham, Nicholas J., *MATLAB Guide*, 2nd ed., Society for Industrial and Applied Mathematics, 2005.

Ht, Brain R., Lipsman, Ronal L., and Rosenberg, Jonathan M., *A Guide to MATLAB for Beginners and Experience Users*, Cambridge University Press, New York, 2001.

Jain, S., *Modelling and Simulation Using MATLAB-Simulink*, Wiley India, New Delhi, 2011.

Kalechman, M., *Practical MATLAB Applications for Engineers*, CRC Press, Florida, 2009.

Kattan, Peter I., *MATLAB for Beginners: A Gentle Approach*, Revised Edition, CreateSpace Independent Publishing Platform, North Charleston (USA), 2010.

Moore, H., *MATLAB for Engineers*, 2nd ed., Prentice Hall, New Jersey, 2009.

Pratap, R., *Getting Started with MATLAB*, Oxford University Press, USA, 2010.

Proakis, John G. and Manolakis, Dimitris G., *Digital Signal Processing: Principles, Algorithms and Applications*, 3rd ed., Prentice-Hall of India, New Delhi, 2003.

The Mathworks Inc., *User Guide Fuzzy Logic Toolbox, MATLAB 2010b*.

Tyagi, A.K., *MATLAB and Simulink for Engineers*, Oxford University Press, New Delhi, 2012.

Index